Applied
BIOLOGY

Applied BIOLOGY

VOL. I

Edited by

T. H. COAKER

*Department of Applied Biology, University of Cambridge,
Cambridge, England*

1976

ACADEMIC PRESS

LONDON · NEW YORK · SAN FRANCISCO

A Subsidiary of Harcourt Brace Jovanovich, Publishers

ACADEMIC PRESS INC. (LONDON) LTD.
24/28 Oval Road,
London NW1

United States Edition published by
ACADEMIC PRESS INC.
111 Fifth Avenue
New York, New York 10003

Library of Congress Catalog Number 76–1065
ISBN: 0 12 040901 1

Text set in 11/12 pt. Monotype Baskerville, printed by letterpress,
and bound in Great Britain at The Pitman Press, Bath

Contributors

CAUGHLEY, GRAEME, *School of Biological Sciences, Zoology Building, University of Sydney, New South Wales, Australia*

GAMBELL, RAY, *Whale Research Unit, Institute of Oceanographic Sciences, c/o British Museum (Natural History), Cromwell Road, London, England*

MATTHEWS, J. D., *Department of Forestry, University of Aberdeen, Aberdeen, Scotland*

MORTIMER, A. M., *School of Plant Biology, University College of North Wales, Bangor, Gwynedd, Wales*

MURTON, R. K., *Institute of Terrestrial Ecology, Monks Wood Experimental Station, Huntingdon, England*

SAGAR, G. R., *School of Plant Biology, University College of North Wales, Bangor, Gwynedd, Wales*

WESTWOOD, N. J., *Institute of Terrestrial Ecology, Monks Wood Experimental Station, Huntingdon, England*

Preface

In duelling, one choses ones weapons; war however is total. Thus it is with the life sciences. The specialist may choose what aspect of a pure problem he will investigate, more often than not fitting his choice to his equipment rather than *vice versa*, and working in a department of botany or zoology which may specialise in only a few aspects of one of those disciplines. It is very rare that the applied problem occurs in such specialised isolation. Real animals depend on plants, real plants on soil, soil modifies and is modified by both. The applied departments are thus of necessity multi-disciplinary and like them, it is with no apology that this, the first volume of a review series, is simply called *Applied Biology*.

This volume, like succeeding ones, contains papers which between them span an enormous field—or widely different fields, if the reader choses to regard them as: one on the survival of seeds, one on tree genetics, the others on birds, grazing mammals and on whales. But every one of these papers is in fact concerned with the problems of populations: what controls them, what predicts them. Food supplies, competition, environment and productivity are the same themes whether we are concerned to conserve whales or trees in order to cull them; to control weeds or birds in order to improve the yield of crops.

Each article seeks to fulfil four aims. They review generally the state of a subject, but select one or more aspect for particular critical discussion; they summarize what is known to be of practical importance and indicate where each author sees the greatest need for future work. We agree with the attitude expressed by more than one of these contributors when they say that they can draw conclusions but their papers cannot be briefly summarized. A judge sums up when the evidence is complete but in applied biology the case will have to be adjourned many times before we reach that stage. We cannot isolate small and controllable systems, but we can only review parts of the major system at a time.

At the end of the day we are concerned with man the animal who interferes and hopes to control, the predator who must learn to conserve. The task is usually stated as 'to apply for the benefit of man', but it is a phrase capable of so many interpretations depending on the length of his sight and the nature of his demand—indeed the form of his demand must determine how far forward he can hope his species may look. I believe readers will find these papers cautiously forward-looking, and realistic as applied biology must always be.

J. W. L. BEAMENT

Contents

An Approach to the Study of the Population Dynamics of Plants with Special Reference to Weeds

G. R. SAGAR and A. M. MORTIMER

School of Plant Biology, University College of North Wales, Bangor, Gwynedd, Wales

I. INTRODUCTION

Comprehension of the processes of population regulation is a primary aim in the study of population biology and the acquisition of actuarial data is necessary for the understanding of demographic behaviour. Although

1

plants have received considerably less attention than animals from demographers this has not prevented the development of two synoptic hypotheses each of which seeks to explain the numerical changes and the degree of numerical constancy that populations are believed to exhibit. According to the first hypothesis the heterogeneity of the physical environment in space and time provides sufficient explanation for observed changes; in contrast, the second view claims regulation through some resource of the environment through competition, predation or parasitism. This review examines the life histories of a few selected plant species and comments on some of the possible mechanisms of population regulation.

II. A WORKING SCHEME

For an examination of the population dynamics of any higher plant species where vegetative multiplication does not occur, the life-cycle may be stylized as in Fig. 1 (after Sagar, 1970, 1974). This presentation shows two routes by which the population of ecologic individuals (independently assimilating plant units) of size A1 in generation Gt may occur in the succeeding generation Gt + 1. The population A2 in generation Gt + 1 comes from genet reproduction (Kays and Harper, 1974) and sometimes from survivors from the previous generation.

Route I is genet reproduction or plant establishment from seed* and may be divided into five intermediate phases viz: B, the total number of viable seeds produced by the population A1; C, the total number of viable seeds falling onto the soil surface (to which are added any seeds arriving by invasion, G); D1 the total number of viable seeds that are present in the "surface seed bank". This seed bank may lose individuals to the "buried seed bank" D2, which includes the "carry-over" of the previous generations' seeds. There may be additions to the surface seed bank from invading seed or to the buried seed bank by sowing contaminated seed; E, the number of seedlings germinated from either seed bank; and F, the number of plants established. Six interphases are recognized, (a) to (h), where, for example, (d) is the probability of a seed giving rise to a seedling within the time-span of a generation. The invasion interphase (g) is further subdivided to distinguish contributions to the seed rain (g1), to the surface seed bank (g2) and to the buried seed bank (g3).

Route II is found in all species except ephemerals and annuals and indicates an interphase probability for the fraction of the population A1 which survives to generation Gt + 1. For an idealized biennial species

* Despite the protestations of van der Pijl (1972) we use the word seed loosely.

the interphase (i) may carry a value of 0·5, for half the plants in the population A1 would flower and die and half remain vegetative and survive into population A2.

Figure 1 needs slight modification for biennial species because of the overlap of generations and is inappropriate for species which have mixed

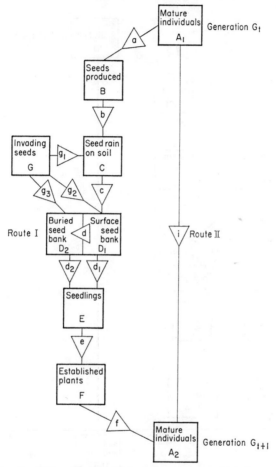

FIG. 1. The generalized life-table for a higher plant species which does not have ramet reproduction.

populations of genets and ramets (Harper and White, 1974; Kays and Harper, 1974), in part because different survival probabilities may be expected for each component and in part because of the difficulties of distinguishing independently assimilating plant units. These special problems are discussed later.

III. Some Examples

A. *Alopecurus myosuroides*

The first species considered is an annual weed of British arable land—
Alopecurus myosuroides Huds. Using the data of Naylor (1972) Fig. 2 can be

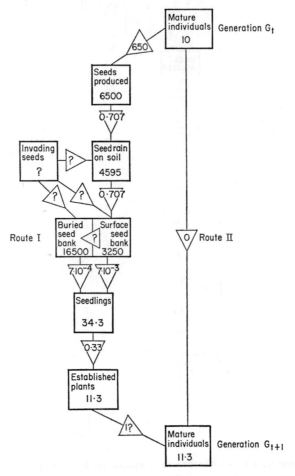

Fig. 2. A life-table for *Alopecurus myosuroides* (after Naylor, 1972).

constructed. A notional population of 10 plants (A1) produces 6500 seeds
(B) by assigning a value of 650 to interphase (a). We have no direct
knowledge of those seeds but we have presumed, since many are not
viable and some will be lost from the system (see later discussion), that

interphase probabilities (b) × (c) equal 0·5; thus 3250 seeds fall into the surface seed bank (D1) to join an estimated 16 500 seeds already in the buried seed bank (D2). The new and the old components of the bank differ in interphase (d), their values being 0·007 and 0·0007 respectively.

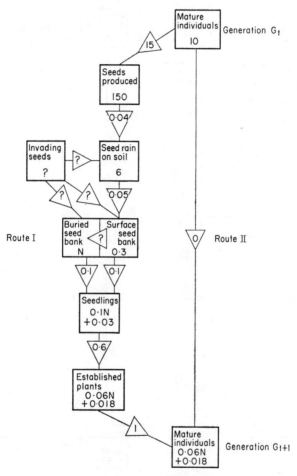

Fig. 3a. Life table for *Avena fatua*. Population increase low. "N" represents buried seed bank. (Sources of values acknowledged in text.)

The combined population at E is 34·3 and interphases (e) and (f) combined remove a further two-thirds giving 11·3 individuals in A2. This population was increasing but at a minute rate by comparison with the potential indicated in interphase (a). Clearly the most powerful brake on the potential expansion appears to be in the soil.

B. *Avena fatua*

For *Avena fatua* L. (Fig. 3) the model becomes much more clumsy because it is no longer possible to use a single flow of Route I. Instead, we have chosen three schemes which from a population point of view may be

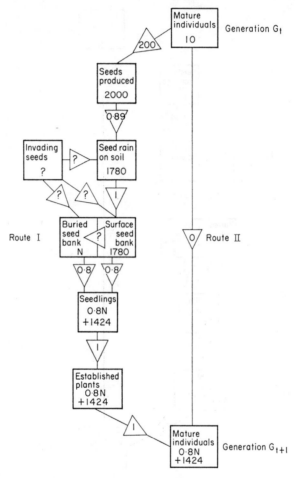

FIG. 3b. Life table for *Avena fatua*. Population increase high. "N" represents buried seed bank. (Sources of values acknowledged in text.)

described as high, low and median. Although the median scheme conforms to the Selman (1970) observations, most of the values assigned to the interphases are notional and should not be taken as real. More probably a threefold increase occurs through a combination of interphase values from best and worst schemes. The most severe (best) regulation is gained by a combination of control over seed output by best choice of companion crop (a) (Chancellor and Peters, 1970), harvest before the seed is shed with collection and removal of straw and trash (b) (Thurston,

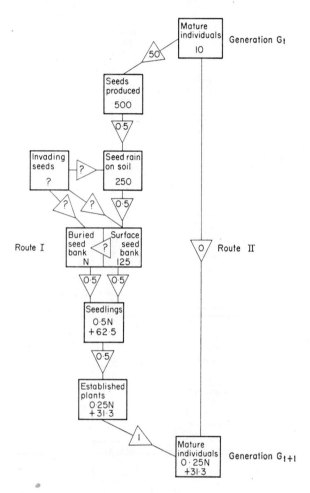

FIG. 3c. Life table for *Avena fatua*. Population increase medium. "N" represents the buried seed bank. (Sources of values acknowledged in text.)

1964), maximum exposure on the soil surface (c) (Wilson, 1972; Wilson and Cussans, 1972), low emergence of seedlings from the soil (d) (Thurston, 1961) and high post-emergence mortality (e) (Chancellor and Peters, 1972). The most rapid rate of expansion arises from minimal crop competition (Chancellor and Peters, 1970), almost total failure to collect seed at crop harvest (Wilson, 1972), immediate incorporation of the seed into the soil (Wilson, 1972), maximum emergence (Marshall

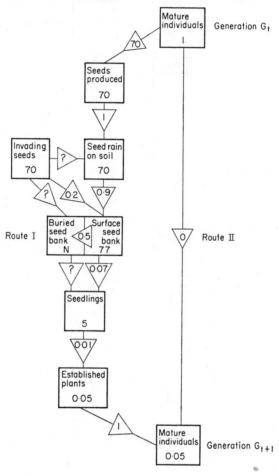

FIG. 4. A life-table for *Poa annua* in an open habitat. Data are numbers 100cm^{-2}. "N" represents the buried seed bank. (After Mortimer, 1974.)

and Jain, 1967) and no subsequent mortality. The greatest losses in practice are at crop harvest, of seeds from the soil surface and through failure of seeds to emerge from the buried seed bank. Inputs of seed (G) by sowing contaminated crop seeds are ignored.

c. *Poa annua*

One of the more complete models for an annual species is for *Poa annua* L. in an open habitat (Mortimer, 1974). The model (Fig. 4) illustrates that the processes regulating population size are most powerful during germination and seedling establishment. In this case it would appear that even if no seeds were buried and all the seeds in the surface seed bank germinated, the measured probability of 0·07 for interphase (d) and 0·01 for interphase (e) would mean that the population would decline because the value for interphase (a) is only 70. However,

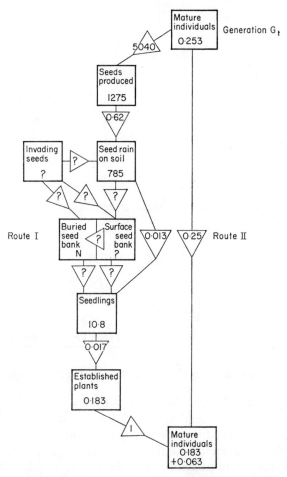

FIG. 5. A life-table for *Senecio jacobaea*. All values in phases are × 10⁻³. (After van der Meijden, 1971.)

P. annua often produces more than one generation a year and interphase values may not be constant throughout the season. In some situations seedling contributions from a large buried seed bank are indicated (Champness and Morris, 1948).

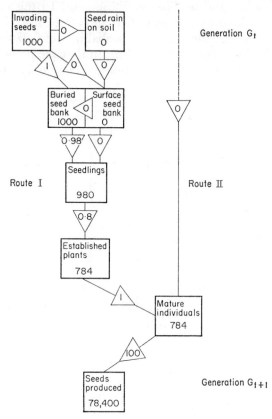

FIG. 6. A life-table for *Daucus carota* grown as a crop for seed (after Hegarty, 1963).

D. *Senecio jacobaea, Daucus carota* AND *Digitalis purpurea*

Biennial species differ little in principle from annuals although Route II does exist. van der Meijden (1971) has recently published a very tentative table of data that allows construction of Fig. 5 for *Senecio jacobaea* L. which is a biennial although in many systems it is frequently perennial. Some assumptions have to be made, notably that the A2 population is the same size as the A1 population and that Routes I and II are synchronous (in fact they are not, Route II is one year ahead).

When this is done large scale loss of seed by failure to germinate and (presumed) loss of seedlings is noted. Although the percentage of seed germinating is similar to that recorded by Cameron (1935) for seed

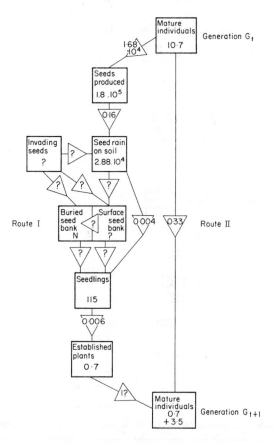

FIG. 7. A life-table for *Digitalis purpurea* (data kindly supplied by E. R. B. Oxley). Values are m⁻². "N" represents the buried seed population which is assumed to be very large.

sown into overgrazed turf, Cameron did not record heavy mortality of seedlings (see later). It is possible that van der Meijden's populations are rapidly expanding. Time will tell. For salutary comparison a model of *Daucus carota* L. grown from seed is presented as Fig. 6. It uses the data of

Hegarty (1973) and has the provisos that the population size and structure is constant from one generation to the next, that half the population
flowers and dies each year and that seed viability is 98 %. It is clear that if
time spent on and in the soil can be reduced to a minimum, rates of

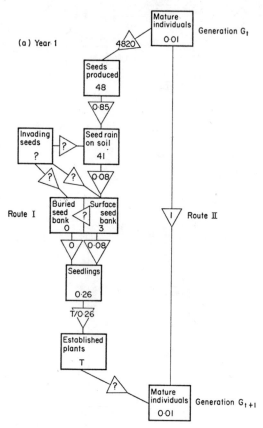

FIG. 8a. A life table for *Quercus petraea* (after Shaw, 1968a, b). Year 1. Data are numbers
m^{-2}

population increase approach the geometric potential. Some complications appear with biennials, not least important being a reduction in the
percentage of plants flowering as density is increased. Oxley (see
Harper and White, 1971) showed this effect for *Digitalis purpurea* L. A
generalized model for this species is given as Fig. 7.

E. *Quercus petraea*

Using the data of Shaw (1968a, b) for two years of observations on
Quercus petraea (Mattuschka) Liebl., this species may be displayed

(Fig. 8). Two points are worthy of note. First, the oak is one of a small number of species in the temperate flora which does not have a persistent seed bank and second, the interphases of maximum individual mortality are those post-dispersal and pre-emergence.

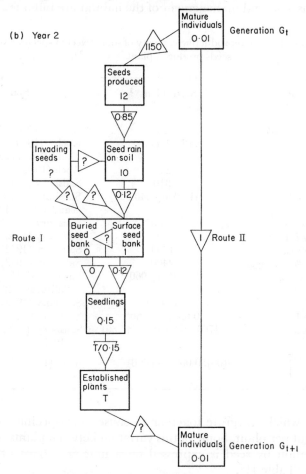

FIG. 8b. A life-table for *Quercus petraea* (after Shaw, 1968a, b). Year 2. Data are numbers m^{-2}.

We hope that these displays make a limited survey of the several interphases legitimate.

IV. ROUTE I. REPRODUCTION BY SEEDS

A. INTERPHASE (a). MULTIPLICATION BY SEEDS

Two approaches are possible. In the first approach, reproductive capacity, *sensu* Salisbury (1942), of individual plants is examined and a short selection of such data is presented as Table I. Examination of species in this way shows not only the clear difference between species but also some of the variability within species. The climatic and edaphic conditions, the density of the species, and density of other species, predation, parasitism and management of the habitat are but a few examples

TABLE I   The reproductive capacity of some selected species (No. of seeds produced plant^{-1} year^{-1}).

Species	Seeds plant^{-1}	Source
Alopecurus myosuroides	43	Koch (1970)
Avena fatua	(16–)22(–184)	Koch (1970), Chancellor and Peters (1970)
Sinapis arvensis L.	219	Koch (1970)
Agrostemma githago	310	Salisbury (1942)
Papaver rhoeas L.	(4–)17 000(–340 000)	Salisbury (1942), Harper and White (1974)
Thlaspi arvense L.	1900	Salisbury (1942)
Senecio vulgaris L.	1100	Salisbury (1942)
Bellis perennis L.	1300	Salisbury (1942)
Taraxacum officinale agg.	2400	Salisbury (1942)
Plantago media L.	9·3–19·4(–960)	Sagar and Harper (1961), Salisbury (1942)
P. major L.	14 000	Salisbury (1942)
P. lanceolata L.	0·85–7·43(–60)	Sagar and Harper (1961)
Senecio jacobaea	(4760–)63 000(–174 230)	Salisbury (1942), Cameron (1935)
Quercus petraea *Q. robur* L.	(0–)50 000(–90 000)	Jones (1959)

of factors which integrate together to cause intra-specific variation in seed output per plant. Some of this variation between plants is hidden if multiplication by seed is expressed on a unit area basis—the second approach (Table II).

This method of expression is almost the seed rain of Harper and White (1971) but not quite, for seed rain falls on the ground and area reproduction occurs above ground. Predation, parasitism and dispersal out of the area, for example, intervene between the two phases B and C (Fig. 1). In Table II a good deal of variation is still evident. For *Quercus petraea* the variation is between seasons and localities (climatic?), and for *Avena fatua* it is between locations and densities but mainly between companion crops, for the range 393–4784 is for a constant density of weed plants (Chancellor and Peters, 1970). The case of *Agrostemma githago* L. is of special interest for over a range of plant densities from 250 to 2400 m^{-2} this weed in pure stand yielded 29 000, 31 000 and 32 000 seeds m^{-2}, a constancy which is matched by cultivated cereals. On the other hand the presence of interfering species increased the range of seed outputs due to different weed densities (Harper and Gajic, 1961). The

TABLE II   The seed output m^{-2} year^{-1}. Some selected species.

Species	Seeds m^{-2}	Authority
Alopecurus myosuroides	2494(6500–7600)	Koch (1970), Naylor (1972)
Avena fatua	198	Koch (1970)
A. fatua	(393–)1000(–4784)	Thurston (1964), Chancellor and Peters (1970)
Sinapis arvensis L.	9198	Koch (1970)
Senecio jacobaea	630 × 10^3	van der Meijden (1971)
Plantago media + grass	122	Sagar and Harper (1961)
— grass	242	
P. lanceolata + grass	143–882	Sagar and Harper (1961)
— grass	1570–2700	Sagar and Harper (1961)
Quercus petraea	11·5–48·2	Shaw (1968a)
	(0–)50(–175)	Jones (1959)
Ranunculus repens L.	205–331	Sarukhán (1970)
Agrostemma githago	6500–29 000	Harper and Gajic (1961)

influence of site, plant density and other species is also seen in the two species of Plantago, *P. lanceolata* and *P. media*. We may add that in pure stands there is a density dependent control of seed output whereby increasing plant densities do not result in increasing output of seeds (Harper, 1960). Indeed, there is some evidence that reductions in seed output per unit area occur at high densities (Harper, 1961), and individuals of biennial and perennial species may react to high density by failure to flower (Harper and White, 1971 citing Oxley's *Digitalis purpurea*; Palmbald, 1968 for *Plantago lanceolata*). In mixed stands density remains an important contributor to seed output per unit area but other species also play a most important part in controlling output; so naturally do soils, climate and any management factors. In addition, predation or parasitism of plants (either indirectly through loss of vegetative parts or directly by predation of sexual reproductive parts) may be very significant (Janzen, 1971; Maun and Cavers, 1971a, b).

B. INTERPHASE (b). LOSSES BETWEEN SEED PRODUCTION AND
ARRIVAL ON THE SOIL SURFACE

Janzen (1969, 1971) has recently given extensive attention to one aspect of this interphase, notably the role and significance of predation of seeds. He claims pre-dispersal losses of seeds ranging from 0–100% with a common range between 10 and 90%. Losses within this range have been reported for *Senecio jacobaea* (22·9%—van der Meijden, 1971), *Quercus petraea* (15·9%—Shaw, 1968a, b), and *Ranunculus repens* (19·9%—Sarukhan, 1970). Data for weeds are hard to find, especially so for annuals. For perennial species qualitative information suggests that there is a frequent loss to the larvae of insect predators (e.g. Barnes, 1932, 1933). Even cursory examinations of the infructescences of perennial dicotyledons in grassland demonstrate the reductions in numbers that may occur. But not all species are equally affected, hence in part Janzen's view that there may be quite specific host plant–predator relationships. Organisms higher than insects also ingest seeds and there is an impressive older literature on the activities of birds, coupled with data on the effects of passage through the gut on viability and germinability of seeds (Krefting and Roe, 1949; Kirk and Courtney, 1972). Arboreal mammals may also take a toll. Unfortunately, quantitative estimates of predation in this interphase are very few. Perhaps annual weeds are less vulnerable than perennials.

All species are likely to lose a fraction of their seed by dispersal and although this may be balanced by immigration through dispersal, in a small study area or in areas where a species shows underdispersion, losses by dispersal may be important in the equation. For example, van der Meijden (1971) reported a 37·7% dispersal loss of seed of *S. jacobaea* from his small plots. Weeds have another hazard—notably loss through being harvested with the crop seed. In a study with important practical conclusions Thurston (1964) showed that of 1000 *Avena fatua* grains produced in a cereal crop 40 were left on the soil after the crop was harvested by a combine-harvester, 50 were present in the straw, 160 in the rubbish, 280 in the first-grade grain and 480 in the second-grade grain. If straw, rubbish and grain were taken from the field only 4% of the weed seeds would remain. By contrast Wilson (1972) also recorded the fate of seeds of this species. At cereal harvest there were *c.* 990 seeds m^{-2} on the oat panicles and *c.* 920 m^{-2} on the ground. After harvest *c.* 1463 m^{-2} were recorded on the ground. Presumably a relatively later harvest and a failure to collect seeds which passed through the combine were responsible for a negligible reduction in the weed seed population. Although the precision of the calculations might be questioned it should be possible to derive harvest-loss figures for many weeds which occur in seed crops from the figures of crop-seed contamination levels published by official seed testing stations (see also Wilson, 1970). These figures have been used (with greater validity) to calculate inputs of weed seeds when crop seeds are sown (see later). It has generally been accepted that a major cause of the loss of *Agrostemma githago* from the British weed flora was improved seed cleaning. At the same time it must follow that collection of the seed (the capsule does not shatter) at harvest time must have made a real contribution to the story. By no means all weeds suffer losses of the magnitude possible for *Avena fatua*. Some flower and set seed below the level of the combine blade, others mature and shed seed before or after harvest and in many crops the machinery of harvesting is totally inappropriate for the collection of weed seeds. Nevertheless the potential for loss of seed between plant and ground must not be ignored.

C. INTERPHASE (c). THE FATE OF SEED ON THE GROUND

The rain of viable seeds onto the ground is the product of A1 × (a) × (b) (Fig. 1). The fates of seeds in the rain are to remain *in situ* at the point of landing on the soil surface; to move along the soil surface away from the original point of dispersal; to become buried; to be predated on the soil surface; to be removed from the ground by agents of long distance dispersal; to be killed; to die or to germinate either on the surface or beneath it.

Of course more than one of the fates listed above may be encountered by the individual seed although predation, death and germination (see later) are terminal. The immediate fate of a seed on dissemination to the ground may depend upon patterns of seed rain to the ground surface. Falínska (1968) found that in a forest herb layer within a continuous seed rain from May until September individual species had different patterns of seed dissemination during the season. Some species (*Anemone nemorosa* L.) shed seeds very early and in large numbers, some disseminated seeds at a constant rate for a longer period of time (*Geranium robertianum* L.) whilst others shed seed twice in the season (*Ranunculus lanuginosus* L.). The time at which the individual seed is shed, the density of seeds of that species and the overall seed density may well have profound effects upon the subsequent fate of the individual.

Superficially, only a small proportion of dispersed seeds appear to remain on the soil surface at the site of landing and a more frequent fate is probably burial. Some species have external seed characteristics which increase the probability of close contact of the proximal (embryo) point of the seed with the ground surface (Heydecker, 1973). Such a position is advantageous since it allows a minimum expenditure of energy on the development of root and phytosynthetic organs although in some other respects shallow burial may be better (see later). The method of entry of seeds into the soil bank is easily explained in an arable agriculture or in horticulture. "In nature" or in a more perennial crop system seed burial is a little more difficult to follow. Seed lying on the surface may become buried under litter—a phenomenon well seen in oak or beech woods where the nuts are shed before the leaves; less spectacularly, similar processes occur in grassland. In neither case is seed buried in mineral soil. Surface-casting earthworms must be responsible for some seed burial either by producing holes down which seeds may fall, by the mineral soil cast material causing burial or by deliberate action of earthworms in moving seeds into the burrow (Darwin, 1881) or in ingesting them and subsequently voiding them in a viable but buried state in the cast (McRill and Sagar, 1973; McRill, 1974).

Loss of seeds or of viability of seeds on a soil surface appears to be very high as long as that surface is not violently disturbed by man. There are examples to illustrate this. Shaw (1968a) reported a maximum ground density of $15 \cdot 14$ acorns m^{-2}; by the end of December the same year the density was $2 \cdot 96$ m^{-2}. In an experiment, seed protected from predators was 70–80% more likely to remain untouched over a similar period. In earlier studies Watt (1919) showed that acorns were almost invariably lost from the soil surface soon after arrival. Burying the acorns slightly improved their survival rate as did certain forms of enclosure. However an enclosure which had bird and rodent proof top and sides, with the sides extending down *below* ground level, ensured complete survival. For *Fagus sylvatica* L. a similar series of experiments led to similar conclusions (Watt, 1923). Beech nuts protected from birds and rodents all remained *in situ*; if exposed to birds or mice they disappeared [mean $0 \cdot 3$% survival if on the surface, $17 \cdot 5$% (range 2–96%) survival if buried under litter, and $56 \cdot 3$% (range 3–97%) survival if buried in soil]. Thus disappearance of oak or beech fruits from the soil surface (and not by local burial!) ranged from 0 to 100% and was most commonly closer to the higher value. The agents of these losses were generally identifiable. Lawrence and Rediske (1962) have made a similar study of *Pseudotsuga menziesii* (Mirb.) Franco. A different situation has more recently been reported for *Avena fatua*. Studying a natural infestation of this weed, Wilson (1972) recorded a density of seed on the ground on 3 September of 682 yd^{-2} (352 yd^{-2} viable). On 29 November the same population had only 349 seed yd^{-2} (only 53 yd^{-2} viable)—a striking reduction. In a subsequent experiment on land not previously infested by the weed *c.* 1000 seeds unit area^{-1} were sown onto the surface of (a) soil, (b) sterilized soil, (c) cultivated soil or (d) mixed into the soil. The results are shown in Table III.

TABLE III Survival of surface-sown seeds of *Avena fatua*. 1000 seeds *unit area*$^{-1}$ sown in September. Seeds recovered on four dates. In parentheses—the number of "full" seeds (89% viable). From Wilson (1972).

Treatment	Date of retrieval			
	5 Oct	5 Nov	16 Dec	25 Feb
On soil surface	928(687)	903(605)	856(171)	738(74)
On sterilized surface	830(639)	894(572)	916(92)	723(29)
On cultivated surface	989(682)	929(641)	854(214)	555(89)
Mixed into soil	914(667)	745(544)	934(588)	970(689)

In the first study there were significant losses in numbers as well as in viability, but in the second viability was the most significant casualty of surface sown seed. Losses of 89% in viable seed in five months are of real interest to the study of the population dynamics of plants.

Bearing in mind *Quercus*, *Fagus* and *Avena fatua* it seems legitimate to enquire about other species, for the propagules of these three are large and fairly obvious to the eye. Far more plants have small seeds which are not so easily spotted on a soil surface. Other data are sketchy by comparison frequently failing to distinguish interphase (c) as discrete from (d) or even (e). Many attempts have now been made to interfere with the population size of plants by deliberately adding seeds into a population. Unless some other form of treatment is superimposed the impact of added seed has either been nil or negligible (measured by subsequent seedling numbers). Values have ranged from 0–15% (generally closer to 0%) for *Plantago lanceolata*, *P. major* and *P. media* (Sagar, 1959, 1970; Sagar and Harper, 1960, 1961), *Bellis perennis* (Foster, 1964), *Rumex crispus* L. and *R. obtusifolius* L. (Cavers and Harper, 1967), and *R. acetosa* L. and *R. acetosella* agg. (Putwain, 1970). Even when seeds of *Plantago lanceolata*, *P. major* and *P. media* were sown on a cultivated soil surface otherwise free of vegetation, recoveries of seeds as seedlings did not exceed 30% for *P. lanceolata* and 5% for *P. major* and *P. media* (Sagar, 1959). The fate of the remaining percentages are technically very difficult to measure. An attempt has however been made for *Plantago lanceolata* (Fig. 9). Seeds were introduced into three experimentally managed habitats and the numbers in various fate categories assessed at intervals. Burial was a common seed fate in all

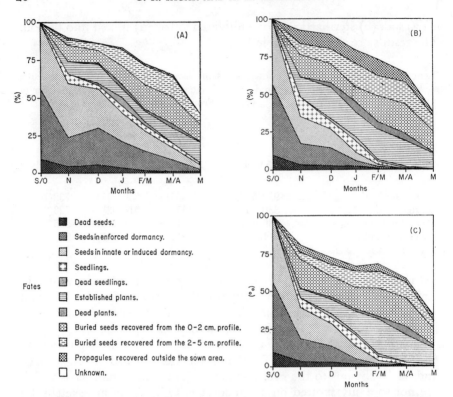

Fates

- Dead seeds.
- Seeds in enforced dormancy.
- Seeds in innate or induced dormancy.
- Seedlings.
- Dead seedlings.
- Established plants.
- Dead plants.
- Buried seeds recovered from the 0-2 cm. profile.
- Buried seeds recovered from the 2-5 cm. profile.
- Propagules recovered outside the sown area.
- Unknown.

FIG. 9. The fates of seeds of *Plantago lanceolata* introduced into a grassland sward (A), upon a ploughed soil surface (B), and onto a soil surface denuded of vegetation (C). (After Mortimer, 1974.)

three habitats, being greater in disturbed sites. Movement along the ground away from the sown area accounted for some of the propagules, more significantly on cultivated soil. Established plants were present in all three habitats at each observation and their numbers often exceeded the numbers of seedlings present. Recruitment to the seedling populations occurred principally in two flushes, during October and December. Six months after sowing greater numbers of established plants were found in disturbed sites than in grassland. A very conspicuous feature of seed behaviour was the changing proportions of seeds in the three dormancy states. In both habitats A and B some seeds in the enforced state were further induced into dormancy. The dynamic nature of dormancy fluctuations in the surface seed population may directly reflect a tactic which optimizes seedling numbers within a climatic regime.

Predation may well be a major fate of seeds on the ground since seeds form critical links in many food chains. The re-interpretation of the allelopathy of sage brush (Muller and Muller, 1964) by Bartholemew (1970) shows how thoroughly small mammals may sweep a soil surface. The story of dove-weed, *Eremocarpus setigerus* (Hook.) Benth. (Cook *et al.*, 1971) and the mourning-dove, *Zenaidura macroura* is a further illustration. Ground feeding birds of many species are known to feed on seeds in season (see Colquhoun, 1951); the order of their contribution to population control is not known. Finally it seems worth commenting that studies of the weed-seed bank show that seeds of annual weeds are far more common than seeds of perennials and that not infrequently there is little correlation between the content of the seed bank and the perennial community found on that soil, the bank in these cases reflecting past vegetation and management systems (Champness and Morris, 1948; Douglas, 1965). Is it possible that seed losses from the soil surface are very great for many perennial species; or are the observations to be correlated with the generally lower seed production of herbaceous perennials? Janzen (1971) has written about the losses although with a particular hypothesis as a framework. He reported predation of seed on the ground, ranging from very light to very heavy and drew attention to the studies of Marshall and Jain (1970) who reported losses of *Avena fatua* due to predators of from 0–65% in a non-agricultural area.

Biological agents, predators and pathogens must account for many of the reported losses. In the experiments of Wilson (1972) with *A. fatua*, which included attempts to keep both predators and pathogens at bay, the causes of the losses remain unclear, although Whybrew (1964) had earlier implicated birds as a possible cause of loss of viability of grains of *A. fatua* for they would presumably be dormant over the observation period (Thurston, 1951, 1953) and subject to relatively low temperatures. Perhaps this species is very vulnerable to wetting and drying. Seed borne pathogens or predators are also possible agents (see Kiewnick, 1963, 1964 and Hampel, 1969).

D. INTERPHASE (d). GERMINATION AND EMERGENCE FROM THE SEED BANK

The seed bank has been a popular and rewarding area of study since Brenchley and Warington (1930, 1933, 1936) first showed how many seeds were present in agricultural soils. Roberts (1970) has provided a succinct review of this subject and it is not necessary to examine it here in very great detail. Populations of seeds appear to have a constant half-life which varies with species and with management. But, if half the seed population disappears during one year, this does not mean that half of the seed produce emerged seedlings. Roberts and Dawkins (1967) for example recorded losses from the bank of 22–36% per annum of which only 0·3–9% were found as emerged seedlings. Table IV is an accumulation of data in this area (see also Forbes, 1963; Thurston, 1966; Ødum, 1974). It should be noted that some of the results confound interphases (c) and (d) and a few may include mortality of emerged seedlings. From the table it is clear that the percentage of seeds that germinate and emerge varies greatly both within and between species. It is equally clear from the work of Roberts and his colleagues that a large part of the seed bank dies either without germinating or germinates and fails to emerge. For many species a significant fraction of the seed bank remains dormant and a proportion of this is likely to contribute to the seedling population of later generations. If the data of Naylor (1972) on *Alopecurus myosuroides* is typical, it appears that the chance of a newly arrived seed producing a seedling is considerably higher than the chance of a seed which has been longer in the bank doing so. The physiology and biochemistry of dormancy has received a great deal of attention but most of the studies have been made in the laboratory. This is not the place to discuss the mechanisms of dormancy except insofar as they affect the proportion of seeds which germinate (to die or to emerge). Seeds in the soil may be in one of four states: germinating or in enforced, induced or innate dormancy (Harper, 1957a), and the relationship between these is shown in Fig. 10. Two comparatively recent developments in the study of the ecology of germination give hope of a fuller understanding of the model.

Black (1969), Wesson and Wareing (1967, 1969), Taylorson (1970) and Courtney (1968) have, from different standpoints, approached the problem of the interconversion of the states of dormancy. Innate dormancy is a fairly temporary state for most species (most often less than two years) and may simply be a temporary measure to prevent immediate post-dispersal germination and to allow the seeds to come to equilibrium with the environment of the bank. Many dormant seeds will then be induced or enforced into dormancy, exchanging between these states (Courtney, 1968; Koch, 1969). Release from the enforced state will come about by the correction of the limiting factor and from exposure to light (Wesson and Wareing, 1967, 1969), to ethylene in the soil (Hall and Wareing, 1972; Olatoye and Hall, 1973) or to carbon dioxide (Grant Lipp and Ballard, 1959). The periodicity of seed germination in the field (Brenchley and Warington, 1930; Chancellor, 1964a; Fryer and Evans, 1968) is an important determinant of the development of a weed flora and has proved of interest to physiologists (e.g. Popay and Roberts, 1970a, b). Seeds left in the bank will be subjected to a further period of vulnerability. Naylor (1970) was able to predict the size of the April field population of seedlings of *Alopecurus myosuroides* from soil samples taken in the previous October but was less successful with September samples perhaps because there was a greater instability in the dormancy states in September.

The second development comes from the extension of the original concept of a safe site (Watt, 1923; Harper et al., 1961). Even, or perhaps

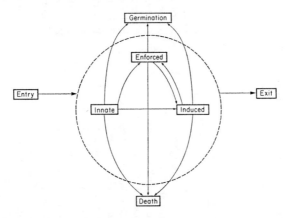

FIG. 10. The states and fates of seeds in the soil (after Roberts, 1970). Within the broken circle, seeds are in dormancy.

especially, when seeds are sown or shed onto a soil surface the site into which they fall markedly affects germination. It is easy to demonstrate this (Harper et al., 1965; White, quoted in Harper and White, 1971; Sheldon, 1974) and to conceive its mechanism; it is much more difficult to prove its relevance for seeds buried in the seed bank, for the seed is still the most accurate sensor we have of its own environment. There are ample continuous variables to admit the species specificity which seems to occur, for in addition to temperature, water economy, depth in soil and light (White and Harper, 1971), gases such as CO_2, O_2 and perhaps ethylene also have marked effects (Mülverstedt, 1963, and Koch, 1969). Janzen (1971) included protection from predation as an additional characteristic of the safe site.

Interphase (e) then shows the distinct contrast between sown agricultural crop seeds, which have only a short experience of the seed bank [and may prove very vulnerable if conditions are not optimal (Heydecker, 1973)] and annual weed seeds whose populations are vulnerable to loss but protected enough to ensure survival over many years. In addition the contrast between populations and species in arable and non-arable communities should be noted. Existing perennial vegetation apparently severely limits the chance of a seed producing a seedling

TABLE IV The chance of a seed in the seed bank producing an emerged seedling

Species	Emerged as seedlings (% of seed present)	Notes	Authority
Avena fatua	21	Over 3 year period	Thurston (1961)
A. fatua	20–80[a]	Over 1 year, unploughed situation (U.S.)	Marshall and Jain (1967)
A. fatua	0–52	Over 1 season laboratory studies in soil	Kiewnick (1963)
Capsella bursa-pastoris (L.) Medic.	46	Over 5 years. Cultivated soil	Roberts and Feast (1972)
C. bursa-pastoris	12	Over 5 years. Undisturbed soil	Roberts and Feast (1972)
Poa annua	50	Over 5 years. Cultivated soil	Roberts and Feast (1972)
P. annua	22	Over 5 years. Undisturbed soil	Roberts and Feast (1972)
Thlaspi arvensis	63	Over 5 years. Cultivated soil	Roberts and Feast (1972)
Th. arvensis	17	Over 5 years. Undisturbed soil	Roberts and Feast (1972)
Papaver rhoeas	34	Over 5 years. Cultivated soil	Roberts and Feast (1972)
P. rhoeas	9	Over 5 years. Undisturbed soil	Roberts and Feast (1972)
Alopecurus myosuroides	0·1–0·15	In one season	Naylor (1972)
Hordeum leporinum	90	In one season, Australia	Smith (1968)
Matricaria recutita L.	4	(Density of seedlings 1280^{-2})	Chancellor (1965)
Senecio jacobaea	0·9[a]	Field population	van der Meijden (1971)
S. jacobaea	0[a]	In short continous turf	Cameron (1935)
S. jacobaea	2[a]	On overgrazed turf	Cameron (1935)
S. jacobaea	20[a]	In hard exposed soil	Cameron (1935)
S. jacobaea	53[a]	On open soil	Cameron (1935)

	0·8 × germination at 10°C		
Daucus carota (c.v.)		Assay in laboratory	Hegarty (1963)
D. carota		In field	
Juncus effusus	11–80	In experiments and field	Lazenby (1955a, b)
J. effusus	10 rarely exceeded[a]	Sown alone	Lazenby (1955a, b)
J. effusus	4–9	Sown with *Trifolium repens*	Lazenby (1955a, b)
J. effusus	3·0	Sown with *T. repens* and *Agrostis tenuis*	Lazenby (1955a, b)
Trifolium pratense L.	0·1	Field study, Australia	Campbell (1968)
T. repens L.	11–31	Field study, Australia	Campbell (1968)
T. subterraneum	7–23	Field study, Australia	Campbell (1968)
Lolium perenne L.	11–41	Field study, Australia	Campbell (1968)
Dactylis glomerata	17–50	Field study, Australia	Campbell (1968)
Phalaris tuberosa L.	12–41	Field study, Australia	Campbell (1968)
Quercus petraea	4–12	Field study	Shaw (1968a, b)
Q. petraea	0·6–1·5[a]	Field study	Watt (1919)
Fagus sylvatica L.	0–100[a]	Field study	Watt (1923)
Narthecium ossifragum (L.) Huds.	8–60[a]	If previous vegetation removed	Summerfield (1973)
N. ossifragum	8–29[a]	If previous vegetation not removed	Summerfield (1973)
Ranunculus repens	0–2	In grassland	Sarukhán (1970)
Chondrilla juncea	3·7	10 days after soil cultivated	McVean (1966)
C. juncea	60	Soil not cultivated	McVean (1966)
	1		

[a] Germinating on the surface (combined interphases c and d).

(Tamm, 1948, 1956; Sagar and Harper, 1961; Cavers and Harper, 1967; Miles, 1974) although there are some exceptions to this rule (Symonides, 1974 on *Spergula vernalis* Willd.). The survival of seeds of some arable weeds for many years in the soil bank under grassland (Chippindale and Milton, 1934; Champness and Morris, 1948) is presumably an indication of the infrequency with which such seeds move out of the induced or enforced states of dormancy.

Table IV has some examples of the order of true losses from the seed bank. Many more examples are available in Roberts (1964) and Roberts and Feast (1972). In Table V the species are listed in the order of

TABLE V   The fates of buried seeds. Seeds deliberately buried and not disturbed for six years. Values given are the cumulated percentages (after Roberts and Feast, 1972).

Species	Emerged as seedlings	Still viable in soil after 6 years	Unaccounted for after 6 years
Spergula arvensis L.	11	13	76
Matricaria recutita	6	17	77
Papaver rhoeas	9	21	70
Senecio vulgaris	19	13	68
Stellaria media (L.) Vill.	15	22	63
Poa annua	22	24	54
Polygonum aviculare agg.	12	39	49
Urtica urens L.	13	39	48
Viola arvensis Murr.	20	38	48
Fumaria officinalis L.	30	31	39
Thlaspi arvensis	17	48	35
Chenopodium album L.	14	53	33

inability to account for the seeds lost. Attention must be directed to the causes of losses of seeds. When crop seeds are sown under unfavourable conditions, failure to emerge is common. Hegarty (1963) quotes figures for carrot seeds (98% viable) of between 11 and 80% emergence. For maize, failure to emerge is temperature related but the mechanism is biological for seed protection by fungicides markedly increases final emergence even after low temperature (Harper, 1956). It seems that the seed which is ready to germinate and the germinated seedling are very vulnerable to attack by microorganisms (see also Kiewnick, 1964). Other agents apart, we must also recognize that seeds vary in their inherent longevity. Studies of seed storage even out of the soil show how rapidly the viability of seeds of many species is lost at high temperatures and relative humidities, especially so when these fluctuate (Barton, 1961). The depth at which seeds germinate will also affect their chance of emergence (Black, 1955, 1956; Chancellor, 1964; Holroyd, 1964; Karssen, 1968, 1970a, b; Koch, 1969). Regrettably it is possible to write only qualitatively on these matters and this is unfortunate, for numerically the seed bank is often the phase of the life cycle where numbers are highest and it has great importance in the survival of species and, indirectly, in their evolution (Major and Pyott, 1966).

The surface of the soil is often an unstable environment and yet seeds do germinate there. Seeds with mucilages appear to have some advantage (Harper and Benton, 1966; Young and Evans, 1973; Evans et al., 1974). Some seeds have morphological adaptations which orientate the seed to optimize the contact between the surfaces of water availability and water uptake. The hygroscopic awn of *Avena fatua* (Thurston, 1960) and of *Danthonia penicillata* (Labill.) Palisot (Simpson, 1952) are well known. A combination of adaptations and mucilaginous hairs is reported to orientate and anchor the seeds of *Blepharis persica* (Burm.) Kuntze (Gutterman et al., 1967). The shapes, sizes and positions of seeds lying on the surface are also important (Watt, 1919; Harper et al., 1970; Evans et al., 1974; Sheldon, 1974). The roles of shapes and sizes are intimately associated with the concept of safe-sites, volumes of environment where germination is possible (Harper et al., 1961; Harper et al., 1965; Evans and Young, 1970, 1972; Evans et al., 1974; Sheldon, 1974). The germination requirements of species are often different; consequently an array of microsites on any natural surface will favour some species more than others. Microsites are not constant in time or space and therefore safe-sites appear and disappear with irregularity. Disturbance by wind or rain or by man, his animals or his machines contribute to the flux. To germinate, seed of the right species must be in the right site at the right time. The right species is a function of the size and shape of the seed in relation to the size and shape of the site and the relationship is not absolute but relative. For example on a given surface, conditions of ample moisture are likely to increase the number of safe-sites above the number available when there is less moisture (Harper and Benton, 1966; Sheldon, 1974) although pathogenic activity may mask the effect. All the physiological requirements for germination may contribute to the definition of the safe site but they must be measured on the scale of the size and with the dimensions of the shape of the seed. The foregoing appears to be as relevant to an understanding of surface seeding techniques for upgrading or re-establishing pastures (e.g.

Charles, 1962; Dowling *et al.*, 1971) as it is to the study of the dynamics of species of a native or adventive form.

E. INTERPHASE (e). FROM EMERGENCE TO ESTABLISHMENT

It is a matter of convenience to recognize a phase of establishment but very difficult to define the attainment of that phase in terms which are workable in the field. Although Watt (1919, 1923) defined the word as the contact of the seedling roots with the substrate and the expansion of cotyledons, for seeds germinating, below ground and showing hypogeal germination, the definition is not always appropriate. We prefer to recognize this stage (rather theoretically) as the achievement of a positive unit leaf rate or net assimilation rate (Evans, 1972) for a significant period. Relatively crudely this would signal the onset of growth by increase in dry weight. The phase is not readily recognizable in the field except by destructive sampling.

The need to recognize establishment as a separate phase is based on two presumptions, the first that the safe site for establishment may differ from the safe site for germination and the second that the agents acting on the population are different from those affecting survival later (post-establishment). In particular the second presumption may be false and observations of massive seedling mortality (i.e. "many more emerge than survive") may arise because there are many more individuals to be seen dying than at later (or earlier) stages. It may be that the whole of post-emergence mortality is represented by the exponential decay curve recognized by Harper (1967) although the data for *Ranunculus bulbosus* L. do show a greater relative rate of loss of seedlings immediately after emergence with a later log constant rate (Sarukhán and Harper, 1973). Resistance to inanition in the seedling state has not received the attention it appears to merit (Chippindale, 1948). Nevertheless because of lack of substantive data it is convenient to consider interphases (e) and (f) together.

F. INTERPHASES (e) AND (f). POST-EMERGENCE FATE

In the simplest type of study, best seen for crop plants, seeds are sown at a range of densities and survival of the seedlings is monitored. Donald (1963) illustrated the effect (Table VI). Greater mortality at higher seedling densities has been reported many times although not universally. Palmblad (1968) in pot tests sowed *Plantago major* at 5, 50, 100 and 200 seeds per pot and recorded seedling mortalities of 7, 6, 10 and 24% respectively. These were intraspecific tests but in the field interspecific effects may be at least as great if not overriding. In Tables VII–X are accumulated data on seedling survival. The arrangement of Table VII is broadly on an annual–perennial basis and the results from experimental introductions of seeds (synthetic) are amalgamated with those gathered by surveys of naturally occurring seedling populations (analytic). More records are available (see e.g. Marshall and Jain, 1969; Bonde, 1968; Caruso, 1970).

From the crude survey there emerges the well-worn dictum that establishment of plants from seed in closed communities is rare (Tamm,

TABLE VI   The effect of density on the survival of wheat plants. Number of plants m^{-2}. (After Donald, 1963.)

Time after sowing	Sowing rate Kg ha^{-1}				
	0·5	2·4	11·8	61·8	365·6
At germination	1·4	7	35	184	1078
At 119 days	1·4	7	35	190	694
at 182 days	1·4	7	35	154	447

1956; Sagar and Harper, 1961; Cavers and Harper, 1967; Putwain et al., 1968; Miles, 1972, 1974; Summerfield, 1973)—hence the shortage of annual plants in closed communities? Competition from other species is frequently used to explain the shortage of genet introductions but it is not always clear whether one is dealing with fewer emerged seedlings or an increased mortality, for seedlings are frequently difficult to see and they disappear rapidly (Miles, 1972). Summerfield (1973) displayed this neatly by demonstrating quite high seedling numbers and survival following the introduction of sown seed but was able to find only 11 naturally occurring seedlings at one site and two at another where natural seed inputs were 16×10^3 and 10×10^3 m^{-2} respectively. Presumably the microenvironment within a closed community is also different from that of an open community and the higher humidities would favour pathogenic attack (e.g. damping off, Gibson, 1956a, b, c; Miles, 1972) and might provide a more suitable environment for potential predators. The causes of seedling death require early and serious attention (see Hampel, 1969).

Drought, frost, and low light intensity have frequently been used to explain some of the losses. Summerfield (1973) emphasizes our shared ignorance by writing: "there is a closely circumscribed combination of environmental conditions that will permit seedling establishment to be

TABLE VII Post-emergence fates of seedlings and young plants

Species	Fates of seedlings and young plants	Authority
Avena fatua	0–60% mortality (in cereal crops)	Chancellor and Peters (1972)
	5–80% mortality (California—*ex* crop)	Marshall and Jain (1969)
Alopecurus myosuroides	60% mortality (in cereal crop)	Naylor (1972)
Desert annuals (Mojave)	Autumn germinating 37–90% mortality	
	Spring germinating 17–56% mortality	Beatley (1967)
Sinapis arvensis	Feb–Mar 48% of deaths due to pathogens. April–May 67% of deaths due to insects (Germany)	Hampel (1969)
Range of heath species	8, 26 and 29% seedlings established in absence of vegetation	Miles (1972)
	0, 2, 0% seedlings established in presence of vegetation	
Panicum virgatum	1·7% survival	Clements *ex* Donald (1963)
Arctic alpines	18% mortality 1st year; 44% 2nd; 72% by end of 3rd	Bliss (1971)
Rumex crispus and *R. obtusifolius*	15–100% mortality depending on habitat	Cavers and Harper (1967)
Plantago spp.	Up to 100% mortality depending on habitat	Sagar and Harper (1960, 1961)
Juncus effusus	5–50% mortality	Lazenby (1955a, b)
Lolium perenne	81–90% mortality in 1·5 years (sown as crop—Australia)	Campbell (1968)
Dactylis glomerata	76–94% mortality in 1·5 years (sown as crop—Australia)	Campbell (1968)
Phalaris tuberosa	25–64% mortality in 1·5 years (sown as crop—Australia)	Campbell (1968)
Fagus sylvatica	75·7–86·3% mortality in 1st year; 82·3–93·4% over 2 years	Watt (1923)
Ilex aquifolium L.	Of 319 seedlings emerged 2 April–10 June, 115 (29·4%) alive after 15 months	Peterken (1966)

TABLE VIII Survivorship of emerged seedlings of *Sinapis arvensis* and *Raphanus raphanistrum* L. % surviving (Blackman and Templeman, 1938). Weeds growing in a crop of oats.

Species	Emerged 20 Apl	6 May	% Surviving 19 May	7 June	23 June
Raphanus raphanistrum	100	73·7	42·1	28·4	24.3
Sinapis arvensis	100	53·7	42·8	29·6	14·3

TABLE IX The fates of seedlings of *Quercus petraea* observed for four years. Numbers of seedlings (Watt, 1919).

	Year 1915	Year 1916 Healthy	Diseased/ damaged	Missing	Year 1919 Surviving	(% surviving from 1915)
Habitat						
Open	661	94	239	328	6	(1)
Rabbits excluded	311	164	111	36	20	(6·4)
Vertebrates excluded	480	207	270	3	130	(27)

TABLE X The fates of seedlings and young plants of *Ilex aquifolium* observed for two seasons (Peterken, 1966).

Seedling classes	No. present At beginning	Two years later
1–2 yr old	732	0
2–4 yr old	33	17
4(–13) yr old	30	13

successful." The only generalization to come readily from study of these interphases is that in a pure species system it is possible to show that increasing densities lead to progressively more severe seedling mortality and that for a few species studied in sufficient detail there appear to be species-specific exponential losses of individuals (Harper, 1967). The plasticity of individuals as a response to increasing density must not be ignored (Ross and Harper, 1972).

G. INTERPHASE (g). INVASION

There are very many means by which seeds may enter a locality adjacent to or even remote from their locality of production, for seeds are a mobile phase of the life cycle. It is not appropriate to review the naturally occurring dispersal mechanisms here and the reader is referred to Ridley (1930), Salisbury (1942), and van der Pijl (1972). Wagner (1965) used a heavily irradiated area in the United States to set up seed traps. The total absence of vegetation in the trap sites precluded contamination by standing vegetation. Examples of seed numbers trapped per hectare are *Erigeron canadensis* L. 915,662, *Phragmites communis* Trin. 216,867 and *Taraxacum officinale* Weber 36,144. All these species have a pappus (see also Sheldon and Burrows, 1973). The importance of seed dispersal in species invasion of new land masses is obvious (Ridley, 1930; see also in Lousley, 1953) and on a more local level the problem of invasion of "weed-free" land from headlands, hedgerows and roadside verges has caused some consternation and stimulated a little study (Way, 1968, 1969). Generally, it has been suggested that the frequency of long distance transport by natural agencies (i.e. excluding man) can easily be exaggerated although significant numbers of cypselas do travel considerable distances (e.g. *Tussilago farfara* L. 4 km; Bakker, 1960). We need to know more about the rate at which areas of vegetation are rained upon by seeds of species which are not already members of the standing community.

Unwitting introduction of seeds by the otherwise deliberate activities of man has received more attention (Horne, 1953; Harper, 1957b; Wellington, 1960; Mackay, 1964; Tonkin, 1968a, b; Elliott, 1972) and the careful records kept by the Official Seed Testing Station are of immense value not only in estimating changes in the weed flora (e.g. Tonkin, 1968a, b) but also as estimates of the numbers of viable seeds likely to be sown directly with contaminated crop seeds. Horne (1953) quoted from a Ministry of Agriculture Committee report that a 1% contamination (by weight) of cereals by *Galium aparine* L. would mean the sowing of 51·1 seeds of this species per m². Other examples are given in Table XI. Changes in the regulations governing the contamination of crop seeds are frequently under discussion. In the context of this whole review, it is the likelihood of a sown seed producing seeds which is the issue but it cannot pass unrecorded that the contaminants are treated (i.e. dressed, sown and fertilized) as though they were crop seeds where the whole husbandry is aimed at maximizing the chance of a seed producing an established plant.

TABLE XI   The number of weed seeds that would be sown inadvertently if they were present as 1% contaminants by weight of (a) cereal grains sown at 188·2 kg ha^{-1} or (b) herbage seed sown at 17·9 kg ha^{-1} (after Anon, 1950).

Species	No. of seeds if present as 1% in 0·45 kg of seed	No. of weed seeds sown m^{-2}
(a) Sown with cereals		
Avena fatua	259	10·8
Agrostemma githago	388	15·9
Raphanus raphanistrum	574	23·9
Polygonum convolvulus L.	648	27·0
Galium aparine	1226	51·1
Agropyron repens	2268	94·6
(b) Sown with herbage crops		
Rumex crispus	3240	12·8
Alopecurus myosuroides	4320	17·16
Holcus lanatus L.	18 144	72·0
Cuscuta sp.	15 120	60·0
Plantago major	22 680	90·0
Poa annua	22 680	90·0
Cerastium vulgatum L.	45 360	180·0

V. ROUTE II. INTERPHASE (i). SURVIVAL OF THE MEMBERS OF A POPULATION

This route does not exist for annuals or ephemerals. Theoretically it is zero during the life of a generation of even-aged uniform monocarpic perennials and is 0·5 for a model biennial. Harper (1967) and Harper and White (1974) have discussed this route at some length and there is little to add beyond repeating the request for information on the causes of mortality. It is fairly clear that many individual plants of perennial species have only short life-spans although there are many obvious exceptions especially amongst the forest trees and perhaps in some species showing vegetative reproduction (Harper, 1961, 1967). Self-thinning of pure species populations (Harper and White, 1971) seems to be a result of interference but in mixed species stands such a mechanism is more difficult to comprehend. The separation of inter- and intra-specific effects in the field situation is of great interest (Sagar and Harper, 1961; Harper, 1964; Putwain and Harper, 1970). It is however perfectly feasible to draw up life-tables of perennial species and when sufficient of these are available some generalizations may be possible.

VI. Reproduction by Ramets

It is reproduction by ramets which makes the numerical handling of plant populations difficult, ecologic individuals no longer being equivalent to genetic ones. Nevertheless many plants do produce offspring vegetatively and studies of this subject have received strong impetus from weed science, for most of the problems of control of perennial herbaceous species are due to the potential of these weeds for this form of reproduction [but see Williams and Attwood, 1970, 1971 on the importance of seeds to a spread of *Agropyron repens* (L.) Beauv]. Although the forms of vegetative reproduction are more varied than the sexual, there are some clear parallels between them. It is for example more convenient for non-genetical work to examine the fate of the bulbils of *Allium* spp. as though they were seeds. Such bulbils become physiologically independent individuals at dispersal.

The identity of the individual becomes especially difficult when considering those species which produce shoots from subterranean organs. In its simplest form the question is "when is a shoot an ecological individual?" Clearly, if vascular connection between the shoots is totally lost, for ecological purposes the two parts are likely to behave as very closely related but separate individuals. Thus for say potato (*Solanum tuberosum* L.), *Oxalis latifolia* H.B.K., *Ranunculus repens* or *Fragaria vesca* L. the identity of the individuals is a problem for only a short period of time and there is a period each year when ecological individuals may be counted. But, for a plant like *Agropyron repens* Beauv. where vascular continuity (judged by the persistence of rhizomes) may persist for more than three years, counts of numbers of above ground shoots are, in one sense, meaningless for the interrelationships of shoots in vascular connection are, in grasses at least, quite different from those of separated shoots (Sagar and Marshall, 1966; Marshall and Sagar, 1968a, b; Nyahoza *et al.*, 1973, 1974). Where vascular connection can be confirmed there is an obvious case for continuing to treat the interconnected parts as an individual, much as might be done if an oak tree was under consideration. On the other hand, the capacity of branches to become separated after periods of longer than one year—a capacity which is normal in, for example, *Agropyron repens* (Sagar, 1960, 1961), some *Carex* spp, *Cirsium arvense* (L.) Scop. (Sagar and Rawson, 1964) or *Pteridium aquilinum* (L.) Kuhn.—at least makes the study of the demography of such species abominably difficult! There is a real need to try to resolve this puzzle. One approach might be to broaden the definition of Route II to include branching when this does not lead, over the life span of the genet, to the loss of vascular continuity between branches. However such a treatment could lead to a simpler view than is necessary for a synthesis of demographic models for species which show ramet reproduction.

A better understanding, although not a universally practical method, emerges if the terms genet and ramet (Harper and White, 1974) are further subdivided. A genet might be unbranched (a unigenet-Type 1) or branched (each branch would be a sub-genet-Type 2); the distinction is important because leaves on an unbranched shoot do not have all the physiological interrelationships which branches may have with each other. Sub-genets would not have their own independent roots. Ramet (Type 4) could remain as a term to include individuals produced by vegetative propagation but would be applicable only when such pro-pagules are totally and permanently independent of the individual from which they were produced. It is proposed that the term incipient ramet (Type 3) be introduced to cover the situations where branches have produced their own root systems but where vascular continuity between branches remains functional so that local deficiencies (e.g. light, water or nutrients) or disasters (e.g. defoliation) are potentially (actually?) shared by the whole plant and not only by the affected branch.

These four types of individuals are comfortable to contemplate from the armchair. It is a totally different matter to assign individuals in the field with certainty to a type and this is especially so if the connections between individuals are below ground. Nevertheless, to understand the interrelationships between plants, these distinctions must not be totally ignored.

In practice, the presentation of the dynamics of species which multiply by vegetative means (i.e. ultimately producing ramets) demands a different display from the one used in Fig. 1.

Figure 11a is an example of a form of presentation which can be useful as a model in such a situation (cf. Sarukhán and Gadgil, 1974). The starting population is in four classes—seeds (unigenets), seedlings (unigenets), emerged shoots (genets of both types, incipient ramets and ramets) and buds (sub-genets, incipient ramets and ramets). The latter are almost as hidden as the seeds in the bank and can only be assessed by destructive sampling. During the course of a season's growth and development components may die, survive, reproduce, multiply or transfer from one class to another as appropriate. Probabilities of each of these events may be measured or calculated and some of the values have clear relationships with the interphases discussed earlier.

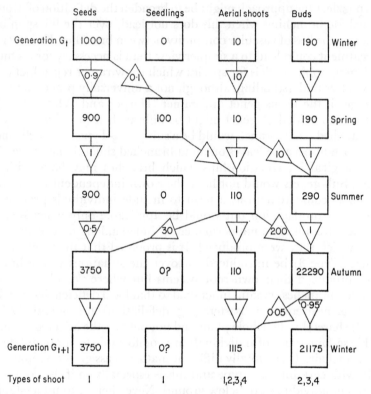

FIG. 11a. Life table for Agropyron repens. An expanding population. (Sources acknowledged in text.)

A. *Agropyron repens*

Figure 11a is drawn to describe the potential of *Agropyron repens* in an unlimited environment such as might occur after cultivation. The population is created by planting 200 buds or rhizomes m⁻² and assuming that 5% of the buds produce emerged shoots, the remainder surviving as buds. To these plants are added 1000 seeds. Despite the best attentions of Williams (1968, 1970, 1971, 1973) and Williams and Attwood (1970, 1971), data on the emergence of seedlings in the field do not appear to be available. It is therefore assumed that 10% of the seed produces emerged seedlings which survive, enter the established plant population and produce rhizomes (with buds) and flowers in their first year (Williams, 1971; Tripathi and Harper, 1973). From studies of this species grown under conditions of a cold glasshouse Tripathi and

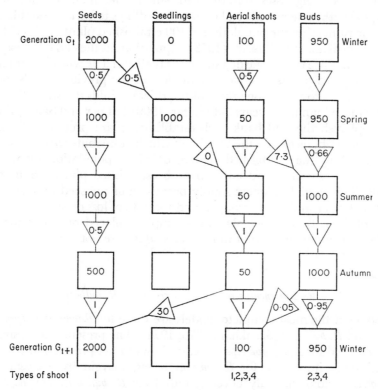

FIG. 11b. Life table for *Agropyron repens*. A regulated population (Sources acknowledged in text.)

Harper (1973) have shown that a seedling may, within a single season, produce more than 200 new rhizome buds and 30 seeds. These values have been used in the model and in addition the originally established plants have produced 10 new buds per shoot during the spring. In the autumn the established shoots die and are replaced by the upturned rhizome tips of the new rhizomes, the terminal apices representing 5% of the total rhizome bud population (Cussans 1970, 1973; Tripathi and

Harper, 1973). It is also assumed that 50% of the seeds in the seed bank die during a year. Using these data, over one generation the seed bank expands from 1000 to 3750 seeds m^{-2}, the established (emerged) plant population from 10 to 1115 and the bud bank from 190 to 21 175. Clearly an unlimited environment can last for only a short time and in Fig. 11b a more stable situation is described. Stability is achieved in part by assuming losses from the seed bank by death and by emergence coupled with an assumed total failure of seedlings to become established. On the ramet side the population of 100 established plants and 950 buds m^{-2} approximate to Cussans (1973) populations at the end of his experiment. They are to be regarded simply as realistic! The winter population of established plants is halved by the loss of the previous year's shoots and during the Spring one third of the rhizome buds die when they become more than three years old (Sagar, 1960; Palmer and Sagar, 1963). To replenish the bud bank each established plant produces rhizomes bearing 7·3 buds to join the bud bank which contributes 5% of its total (all new) to the established (emerged) plant population by winter. During the summer and autumn each established plant produces 30 seeds. This model balances simply because half the seed population is lost each year and then recouped and the rate of loss of buds equals the rate of gain. Established plants are simply replaced on a one for one basis. It is unfortunate that more precise data are not available.

B. *Ranunculus repens, R. acris* AND *R. bulbosus*

Some of the most complete models are those for *Ranunculus repens, R. acris* and *R. bulbosus* (Sarukhán, 1970, 1974). The presentation is similar to that used for *Agropyron repens*, i.e. it allows ramet production which is continually important for *Ranunculus repens*, marginally necessary for *R. acris* L. and virtually never required for *R. bulbosus*. For *R. repens* (Fig. 12) the size of the ramet bank is estimated from knowledge of the population of mature plants that undergo ramet production. The model indicates the changes in interphase probabilities over the season and the very great importance of ramet reproduction in contributing to the population. During the season shown 76% of the recruits to this final population were ramets. The survival rate of ecologic individuals from generation Gt to Gt + 1 may be unusually low because in this species a mother plant having produced a ramet frequently dies. *Ranunculus acris* (Fig. 13) and *R. bulbosus* (Fig. 14) differ from *R. repens* in reproducing by ramets to a small degree or not at all. These two models illustrate yet again the low probability of a seed producing a seedling.

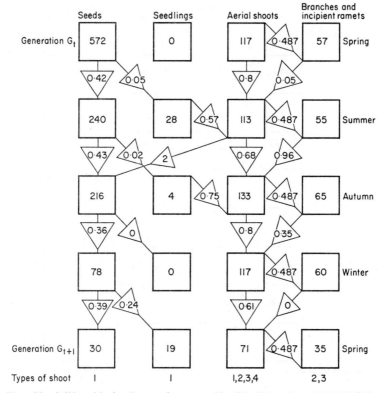

FIG. 12. A life-table for *Ranunculus repens*, Site B1. (After Sarukhán, 1971.)

c. *Plantago lanceolata*

The dynamics of the perennial *Plantago lanceolata* are summarized in Fig. 15. The model is precarious because the data are from two different populations (Sagar, 1959, 1970 and Mortimer, 1974). The half-life of established plants is 13·5 months and replacement is by ramets or by seeds and seedlings.

In general, vegetatively produced offspring seem to have a greater chance of survival than do seeds, perhaps because the numbers produced are almost always fewer and maternal support often continues. The studies of Putwain *et al.* (1968) on *Rumex acetosa* L. and *R. acetosella* L., of Foster (1964) on *Bellis perennis* L. and of Sarukhán (1970, 1974) and Sarukhán and Harper (1973) on *Ranunculus repens* L. all point to the great importance of vegetative propagation in the maintenance of the population. Harberd (1961) also reached a similar conclusion for *Holcus*

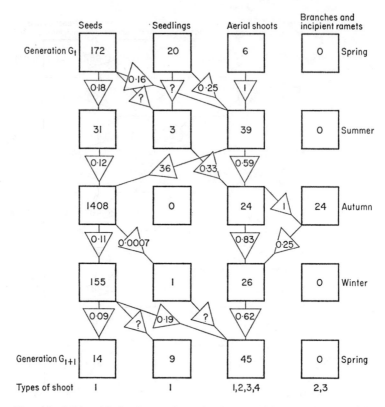

Fig. 13. A life-table for *Ranunculus acris*, Site G2. (After Sarukhán, 1971.)

mollis L. and *Festuca rubra* L. following a search for genetic variability. All these studies were made in existing more or less closed communities but even on arable land the persistence of such species as *Cirsium arvense* Scop., *Agropyron repens* (L.) Beauv., *Oxalis* spp. and *Rumex crispus* L. depends on the potential for vegetative reproduction.

There seems to have grown up a view that perennial weeds are more difficult to control than annual weeds because of their potential to regenerate. Yet this potential is little different, in the ecologic sense, from the potential of the seed bank in the soil. The difference between the two may lie in the size of the propagule—most frequently in vegetative reproduction the daughter is far better endowed with reserves for emergence and early growth, than is the seed of that same species. The vegetative propagule may show greater plasticity than the seed. Furthermore, in many cases the offspring remains attached to the mother plant

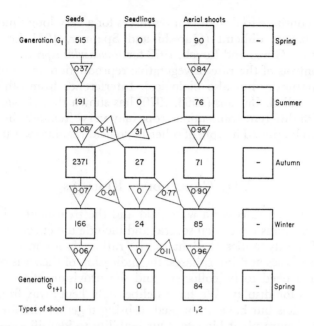

Fɪɢ. 14. A life-table for *Ranunculus bulbosus*, Site G1. (After Sarukhán, 1971).

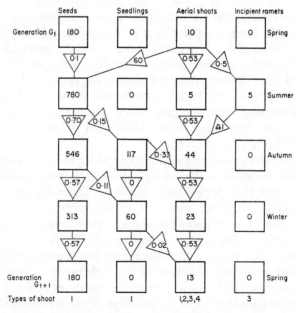

Fɪɢ. 15. A life-table for *Plantago lanceolata*. (After Sagar, 1959 and Mortimer, 1974.)

and may continue to draw upon resources for a very long time if establishment proves difficult (Qureshi and Spanner, 1971 for *Saxifraga sarmentosa* L.; Ginzo and Lovell, 1973 for *Ranunculus repens*).

The controls of the rate of vegetative reproduction are climatic and edaphic naturally but also biological. Interference from other species has been studied. Cussans (1968, 1970) has shown that *Agropyron repens* grown with different companion crops may vary "tenfold" in its vegetative reproduction. The role of other biological regulators is unclear.

VII. Concluding Remarks

We have tried to cover a wide field and the treatment is inevitably uneven. Our aims have been several and include the encouragement of studies of the dynamics of plant species rather than concentration on particular phases and interphases, the indication of the sorts of information which need to be collected, and the provision of two practical frameworks for display. We have deliberately kept away from mathematical models but have attempted to bring together the literature of applied and pure plant biology. Our inability to identify precisely the regulators of populations (in the necessary sense of density-related agents or agencies) is thoroughly displayed. Such evidence as is available yields no generality; species will have to be examined separately. For weeds of arable land the principles of natural regulation may rarely apply; but studies of weeds of grasslands are perhaps more likely to yield evidence of some biologically based controlling mechanisms. The sort of data yielded from the very detailed accounting systems of the kind used by Sarukhán (1970, 1974) and Sharitz and McCormick (1973) lend strength to the hope that we may one day understand the way plant populations are regulated when integrated control methods (e.g. Hussey, 1970) might be evolved.

It is of more than passing interest to consider the philosophy of those who work in the area of the biological control of weeds for their approaches suggest that populations of species generally explode in new environments not only because of new edaphic or climatic conditions but also because of escape from some predator or pathogen (see e.g. Huffaker, 1957, 1964, 1971; de Bach, 1964; Wapshere, 1970; Hasan and Wapshere, 1973). If this view is correct, then the regulation of population size in the native habitat seems more likely to be through agents acting from above in the food chain than through limits of the resources below. Such a view is very attractive for it reduces the problem of plant communities which have many species all apparently co-habiting—a situation difficult to hold in equilibrium when plants have so few resources of the De Wit (1960) "space" type (Harper *et al.*, 1961).

Plant populations are usually regulated. It is time that we understood more about the means and mechanisms.

Acknowledgements

The senior author thanks Prof. Dr Werner Koch for hospitality, kindness and facilities at Universität Hohenheim when the preparatory work for this paper was in progress. We thank Mrs Venesoen for her invaluable help in translating our hieroglyphics into type.

References

Anon (1950). "Seeds—Report on qualitative control of seeds". HMSO, London.
Barnes, H. F. (1932). *J. anim. Ecol.* 1, 12–31.
Barnes, H. F. (1933). *J. anim. Ecol.* 2, 98–108.
Bakker, D. (1960). *In*: "Biology of Weeds" (J. L. Harper, Ed.), pp. 205–222. Blackwell Scientific Publications, Oxford.
Bartholemew, B. (1970). *Science, N.Y.* 170, 1210–1212.
Barton, L. V. (1961). "Seed Preservation and Longevity". Leonard Hill, London.
Beatley, J. C. (1967). *Ecology,* 48, 745–750.
Black, J. N. (1955). *Aust. J. Agr. Res.* 6, 203–211.
Black, J. N. (1956). *Aust. J. Agr. Res.* 7, 98–109.
Black, M. (1969). *Symp. Soc. Exptl. Biol.* 23, 193–217.
Blackman, G. E. and Templeman, W. G. (1938). *J. agric. Sci.* 27, 247–271.
Bliss, L. C. (1971). *A. Rev. Ecol. Syst.* 2, 405–438.
Bonde, E. K. (1970). *Ecology* 49, 1193–1195.
Brenchley, W. E. and Warington, K. (1930). *J. Ecol.* 18, 235–272.
Brenchley, W. E. and Warington, K. (1933). *J. Ecol.* 21, 103–127.
Brenchley, W. E. and Warington, K. (1936). *J. Ecol.* 24, 479–501.
Cameron, E. (1935). *J. Ecol.* 23, 265–322.
Campbell, M. H. (1968). *Aust. J. exp. Agric. Anim. Husb.* 8, 470–477.
Caruso, J. L. (1970). *Ecology,* 51, 553–554.
Cavers, P. A. and Harper, J. L. (1967). *J. Ecol.* 55, 59–71.
Champness, S. S. and Morris, K. (1948). *J. Ecol.* 36, 149–173.
Chancellor, R. J. (1964a). Proc. 7th Brit. Weed Control. Conf. 599–606.
Chancellor, R. J. (1964b). Proc. 7th Brit. Weed Control Conf. 607–613.
Chancellor, R. J. (1965). Rept. A.R.C. Weed Res. Org. for 1960–64, 15–19.
Chancellor, R. J. and Peters, N. C. B. (1970). Proc. 10th Brit. Weed Control Conf. 7–11.
Chancellor, R. J. and Peters, N. C. B. (1972). Proc. 11th Brit. Weed Control Conf. 218–225.
Charles, A. H. (1962). *Herb. Abst.* 32, 175–181.
Chippindale, H. G. (1948). *Nature, Lond.* 161, 65.
Chippindale, H. G. and Milton, W. E. J. (1934). *J. Ecol.* 22, 508–531.
Colquhoun, M. K. (1951). *A.R.C. Report Series* 10, 1–69.
Cook, A. D., Atsatt, P. R. and Simon, C. A. (1971). *Bioscience* 21, 277–281.
Courtney, A. D. (1968). *J. app. Ecol.* 5, 675–684.

44 G. R. SAGAR AND A. M. MORTIMER

Cussans, G. W. (1968). Proc. 9th Brit. Weed Control Conf. 131–136.
Cussans, G. W. (1970). Proc. 10th Brit. Weed Control Conf. 1101–1107.
Cussans, G. W. (1973). Weed Res. 13, 283–291.
Darwin, C. R. (1881). "The Formation of Vegetable Mould—through the action of worms with observations on their habits." Faber and Faber, London.
De Bach, P. (Ed.) (1964). "Biological Control of Insect Pests and Weeds." Chapman and Hall, London.
De Wit, C. T. (1960). Versl. Landbouwk. Onderz. 66, 1–82.
Donald, C. M. (1963). Adv. Agron. 15, 1–118.
Douglas, G. (1965). J. Brit. Grassld Soc. 20, 91–100.
Dowling, P. M., Clements, R. J. and McWilliam, H. R. (1971). Aust. J. agric. Res. 22, 61–74.
Evans, C. G. (1972). "The Quantitative Analysis of Plant Growth." Blackwell Scientific Publications, Oxford.
Evans, R. A. and Young, J. A. (1970). Weed Sci. 18, 697–703.
Evans, R. A. and Young, J. A. (1972). Weed Sci. 20, 350–356.
Evans, R. A., Young, J. A. and Kay, B. L. (1974). Weed Sci. 22, 185–187.
Elliott, J. G. (1972). Proc. 11th Brit. Weed Control Conf. 965–976.
Falinska, K. (1968). Ekologia Polska. Seria A. 161, 395–408.
Forbes, N. (1963). Exptl. Husb. 9, 10–13.
Foster, J. (1964). "Studies on the population dynamics of the daisy (Bellis perennis L.)". Ph.D. Thesis, Univ. Wales.
Fryer, J. D. and Evans, S. A. (Eds) (1968). "Weed Control Handbook". Vol. 1 (5th Ed.). Blackwell Scientific Publications, Oxford.
Gibson, I. A. S. (1956a). E. Afr. Agric. J. 21, 96–99.
Gibson, I. A. S. (1956b). E. Afr. Agric. J. 21, 165–166.
Gibson, I. A. S. (1956c). E. Afr. Agric. J. 21, 183–188.
Ginzo, H. D. and Lovell, P. H. (1973). Ann. Bot. 37, 765–776.
Grant Lipp, A. E. and Ballard, L. A. T. (1959). Aust. J. Res. 10, 495–499.
Gutterman, Y., Witztum, A. and Evanari, M. (1967). Israel J. Bot. 16, 213–234.
Hall, M. A. and Wareing, P. F. (1972). Proc. 11th Brit. Weed Control Conf. 1173–1182.
Hampel, M. (1969). "Untersuchungen über Ursachen und Verbreitung von Keimlingskoankheiten an Unkräutern." Diss. Univ. Hohenheim.
Harberd, D. J. (1961). New Phytol. 60, 184–206.
Harberd, D. J. (1967). New Phytol. 66, 401–408.
Harper, J. L. (1956). New Phytol. 55, 35–44.
Harper, J. L. (1957a). Proc. 4th Int. Congr. Crop Prot. Hamburg. 415–420.
Harper, J. L. (1957b). Outlook Agric., 197–205.
Harper, J. L. (1960). In: "Biology of Weeds" (J. L. Harper, Ed.), pp. 119–132. Blackwell Scientific Publications, Oxford.
Harper, J. L. (1961). Symp. Soc. Exptl. Biol. 15, 1–39.
Harper, J. L. (1964). Proc. 11th Int. Congr. Genetics. 465–482.
Harper, J. L. (1967). J. Ecol. 55, 247–270.
Harper, J. L. and Benton, R. A. (1966). J. Ecol. 54, 151–166.
Harper, J. L., Clatworthy, J. N., McNaughton, I. H. and Sagar, G. R. (1961). Evolution 15, 209–227.
Harper, J. L. and Gajic, D. (1961). Weed Res. 1, 91–104.
Harper, J. L. and White, J. (1971). Proc. Advanc. Stud. Inst. Dyn. Numbers Pop., Oosterbeek, 1970, 41–63.
Harper, J. L. and White, J. (1974). A. Rev. Ecol. Syst. 5, 419–463.

Harper, J. L., Williams, J. T. and Sagar, G. R. (1965). *J. Ecol.* **53**, 273–286.
Harper, J. L., Lovell, P. H. and Moore, K. (1970). *A. Rev. Ecol. Syst.* **1**, 327–356.
Hasan, S. and Wapshere, A. J. (1973). *Ann. appl. Biol.* **74**, 263–399.
Hegarty, T. W. (1963). *In*: "Seed Ecology". (W. Heydecker, Ed.), pp. 411–431. Butterworths, London.
Heydecker, W. (Ed.) (1973). "Seed Ecology", Butterworths, London.
Holroyd, J. (1964). Proc. 7th Brit. Weed Control Conf. 621–627.
Horne, F. R. (1953). Proc. 1st Brit. Weed Control Conf. 372–398.
Huffaker, C. B. (1957). *Hilgardia* **27**, 101–157.
Huffaker, C. B. (1964). *In*: "Biological Control of Insect Pests and Weeds". (P. De Bach, Ed.), pp. 631–649. Chapman and Hall, London.
Huffaker, C. B. (Ed.) (1971). "Biological Control. Proc. AAAS Symposium on Biological Control". Plenum Press, New York.
Hussey, N. W. (1970). Rep. Roy. Soc. Meet. Brit. Nat. Cttee Biol. 16–21.
Janzen, D. H. (1969). *Evolution* **23**, 1–27.
Janzen, D. H. (1971). *A. Rev. Ecol. Syst.* **2**, 465–492.
Jones, E. W. (1959). *J. Ecol.* **47**, 169–222.
Karssen, C. M. (1968). *Acta bot. Neerl.* **14**, 293–308.
Karssen, C. M. (1970a). *Acta bot. Neerl.* **19**, 95–108.
Karssen, C. M. (1970b). *Acta bot. Neerl.* **19**, 187–196.
Kays, S. and Harper, J. L. (1974). *J. Ecol.* **62**, 97–105.
Kiewnick, L. (1963). *Weed Res.* **3**, 322–332.
Kiewnick. L. (1964). *Weed Res.* **4**, 31–43.
Kirk, J. and Courtney, A. D. (1972). Proc. 11th Brit. Weed Control Conf. 226–233.
Koch, W. (1969). "Einfluss von Unweltfaktoren auf die Samenphase annueller Unkräuter insbesondere unter dem Gesichtspunkt der Unkräutbekämpfung". Eugen Ulmer, Stuttgart.
Koch, W. (1970). "Unkräutbekämpfung". Eugen Ulmer, Stuttgart.
Krefting, L. W. and Roe, E. I. (1949). *Ecol. Monogr.* **19**, 269–286.
Lawrence, W. H. and Rediske, J. H. (1962). *For. Sci.* **8**, 210–218.
Lazenby, A. (1955a). *J. Ecol.* **43**, 43–119.
Lazenby, A. (1955b). *J. Ecol.* **43**, 595–605.
Lousley, J. E. (Ed.) (1953). "The Changing Flora of Britain". B.S.B.I. London.
Mackay, D. B. (1964). Proc. 7th Brit. Weed Control Conf. 583–591.
McRill, M. (1974). Proc. 12th Brit. Weed Control Conf. 519–523.
McRill, M. and Sagar, G. R. (1973). *Nature, Lond.* **243**, 482.
McVean, D. N. (1966). *J. Ecol.* **54**, 345–365.
Major, J. and Pyott, W. T. (1966). *Vegetation* **13**, 253–282.
Marshall, C. and Sagar, G. R. (1968a). *Ann. Bot.* **32**, 715–719.
Marshall, C. and Sagar, G. R. (1968b). *J. exptl. Bot.* **19**, 785–794.
Marshall, D. R. and Jain, S. K. (1967). *Ecology* **48**, 656–659.
Marshall, D. R. and Jain, S. K. (1969). *J. Ecol.* **57**, 251–270.
Marshall, D. R. and Jain, S. K. (1970). *Ecology* **51**, 886–891.
Maun, M. A. and Cavers, P. B. (1971a). *Can. J. Bot.* **49**, 1123–1130.
Maun, M. A. and Cavers, P. B. (1971b). *Can. J. Bot.* **49**, 1184–1848.
Miles, J. (1972). *J. Ecol.* **60**, 225–234.
Miles, J. (1974). *J. Ecol.* **62**, 675–687.
Mortimer, A. M. (1974). "Studies of germination and establishment of selected species with special references to the fates of seeds." Ph.D. Thesis. Univ. Wales.
Muller, C. H. and Muller, W. H. (1964). *Science, N.Y.* **144**, 889–890.

Müllverstedt, R. (1963). *Weed Res.* **3**, 154–163.
Naylor, R. E. L. (1970). *Weed Res.* **10**, 296–299.
Naylor, R. E. L. (1972). *J. appl. Ecol.* **9**, 127–139.
Nyahoza, F., Marshall, C. and Sagar, G. R. (1973). *Weed Res.* **13**, 304–309.
Nyahoza, F., Marshall, C. and Sagar, G. R. (1974). *Weed Res.* **14**, 251–256.
Ødum, S. (1974). Proc. 12th Brit. Weed Control Conf. 1131–1144.
Olatoye, S. T. and Hall, M. A. (1973). *In:* "Seed Ecology" (W. Heydecker, Ed.), pp. 233–248. Butterworths, London.
Palmblad, I. G. (1968). *Ecology* **49**, 26–35.
Palmer, J. H. and Sagar, G. R. (1963). *J. Ecol.* **51**, 783–794.
Peterken, G. F. (1966). *J. Ecol.* **54**, 259–269.
Popay, A. I. and Roberts, E. H. (1970a). *J. Ecol.* **58**, 103–122.
Popay, A. I. and Roberts, E. H. (1970b). *J. Ecol.* **58**, 123–139.
Putwain, P. D. (1970). Proc. 10th Brit. Weed Control Conf. 12–19.
Putwain, P. D., Machin, D. and Harper, J. L. (1968). *J. Ecol.* **56**, 421–431.
Putwain, P. D. and Harper, J. L. (1970). *J. Ecol.* **58**, 251–264.
Qureshi, F. A. and Spanner, D. C. (1971). *Planta (Berl.)* **101**, 133–146.
Ridley, H. N. (1930). "The Dispersal of Plants throughout the World." Reeve, Ashford.
Roberts, H. A. (1964). *Weed Res.* **4**, 296–307.
Roberts, H. A. (1970). Rep. natn. Veg. Res. Stn for 1969. 25–38.
Roberts, H. A. and Dawkins, P. A. (1967). *Weed Res.* **7**, 290–301.
Roberts, H. A. and Feast, P. (1972). *Weed Res.* **12**, 316–324.
Roberts, H. A. and Feast, P. (1973). *J. appl. Ecol.* **10**, 133–143.
Ross, M. A. and Harper, J. L. (1972). *J. Ecol.* **60**, 77–88.
Sagar, G. R. (1959). "The biology of some sympatric species of grassland." D.Phil. thesis, University of Oxford.
Sagar, G. R. (1960). Proc. 5th Brit. Weed Control Conf. 259–263.
Sagar, G. R. (1961). *N.A.A.S. q. Rev.* **53**, 10–16.
Sagar, G. R. (1970). Proc. 10th Brit. Weed Control Conf. 965–979.
Sagar, G. R. (1974). *In:* "Biology in Pest and Disease Control". (D. Price-Jones and M. E. Solomon, Eds), pp. 42–56. Blackwell Scientific Publications, Oxford.
Sagar, G. R. and Harper, J. L. (1960). *In:* "Biology of Weeds". (J. L. Harper, Ed.), pp. 236–245. Blackwell Scientific Publications, Oxford.
Sagar, G. R. and Harper, J. L. (1961). *Weed Res.* **1**, 163–176.
Sagar, G. R. and Marshall, C. (1966). Proc. 9th Int. Grassld Congr. **1**, 493–497.
Sagar, G. R. and Rawson, H. M. (1964). Proc. 7th Brit. Weed Control Conf. 553–562.
Salisbury, E. J. (1942). "The Reproductive Capacity of Plants". Bell and Sons, London.
Salisbury, E. J. (1961). "Weeds and Aliens". Collins, London.
Sarukhán, J. (1970). Proc. 10th Brit. Weed Control Conf. 20–25.
Sarukhán, J. (1971). "Studies on plant demography". Ph.D. thesis. University of Wales.
Sarukhán, J. (1974). *J. Ecol.* **62**, 151–177.
Sarukhán, J. and Gadgil, M. (1974). *J. Ecol.* **62**, 921–936.
Sarukhán, J. and Harper, J. L. (1973). *J. Ecol.* **61**, 675–716.
Selman, M. (1970). Proc. 10th Brit. Weed Control Conf. 1176–1188.
Sharitz, R. R. and McCormick, J. F. (1973). *Ecology* **54**, 723–740.
Shaw, M. W. (1968a). *J. Ecol.* **56**, 565–583.
Shaw, M. W. (1968b). *J. Ecol.* **56**, 647–660.

Sheldon, J. C. (1974). *J. Ecol.* **62,** 47–66.
Sheldon, J. C. and Burrows, F. M. (1973). *New Phytol.* **72,** 665–675.
Simpson, M. (1952). *N.Z. Jl. Sci. Technol.* **34,** 360–364.
Smith, D. F. (1968). *Aust. J. exp. Agric. Anim. Husb.* **8,** 478–483.
Summerfield, R. J. (1973). *J. Ecol.* **61,** 387–398.
Symonides, E. (1974). *Ekol. pol.* **22,** 379–416.
Tamm, C. O. (1948). *Bot. notiser.* **3,** 305–321.
Tamm, C. O. (1956). *Oikos* **7,** 273–292.
Taylorson, R. B. (1970). *Weed Sci.* **18,** 265–269.
Thurston, J. M. (1951). *Ann. appl. Biol.* **38,** 812–832.
Thurston, J. M. (1953). Proc. 1st Brit. Weed Control Conf. 240–248.
Thurston, J. M. (1960). *In:* "Biology of Weeds". (J. L. Harper, Ed.), pp. 69–82. Blackwell Scientific Publications.
Thurston, J. M. (1961). *Weed Res.* **1,** 19–31.
Thurston, J. M. (1964). Proc. 7th Brit. Weed Control Conf. 592–598.
Thurston, J. M. (1966). *Weed Res.* **6,** 67–80.
Tonkin, J. H. B. (1968a). Proc. 9th Brit. Weed Control Conf. 1–5.
Tonkin, J. H. B. (1968b). Proc. 9th Brit. Weed Control Conf. 1199–1204.
Tripathi, R. S. and Harper, J. L. (1973). *J. Ecol.* **61,** 353–368.
van der Meijden, E. (1971). Proc. Advan. Stud. Inst. Dyn. Numbers Pop. Oosterbeek 1970, 390–404.
van der Pilj, L. (1972). "Principles of Dispersal in Higher Plants." 2nd Ed. Springer-Verlag, Berlin.
Wagner, R. H. (1965). *Ecology* **46,** 517–520.
Wapshere, A. J. (1970). Proc. 1st Int. Symp. Biol. Control Weeds, 81–89.
Watt, A. S. (1919). *J. Ecol.* **7,** 173–203.
Watt, A. S. (1923). *J. Ecol.* **11,** 1–48.
Way, J. M. (1968). Proc. 9th Brit. Weed Control Conf. 989–994.
Way, J. M. (1969). "Road Verges, their Function and Management". Nature Conservancy, Monks Wood.
Wellington, P. S. (1960). *In:* "Biology of Weeds" (J. L. Harper, Ed.), pp. 94–107. Blackwell Scientific Publications.
Wesson, G. and Wareing, P. F. (1967). *Nature, Lond.* **213,** 600–601.
Wesson, G. and Wareing, P. F. (1969). *J. exp. Bot.* **20,** 414–425.
Whybrew, J. E. (1964). Proc. 7th Brit. Weed Control Conf. 614–620.
Williams, E. D. (1968). Proc. 9th Brit. Weed Control Conf. 119–124.
Williams, E. D. (1970). *Weed Res.* **10,** 321–330.
Williams, E. D. (1971). *Weed Res.* **11,** 159–170.
Williams, E. D. (1973). *Weed Res.* **13,** 24–41.
Williams, E. D. and Attwood, P. J. (1970). *N.A.A.S. q. Rev.* **89,** 42–46.
Williams, E. D. and Attwood, P. J. (1971). *Weed Res.* **11,** 22–30.
Wilson, B. J. (1970). Proc. 10th Brit. Weed Control Conf. 831–836.
Wilson, B. J. (1972). Proc. 11th Brit. Weed Control Conf. 242–247.
Wilson, B. J. and Cussans, G. W. (1972). Proc. 11th Brit. Weed Control Conf. 234–241.
Young, J. A. and Evans, R. A. (1973). *Weed Sci.* **21,** 52–54.

The Development of Forest Science

J. D. MATTHEWS

Department of Forestry, University of Aberdeen, Aberdeen, Scotland

I. INTRODUCTION

A. THE SCOPE OF FOREST SCIENCE

A *forest* is a biological community dominated by trees and other woody vegetation and the major task of *forestry* is to provide raw materials from forests—mainly timber but also a wide variety of other products including forage, litter, bark, tanstuffs, medicinal and edible plants, resin, gums, latex, dyestuffs, honey, fruits and seeds.

But the activities covered by the term *forestry* extend over a much wider field. In many places forests are valued primarily for the direct protection they afford to water supplies. Over vast areas of the world maintenance of forests or some other form of vegetal cover is the only cheap and practical means of preserving the soil from erosion and maintaining its fertility, and the systematic use of vegetation for this protective purpose is an important function of forest services in many countries.

The influence that forests exert by providing shelter from strong and dessicating winds is of great importance in growing certain economic crops and husbanding certain animals. In some countries forest services have become involved in rural development and land use together with other agencies engaged in similar work. Production of a sustained supply of raw material from forests can stimulate local industries thus providing employment and improving the living standards of people.

Forests also contribute to landscape beauty and to sport and recreation. The aesthetic values are seen and enjoyed in parks and the artistic placing of trees in the landscape (Schlich, 1916). Forests often contain a valuable store of wildlife attractive to hunters and fisherman and important to conservationists. Forest roads can provide access for tourists to beautiful places hitherto difficult to reach.

One comprehensive definition of the broad scope of forestry was provided recently in the "National Statement by the Schools of Forestry at Canadian Universities" (Science Council of Canada, 1973) and with only small alterations serves well to introduce this paper:

Forestry is the science, business and art of managing and conserving forests and associated lands for continuing economic, social and environmental benefit. It involves the balanced management of forest resources for optimum yields of wood products, abundant wildlife, plentiful supplies of pure water, attractive scenic and recreational environments in wild, rural and urban settings, and a variety of other services and products. Forestry draws upon knowledge and experience from many disciplines and other professions.

In protection forests and wilderness areas the practical solution to the tasks of forestry lies in carefully maintaining the original natural balance; in production forests it is found in the systematic and sustained formation, harvesting and utilization of forest stands. Mere harvesting and utilization of timber and other resources is exploitation; thus the essence of genuine forest management lies in the conservation and continual use of forests (Heske, 1938) The general task of *forest science* is to seek understanding of and solutions to the problems encountered in organizing the use of the natural resources of forests on a permanent basis. Forest science is the systematic application of science to the technical, economic and social questions of forestry.

Fuller use of the productive capacity of forests is essential for a permanent world supply of timber and other forest products. The mounting demand for forest products can only be met by balancing out harvesting and growth, so as to sustain yield, and by increasing growth. The latter is one of the most important detailed tasks of forest science; another is to show how better to use forest resources.

The practice of sustained yield forestry, whether for protection or production, has called into existence a number of disciplines in which the findings and methods of the basic sciences are brought to bear on forestry problems.

There is a group of disciplines directly concerned with the production of timber and other products and these are *forest botany, forest genetics, tree physiology, forest soil science, forest ecology* and *wood science* (which deals with the structure and properties of timber). Forests and forest produce must be protected from injury by insects, fungi and inorganic agencies such as fire, and this is the concern of forest protection, often subdivided as *forest zoology* and *forest pathology*.

Central to the management of forests and associated lands, whether it is concerned with timber production, wildlife habitats, water supplies, recreation or landscape are *silviculture, forest economics* and *forest yield studies* the latter being the study of the organic production, structure, increment and yield of forest stands. It is in silviculture that much of the growing store of scientific knowledge about trees is applied. Troup (1928) defined a silvicultural system as "the process by which the crops constituting a forest are tended, removed and replaced by new crops, resulting in the production of woods of a distinctive form". A silvicultural system embodies three main ideas: (i) the method of regeneration of the individual crops constituting the forest; (ii) the form of crop produced; (iii) the orderly arrangement of the crops over the whole forest, with special reference to silvicultural and protective considerations and the economic utilization of the produce.

The practical application of silvicultural systems is closely connected with the requirements of *forest management* and the general framework of the scheme, including the division of the forest, the allotment of areas for felling and the regulation of the yield, is the concern of *forest management*.

The timber and other produce must be harvested, converted, manufactured, processed, and graded for presentation to markets. These are technologies and although essential to forestry are outside the scope of this paper. It is not possible here to describe and discuss the development of every aspect of forest science so attention has been concentrated on some parts of those disciplines closely connected with growth increment and yield. Each topic is defined, its development outlined, some recent results are reported and past, present and future application in silviculture and forest management discussed. But first it is necessary to look at the origins of forest science and the scale and geographic distribution of the present investment in it.

B. THE ORIGINS OF FOREST SCIENCE

The origins of forest management and forest science lie in Central Europe (Mantel, 1964). This is mainly because the people of that region depended on the forest for some of their food, their domestic animals found pasture in the forest and wood provided the most important material for buildings and fuel. Thus from earliest times the Central European forest met vital needs of the community and care was taken to conserve it.

It appears that for a long period the favourable climate of the region enabled the Central European forest to regenerate itself even in the face of human use but the increases in population during the sixteenth and especially in the eighteenth centuries eventually led to fears of a wood shortage and hence disaster due to lack of domestic fuel and adverse effects on industry and trade. Then it became necessary to plan the management of forests, raise the yield of timber and other products, control the rate and type of utilization, and conserve the area of forest. So it was that permanent forest administrations staffed by professional foresters first appeared in Central Europe and forest science began to systematize and improve the techniques arrived at by accumulated practical experience.

As Mantel (1964) points out, the history of forest management and forest science varies greatly between countries within Europe and from region to region in the world. After the setbacks caused by the numerous wars of the seventeenth century, the eighteenth century brought important advances in forest management in France and Germany. By the end of that century Denmark, Belgium, the Netherlands, Austria and Switzerland had forest administrations responsible for planned management of forests; and, as conditions in the European timber market allowed an economically profitable opening of forests, their example was followed in the nineteenth century by the northern, eastern and southern countries of Europe. During the nineteenth century also, the United States and India began regulating the exploitation of their forests. In Japan older ideas and techniques of conservation and forest management were combined with those of France and Germany after the political revolution of 1868 to make a national policy for forestry (Shioya, 1967).

The first task of forest scientists was to provide the basic information for developing systems of silviculture, the measurement of growth and regulation of yield, the utilization of timber in buildings and for other purposes, especially fuel, the control of game birds and animals and the use of forests by domestic animals. The developing science of forestry drew for information and innovation on three main sources: first, the recorded practical experience of those who planted, tended and felled trees and prevented illegal and improper fellings; second, the financial and administrative skills of the officials of the kings and princes, who developed the principles of forest economics; and, third, from mathematicians and natural scientists.

Three French scientists are credited with early achievements in forest science. René Antoine Ferchault de Réaumur (1683–1757) proposed experiments into the yield of forests as the basis for compiling yield tables which predict output and permit determination of the length o the rotation period. George Louis Leclerc, Comte de Buffon (1707–1788), attempted site evaluation on his estates, began experiments concerning tree growth, established plantations of broadleaved trees and cultivated conifers in his nurseries. In the field of wood science "it was probably Buffon who first recognized the correlation between the density and the strength of wood" (Mantel, 1964). The most significant contributions were made by Henri Louis Duhamel de Monceau (1700–1788). In five major works published between 1755 and 1767, Duhamel described the results of biological, physical and chemical experiments on the anatomy and physiology of trees, forest botany and ecology, the yields obtained from various silvicultural systems, wood science and technology and timber harvesting. These works were translated into German and published in that country.

These promising beginnings of forest science in France were checked by the period of war and unrest in the late eighteenth and early nineteenth centuries. The centre of development moved to Germany where an outstanding group of men combined practical experience with scientific method to develop systems of silviculture and yield control, and provide forest economics with a firm theoretical foundation.

The special contribution of Georg Ludwig Hartig (1764–1837) was the uniform shelterwood system of regeneration arranged by fixed areas called "compartments" and with yield regulated by volume. Heinrich von Cotta (1763–1844) was the most influential of the group. According to Mantel (1964) his publications on forest management and silviculture "constitute the essence of the young science of forestry in the first half of the nineteenth century" and his lectures given from 1785 at Zillbach and from 1811 onwards at Tharandt, as director of the "Forstlichen Akademie" drew students from many countries.

An outstanding early contribution to knowledge of annual and periodic growth increment in oak (*Quercus* species) and the effects on this increment of thinnings made to adjust the stocking of trees and favour those with an economically desirable balance of stem and crown was that of Christian Ditlev Frederik, Viscount Reventlow (1748–1827). Reventlow was Lord Chancellor of Denmark around 1800 and had become acquainted with forestry during travels as a young man in France and England. He studied the writings of Duhamel de Monceau and John Evelyn (1620–1706) on oak and beech (*Fagus sylvatica* L.) and after inheriting estates on Lolland, and in association with the Hanoverian forester Georg Wilhelm Bruel (1752–1829), began his investigations into the silviculture and management of oak forests. The manuscript of *A Treatise on Forestry* was completed in 1816 and remained unpublished until 1879 (Society of Forest History, 1960) but Reventlow's principles for controlling competition in stands of oak by regular thinnings and the favouring of well-developed stems clear of dead branches had been put into practice in 1812 on the Brahetrolleborg estate on Funen by another Hanoverian forester C. V. Opperman (1784–1861). He established a sample plot for the study of growth increment in a young stand of oak raised by direct sowing of acorns on old farm land in 1785. The resulting plantation probably is the oldest sample plot for the systematic recording of growth increment in the world.

C. THE INTERNATIONAL UNION OF FORESTRY RESEARCH ORGANIZATIONS

A very important event in the development of forest science was the founding in 1892 of the International Union of Forestry Research Organizations (IUFRO). The idea sprang from the need to unify forest research and standardize the methods of measurement used in experiments thus making the results more readily comparable. The idea of close personal relations among forest scientists of different countries leading to the development of uniform principles and standard forms for experimentation and publication of results was brought forward by Professor Böhmerle of Austria at an international agriculture and forestry congress held in Vienna in 1890 (Speer, 1973). A resolution tabled by Professor Schuberg of Germany and adopted by the Congress brought into being a working group which met at Badenweiler in 1890 during the Congress of the Union of German Forestry Research Establishments (which had existed since 1872) and wrote draft Statutes. In 1892 IUFRO was formally established at Eberswalde in Germany.

The first Congress of IUFRO, held in 1893 at Vienna, was attended by eighteen delegates from Austria, Germany, Switzerland, Italy and Hungary. At the second Congress in Germany at Brunswick two more countries, Russia and Sweden, were represented and at the third Congress in 1900 at Zurich, Switzerland there were twenty-two participants from seven countries.

The Union then grew steadily. In addition to the forest research organizations of the founding nations (Austria, Germany and Switzerland), those of Belgium, Denmark, Great Britain, Italy, Japan, Russia and Hungary were admitted as members. The Statutes were redrawn during the fourth Congress at Vienna in 1903 and provision made for raising funds by subscriptions from the member organizations. By 1910 Bulgaria, Holland, Portugal, Rumania, Sweden and the United States had all been admitted to the Union and, although the outbreak of the first World War prevented the seventh Congress being held, IUFRO had become a world wide organization. In addition to standardization of terminology and bibliography the members had made arrangements for international exchange of seed for research into racial hereditary adaptation to diverse environments which later became an important part of the work of IUFRO.

After the war IUFRO lapsed but a resolution for its re-establishment was adopted during the first World Forestry Congress at Rome 1926 and the seventh Congress was held in Stockholm in 1929. The title became the International Union of *Forestry* Research Organizations to emphasize the broadened scope of the membership and aims—which were to advance international co-operation in all branches of forestry and forest products research.

In 1929 the member institutes were located in 33 countries distributed over all five continents. The Statutes of that year provided for a permanent Committee of seven members which became the managing board of IUFRO between Congresses. At Stockholm most of the papers were presented to and discussed by four special sections: forestry, forest ecology, forest soil science and forest entomology.

The eighth Congress was held at Nancy, France in 1932 and the ninth at Budapest, Hungary in 1936. The second World War prevented the tenth Congress being held in Finland in 1940, but at a meeting held in Helsinki in 1947 delegates from Finland, Great Britain, Italy, Sweden and Switzerland agreed that the tenth Congress should be held in Zurich, Switzerland in 1948.

The Food and Agriculture Organization had been established by the United Nations after the war and had taken over several international forestry organizations, but the suggestion that FAO should also absorb IUFRO was resisted and, after discussion, FAO agreed to provide a Secretariat in Rome for a fully independent Union. In 1957 FAO asked to be relieved from this obligation and in 1958 awarded to IUFRO the status of technical adviser. This soon led to close and fruitful co-operation between the two organizations whereby FAO financed many research projects undertaken by member organizations while IUFRO has advised FAO and carried out a large number of research contracts.

At the tenth Congress of IUFRO at Zurich in 1949 the number of member organizations had fallen to forty-seven but contacts with others were gradually re-established and by the eleventh Congress in Rome 1953 the Union had more than one hundred members.

TABLE I   Membership of International Union of Forest Research
Organizations 1929–74

Year of Congress	Member Organizations	Number of Countries
1929	141	33
1940	47	23
1953	101	43
1956	139	46
1961	163	53
1967	180	60
1971	240	71
1975[a]	292	77

[a] The 16th Congress of IUFRO was held in Norway in 1976.
Source: Annual Reports of the International Union of Forest Research Organizations.

Twelve research sections were formed each headed by a Section Leader who encouraged and guided the formation and work of international Working Groups. This system proved very successful and was reinforced during the twelfth Congress, held at Oxford in 1956; by the thirteenth Congress at Vienna in 1961 there were over 80 Working Groups. The new Statutes adopted at Vienna added to the Permanent Committee an Enlarged Committee comprised of the leaders of the scientific sections to co-ordinate their work.

The Union now began to enlarge rapidly. More than 1000 forest scientists attended the fourteenth Congress at Munich in 1967. Eight years later the number of forest scientists employed in member organizations was 6860 and in 1975 there were some 9000 scientists in those organizations engaged on forestry, forest operations and forest products research. A new scheme of management was needed and new Statutes were adopted which provided for six research divisions as follows:

Division 1   Forest Environment and Silviculture
Division 2   Forest Plants and Forest Protection
Division 3   Forest Operations and Techniques
Division 4   Planning, Economics, Growth and Yield, Management and Policy
Division 5   Forest Products

Division 6   General Subjects (Recreation, Landscape, Statistics, Terminology, Information, Education and History of Forestry)

There are 41 groups of subjects and 17 groups of projects and the detailed work is done by 166 Working Parties (IUFRO, 1975).

In 1971 the Permanent Committee was replaced by an Executive Board and in 1973 the re-organization was completed by the establishment of a Permanent Secretariat in Vienna.

The aim of the Union is to promote international co-operation in forestry by:

(i)   encouragement of close personal relations among forestry research workers of all countries;
(ii) promotion of informal exchanges in ideas and experiences, especially within the individual Working Parties;
(iii) improvement of forestry concepts and of research methods;
(iv) promotion of forestry research of high priority on an international scale;
(v)   collaboration with other international organizations by providing scientific advice and guidance on forestry problems;
(vi) preparation of a uniform classification system for forestry literature;
(vii) development of standard references for forestry terminology.

Reliable figures concerning the total number of forest research organizations in the world are not available but it is possible to attempt an estimate from the "World Directory of Forest and Forest Products Research Institutes" compiled by the Food and Agriculture Organization (FAO, 1963) and from the annual reports of IUFRO. The results appear in Table II. It is likely that the estimate is too low because, for example, no account is taken of the separate institutions and research units in eastern Europe administrated by such organizations as the Academy of Agricultural Sciences and Academy of Science in Russia.

In closing this Introduction it is desirable to emphasize the very valuable work being done for forest science by the Commonwealth Forestry Bureau, based in the Commonwealth Forestry Institute at Oxford (CAB, 1960). *Forestry Abstracts*, which first appeared in 1938, is not the sole abstracting medium but it has gained a high reputation throughout the world for the broad scope and accuracy of its abstracting service. During the period 1964–74 every aspect of forest science was covered but it is interesting to consider the frequency of mention (by numbers of abstracts) which was, in descending order, systematic forest botany, forest protection (entomology and pathology), structure, properties and preservation of wood, forest ecology, forest hydrology and soil science, forest genetics and tree physiology. Topics from some of these important fields will now be considered; they have been chosen to demonstrate the broad scope of forest science.

TABLE II   Estimated number of forestry research organizations, 1975

Continent	Federal and state research institutes	Private research institutes	Universities and colleges	Totals
Africa	30	2	4	36
Asia	30	1	23	54
Australasia	15	2	4	21
Europe	103	14	44	161
North America	42	6	37	85
South America	26	3	11	40
Totals	**246**	**28**	**123**	**397**

II. SYSTEMATIC FOREST BOTANY

From the beginning of forest science there has been work on the taxonomy and distribution of the woody, herbaceous and other vegetation of the forest. This has been done primarily by members of Government forest services and forestry departments of Universities and by botanists in botanical gardens and arboreta. The output of published papers and books has been and continues to be large and it is possible only to indicate its scope and record some notable events.

Early publications listing or describing the forest trees of North America are Marshall's *Arbustrum Americanum* of 1785, Wangenheim's illustrated German work on North American woody species in 1787 and F. A. Michaux's *North American Sylva* in 1817–19 (Little, 1953). In 1880 and 1883 Charles Sprague Sargent published a detailed catalogue of the forest trees of the United States. This included the work of several field agents of the United States Government in different regions and was followed by Sargent's *Silva of North America* in 14 volumes (1891–1902) which described and illustrated 585 native tree species. In the United States the Forest Service led in the nomenclature of the trees of that country, their object being to arrive at uniform, stable scientific and vernacular names of trees. The work of the Forest Service's dendrologists is recorded by Little (1953) in his *Check List of Native and Naturalised Trees of the United States (including Alaska)*.

When confronted with the vast botanical riches of South America, Africa, Asia and Australasia early foresters and botanists often concentrated on species likely to be of economic value. The scope was gradually extended and some fine examples of tree floras from Africa are given in *The Indigenous Trees of the Uganda Protectorate* first published by W. J. Eggeling in 1940 and revised by Eggeling and Dale (1951), the *Flora of West Tropical Africa* (Hutchinson *et al.*, 1954) and *The Forest Flora of Northern Rhodesia* (White, 1962). A remarkable recent publication is the three volumes of *Trees of Southern Africa* (Palmer and Pitman, 1972).

An event of great significance for taxonomy in Africa was the formation of a special international association, the Association pour l'Étude Taxonomique de la Flore d'Afrique Tropicale (A.E.T.F.A.T., 1954) which has published an annual index of papers on systematic phanerogamy and new taxa for Africa south of the Sahara. The first three issues appeared in 1954, 1955 and 1956 and the Indices for the succeeding years have listed many thousands of new names (new combinations, genera, species, sub-species and varieties) indicating the progress being made in the preparation of African floras. In 1960 the first volume of *Flora Zambesiaca* appeared (Excell and Wild, 1960) and a richly illustrated handbook dealing with the woody plants of Kenya (Dale and Greenway, 1961) was full of information useful to foresters.

Bor's *Manual of Indian Forest Botany* (Bor, 1953) was written to acquaint forest managers with the elements of systematic botany and a fine example of the work of a forest officer in this field is *Forest Trees of Sarawak and Brunei and their Products* by Browne (1955). Ashton (1964) published a *Manual of the Dipterocarp Trees of Brunei State* and Meijer and Wood (1964) dealt with the *Dipterocarps of Sabah (North Borneo)*. Further east a Japanese dendrological work (Anon, 1964) proved of interest to a wide circle of foresters and arboriculturists not least for its beautiful full page colour plates of 100 important species, with distribution maps.

A work on the *Trees of Surinam* (Lindemann and Mennaga, 1963) was noteworthy for its inclusion of keys based on vegetative characters and wood anatomy and Turrill (1942) has pointed out that anatomy and cytology are also kinds of morphology. Other outstanding compilations are *The Anatomy of the Dicotyledons* by Metcalfe and Chalk (1957) and the *Anatomy of the Monocotyledons* by Metcalfe (1960) and Tomlinson (1961).

Monographs of genera and species are abundant and they have particular value in transcending country or regional boundaries to give a broad picture. The *Eucalypts* (Penfold and Willis, 1961) deals with a very important genus and the recent "Forest Tree Series" from the

Australian Forestry and Timber Bureau (Hall, 1970) will, when complete, provide a comprehensive account of all the Eucalyptus species in Australia.

Concerning the usefulness of cytology in systematic forest botany the species of *Taxus* provide a common example of a gymnosperm genus having stable chromosome numbers. The eight species have $x = 12$ with very minor differences between them in the number of chiasmata. By contrast the Podocarpaceae are revealed by the data of Hair and Beuzenberg (1958) as being unusual among gymnosperms in having a surprising variation in chromosome numbers from $2n = 38$ to $2n = 18$. Chromosome counts given by Barlow (1959a, b) for 37 species of *Casuarina* conform with a suggested division of this genus into major groups.

The use of chemotaxonomy to supplement orthodox methods in taxonomic research is not new but has received increasing attention during the past 20 years. Two works of unusually wide scope appeared in 1962 and 1963. The first (Swain, 1963) consisted of surveys by 17 authors of various general aspects of the subject and of particular classes of components. The other (Hegnauer, 1962) is a five volume work arranged systematically by families, giving for each its botanical characteristics, distribution, systematics and phytochemistry.

Larsen (1937) has recorded many of the early attempts at artificial crosses within and between tree species. Twenty-five years later the body of information about natural and artificial hybrids had grown sufficiently large for Wright (1962) to attempt the first general survey of the relations between inter-species crossing patterns, geographic distribution and comparative morphology. This kind of work has continued throughout the world and recently Critchfield (1975) and Zauffa (1975) summarized the situation for *Pinus* and *Populus* respectively. About four-fifths of the 95 to 100 species in *Pinus* have been involved in one or more attempts at hybridization and about 100 successful hybrid combinations have been produced. In most instances crossing is possible only between those species that resemble each other most closely in morphological characters, but *Pinus* does appear to differ from many herbaceous plant genera in that most inter-specific hybrids are vigorous and fertile. Hybrid sterility is uncommon.

The genus *Populus* has proved particularly difficult from the viewpoint of systematic botany due to the wide geographic distribution of some species, the frequent introgressive hybridization, the long period of cultivation, extending over 300 years, and ease of vegetative propagation. The International Code of Nomenclature for Cultivated Plants is now widely applied to the naming of poplar cultivars.

The taxonomic inventory of the forest resources of the tropical and sub-tropical regions still is incomplete and the products of forest tree breeding are steadily increasing in number and in use, so that there is no doubt of the continued need for systematic forest botany as a branch of forest science.

III. Wood Science

In 1673 and 1674 Nehemiah Grew (1641–1712) gave a series of illustrated lectures to the Royal Society of London on "The Anatomy of Tree Trunks." Using a microscope Grew analysed the structure of oak, pine, walnut (*Juglans* species) and beech and on this basis described some suitable uses for the timber of these species. This probably was the first occasion a trained botanist had tried to use his scientific knowledge to explain the mechanical properties of wood (Sharp, 1975).

The contributions to wood science of Buffon and Duhamel de Monceau in the eighteenth century have already been noted (Section I, B). As the optical microscope and its use were improved, as X-ray diffraction was developed and as the electron microscope became available so progressively has the knowledge and understanding of the structure of wood cell walls improved (Preston, 1974). One of the principal aims of the wood anatomist is to elucidate the structure of timber in its relation on the one hand to conditions of growth and on the other hand to technical properties (Clarke, 1940). This is a very big field of study (see Stamm, 1964) but two important aspects of it have been selected to illustrate developments in wood science.

A. THE PHYSIOLOGICAL BASIS FOR THE SPECIFIC GRAVITY OF TIMBER

Larson (1969, 1973) has summarized existing ideas about the physiological mechanism causing the variation in specific gravity of conifer timbers. Specific gravity measures the proportion of wood substance in a given volume of timber and is commonly used to estimate the strength of timber or the yield of pulpwood. Considering only tracheids, which comprise the bulk of coniferous timbers and assuming the specific gravity of wood substance to be relatively constant the variable factors contributing to specific gravity are tracheid wall thickness and lumen diameter. It has been shown by Coggans (1965) and Rendle (1960) that tangential tracheid wall thickness and radial lumen diameter account for most of the variation in specific gravity of conifer timbers.

Earlywood and latewood are defined by the relative changes in wall thickness and radial diameter of the tracheids as they vary seasonally within a growth ring. "Latewood percentage is simply an arbitrary measure of these changes and the high correlation between latewood percentage and wood specific gravity is directly attributable to the seasonal changes in tracheid dimensions. The physiological basis for wood specific gravity can therefore be sought most easily by following the processes that contribute to the seasonal variability in tracheid wall thickness and radial diameter" (Larson, 1973). In conifers it is the seasonal or periodic development of the needles that regulates differentiation of the tracheids, thus producing the growth ring. This relationship can be described by following the seasonal course of growth.

At the beginning of each growth period a hormonal stimulus produced by the developing buds activates the dormant or quiescent cambium. Cambial activity begins first beneath the active buds and progresses downwards along each branch, down the main stem and into the roots. The first xylem cells produced by the newly activated cambium are large-diameter thin-walled tracheids classified as earlywood. "The large diameter of these tracheids is presumably due to a growth hormone, auxin, produced by the developing needle primordia within the buds and transported downward through the cambial region" (Larson, 1973). The thin walls of earlywood tracheids are due to competition for food between meristems of the tree. Competition is particularly severe when the new shoots are elongating and both stored foods and photosynthetic foods currently produced by older needles are moved to these very active terminal meristems.

Earlywood formation normally continues as long as the shoot is extending and the new needles are elongating rapidly. When shoot growth ceases and needle elongation slows down, auxin production declines and the reduced auxin gradient down the stem results in the formation of narrow-diameter latewood tracheids. The formation of thick-walled latewood is correlated with a change in competition for foods as the new needles begin to mature and export excess products of photosynthesis. New assimilates from both old and new needles are available for wood formation and thick-walled latewood tracheids appear in the developing annual growth ring.

The physiological mechanisms that determine tracheid structure are also related to their function. Transport of water and mineral nutrients from the roots to needles of the crown occurs primarily in the earlywood. The thickwalled latewood tracheids are so constructed and timed in their development that they give strength to the stem and support for the crown when it attains full expansion during each period of growth.

Now the processes regulating radial lumen diameter and tracheid wall thickness are independent and the varying patterns in structure of growth rings observed within trees are caused both by the timing of the physiological processes and by their subsequent interactions at points in the stem increasingly further removed from the active crown. When the decline in auxin production coincides with the export of assimilates from the new needles both tracheid dimensions will change simultaneously and the transition from earlywood to latewood will be abrupt. Such abrupt transitions are common in mature trees. Frequently however the two processes overlap in time and a broad transition zone is produced consisting of tracheids that can be classified neither as true earlywood or true latewood. Transition wood is common in young trees and in the growth rings of fast-growing older trees. The occurrence of transition wood contributes to much of the seasonal variation in growth ring structure at different positions within a tree and also to the variation in specific gravity between trees grown under different environments (Gordon and Larson, 1968).

In young coniferous trees the growth rings nearest the pith are almost totally without latewood and consist of tracheids with relatively large radial diameters and thin walls. The full vigorous crowns of young trees usually encompass the entire stem and so auxin production is high and competition for limited food supplies is intense. Thus crown-formed timber is almost devoid of latewood.

As the tree becomes older and grows in height the crown approaches its full size and the translocation pathways down the stem lengthen. The effects of these factors on wood specific gravity can be followed by examining a cross sectional disk taken from the basal section of an older tree with moderate growth rate. The percentage of latewood increases rapidly in the first few rings outward from the pith, then more slowly, and finally fluctuates in response to growth conditions.

If a single annual increment is followed from stem apex to base in an older tree one first encounters crown-formed wood, then transition wood near the base of the live crown and finally mature wood with a well-defined earlywood–latewood transition in the branch-free stem. In each succeeding annual increment that is added to the stem by the cambium the point at which transition wood merges into mature wood moves progressively upwards as the tree grows in height.

The conditions of site and silvicultural practice strongly affect tracheid dimensions and hence the specific gravity of the timber. Because of the physiological processes involved the direct effect of environment is on the needles; that on the tracheids is indirect (Larson, 1964). When environmental conditions are altered the first discernible change is usually a decrease or increase in the number of tracheids comprising the growth ring. If the physiological response to external conditions is sufficiently intense or persistent the structure of the tracheids comprising the earlywood–latewood transition will be modified —either in the last-formed earlywood or first-formed latewood or both depending on the time during the growing season when the environmental influence occurs and on the intensity of the response.

An abrupt transition from earlywood to latewood is very often connected with a reduction in tree growth because the cessation of needle elongation and maturity of photosynthesis tend to coincide when the vigour of the live crown declines. Growth acceleration due to such silvicultural treatment as thinning, application of fertilizers or irrigation causes an increase in width of the growth ring and, if sustained, a change in the earlywood–latewood transition zone. It is the change in this zone that most strongly influences wood specific gravity.

Conditions highly favourable for tree growth encourage needle elongation and/or meristematic activity of the needle bases resulting in a prolongation of auxin synthesis and the formation of large-diameter tracheids. But the needles of fast-growing trees may begin exporting assimilates while auxin production is still high, since photosynthetic maturity is not necessarily correlated with the cessation of needle elongation. The net result of these overlapping events is a broad transition zone that grades imperceptibly from earlywood to latewood with a very gradual increase in wall thickness and decrease in radial lumen diameter. The specific gravity of fast-grown timber therefore reflects more strongly the width and structure of the transition zone than the width of either earlywood or latewood alone.

Thus far this account has been concerned with the relation between needle and cambial development in the elongating shoot and between the performance of mature needles and cambial growth on the stem, and with how this relationship is modified by site conditions and silviculture. But the relation between needle and cambial development is also under genetic control and so the possibility exists of influencing the specific gravity of timber by selection and breeding. Important benefits can accrue from reduced variability in specific gravity within and between annual growth rings because an even distribution results in even-textured timber which in turn tends to give less degrade in drying, less splitting on nailing, improved surface-finish on planing and, in the manufacture of pulp and paper, more uniform sheet properties. There is good evidence for the existence of inherent variation in specific gravity of coniferous and broadleaved timbers and new cultivars with desirable properties are being produced (Zobel, 1964; Harris, 1970). Up to the present time the assessment of specific gravity has been based on the examination of small samples of timber taken from the parent trees and progenies. Now there is the possibility that characteristics of needle and shoot growth might become the basis for selection.

B. THE MOVEMENT OF FLUIDS AND GASES THROUGH TIMBER

One aspect of wood science which has many theoretical and practical uses concerns the movement of liquids and gases through timber. Tree physiologists studying the movement of water from the roots to the crown of living trees require knowledge of the effect of the fine structure of timber on fluid flow (Jarvis, 1974). The process of drying timber involves a complex combination of gaseous diffusion and liquid flow, and treatment of timber with preservative liquids, fire retardants, dimensional-stabilizing agents and the chemicals used in pulping processes all involve the passage of fluids through timber.

The most important application of this aspect of wood science is in timber preservation. A progressively greater proportion of timber must be treated to meet the needs of those who use it but satisfactory penetration of the seasoned sapwood of some species and the heartwood of a great many species is a major problem. Its solution lies in studying the paths followed by liquids and gases in timber and the nature of the resistance to flow and diffusion.

In conifers, water moves longitudinally through the lumina of the tracheids, passing from one tracheid to the next through the bordered pits. It is probable that the same path is followed by preservative fluids when penetrating timber from a transverse surface. The path followed by treatment fluids in the radial direction is less well known though it seems likely that ray tracheids, when they are present, play a major part in radial movement. "Because tracheid lumina provide an unobstructed pathway for flow it follows that the bordered pits will largely control the movement of fluids in conifer wood" (Petty, 1970).

There are about 100 bordered pits in each earlywood tracheid but only about ten in each latewood tracheid. The structure of a typical earlywood bordered pit appears in Fig. 1. In green timber, water may pass from one pit aperture to the other through the pit chamber and the pit membrane pores. Following suitable preparation of the timber for electron microscopy the pores can be identified as gaps in a network of microfibrils through which the water flows. When timber is dried the structure shown in Fig. 1 may be modified by "aspiration" in which the torus moves across the pit chamber to seal one of the pit apertures and is bound by hydrogen bonding to the pit border (Petty, 1972) thus preventing fluid flow through the pit (Fig. 2). Green timber from the heartwood region of the tree stem has a low moisture content and most of the bordered pits are aspirated—this presumably occurring as the wood dries during the conversion to heartwood. The result is that heartwood always is less permeable to fluids than sapwood. Moreover, the pores in heartwood may be blocked by extractives deposited on the pit membranes.

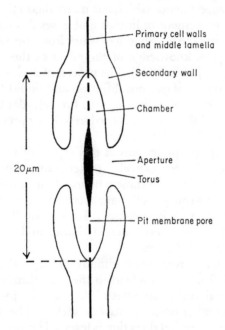

FIG. 1. Diagrammatic representation of an earlywood bordered pit in section transverse to the pit membrane.

When green sapwood is oven-dried its permeability to water falls to about 1–10% of the value for green timber. Most of the early wood pits become aspirated during drying but many of the latewood pits remain unaspirated. Petty (1970) considers that this difference is due to the greater cell-wall thickness and small pit diameter in latewood, which in turn mean that the surface-tension forces generated during drying are insufficient to counteract those of mechanical resistance; so the torus is not pulled across the pit chamber but remains in its central position. This explains why in dry sapwood the latewood but not the earlywood is permeable and why the observed permeability of the timber as a whole is low. If the water in green sapwood is replaced before drying with a fluid which does not promote hydrogen bonding between torus and border, aspiration of many earlywood pits is prevented and the dried timber has a very high permeability.

Several methods have been devised to estimate the nature and size of the components of resistance to flow of liquids and diffusion of gases in timber. Gas flow techniques enable the radii and numbers of pit membrane pores, tracheid lumina and pit apertures to be estimated. These values may be inserted in liquid flow equations (such as Poisenille's equation) to predict the liquid permeabilities of these structures.

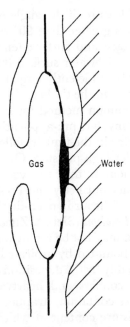

Gas   Water

FIG. 2. Aspirated bordered pit showing how the pit acts as a safety valve in the transpiration stream in the living tree to prevent spread of gas bubbles. The membrane is bound to the wall of the chamber by hydrogen bonding.

Petty (1970) measured gaseous flow at several mean pressures and was able to demonstrate the smaller but still important resistance of the tracheid lumina and the larger resistance of the pit membrane pores. He was also able to calculate the mean radius and number of the lumina and pit pores. In air dried sapwood of Sitka spruce [*Picea sitchensis* (Bong.) Carr.], which is notoriously difficult to treat with preservatives, only 7 % of the tracheids were conducting. There were 250 pit membrane pores of radius 0·14 μm in series with each conducting tracheid lumen (Petty, 1970). This calculation probably corresponds to all the early-wood pits being aspirated and conductivity occurring through two to five unaspirated pits in each conducting latewood tracheid.

There are three other features of the fine structure of conifer timber that affect the movement of fluids and gases and these must be considered when devising preservation processes. The first is structural blockage by extractives of flow paths in heartwood, the second is the possible presence of air–liquid menisci blocking the pit membrane pores, and the third is the nature of the internal surface of the cell-wall lining and lumina and bordered pits.

Concerning the third feature, if the angle of contact of water on the surface of the cell walls is greater than 90° the water will behave like mercury on a glass surface and surface tension forces will resist the passage of an advancing air–water surface through the pit membrane pores. These forces may be sufficiently large to prevent penetration of a water-borne preservative into the timber.

Probably the most common method for saturating seasoned timber with a preservative fluid involves pre-application of a vacuum to remove the air from the void space in the timber, followed by immersion of the timber in the liquid under high pressure. One assumption made in this vacuum/pressure treatment is that the vacuum removes all the air contained in the void space but Petty and Preston (1969) showed that a considerable proportion of the air in oven-dry heartwood of such species as Japanese larch [*Larix leptolepis* (Sieb. & Zucc.) Endl.], Douglas fir and *Eucalyptus maculata* Hook. may not be removable in a vacuum because it is "trapped" in regions bounded by aspirated bordered pits which are hermetically sealed probably by the deposition of extractives (see above).

In sapwood of most conifers and heartwood of some species the proportion of void spaces containing trapped air varies with moisture content. Above the moisture content at which condensation occurs in the pit membrane pores little or no air can be removed because of blockage by air–water menisci and very high pressures are needed to displace them. Thus in conifer timber with pores of less than 1 μm radius all the air in the void space is effectively trapped at moisture contents greater than 30%; seasoning to well below this figure should ensure removal of a high proportion of air from the void space but unfortunately will also ensure that most of the bordered pits become aspirated, reducing permeability to a low level. The solution to this dilemma for sapwood lies in some kind of solvent-drying which maintains the high permeability of greenwood during seasoning.

Petty and Puritch (1970) compared the effects of air and solvent drying of the sapwood of the Grand fir (*Abies grandis* Lindl.). The water in the green sapwood was replaced, before drying, by a series of organic liquids of progressively lower surface tension and swelling power (for example, methanol, acetone, and pentane). After solvent drying 83% of both earlywood and latewood tracheids were conducting compared with only latewood tracheids (32 % of the total) after air drying. There were 27 000 pit membranes pores per conducting tracheid in solvent-dried sapwood but only 600 in air-dried sapwood. Petty and Puritch (1970) went on to predict the permeability of the timber of Grand fir to liquids and considered that solvent dried sapwood timber should be 31 times more permeable than air dried.

In present practice drying and preservation are separated and there would be great advantages in combining the two. In a proposal made by Petty (1975) a solvent such as methanol, containing dissolved preservatives diffuses rapidly into green timber. The solvent subsequently is evaporated quickly and recovered leaving the preservative distributed throughout the timber. In this process, unlike many others, the preservative may penetrate completely both heartwood and sapwood and enter the cell walls.

IV. FOREST YIELD STUDIES

Production techniques in forestry depend on the use and systematic control of growth processes in the course of which quantities of timber and other organic substances are produced. The purpose of forest yield studies is to examine quantitatively the rates of growth processes and their relation to time, site, economics and methods of utilization. Every year an individual tree or stand grows in volume, mass and surface area and this is the *increment*. Part of the increment is harvested and this is the *yield*. Thus forest yield studies are concerned also with the quantities, form and dimensions of the harvested timber and other organic substances that contribute to the yield.

Forest managers require knowledge of the existing stock of their forests and of the yields to be expected in future. Thus almost all the notable forest scientists of the eighteenth and early nineteenth centuries studied yield. According to Assmann (1970), Chr. von Seebach (1793–1865) was one of the first to study yield by systematic scientific methods. M. R. Pressler (1815–86) devised methods and instruments to determine timber volume and increment of growing trees and stands. Robert Hartig (1839–1901) constructed stand yield tables and was a pioneer of tree physiology.

From about 1870 the forest research institutes set up experiments on the factors affecting increment and yield and soon amassed quantities of data which were presented in the form of stand volume yield tables. At this time yield studies were auxiliary to forest mensuration and management but as more information was gained about growth processes the synthesis of some biological principles of forest growth and yield in relation to site and silvicultural treatment began.

The production of timber represents only a small part of the organic accretion in a forest but the concentration on the technically utilizable timber restricted the contribution to forest science made by the early workers. It was the Danish plant physiologist Boysen-Jensen (1932) who first classified the organic production of tree stands and calculated approximate quantities. In the production equation of Boysen-Jensen net assimilation by the leaves appears as the gross production of the stand; net production is that quantity remaining after deducting the several components of loss and appears as woody increment plus seeds.

This work was continued in Denmark by Mar:Møller (1945) who produced "production spectra" for beech and Norway spruce [*Picea abies* (L.) Karst.] which show the changing proportions of organic production with age. Table III gives the data for beech compiled by

TABLE III   Components of organic production of a Danish stand of beech quality class II. Mean annual increment at 100 years 80 m³ of timber (more than 7 cm diameter per hectare)

| | Annual production in tonnes of dry matter/ha at ages: | | | |
	10	30	60	90
Total gross assimilation	15·9	23·2	23·2	20·9
Losses by:				
Respiration of leaves	4·0	4·7	4·7	4·7
Leaf shedding	2·2	2·7	2·7	2·7
Respiration of roots, stem and branches	3·6	4·8	5·6	5·1
Shedding of branches and roots	0·5	1·2	1·2	1·2
Total	**10·3**	**13·4**	**14·2**	**13·7**
Net increment of trees (including roots)	5·6	9·8	9·1	7·2

Source: Mar:Møller, Müller and Nielsen (1954).

Mar:Møller *et al.* (1954) and it will be seen that gross production reaches a maximum between 30 and 60 years and then declines markedly with increasing age. Leaf respiration losses appear relatively low. The respiration losses of branches and stems decrease rapidly as their diameters increase. Thus the combined losses from stems, branches and roots after the age of 60 years remain almost constant at 24% of gross assimilation. At the age of 30 years net increment reaches a maximum of about 42% of gross assimilation after which it declines slowly. At 90 years the proportion is only 34%.

Much fine work on the organic production of forest stands and its components was done in Switzerland from 1929 to 1953 by Hans Burger (1889–1973). This work has been compiled and reviewed by Trendelenburg and Mayer-Wegelin (1955) and Table IV presents some data of Burger relating to foliage mass and current annual volume increment on Norway spruce. In this species fresh weight of needles per hectare

TABLE IV   Needle fresh weight and current annual increment of pure fully stocked Norway spruce stands by site quality and age

	Quality class I		Quality class III		Quality class V	
Age	Fresh needle weight (tons)	CAI in volume (m^3)	Fresh needle weight (tons)	CAI in volume (m^3)	Fresh needle weight (tons)	CAI in volume (m^3)
40	40	23	35	17	26	9
60	35	22	32	16	29	11
90	31	16	30	12	27	8
120	29	11	28	7	26	4

decreases with increasing age. On a given site the culmination of volume increment evidently coincides with maximum fresh needle weight.

Between Site Quality Classes I and III there is little difference in foliage mass but the yield of timber per 1000 kg of fresh needle weight dropped from 0·59 to 0·48 m^3 at 40 years; 0·62 to 0·50 m^3 at 60 years; 0·53 to 0·40 m^3 at 90 years and 0·38 to 0·25 m^3 at 120 years thus reflecting the reduction in site quality from I to III.

The next step was to study primary production of whole forest ecosystems (Ovington, 1962) and this became one theme of the International Biological Programme (Duvigneaud, 1971). Primary production is the total mass produced by an autotrophic plant community per unit of area and time. The measures of production are dry matter, weights of nutrient elements within the biomass and the amount of energy fixed—all per unit of area and time. Energy budgets for forest ecosystems are not numerous but separate budgets for water, carbon, nitrogen and the various mineral elements have often been prepared (Bakuzis, 1969). Estimates of total biomass are now appearing in increasing numbers because the rising world demand for timber and the other resources of forests and associated lands has stimulated research into the structure and function of forest ecosystems and made necessary comprehensive estimates of total production and yield of forest resources.

Although volume is a satisfactory unit for measurement and sale of the merchantable portion of a stem it is not suitable for small branches, small roots or leaves (Young, 1973). Dry weight has been used in studies of the production of seedlings and young plants and has greatly improved understanding of the physiology of tree growth, the components of yield and response to experimental variations of water, nutrients, heat and light. But estimating the weight, fresh and dry, of large trees and whole stands is a formidable undertaking which has demanded improvements in sampling techniques and statistical analysis to become practicable (Young, 1973). Forest biomass data are being collected for several purposes: (i) to check estimates of stand growth based on studies of physiological processes (photosynthesis, respiration and decomposition) in relation to environmental variables (moisture, nutrients, light and heat); (ii) to provide data and samples for work on the uptake, storage, return and loss of water and nutrients in forest ecosystems; (iii) to supplement existing estimates of timber and fibre yield of standing crops of trees, as in the construction of dry weight yield tables.

In a full study of forest biomass all the components are measured and weighed fresh and dry to determine moisture contents. With careful sampling and regression analysis the total number of trees required to construct tables of tree and stand biomass can be kept small (perhaps 15 to 30 per stand). The components of trees often are grouped thus (Newbould, 1967):

bud scales, flowers, fruit and other minor components
leaves, perhaps with current year's extension growth (twigs)
branches
stems
roots.

The total production of the forest ecosystem is the sum of these components plus those of shrubs and ground flora. Estimates of the biomass of epiphytes on large trees demand a method for describing and sampling the branch system of the trees. Examples of estimates of total biomass and net production appear on Tables V and VI. Another unit of measurement in studies of forest ecosystems is surface area (Boyce, 1975; Whittaker and Woodwell, 1967). Its use also creates problems of sampling in large trees and stands but has several advantages over weight. Surface area data are being collected: (i) to provide data for the standard physiological analysis of growth of trees and crops (Evans, 1970); (ii) in studies of experimental watersheds, particularly in relation to the uptake, storage, return and loss of water in forest hydrology.

TABLE V Biomass of a Japanese plantation of larch [*Larix leptolepis* (Sieb. and Zucc.) Endl.] age 39 years

Components	Total biomass in tonnes of dry matter per hectare				
	Larch overstorey	Broadleaved understorey	Shrub layer	Ground vegetation	Totals
Above ground	164·44	3·20	0·83	0·96	169·43
Foliage	3·59	0·31	0·11	0·36	4·37
Woody parts	160·85	2·89	0·72	0·60	165·06
Stems	145·35	1·92	—	—	—
Branches	15·50	0·97	—	—	—
Below ground	34·84	0·84	0.87	1·39	37·94
Totals	199·28	4·04	1·70	2·35	207·37

Source: Satoo, T. (1971).

TABLE VI Net production above ground of conifer stands in Japan

Species	Production in tonnes per hectare per year				
	No. Plots	Foliage	Branches	Stems	Tree
Abies sachalinensis Mast.	3	2·3	1·8	6·3	10·4
A. veitchii Lindl.	7	3·8	2·3	6·6	12·8
A. veitchii Lindl. + *A. mariesii* Mast.	1	3·9	1·3	4·2	9·4
Larix leptolepis (Sieb. and Zucc.) Endl.	4	4·5	3·1	7·4	15·0
Picea glehnii (Schmidt) Mast.	1	2·3	0·5	4·6	7·4
Pinus densiflora (Sieb and Zucc.)	37	4·7	2·8	6·6	13·5
Chamaecyparis obtusa (Sieb. and Zucc.) Endl.	1	7·2	5·3	7·6	20·1
Thujopsis dolobrata (L.f.) (Sieb. and Zucc.)	3	3·6	1·8	9·3	14·7
Picea abies (L.) Karst.	5	4·1	1·1	6·0	11·2

Source: Satoo, T. (1971).

Each of the units volume, weight and surface area have their advantages; all three are being related by regression to diameter at breast height and total height of trees to establish common ground in research and make the results available to forest practice. As Delvaux (1971) points out, the stand volume yield tables prepared in many countries can be used to estimate primary production and hence to prepare forest energy balances.

As already noted the incentive for many studies of primary production is the need to make more complete use of forest resources. According to Alestalo (1973) about 20 million tons of timber are harvested each year in Finland. At present 4·4 million tons of branchwood, 2·1 million tons of foliage and 1·9 million tons of bark go to waste and their utilization plus that of the roots could add greatly to the economy of Finland. Tree foliage is a potential source of essential oils, glucosides, glucose, vitamins, pharmaceuticals, fodder and fuel and with an increased use of whole-tree harvesting it might become possible to deliver foliage for processing at a suitable price. But increased utilization of foliage, branchwood and roots in addition to stemwood and all the other components of forest eco-systems will greatly affect their structure and function and this aspect of forest yield studies is attracting much attention. Mälkönen (1973) calculated the amounts of nutrients removed after clear cutting of trees by two methods from two sites in Finland, one bearing Scots pine (*Pinus silvestris* L.) and the other Norway spruce. The results suggest that a change from the present harvesting of timber to *whole tree* harvesting would reduce the stock of nitrogen and phosphorous at the site by 2·5 times as much in Scots pine and 4 to 5 times as much in Norway spruce. In order to maintain the fertility of forest soils it may be necessary, as a result of the increased efficiency of timber harvesting, to replace the nutrients by applying fertilizer. Because part of the nutrients given as fertilizers are leached away, larger quantities of fertilizer nutrients than are contained in the harvested timber must be used. "Thus logging residues are by no means a gratuitous source of raw material" (Mälkönen, 1973).

V. FOREST GENETICS

A. GENECOLOGY OF FOREST TREES

Genecology is the study of the ecology of populations or, more pre-cisely, of the interactions of genotype with environment at the level of populations. The principal technique used is comparative culture, under similar external conditions, of plant material originating from geo-graphically or environmentally different sites and in forest science the term *provenance* is used to denote a population originating from a given site.

The term is useful because it does not presume that provenances will differ from one another in any respect other than their diverse native sites. The existence of more or less discrete populations and their morphological, physiological and genetical status is revealed by the *provenance test.*

Langlet (1971) has reviewed developments in genecology from 1745 to 1942 thus embracing two centuries of research. He writes: "Long before the term genecology was introduced it was established that there may exist within the species racial hereditary adaptation to diverse environments, that is, an ecologically conditioned diversity." Once the concept of species was fixed and became a generally adopted convention, reports of adaptive subspecific differences began to appear. One of the earliest relating to forest trees is that of Linneaus in *Arboretum suecica,* 1759, that yew trees (*Taxus baccata* L.) brought in from France had proved less winter hardy than indigenous Swedish yews.

Langlet (1971) points out that much of the work on the genecology of forest trees is virtually unknown, mainly because the results were produced for consideration and application in silvicultural practice.

H. L. Duhamel du Monceau has already been credited (Section I, B) with the founding of experimental taxonomy in forestry. He is also named by Langlet (1971) as the real pioneer of forest provenance research and experimental studies of intraspecific variation. As Inspector-General of the French Navy, and because of the lack of suitable material for the masts of naval vessels, Duhamel established from 1745 to 1755 comparative plantings of Scots pine from the Baltic Provinces and neighbouring parts of Russia, from Scotland and several regions of Central Europe. No detailed account of these investigations was published but at the beginning of the 1820's another Frenchman Pierre Philippe Andre de Vilmorin began comparative plantings of Scots pine on his estate of Les Barres. He gathered seed of 30 different provenances from many parts of the range of Scots pine and in dividing his material into five groups by form of stem and crown emphasized the absence of regional boundary lines between these groups, thus making "the first distinct statement about continuous spatial diversity in plants" (Langlet, 1971).

de Vilmorin's plantations attracted great attention in forestry and stimulated others to plant tests of diverse provenances of many tree species, but the next genecological investigations to be noted here are those of Cieslar who between 1887 and 1907 made provenance studies in Norway spruce that have become classical in forest science. He collected seed of Norway spruce at different altitudes in the Tyrol and established comparative tests on sites at 227, 795 and 1380 m where he assessed characters of tree growth and habit, needles, roots and injury by frost.

Cieslar (1907) was able to establish that at the lowest site near Vienna, Norway spruce of lowland provenance produced more wood per unit weight of needles than did spruce of high altitude provenance. Cieslar also studied other species and his test of 21 provenances of oak, sown in 1904, was probably the first provenance test of a broadleaved tree species. The acorns were gathered from only one or two trees to represent each provenance (only one provenance was represented by a mixture of acorns) but Cieslar (1923) was able to establish that northern provenances differ from southern in that they flush later in spring and so are less damaged by late frosts, they develop fewer "Lammas" or late season shoots, grow more slowly and have more leathery leaves. Early discolouration of the foliage distinguishes northern and also continental provenances.

Engler (1905, 1908, 1913) in Switzerland repeated and extended the experiments of Cieslar and tested provenances of Scots pine, Norway spruce, European Silver fir (*Abies alba* Mill.), European larch (*Larix decidua* Mill.) and Sycamore (*Acer pseudoplataus* L.) collected from different sites and elevations in the Alps. The plants were set out at different elevations, the Norway spruce at 18 sites from 470 to 2150 m (Engler, 1905). Engler also sowed Norway spruce seeds collected from trees of lowland origin which had been grown earlier in highland areas in comparison with seeds from indigenous highland spruce and with seeds collected in the lowland, thus anticipating many later experiments with other plants designed to demonstrate natural selection.

The practical need for provenance research was one of the reasons for the establishment in 1902 of the Swedish Forest Research Institute. The first Scots pine provenance trial of this Institute included more than 30 different Swedish provenances originating from 56°40' to 67°15' North latitude, most of them were tested at two experimental sites in Southern Sweden. Schotte (1906) found that the size of one year seedlings decreased with increasing latitude of their original habitat. In 1909 Schotte and Wibeck had Scots pine seeds collected from 20 stands in different parts of Sweden from 56°50' to 60°1' North latitude and the plants were set out in provenance tests on 13 sites from 60°45' to 67°12' North latitude. This experiment permitted assessment of the effects of transfer northwards on the development of plants, and the permissible distance of transfer of Scots pine seed and plants in Sweden has since been defined in the horizontal as well as the vertical direction.

The subsequent investigations of Langlet (1934, 1971) in Sweden were made on Scots pine seedlings from many hundreds of European and Swedish provenances. He demonstrated that "the dry matter percentage of the needles during the autumnal process of hardening may exhibit a remarkably strong correlation with the length of the growing season at the particular native habitats, as expressed in the latitude and the number of days, or rather by nycthemerons, with a normal average temperature of +6°C or above. Other features conditioning winter-resistance such as the relative quality of reducing substances ('sugar content') of chlorophylls, fats, total proteins, catalase, etc., co-vary with the dry matter content" (Langlet, 1936).

In Norway spruce different provenances seem to be adapted to the local frequency of late spring frosts rather than to the general climate of the region. The high altitude provenances from the Alps, as well as those from high-latitude regions, generally flush early, whilst spruces from the eastern part of Central Europe, i.e. eastern Poland, part of the Baltic States and adjacent regions of the Soviet Union, flush rather late, even extremely late in the spring and thus mostly escape damage by late spring frosts. It has also been possible to demonstrate for Norway spruce in Sweden that the difference in yield per hectare between what are called "German" and "Swedish" provenances steadily increases at least up to 70 to 80 years.

The natural range of the major tree species in Europe transcends the boundaries of countries, and in 1907 the International Union of Forest Research Organisations organized the first international provenance test of Scots pine. Schwappach (1911) assessed the test on one of the German sites and found considerable differences in growth and resistance to the needle cast disease *Lophodermium pinastri* Desm. An international test of provenances of Norway spruce was established in 1938 and the most comprehensive international experiment is that known as the "IUFRO Experiment of 1964/68" which comprises 1100 provenances of Norway spruce and has been planted on 20 sites within 13 countries (Dietrichson, 1973). The planning of assessments and comparison of results are done by a Working Group within Division 2 of IUFRO.

Since the end of the Second World War the number of provenance tests has risen very greatly to include most of the commercially important species of the temperate regions and also several sub-tropical and tropical species. Much attention has been paid to the problems encountered in such tests, particularly how the natural range of a widely distributed species can most effectively be sampled and how to sample the parent populations to reduce uncertainty about the variance found in them. The tendency has been to increase the number of populations sampled, and the subsequent establishment of the plants on a wide range of sites has not only increased the information gained from provenance tests but has also made an important contribution to gene conservation (Last, 1975).

Attention has also been given to developing experimental techniques which reduce the variation related to such factors as seed size induced in batches of young plants by variations in time of sowing, speed of germination and density of stocking. The characters assessed in provenance tests are related as closely as knowledge permits to final survival, yield and reproduction, bearing in mind the large final size of trees and the long period to maturity. With accumulating experience gained from older provenance tests increasing reliance is being placed on assessments of juvenile survival and yield to indicate final survival and yield.

Callaham (1964) summarized the results of numerous provenance tests in the following way:

(i) A diverse environment throughout the range of a species leads to a genetically variable species; widespread species tend to be more variable than species restricted in their range.

(ii) Patterns of inherent variation parallel patterns of environmental variation. Discontinuities in patterns of inherent variation are related to breaks in the distribution of a species or rapid changes in environmental factors.

(iii) Populations of a species which grow in different climatic regions may differ in inherent adaptation to environmental factors. In one region a certain factor of the environment will be critical; in other regions this factor may be less important than some other critical factor.

(iv) Sympatric species will be similar but not identical in their inherent adaptations to the same environment. Limiting factors generally are not always the same for co-habitating species.

(v) Provenance studies of native species undisturbed by man generally show the local seed source to be the best adapted but not necessarily the most productive. Introduced or exotic populations do not equal local populations in adaptation to the unique combination of factors of the local environment.

(vi) Performance is unpredictable for species grown for a long time under cultivation or disturbance by man or for species transferred to radically different environments.

In spite of tremendous exploitation of the forests of the world and the widespread use of exotic species in plantations the growing stock remains close to the wild beginnings and many stands still are growing in the regions and on the sites where they evolved. It might be possible through provenance research to observe evolution at work, to assess the rate and mode of adaptive processes and learn more about the nature of adaptive responses, but the difficulties of experimentation and interpretation are great. It can however be stated that provenance tests have indisputable value in indicating suitable sources of seed for commercial plantations, conserving genes, providing a basis for tree breeding through selection within provenances and hybridization between provenances, and in giving tree physiologists known material for their work.

B. APPLICATION OF GENETICS IN TREE BREEDING

One of the most recent developments in forest science, dating mainly from the 1920's has been the application of genetics to the breeding of new cultivars of trees which are superior to the planting stock currently available. Two major problems which delayed the development of forest genetics and tree breeding are the large size and long generation time of trees and the fact that some economically important characters do not appear until maturity (Libby *et al.*, 1969). These problems remain but their solution lies in drawing information from the growing store of knowledge about how trees grow.

The starting point in tree breeding is the study of genetic variation of trees and stands, whether natural or artificial, indigenous or introduced. The tree breeder then selects desirable trees or genes and propagates them as grafts, rooted cuttings or seedlings. Finally he uses these genotypes to produce cultivars for planting and eventual harvest.

Whether studies of genetic variation precede or follow the start of a breeding programme the information they provide will increase its effectiveness.

1. *Selection of individual trees and families*

According to Libby (1973) one common approach to selection is to identify the trees growing fastest in stem height, diameter and volume in each of many stands. Another is to assess trees by how well they are using the space available to them in producing stem-wood and select those which appear most "efficient." A third alternative is to concentrate on the distribution of dry matter between foliage, branches, seed or fruit, stem and roots, selecting those trees which have a high proportion of the total in the stem. A fourth set of selection criteria accepts no increase in total volume harvested but concentrates on stem straightness, the absence of spiral grain, and branching characters, particularly number, size, angle of insertion and distribution—the object being to increase the value of the stemwood and ease of harvesting. Similarly the characters of wood tracheids and fibres together with specific gravity are used as criteria for selection with the object of gaining better performance of the products made from the harvested timber.

Breeding for resistance to disease, insect attack and such features as resistance to winter cold or drought results in higher yields of timber and successful adaptation to a wider range of sites. With the extensive use of such techniques as site cultivation, supplementary nutrition, control of weeds and plantation layouts designed for mechanical harvesting, increasing attention is being paid to breeding for genotypes which respond to these cultural treatments.

In the majority of breeding programmes several goals are combined by selecting for several characters simultaneously. The characters included in the selection index are weighted by their relative importance and, as the information becomes available, by the genetic variances and co-variances of the characters. Great importance attaches to "early test" procedures in which seedlings and young trees are assessed for characters in the juvenile phase which are closely correlated with those of practical importance at or near the time of harvest.

2. Formation of clone banks

It is not generally convenient to gather large amounts of seed from the selected trees, or to do controlled pollinations on them, because they are widely dispersed and in places difficult to reach. Therefore they or their genes are gathered together in at least two convenient locations and protected against loss.

When a shoot is cut from a tree and rooted or grafted the tree's genotype remains intact in the cutting or graft. In sexual reproduction the genotype divides and is recombined in embryos within seeds. Grafts, cuttings or seedlings can be considered as "packages" of genes that can be detached from selected trees and used or tested in another place (Libby, 1973).

In the gene banks the trees produced by grafting, rooting cuttings or raising seedlings can be kept small for easy access. The phenology of pollen shedding and period of receptivity of female flowers is monitored and controlled crosses are made. The grafts, rooted cuttings or seedlings can be used for further propagation to establish seed orchards. In the gene banks only a few individuals are needed to represent each original tree and these can be planted in a systematic layout. The soil and climate of sites for gene banks must encourage early and abundant flowering and regular seed production. The number of genotypes or families should be large (from 100 to 1000) and include interesting and potentially valuable trees in addition to those of immediate use in the breeding programme.

3. Production of improved cultivars

A simple and effective procedure for producing new cultivars of trees is phenotypic mass selection. Very few outstanding individuals or families are selected from a large population and set out as grafts, rooted cuttings or seedlings in seed orchards or in stool beds or hedges planted as sources of material for clonal propagation.

In many seed orchards matings are by open pollination so that an important characteristic of the site is isolation from foreign pollen. Within the seed orchards the genotypes or families are assigned to their positions either randomly or by some system which encourages many different matings between genotypes or families with similar flowering times. The site and climate of seed orchards should favour early, continued and abundant flowering and seed production and be accessible for management and protection.

In some seed orchards the matings are made by controlled pollination. Specific recombinations of genes are required and repeated systematic layouts are used to facilitate this. In stool beds and hedges planted as sources for further vegetative propagation of clones no recombination of genes is sought and a blocking of genotypes is sufficient.

Another kind of seed orchard which is becoming more important is the seedling seed orchard. The seed has come from the original selections or is derived from controlled matings in gene banks and the seedlings are planted out at close spacing so that thinnings must be done before seed production commences on the survivors. Advantage can be taken of known family relationships to make the selection more efficient than phenotypic mass selection.

Seedling seed orchards are useful for species that do not root well from cuttings, have graft incompatibilities or produce more seed from seedlings than from grafts. Some disadvantages are the need to select rather early so that flowering is not delayed by dense stocking (resulting in selection for characters of the young tree rather than of the harvested tree) or the need to make the selection under non-forest conditions (resulting in selection of inappropriate trees if genotype–environment interactions are important).

A special kind of seedling seed orchard devised in Finland for production of seed of cultivars of *Betula* consists of seedlings planted under cover in very large polythene plant houses. The seedlings are encouraged to grow almost continuously and begin flowering and seed production at 18 months or two years (Lepisto, 1973).

4. *Testing and advanced generation selection*

Once the initial selected genotypes and families are assembled in gene banks and seed orchards, tests of the parents and their progenies on a range of representative forest sites are begun. The justifications for raising families of the original parents, planting them on one or more representative forest sites and making assessments over many years are: (i) to assess the selected trees and their relatives for the desired characters; (ii) on the basis of the information gained under (i) to increase or remove those selected trees that have been established in seed orchards, thus raising the value of the cultivars produced in these orchards; (iii) to provide a large number of trees and families for recombination of genes and continuing selection.

Progeny tests are justified under (i) when selection is based largely on the non-additive component of genetic variation, when important characters such as disease resistance can be assessed at an early age, or if the juvenile–adult correlations of desired characters are high. In these special cases the mating design should be polycross or multiple tester.

Because continuing selection is the most important reason for planting individual genotypes and their families their numbers must be large so as to provide a broad genetic base and generate sufficient selection differential for a large genetic gain in each generation of selection. The plantations should be located in sites representative of those on which the cultivars will be used. If a strong genotype–environment interaction is expected the genotypes and families should be replicated over several different site types. The design of the experiments include randomization, blocking and replication and the subsequent selection is based on the statistical analysis of assessment data.

5. *Anticipated and realized gains*

Most breeding programmes have not reached the point at which estimated gains can be checked against realized gains but tree breeding has been accepted as justified if improvements of 5–10% occur during the first generation of selection. Gains of 10–20% appear common and in specified situations superiority greater than 20% appears to be developing.

VI. CONCLUSION

As already noted it has been possible to discuss only some aspects of forest science related to increment and yield briefly. Nothing has been said about the essential work on protection of forests from damage by insects, fungi, animals and such agencies as fire and wind. The important findings of forest soil science have not been discussed and the growing amount of research being done in all aspects of forest science in the tropical regions has been mentioned only in connection with systematic forest botany. In spite of these and other gaps sufficient has been said to illustrate the development of *forest science*, and it remains to state this development in relation to that of *forestry*.

In forestry as it originated and developed in central Europe the existing forest was usually the starting point for silviculture. A line of thought which can be described as the biological approach to forestry was, and is, pursued. The advocates of this line require that all silvicultural operations in protection and production forests be examined within the framework of the natural forest and they assume that each site has its natural limits of productivity which cannot permanently be exceeded. In consequence the emphasis in the classical systems of silviculture is on adjustments to rather than on radical changes in the process of growth.

Contrasting with this natural forestry is artificial plantation forestry. In many countries in the northern and southern hemispheres plantations are usually established on soils not bearing forest or they replace a forest type which, because of its composition, is not suitable as a source of raw material for industry. Timber-growing in these plantation forests has given rise to a less natural approach to silviculture. The basic concept of the forest as an ecosystem is not forgotten but the emphasis has shifted to developing techniques by which an increased production of a standardized raw material can be obtained. Some of these techniques are based on the accumulated knowledge gained by forest science, examples being (Matthews, 1975; Giordano, 1971): from *Genetics*— selection of suitable provenances and production of improved cultivars; from *Forest Soil Science*—improved nursery techniques and site improvement by cultivation and drainage; from *Tree Physiology*—quicker establishment of trees by the adjustment of spacing, nutrition and control of weeds; from *Forest Yield Studies*—regular tending, including thinning, pruning and supplementary nutrition; from *Entomology and Pathology*—improved protection against pests and diseases and biological control of pests and diseases; from *Wood Science*—standardization of the properties of timber and improvement of its performance in use.

There are several conditions which must be fulfilled if intensive systems of plantation silviculture are to succeed. The tree species must be adapted to growth in pure plantations on a range of sites, it must respond to the treatments applied and it must remain healthy and not be susceptible to diseases and pests. There must be ample land available to achieve economies of scale. The timber must be utilizable in a range of products and there must be suitable wood-using industries and outlets for the products. There are many successful examples of these intensive systems of plantation siliviculture based on species of poplar, pine (*Pinus radiata* D. Don and *P. taeda* L.), spruce [*Picea sitchensis* (Bong.) Carr], eucalypt

(*Eucalyptus globulus* Labill.) and teak (*Tectona grandis* L.f.). There are also many successful examples of the classical systems of silviculture, especially in the protection forests of the mountainous regions of the world. These two main areas of forestry, which are also applied in many intermediate forms, will no doubt continue to be adapted to changing needs and forest science will continue to play a vital role in showing how to increase growth and make better use of forest resources.

The pace of development in forest science appears to have depended on the availability of trained manpower and improvements in the techniques of research such as equipment, instrumentation and design and analysis of experiments. Much was done in early years by trained people using simple techniques; much more can be done today with the aid of air-conditioned plant houses, accurate instruments and direct links to computers. At present insufficient is known about how trees react to the site and how they affect the site, particularly the soil. As more is learned about how trees grow so will foresters be better able to grow trees.

Acknowledgements

I acknowledge with thanks the assistance of my colleagues in the preparation of this paper, particularly W. D. Holmes, J. A. Petty, M. S. Philip, J. S. Murray, S. Thompson and Miss Anne Anstead.

References

A.E.T.F.A.T. (1954). "Index of the Papers on Systematic Phanerogamy and of the New Taxa Concerning Africa South of the Sahara." Association pour L'Etude taxonomique de la Flore de L'Afrique Tropicale, pp. 70.

Alestalo, A. (1973). "On the Possibilities of the Utilization of Needles and Bark." IUFRO Biomass Studies, University of Maine, Orono, 429–442.

Anon (1964). "Illustrated Important Forest Trees of Japan." Chikyu Shuppan Co. Ltd. Tokyo, pp. 217.

Ashton, P. S. (1964). "A Manual of the Dipterocarp Trees of Brunei State." Oxford University Press, London, pp. 242.

Assmann, E. (1970). "The Principles of Forest Yield Study." Pergamon Press, Oxford, pp. 566.

Bakuzis, E. V. (1969). Foresty viewed in an ecosystem perspective. *In* "The Ecosystem Concept in Natural Resourse Management, (Ed. G. M. von Dyne), pp. 189–258. Academic Press, New York and London.

Barlow, B. A. (1959a). Chromosome numbers in the Casuarinaceae. *Aust. J. Bot.* 7, 3, 230–237.

Barlow, B. A. (1959b). Polyploidy and apomixis in the *Casuarina distyla* species group. *Aust. J. Bot.* 7, 3, 238–251.

Bor, N. L. (1953). "Manual of Indian Forest Botany." Oxford University Press, pp. 441.

Boyce, S. G. (1975). The use of bole surface in the estimation of woodland production. *In* "A Discussion on Forests and Forestry in Britain." Phil. Trans. Roy. Soc. Lond. B. *Biological Sciences* **271, 911,** 139–148.

Boysen-Jensen, P. (1932). "Die Stoffproduktion der Pflanzen." Fischer, Jena, pp. 108.

Browne, F. G. (1955). "Forest Trees of Sarawak and Brunei and their Products." Government Printing Office, Kuching, Sarawak, pp. 369.

Burger, H. (1939). Baumkrone und Zuwachs in Zwei Hiebsreifen Fichtenbeständen. *Mitteilungen der Schweizerischen Anst. Forst. Versuchs.* **21,** 1, 147–176.

CAB (1960). "The Work and Growth of the Commonwealth Forestry Bureau, Oxford 1939–1959." Commonwealth Agricultural Bureaux, pp. 27.

Callaham, R. Z. (1964). Provenance research: investigation of genetic diversity associated with geography. *Unasylva* **18,** 2/3, 40–50.

Cieslar, A. (1887). Uber den Einfluss der Grösse des Fichtensamen auf die Entwicklung der Pflanzen nebst einigen Bemarkungen über Schwedische Fichten-und Weissfahrensamen. *Zbl. ges. Forst.* **13,** 149–153.

Cieslar, A. (1907). Die Bedeutung Klimatischer Varietäten unserer Holzarten für den Waldbau. *Zbl. ges. Forst.* **33,** 1–19, 49–62.

Cieslar, A. (1923). Untersuchungen über die Wirtschaftliche Bedeutung der Herkunft des Saatgutes der Stieleiche. *Zbl. ges. Forst.* **49.**

Clarke, S. H. (1940). "The Importance of the Plant Cell Wall to the Forester and Wood Anatomist." *Forestry Abstracts* **2,** 1, 1–4.

Coggans, J. F. (1965). "Variation of Tracheid Width and Wall Thickness within and between Trees of Southern Pine species." Proceedings IUFRO Section 41. 2 Division of Forest Products, CSIRO, Melbourne, Australia.

Critchfield, W. B. (1975). "Interspecific Hybridisation in *Pinus*: a Summary Review." Proceeding Fourteenth Meeting Canadian Tree Improvement Association, Part 2 Canadian Forestry Service, Ottawa, 99–105.

Dale, I. R. and Greenway, P. J. (1961). "Kenya Trees and Shrubs." Buchanan Kenya Estates Limited Nairobi and Hatchards, London, pp. 654.

Delvaux, J. (1971). Des Tables de Production aux Bilans Energétiques. *In* "Productivity of Forest Ecosystems." UNESCO, Paris, 177–184.

Dietrichson, J. (1973). Meeting of the Working Party 2. 02.11 on Norway spruce Provenances. International Union of Forest Research Organisations. Norwegian Forest Research Institute, pp. 54.

Duvigneaud, P. (1971). Concepts sur la Productivité Primaire des Ecosystèmes Forestiers. *In* "Productivity of Forest Ecosystems." UNESCO, Paris, 111–140.

Eggeling, W. J. and Dale, I. R. (1951). "The Indigenous Trees of the Uganda Protectorate. "Second Edition. Government Printer, Entebbe, Uganda, pp. 491.

Engler, A. (1905). Einfluss der Provenienz des Samens auf die Eigenschaften der Forstlichen Holzgewächse. *Mitteilungen Schweizerische Centralanstalt für des Forstliches Versuchs.* **8,** 81–236.

Engler, A. (1908). Tatsachen, Hypotheson und Irrtümer auf dem Gebeite der Samenprovenienzfrage. *Forstwissenschaftliches Centralblatt* **30,** 295–314.

Engler, A. (1913). Einfluss der Provenienz des Samens auf die Eigenschaften der forstlichen Holzgewächse Zweite Mitteilung. *Mitteilungen Schweizerische Centralanstalt für des Forstliches Versuchswesen* **10,** 191–386.

Evans, G. C. (1970). "The Quantitative Analysis of Plant Growth." Studies in Ecology I. Blackwell, Oxford. pp. 734.

Excell, A. W. and Wild, H. (1960). "Flora Zambesiaca." Mozambique, Federation of Rhodesia and Nyasaland, Bechuanaland Protectorate. Volume One, Part One

86   J. D. MATTHEWS

1960, Part Two 1961. Crown Agents for Overseas Governments and Adminstrations, London, pp. 581.

FAO (1963). Forestry Research: a world directory of forest and forest products research institutions. Forestry Occasional Paper 11. Food and Agriculture Organization, Rome, Italy, pp. 422.

Giordano, E. (1971). "Intensive Culture of Forests." Proceedings Fifteenth Congress of IUFRO, Gainesville, Florida, 102–108.

Gordon, J. C. and Larson, P. R. (1968). The seasonal course of photosynthesis, respiration and distribution of ^{14}C in young *Pinus resinosa* trees as related to wood formation. *Pl. Physiol.* **43**, 1617–1624.

Hair, J. B. and Beuzenberg, E. J. (1958). Chromosomal evolution in the *Podocarpaceae*. *Nature, Lond.* **181**, (4623), 1584–1586.

Hall, N. (1970). "Narrow-leaved Black Peppermint. *Eucalyptus nicholii*, Maiden and Blakely." Forest Tree Series 1. Forestry and Timber Bureau, Canberra, Australia, pp. 4.

Harris, J. M. (1970). Breeding to improve wood quality. *In* "Second World Consultation on Forest Tree Breeding." Washington D.C. 1969. *Unasylva*, **24**, 2/3, 1–132.

Hegnauer, R. (1962). "Chemotaxonomy of Plants. A Survey of the Distribution and Systematic Significances of Plant Constituents." I. Thallophytes, Bryophytes, Pteridophytes and Gymnosperms. Birkhäuser Verlag, Basel, Stuttgart, pp. 517.

Heske, F. (1938). "German Forestry." Yale University Press, New Haven, pp. 342.

Hutchinson, J., Dalzeil, J. M. and Keay, R. W. J. (1954). "Flora of West Tropical Africa." Second Edition. Crown Agents for Overseas Governments and Administrations, London, pp. 828.

IUFRO (1975). International Union of Forestry Research Organisations, Annual Report 1975, Vienna, pp. 67.

Jarvis, P. G. (1974). Water transfer in Plants. *In*: "Heat and Mass Transfer in the Environment of Vegetation" pp. 1–21. Scripta Book Co. Washington D.C., U.S.A.

Langlet, O. (1934). Om Variationen hos Tallen (*Pinus silvestris* L.) och dess Samband med Klimatet. *Svenska Skogsvärdsföreningens Tiskrift* **32**, 1–2, 87–110.

Langlet, O. (1936). Studier over Tallens Fysiologiska Variabilitet och det Samband med Klimatet. *Meddelanden frau Statens Skogsforsöksanstalt* **29**, 219–420.

Langlet, O. (1971). Two hundred years of genecology. *Taxon* **20**, 5/6, 653–721.

Larsen, C. S. (1937). "The Employment of Species, Types and Individuals in Forestry." Royal Veterinary and Agriculture College Yearbook. C. A. Reitzel, Copenhagen, pp. 154.

Larson, P. R. (1964). Some indirect effects of environment on wood formation. *In* "The Formation of Wood in Forest Trees" (M. Zimmermann, Ed.), pp. 345–365. Academic Press, New York and London.

Larson, P. R. (1969). "Wood Formation and the Concept of Wood Quality." Yale University, School of Forestry, Bulletin 74, pp. 54.

Larson, P. R. (1973). The physiological basis for wood specific gravity in conifers. *In* "Wood in the Service of Man". IUFRO Division 5, Forest Products, Republic of South Africa, 672–680.

Last, F. T. (1975). "Some Aspects of Genecology of Trees." East Malling Research Station, Report for 1974, Maidstone, Kent, 25–40.

Lipisto, M. (1973). "Accelerated Birch Breeding in Plastic Greenhouses." *Forestry Chronicle* **49**, 4, 1–2.

Libby, W. J., Stettler, R. F. and Seitz, F. W. (1969). Forest genetics and forest tree breeding. *A. Rev. Genet.* **3**, 469–494.

Libby, W. (1973). Domestication strategies for forest trees. *Can. J. For. Res.* **3**, 2, 265–276.

Lindemann, J. C. and Mennega, A. M. W. (1963). "Trees of Surinam: recognition of Surinam species by wood and vegetative characteristics." Diensts Lands Bosbeheer Suriname, Paramibo.

Little, E. L. (1953). "Check List of Native and Naturalised Trees of the United States (including Alaska)." Agriculture Handbook 41, Forest Service, Washington, pp. 472.

Malkönen, E. (1973). "Effect of Complete Tree Utilization on the Nutrient Reserves of Forest Soils." IUFRO Biomass Studies. University of Maine, Orono, 375–386.

Mantel, K. (1964). History of the international science of forestry, with special consideration of Central Europe. *Int. Rev. For. Res.* **1**, 1–37.

Mar:Møller, C. (1945). Untersuchungen über Laubmenge, Stoffverlust und Stoffproduktion des Waldes. *Forstlige Forsøgsvaesen i Danmark* **17**, 1–287.

Mar:Møller, C., Muller, D. and Nielsen, J. (1954). Graphic presentation of dry matter production of European Beech. *Forstlige Forsøgsvaesen i Danmark* **213**, 327–335.

Matthews, J. D. (1975). Prospects of improvement by site amelioration, breeding and protection. "A Discussion on Forests and Forestry in Britain." *Phil. Trans. Roy. Soc. Lond. B* **27**, 911, 115–138.

Meijer, W. and Wood, G. H. S. (1964). "Dipterocarps of Sabah (North Borneo)." Sabah Forest Record 5, pp. 344.

Metcalfe, C. R. (1960). "Anatomy of the Monocotyledons." I. Graminae. Clarendon Press, Oxford, pp. 731.

Metcalfe, C. R. and Chalk, L. (1957). "Anatomy of the Dicotyledons." 2 volumes. Clarendon Press, Oxford.

Michaux, F. A. (1817–19). "The North American Sylva or a Description of the forest trees of the United States, Canada and Nova Scotia." 3 volumes. Philadelphia.

Newbould, P. J. (1967). "Methods for Estimating the Primary Production of Forests." Blackwell, Oxford, pp. 62.

Ovington, J. D. (1962). Quantitative Ecology and the Woodland Ecosystem Concept. *Adv. Ecol. Res.* **1**, 103–192.

Palmer, E. and Pitman, N. (1972). "Trees of Southern Africa." 3 volumes. A. A. Balkema, Capetown.

Penfold, A. R. and Willis, J. L. (1961). "The Eucalypts." Leonard Hill (Books) Ltd., London, pp. 551.

Petty, J. A. (1970). The relation of wood structure to preservative treatment. *In*: The Wood We Grow. *Forestry*, 29–35.

Petty, J. A. (1972). The aspiration of bordered pits in conifer wood. *Proc. Roy. Soc. Lond., B*, **181**, 395–406.

Petty, J. A. (1975). United Kingdom Patent Application 17248/75.

Petty, J. A. and Preston, R. D. (1969). The removal of air from wood. *Holzforschung* 23, 1, 9–15.

Petty, J. A. and Puritch, G. S. (1970). The effects of drying on the structure and permeability of the wood of *Abies grandis*. *Wood Sci. Technol.* **4**, 140–154.

Preston, R. D. (1974). "The Physical Biology of Plant Cell Walls." Chapman and Hall, London, pp. 491.

Rendle, B. J. (1960). Juvenile and adult wood. *J. Inst. Wood Sci.* **5**, 58–61.

Sargent, C. S. (1891–1902). "The Silva of North America: a Description of the trees which grow naturally in North America exclusive of Mexico." 14 volumes. Boston and New York.

Satoo, T. (1971). Primary production relations of coniferous forests in Japan. *In* "Productivity of Forest Ecosystems." pp. 191–205. UNESCO, Paris.

Schlich, W. (1916). Forestry in the United Kingdom. *Q. J. Forest.* **10**, 3, 165–185.

Schotte, G. (1906). Uber die Variation des schwedersiche Kiefenzapfens und Kiefern samens. *Naturwiss. Z. Forst. and wirts.* **4.**

Schwappach, A. (1911). Wolchen Einfluss haben Herkunft und Keimkraft des Kiefernsamens auf Wachstum und Ertrag der aus ihnen hervorgegangenen Bestande? *Deutsche Forst Zeitung* 1911.

Science Council of Canada (1973). "A National Statement by the Schools of Forestry at Candian Universities." Ottawa, pp. 4.

Sharp, L. (1975). Timber, science and economic reform in the seventeenth century. *Forestry* **48**, 1, 51–86.

Shioya, T. (1967). A short history of forestry and forestry research in East Asia. *Int. Rev. Forest. Res.* **2**, 1–42.

Society of Forest History (1960). "A Treatise on Forestry by CDF Reventlow." Hørshelm, Denmark, pp. 142.

Speer, J. (1973). IUFRO 1892–1972. International Union of Forestry Research Organisations, Ås, Norway, pp. 25.

Stamm, A. J. (1964). "Wood and Cellulose Science." Ronald Press Company, New York, pp. 549.

Swain, T. (1963). "Chemical Plant Taxonomy." pp. 543. Academic Press, London and New York.

Tomlinson, P. B. (1961). "Anatomy of the Monocotyledons." II. Palmae. Clarendon Press, Oxford, pp. 453.

Trendelenburg, R. and Mayer-Wegelin, H. (1955). Das Holz als Rohstoff. Second edition, Hanser Munich, pp. 541.

Troup, R. S. (1928). "Silvicultural Systems." Second edition (E. W. Jones, Ed.), Clarendon Press, Oxford, pp. 256.

Turrill, W. B. (1942). Taxonomy and phylogeny. Part 2. *Bot. Rev.* **8**, 8, 473–532.

White, F. (1962). "Forest Flora of Northern Rhodesia." Oxford University Press, pp. 455.

Whittaker, R. H. and Woodwell, G. M. (1967). Surface area relations of woody plants and forest communities. *Am. J. Bot.* **54**, 8, 931–939.

Wright, J. W. (1962). "Genetics of Forest Tree Improvement." FAO Forestry and Forest Products Studies 16, Food and Agriculture Organisation, Rome, Italy, pp. 399.

Young, H. E. (1973). "Growth, Yield and Inventory in Terms of Biomass." IUFRO Biomass Studies, University of Maine, Orono, 1–9.

Zauffa, L. (1975). "A Summary Review of Interspecific Breeding in the Genus *Populus* L." Proceedings Fourteenth Meeting, Canadian Tree Improvement Association Part 2. Canadian Forestry Service, Ottawa, 107–123.

Zobel, B. J. (1964). Breeding for wood properties in forest trees. *Unasylva* **18**, 2/3, 89–103.

Birds as Pests

R. K. MURTON and N. J. WESTWOOD

Institute of Terrestrial Ecology,
Monks Wood Experimental Station, Huntingdon, England.

I. INTRODUCTION

Only two decades ago it was still fashionable to formulate lists of birds using a utilitarian classification of those harmful and those beneficial to man. Neither category has validity and the modern approach requires appreciation of the complex ecosystems of which birds are but one component. Weeds have sometimes tritely been defined as good plants in the wrong place and it might be tempting to apply the same label to pestiferous birds. This would be an over-simplification for birds, more than any other animal taxon, evoke strong but ambivalent emotions in people and the problems they pose as pests must be assessed in the wider context of wildlife management, which embraces the concept of conservation, and pays due regard to public opinion. The situation is highlighted in such drastically man-altered habitats as Trafalgar Square, London, or St Peter's, Rome, where feral pigeons (*Columba livia* Gmein var.) give pleasure to many people yet at the same time provide potential health hazards which concern medical officers of health.

For this review we could have treated problem birds entirely in a systematic manner listing for each species its virtues and vices, but this would have meant much repetition. Another approach might have involved itemizing field crops and situations and detailing the species that can cause problems; discussions of control techniques could then have been dealt with in a separate category. Each treatment we considered confronted us with the difficulties that certain species may pose several distinct problems, while the same control techniques may be applicable under quite different ecological situations. Since we wanted to emphasize the biological and evolutionary context of the subject we opted for a compromise. Birds may pose problems simply because of their physical presence, because of their rôle in harbouring or transmitting disease organisms, or more usually because of their depredations to crops or livestock. Under such broad categories we have focused attention on the most important species, aiming to give details of general biology, the harm caused to man and the ecological context. In this way a topic is expanded only when critical scientific studies have been made and we neglect the countless repetitions of unsupported statements which unfortunately prevail in this field. Much may be known about the damage caused by one species whereas knowledge of the effectiveness of control techniques may have been gained from work on totally different species. We have tried to synthesize the subject so that complete examples are given, that is, the reader can assess the scale of a problem and set it against the appropriate ecological background. Of course, a detailed financial costing ought to precede all situations where money is spent in attempts to mitigate bird damage but it is soon clear that this ideal has rarely been achieved. The research and development of control techniques is also elaborated with reference to the species and context in which major advances have been achieved, even though the particular technique be applied in other situations. For the benefit of readers wishing to locate the literature dealing with control techniques we conclude with a table which categorizes the methods referred to in the text by page number. It should be emphasized, however, that a technique may have been used successfully in a very limited context. The literature abounds with reports and proceedings of bird control seminars referring to numerous project plans and case histories but, as with damage assessment, there is a paucity of scientifically documented examples which relate expenditure on control efforts to the cost of damage and thereby demonstrate tangible returns.

II. Problems Posed by the Physical Presence of Birds

A. BIRD SONG

If nightingales (*Lucinia megarhynchos* Brehm) were to sing regularly in Berkeley Square, it is probable that some residents would complain to the local authorities about disturbance to their sleep. Not all light sleepers appreciate the "dawn chorus"! The collared dove [*Streptopelia decaocto* (Frivaldszky)] is an Indian–Turkestanian faunal component which had expanded its range to the Balkans during the 16th and 17th centuries. Its population was relatively stabilized in this outpost until the early 1930's since when a dramatic expansion across Europe occurred which brought the first breeding pair to Britain in 1955, although it is not clear whether a pair in 1952 were escapes or wild birds (Fisher, 1953; May and Fisher, 1953; Nowak, 1971). Numbers increased exponentially in Britain from one pair in 1955 to an estimated 15–25 thousand pairs in 1970 (Hudson, 1965; 1972). The species has occupied an apparently vacant niche, perhaps created by the demise of the dovecote pigeon (see Murton, 1968), living close to man and feeding on grain spillage, and scavenging on the food provided for poultry or other domestic stock (Stolt and Risberg, 1971). It has invaded urban habitats, living alongside the feral pigeon, where it depends on spillage from provender and food storage mills, and has also successfully established itself in various residential areas, including holiday resorts, where the public feed the birds. From such places have come complaints of it disturbing people by its repetitive and monotonous calls.

B. BIRD STRIKES ON AIRCRAFT

1. *Damage caused*

After years spent learning to emulate the flying ability of birds, man has rapidly become a competitor for air-space. Early aeroplanes mostly flew slowly enough on landing or take-off to be avoided by birds while at height bird density is low and the risks of a collision negligible. The emergence of high speed jets having rapid take-off and landing speeds, compounded by increases in air traffic at the major airports has markedly increased the bird-strike risk. The first major disaster caused by birds was in 1960 at Boston, U.S.A., when a turbo-propellor Electra collided with a flock of starlings (*Sturnus vulgaris* L.—a species introduced to N. America by man) at take-off and 62 out of 72 people aboard were killed in the subsequent crash. In 1962, a turbo-propellor Viscount collided with two whistling swans [*Cygnus columbianus* (Ord)] and crashed near Baltimore, U.S.A., killing 17 people. Since this time around 100 people have died in the United States alone in a series of smaller accidents involving birds.

Quite apart from the direct risk to human life, the costs of replacement or repair to damaged engines and superstructures and of accident prevention are enormous. A relatively small incident at take-off may necessitate a pilot relanding for safety reasons, after first jettisoning expensive fuel, and have serious repercussions from a time-table and passenger good-will viewpoint. Indeed, the financial costs of the damage caused by bird strikes exceeds that of any of the other economic problems posed by birds. Not surprisingly, more money is invested in bird-strike research than any other project involving avian pests; nevertheless, the amount is less than that spent, in the field of aviation, on lightning strikes, encounters with hail or fuel contamination, all these being less serious problems than the bird hazard.

The scale of the problem can be judged by the fact that in five years Trans-Canada Airlines experienced a total of 486 strikes. Up to November 1968 twenty-three engines had to be changed because of birds and direct costs since 1959 have been reckoned at nearly $Can. 2 million. Much publicity has been given to bird-strikes in Canada (Harris, 1965; Bird, 1966; Gunn and Solman, 1968; Associate Committee on Bird Hazards to Aircraft, 1971–2; Canadian Wildlife Service Report, 1971; Solman, 1973) where the current average strike rate is 4·70 per 10 000 aircraft movements compared with a world average of 3·80 and a rate in Britain of 3·33 (Civil Aviation Authority, 1973). Early figures quoted by Cook-Smith (1965) were perhaps underestimates but they indicated that 145 strikes were actually reported at United Kingdom civil aerodromes in the period 1946–1963, with 96 (66%) occurring at take-off or landing. A figure of around four-fifths is probably more realistic judging from world statistics which show this to be the proportion of incidents to civilian aircraft which occur near airfields, whereas only one fifth occur away from airfields above 5000 ft

(1524 m). For military aircraft the situation is reversed and four-fifths occur away from airfields, primarily because of the low altitude and high speed of military operations (Solman, 1973). British European Airways experienced an average of nine strikes per month between June and September 1967, while between 1958 and 1963 B.O.A.C. had to change 81 engines as a result of bird ingestion and of these instances 40 had not been detected during flight and were only discovered during maintenance (Brown, 1965). B.O.A.C. quoted a cost of £1 million for engine repair over five years.

Up to date figures for bird-strikes involving all United Kingdom registered civil aircraft weighing more than 5700 kg and details of all major accidents throughout the world since 1947 have been produced by the Civil Aviation Authority (1973). The report shows that in seventeen cases where costs could be worked out properly they averaged £10 000 per incident. The report confirms that most strikes occur at low levels round airfields, with relatively few at night and a particularly high risk at dawn. The highest absolute number of strikes is noted in July and August when aircraft traffic is greatest, but the highest strike-rate in Britain is in October, November and January. This corresponds to the season of late autumn migration and the influx of gulls (Laridae) which winter inland, particularly round urban conurbations (Hickling, 1967). The number of incidents during spring migration is not particularly high, presumably because spring migration occurs more rapidly than the autumn passage and migrants do not linger round airports and other places to the same extent. In Canada, the incidence of bird-strikes is closely related to the spring and autumn migration seasons (Fig. 1; see also Bridgman, 1965; Bird, 1966; Fowler, 1967; Seubert, 1968).

The species most involved in bird-strikes vary with the locality but on a world wide basis, and in Britain and Europe, *Larus* gulls have proved to be the biggest nuisance (Drury, 1963; Hardenberg, 1965; Murton and Wright, 1968; Cogswell, 1969; Seubert, 1968). In Canada, waterfowl (Anatidae) and waders (Charadriformes) have assumed proportionately more importance and birds of prey, including the snowy owl [*Nyctea scandiaca* (L.)] have been a problem (Hughes, 1965; 1966). At Kai Tak airport, Hong Kong, the black kite [*Milvus migrans* (Boddaert)] is the chief concern and numbers increase markedly in winter due to immigrants from mainland China (Romer, 1969). Black kites are also the biggest nuisance at Townsville, Queensland (Lavery, 1969). In India, vultures (Accipitridae) make use of the wide open spaces and of thermals rising from the tarmac runways. Waders are also a problem at Auckland, New Zealand and their occurrence on the airfield depends much on the tide level in a nearby harbour (Saul, 1967; Roberts and Saul, undated).

Two main kinds of bird-strike can occur. The first involves a straight-forward collision with the airframe and superstructure, and the second, ingestion into the engine. A four-pound (1·81 kg) bird hitting an aircraft travelling at 500 mph is equivalent to the impact of a ton weight (0·907 tonnes) falling from 22 ft (6·7 m) over the same area (Stables and New, 1968), or a four-pound bird when hit at 300 mph produces an almost instantaneous blow to an area of six inches (15 cm)

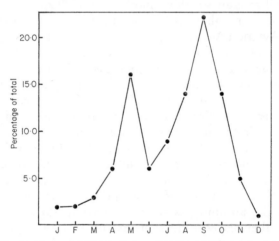

Fig. 1. Monthly incidence of 711 collisions between birds and aircraft in Canada 1966–1970. (From Solman, 1973).

diameter of about 15 tons (= 13·6 tonnes); doubling the speed increases the impact four-fold (Solman, 1973). At Foulness, once proposed as the site for London's third airport, estimates indicate a population of 3000 gulls, 8000 brent geese [*Branta bernicla* (L.)] and 15 000 waders, pro-viding a total biomass of about 25 tons. Large birds can obviously cause the most damage but their frequency of occurrence is lower than for lighter birds. Plotting bird-strike incidence against the average weight of species shows that a marked change in slope occurs with birds weighing above or below about four pounds (1·81 kg) (Fig. 2). Data for small birds are lacking because many incidents are not reported or identified. Because of the above relationship, the Air Registration Board required wind screens and engines to be made safe against birds of up to 1·81 kg weight up to the maximum aircraft speeds employed at 8000 ft (2439 m) altitude (Stables and New, 1968). Stables and New (1968) give details of testing procedures, including the use of the bird-gun at Farnborough used to fire chickens at wind screens and air-frames.

In the second kind of bird strike, that of ingestion into the engine, flocks of small birds can be a hazard, and the risk is related to the size of flock and its configuration. Piston engine aircraft suffer relatively little from this kind of damage which is much more acute for turbine

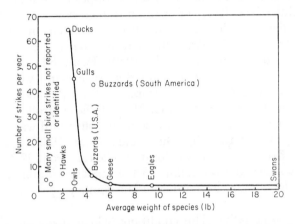

FIG. 2. Incidence of bird strikes on aircraft in relation to weight of bird. (After Stables and New, 1968).

engines. The impact of a single small bird can bend a turbine blade slightly and resultant stresses can lead to vibration and eventual failure; a flock can result in engine seizure. The aerodynamics of air-craft affect the risk of an air-strike and those like the VC10 with tail mounted engines are less at risk than those with engines sited in the wings like the Comet 4 while pod-mounted engines as in the Boing 707 and 747 are intermediate.

Damage to military aircraft is probably proportionately greater than to civil planes but for security reasons details are not readily published (Brink, 1969; Hart, 1969; Hild, 1969a). Gunn and Solman (1968) mentioned that the Canadian Air Force lost seven F104 Star Fighter jets (each at the time worth £0·75 million) and possibly two others, as a direct result of bird collisions; the pilots were saved by their ejector seats. Stables and New (1968) claimed that the Royal Air Force had an annual repair and replacement bill amounting to about £1 million due to bird-strikes. The Royal Navy suffers more for the aerodromes are often near sea-bird concentrations, and aircraft carriers often have attendant gull flocks (Brown, 1965).

2. Control techniques

(a) *Warning procedures*. In Britain and North America considerable attention is devoted to defining the flight paths of gulls (e.g. Bourne, 1969; Lloyd-Evans, 1970) and other birds and the times of risk in order to warn air controllers of dangerous situations (Associate Committee on Bird Hazards to Aircraft, 1971–2). Plan-position radars (PP1) and range height radars (RH1) of medium to high-power surveillance and set at low angles of elevation, are effective for detecting echoes from birds (Sutter, 1957; Harper, 1957) and have been used extensively for studies of bird migration (Lack, 1959; Eastwood, 1967); refined methods can enable the size of individual species to be estimated and their wing beat frequencies measured (Schaefer, 1968). Radar has proved a valuable tool in the hands of air traffic controllers; planes can be directed to avoid bird concentrations and such bird warning systems are in regular use (Bird, 1965; Gunn and Solman, 1968; Grimes, 1972). Solman (1973) reports a reduction in strike-rate from 22 per 10 000 h of flying to 7 per 10 000 h following the implementation of a warning system by the military authorities of one country.

(b) *Habitat manipulation*. The conditions which make airfields attractive to birds may be altered, and this provides one of the best examples of how habitat manipulation can be a feasible means of reducing bird damage (Munroe and Harris, 1963; Solman, 1966, 1970; Wright, 1968; Austin-Smith and Lewis, 1969; Hild, 1969b). It is often the case that refuse dumping grounds are near to airports as both are usually sited on "waste" ground away from cities and this was the case at London Airport, where the proximity of large reservoirs serving as roosting sites has compounded the problem (Bourne, 1969; Sage, 1970); removal of garbage causes a loss of gulls (Drury, 1963; Hickling, 1969). The Canadian authorities spent $Can. 10 million in modifying international and other airports and were able to reduce the annual repair cost to planes damaged by birds by nearly a half, from $Can. 240 000 to $Can. 125 000 (Harris, 1965; Solman, 1973). Cutting vegetation can make the habitat less attractive for small rodents and thereby eliminate hunting areas for avian predators such as buzzards (*Buteo* spp.) and short-eared owls [*Asio flammeus* (Pontoppidan)]. Thus on Vancouver airfield, 500 owls, mostly short-eared owls, were trapped over a three year period (Lewis, 1967). In other circumstances, it may be advantageous to encourage long grass, as at Auckland, New Zealand (Saul,

1967), so that each situation has to be evaluated on its own merits according to the species causing risk. If grazing by domestic animals is allowed the droppings encourage insects and in turn birds. Wood pigeons (*Columba palumbus* L.) are only attracted to grasslands supporting clovers (*Trifolium* spp.) and certain weeds and these can be killed by selective herbicides. In Holland, allowing grass to grow longer than four inches (10·16 cm) caused a marked reduction of gull numbers, and although redshanks [*Tringa totanus* (L.)] became more common they were less of a problem than gulls and other species (Hardenberg, 1965). In many cases, crops are grown in the close vicinity of airport runways and this can attract birds.

The actual concrete or tarmac runways can be attractive to birds for resting or roosting. They may be 10°C above ambient temperature because of solar radiation while adjacent grass can be 3–6°C below ambient due to evaporation. Birds therefore derive advantages in that by resting in such places they need use less of their food reserves for thermo-regulation. There is some evidence that herring gulls (*Larus argentatus* Pontoppidan) prefer warmer sites if given a choice (Kuhring, 1965) and the same explanation applies to such urban roosting species as the starling (Potts, 1967).

(*c*) *Physical scaring techniques*. Birds which, in spite of cases of successful management, do settle on or near airport runways must be dispersed before planes land or take-off. Quite complicated arrangements exist at most major airports and operators stationed at strategic points for bird scaring are in constant communication with the central control room. Simple scaring devices ranging from the use of dogs, various noise machines, shellcracker cartridges and the pyrotechnics of Very lights and fireworks may be employed with varying success (Brough, 1968). Advantage is sometimes taken of the birds' fear of natural enemies and trained birds of prey, especially peregrine falcons (*Falco peregrinus* Tunstall), have been used (Solman, 1965) as at Lossie-mouth, Scotland. Falconry requires specialist personnel and wild stocks of most raptorial birds are presently insufficient to satisfy more than a small demand. Artificial models have been used as an alternative and even some which are radio-controlled have been tried; in all there has been only a limited success, for the birds rapidly habituate (Brough, 1968). Orange runway light has been claimed to reduce the bird-strike risk (van Tets *et al.*, 1969a, b).

(*d*) *Bio-acoustic scaring techniques*. Many avian vocalizations function to proclaim territories and attract mates or serve to integrate flock movements, while alarm calls are used to draw attention to danger but they do not necessarily stimulate escape behaviour. In addition, some species possess so-called distress calls (Frings and Jumber, 1954) which are quite unlike the normal alarm notes of the bird; distress calls often have frequencies which make the localization of their source easy whereas alarm calls have features which make the performer difficult to locate (Brémond, 1963, 1965; Boudreau, 1968). Distress calls may be given when the bird has actually been caught by a predator and they have a ventriloquial quality which may function to distract the predator causing it momentarily to release the victim; this occurred once when Perrins (1968) was removing a great tit (*Parus major* L.) from a mist net and he was surprised enough to let the bird escape from his hand. Since these calls are usually only emitted in nature when a bird has actually been caught it would be expected that their effectiveness should be reinforced if accompanied by some simulation of a predator holding prey. Initial experiments using recorded distress calls to scare birds were done in the United States by Frings (1954, 1962) and Frings and Jumber (1954) and the method has subsequently been extensively developed in a number of countries as a means of crop protection (Busnel and Giban, 1960, 1965, 1968; Frings and Frings, 1962, 1963; Wright, 1965, 1969; Brough, 1965, 1968, 1969).

The distress call of *Sturnus vulgaris* is a long drawn out scream which is capable of making other starlings take immediate flight. Five sounds (starling-distress, -escape, -drug-induced, -feeding and the human voice) played to starlings in acoustic chambers induced a differential acceleration of heart rate and required specific times for habituation to develop; the distress call produced the biggest alteration in heart rate and required most time for habituation (Thompson *et al.*, 1968). Bird vocalizations are complex and different frequency components clearly serve different functions. Some may evoke reflex reactions and others require the addition of a visual stimulus. The distress calls of various gulls, rook (*Corvus frugilegus* L.), jackdaw (*C. monedula* L.) lapwing [*Vanellus vanellus* (L.)] initially cause the birds to approach the sound source and indulge in mobbing behaviour. This phase is followed by dispersal away from the sound and temporary vacation of the area. On airfields the first response phase can be an embarrassment and operators need to use their experience to allow time for the dispersal phase to develop.

The quality of distress call recordings influences their effectiveness and considerable research effort has been devoted to improving equipment and maintaining high-fidelity over distance (Brémond *et al.*, 1968). A sound intensity of around 115 dB generated 1 m from the loudspeaker will give a suitable signal over about 1 km² (Busnel and Giban, 1968). Busnel and Giban (1968) point out that a variation of 5% in the rise time of a signal transient can alter the reaction of an insect by 50% and the perceptive ability of birds is unlikely to be less specific. This means that filters, modulators, speed adjusters, frequency and time transposers are all important variables in wiring circuits. This is especially the case in the wild where birds experience high levels of background sound.

Vocalizations which are used for advertisement and mate selection often show marked intra-specific variations related to habitat and geographical area and they contain many components which are learned (Nottebohm, 1969, 1970). Some claims have been made that the same applies to distress calls and that, for example, dialect differences in herring gull recordings made in N. America made them ineffective in Holland. This viewpoint is not supported by the concensus of evidence which indicates a degree of interspecific effectiveness for these noises. Birds do habituate to repeated distress calls, especially when unassociated with any reinforcing stimulus, and they are more effective if combined with noxious stimuli (Brough, 1968). Nevertheless, distress calls appear to be more effective than other scaring techniques. Wright (1965) reported that gull distress calls kept an airfield clear for 12 months with little evidence of habituation, whereas with acetylene bangers and other noise machines habituation occurred after only two days. Distress calls repelled starlings 11 times more effectively than pure tones at the same decibel level (Langowski et al., 1969). Using distress calls, it is easier to scare birds which have come to roost or rest than to disperse breeding concentrations, while food shortage makes birds more persistent since alternative sources are unavailable (Brough, 1968). For work on airfields it has proved convenient, and more effective, to install tape decks, amplifiers and loud-speakers in a mobile vehicle.

Birds are supposedly disturbed by high frequency sound waves, that is, ultrasonics, but there is little evidence that they can detect sound waves much above the frequency detectable by man. Experiments have produced unconvincing results using frequencies of 16–40 kc. Propagation of such signals needs much power and it is difficult to project the sounds over long distances. Their use has been tried on airfields (Tanner, 1965; Tanner et al., 1967, 1969).

3. *Road casualties and incidental collisions*

For completeness it should be mentioned that birds sometimes fly into windows and other structures and cause damage. Exceptionally they may fly into people and cause injury. It is not unusual for swans e.g. mute swans [*Cygnus olor* (Gmelin)] and other large birds to collide with overhead power or telephone cables and to cause considerable damage and the subject has been reviewed by Turček (1960). Road casualties among birds are common and have given concern to people motivated towards the welfare of birds and a considerable literature pertains to the subject (Hodson, 1960, 1962; Finnis, 1960; Dunthorn and Errington, 1964; Hodson and Snow, 1965; Hansen, 1969). Between 10–20% of the ringing recoveries of many passerines result from road accidents, indicating the scale of the situation. Only exceptionally do collisions result in broken windscreens or otherwise contribute to accidents but collated statistics are not available.

C. GULLS

1. *Increase in numbers*

An enormous increase in the numbers and a range expansion of gulls has occurred during the present century in the North Temperate region. Nesting colonies of herring gulls and lesser blackbacked gulls (*Larus fuscus* L.) in Britain have increased at rates of 10–20% per annum during recent decades (Brown, 1967; Parslow, 1967; Hickling, 1969; Harris, 1970) and there has been a marked increase in the numbers of gulls—these two species and also black-headed gull (*L. ridibundus* L.)—wintering inland (Hickling, 1967). An increase of 21 to 55%, according to species, was noted in the winter population roosting on London reservoirs between 1963 and 1969, emphasizing the increased hazard to aircraft (Sage, 1970), while public health officials concern themselves with health risks from the contamination of drinking water by faeces. Similar trends apply in continental Europe (Bruyns, 1958; Rooth and Timmerman, 1962–6; Goethe, 1969; Gloe, 1971) and some of the rarer species have also prospered and spread in range including the mediterranean gull (*L. melanocephalus* Temminck) (Blondel and Isenmann, 1973; Krivenko *et al.*, 1973). In North America the population of herring gulls has been approximately doubling in size every generation (12–15 years) since the 1880's (Kadlec and Drury, 1968; Drury and Nisbet, 1972). The increased availability of human refuse has been important (Poulding, 1954; Harris, 1964; Drury and Nisbet, 1972) and at various colonies chicks fed on garbage have grown faster than those receiving only natural foods (Spaans, 1971; Drury and Nisbet, 1972). In addition, the expansion of the fishing industry and the availability of offal has been a factor, and gulls have shown a capacity to exploit new feeding sites, for example, gulls wintering inland feed on earthworms and cereal grain on farmland (D. Lloyd, unpublished observations; Vernon, 1970).

The success of gulls at their breeding colonies can have deleterious effects on other species nesting near them in terms of competition for nesting space and food and also because gulls predate the eggs and chicks of other species. The problem is serious at some nature reserves and the topic has been comprehensively reviewed by Thomas (1972).

2. *Control Techniques*

In addition to scaring with noise machines or distress calls (see above) the following deserve mention.

(*a*) *Eliminating adult birds.* Thomas mentions rocket or cannon netting, trapping and catching birds at night by dazzle-net techniques, as methods to use at nature reserves but they are of limited application. Attempts have been made to poison herring gulls with strychnine in Holland (Bruyns, 1958) and Germany (Drost, 1958), but the work of Bruyns shows that even a very intensive slaughter campaign did little more then prevent the population increase that would otherwise have occurred. His culls were nullified by immigrant gulls from other areas which moved in to take advantage of the vacuum. This problem has been discussed in relation to the dispersal pattern of New England herring gulls (Nisbet and Drury, 1969). Baits treated with stupefying substances have been used as alternatives to poisons (see p. 137) and suitable techniques have been described by Borg (1955), Patterson (1965), Caithness (1968) and Stenman *et al.* (1972).

(*b*) *Destruction of eggs and young.* The adult death rate of gulls is of the order of 5–10% per annum so adults live for about ten years. The natural wastage rate of eggs is, therefore, extremely high so that regulation of the birth rate must be very efficient to achieve worthwhile results at reasonable cost. A once favoured method was to prick eggs but unless done carefully this causes the birds to desert and relay, thereby defeating the object of the exercise: for the same reason there is no point in simply smashing eggs. When 22% of the herring gulls on Skomer Island, Wales, had their eggs pricked, chick production *in the area of operation* was reduced by 85% (Corkhill, 1970). The classic work was done by Gross (1950 and unpublished observations) in Maine and Massachusetts between 1938 and 1953. For five years he pricked eggs but these rotted and were replaced so he changed in 1940 to spraying eggs with a mixture of 10% formaldehyde in water and a carrier oil; these eggs were killed without rotting. The annual number of eggs treated at 21 island colonies fell from over 30 000 in 1940 to around

10 000 in 1952. This rate of decrease was higher than could be accounted for by mortality indicating that the gulls deserted breeding stations where they were unsuccessful. Colonies in a nearby area increased more slowly than the regional average (Kadlec and Drury, 1968). Gross's programme coincided with a slight decline in wintering gull populations in eastern North America, and its main effect was to stimulate both adults and immatures to move to new colonies (Nisbet and Drury, 1971). A programme of egg pricking from 1959–63, and then the removal of eggs and nests in 1964 led in 1965 to the black-headed gull population on Havergate Island, England, being reduced from 3000 to 500 pairs (Olney, 1965). But as noted by Murton (1971a) it is likely that the gulls simply moved to another colony on the mainland and that the apparent reduction in population size was an artifact and not the result of a lowered fecundity.

D. BIRD DAMAGE TO STRUCTURES

1. *Damage caused directly by birds*

Woodpeckers (Picidae) use dead trees for food searching, territorial drumming and boring their nesting holes. They do not always distinguish wooden telegraph poles and can cause considerable damage by weakening and facilitating fungal infection. In Czechoslovakia one wooden post per mile had been damaged by great spotted woodpeckers [*Dendrocopos major* (L.)] or the closely related syrian woodpecker [*D. syriacus* (Hemprick and Chrenberg)] (Turček, 1960). The latter is much more a bird of cultivated country than the great spotted and has been undergoing a range expansion in S.E. Europe similar to, but slower than, that of the collared dove, possibly helped by the development of agriculture (Nowak, 1971). It has been suggested that woodpeckers are attracted to telegraph poles by the humming of the wires, which sounds to them like an insect. There is no evidence for this suggestion and it seems unlikely that a response should occur in such a non-adaptive situation. Green woodpeckers (*Picus viridus* L.), and other species, occasionally drill holes through beehives to get at the occupants but this probably involves a different stimulus situation for an important natural food is ants (Formicoidea) obtained by breaking open the nests. In the tropics several species feed on termite mounds. Green woodpeckers have occasionally caused serious damage to roof shingles; individuals at a locality in southern England did considerable damage to a church spire and other examples are on record (Murton, 1971a). Often it is only one or two individuals which acquire such habits and if the particular culprits are removed no more damage occurs.

Many woodpecker species feed on invertebrate foods, or fruit and nuts, but particularly in the New World some forms are adapted to feeding on tree sap and have their tongues modified into brush-like ends (Beeker, 1953). These species can ring valuable forest trees when they break the bark to obtain sap and the common sapsucker [*Sphyrapicus varius* (L.)] of North America can be troublesome. To a lesser extent some of the European species cause similar damage (Turček, 1954), while *Hypopicus hyperythrus* (Vigors) in Thailand is convergent with the sapsuckers and causes similar damage (Zusi and Marshall, 1970).

Birds have a well developed capacity to copy each other and to learn feeding methods by social facilitation (Murton, 1971b) and there is always a risk of a new habit becoming established. This happened with the spread of the habit whereby blue tits (*Parus caeruleus* L.), great tits and other species to a lesser extent, have, since about 1921, learned to open milk bottles to get at the cream (Fisher and Hinde, 1949; Hinde and Fisher, 1951). The movements involved in opening bottles are used in natural food searching and odd individuals apparently independently acquired the habit of trying milk bottles—the basic need was for the bird to search a milk bottle as it would a tree stump. Once the habit was acquired at any one centre it rapidly spread locally, presumably because of social facilitation. Tits also cause damage by paper tearing, a habit of much greater antiquity but probably also related to the natural feeding movements of tearing bark to reveal hidden invertebrates (Cramp *et al.*, 1960; Logan-Home, 1953; Murton, 1971a). In Northern Australia, the brolga [*Grus rubicunda* (Perry)] has developed the habit of pecking holes in plastic tubing used for irrigation projects (Ridpath, personal communication); it is not clear whether the birds use these as a source of water or whether the pipes provide sign stimuli resembling natural food. Syrian woodpeckers were reckoned to cause £1 million worth of damage in Israel in 1972 in the same way (Wolf, 1973).

2. Damage caused by nests

Hole nesting species may resort to artificial sites such as drain pipes, ventilator shafts, chimneys and other crevices in buildings. Blocked pipes can cause flooding or increase fire hazards and common culprits are the house sparrow [*Passer domesticus* (L.)], starling and the tits. Nests at first harbour many ectoparasites but once deserted by the owners various scavengers become dominant, several being important pests of stored products including various clothes and house moths (Lepidoptera), Ptinid beetles and mites (Woodroffe and Southgate,

1951–2; Woodroffe, 1953; Rao and Rajagopalan, 1970). In the interests of hygiene nesting birds have to be prevented from using provender stores or food manufacturing factories.

Some birds build bulky nests which are positioned on pylons and telegraph poles in lieu of, or even in preference to, natural tree sites. Schmidt (1973a) reviews the use made by birds or electric pylons and cables as song posts, feeding and nesting sites. The quaker or monk parakeet (*Myiopsitta monachus* (Boddaert)) of South America is the only parrot which builds its own nest instead of using tree cavities. Enormous stick structures are shared by several pairs each having an individual nest chamber connected with a common entrance chamber. In the Argentinian chaco region the tall pylons supporting power lines are preferred to the lower thorn scrub vegetation and short circuits are not infrequently caused as a result.

3. *Damage caused by faeces*

Faecal material may contain disease organisms and these are considered in the next section. The physical presence of bird droppings defaces statues and buildings, especially the older styles of architecture characterized by crevices, buttresses and much ornamentation. Faecal material is also corrosive particularly to limestone. During the cleaning of public buildings in Paris the workmen sometimes removed layers of pigeon excreta which was a metre thick on some ledges (Murton, 1971a). Droppings mixed with dirt and feathers can provide an effective block for drains and gutters while dried material breaks down into a fine dust which is breathed by the passer-by. It is estimated that New York citizens inhale 3 μg of pigeon dust per person daily. Bird droppings make ledges and pavements slippery for workmen and pedestrians. Fouling of pastures by goose droppings is considered on page 141.

The habit of urban roosting by large concentrations of birds can constitute a major problem by their fouling, the immense flocks of starlings which resort to some cities from surrounding rural areas being an example. The habit in starlings began independently in various towns at the end of the 19th century in Europe, and has subsequently arisen in Australia and N. America. The increase in the incidence of urban roostings by starlings in Britain has been well documented by Potts (1967) and records for other species summarized by Murton (1971a).

4. *Urban birds*

Descendants of domesticated rock doves compose the free-living populations of feral pigeons (*Columba livia* var.) which have long been inhabitants of towns and villages throughout Europe and, following introduction, many urban areas throughout the world from North America to Australia. The harm done by their faeces has been mentioned and they will feature prominently in the next section which deals with disease transmission. It is convenient here to mention the food they steal from grain stores and provender plants. M. M. Senior (1961 and unpublished observations) reported an estimated loss from one warehouse containing maize, milo and palm kernels of 3 tons/week (2·7 tonnes) and some food preference trials undertaken on the floor of the same warehouse were stopped when the amount of bait taken by the pigeons reached a total of 272 kg/day. Local authorities and pest control firms in many towns attempt to reduce pigeon numbers by trapping or, as in Britain since 1961, by catching the birds with stupefying (narcotic) baits (Ridpath et al., 1961; Thearle, 1969a, b; Thearle et al., 1971). To define the cost effectiveness of such schemes a detailed investigation was undertaken in the Salford Docks, Manchester, of the breeding and feeding biology, mortality rate and social organization of the species (Murton et al., 1972a, b; 1973, 1974d; Thearle, 1968, 1970).

Attempts to control population size by trapping or use of baits treated with stupefying chemicals were shown to be relatively ineffective. The equivalent of more than all the birds present at any one time had to be killed per annum to hold the population at about one-half its potential size (Murton et al., 1972a). Control efforts were nullified by constant immigration, particularly of juveniles. Thus the dockland authorities were paying the cost of slaughtering pigeons from outside the area where damage mattered. It was recommended that attention and resources be centred on removing the food spillage which was shown to support the existing population (that is, port hygiene) and the proofing of buildings was considered the best answer to the town pigeon problem which is not readily solved by other means.

(a) *Reproduction inhibitors.* The successful control of the screw worm fly and some other insects following the release of sterile males prompted Elder (1964) to find a means of inhibiting reproduction in pest birds. It is not feasible to "swamp" a population of birds by releasing sterile males and instead efforts were devoted to sterilizing wild subjects by feeding oral contraceptives. Davis (1962) showed that triethylene-melamine (TEM) would inhibit gonad growth in starlings, and Elder (1964) tested this and other agents. One of the most successful was an anti-cholesterol compound, 22, 25-diazacholesterol dihydrochloride manufactured by G. D. Searle & Co. Ltd. as compound SC12937

(Lofts *et al.*, 1968; Woulfe, 1970; Sturtevant and Wentworth, 1970). Many other anti-fertility agents have been proposed including Sudan Black B (Wetherbee *et al.*, 1964; Becker, 1968) but have mostly been tested in laboratory trials (Jones *et al.*, 1972). Few objective field trials have been conducted in which it could unequivocably be shown that population size was reduced as a result of inhibition of reproductive output as distinct from direct mortality induced by the birds receiving toxic doses of the agents used (*c.f.* Wofford and Elder, 1967; Woulfe, 1970; Schortemeyer and Beckwith, 1970). In the free-living population studied at Manchester it was discovered that only around one third of the population actually bred so that indiscriminate dosing of birds was wasteful. Allowing for this fact, and the natural wastage of birds due to mortality (adult death rate is 34% per annum) meant that any campaign to dose the population would have to involve over 80% of the birds. Achievement of such a high efficiency poses considerable practical difficulties and it could be more effective to kill the birds directly with poisons (Murton *et al.*, 1972). Moreover, the sterility agents at present available for field application are not permanent and birds require re-dosing after intervals of about six months. Murton (1974a) has given graphs to show the rapid decline in efficiency when only a proportion of the population (p) can be effectively dosed and n treatments are needed for the drug to be effective. The same arguments apply to attempts to induce sterility at the embryo stage by spraying eggs with anti-fertility substances such as "mestranol" (3-methoxy- 17α-ethymylestra-1,35(10)-trien-17β-ol) (Wentworth *et al.*, 1968).

III. Birds In Disease Transmission

Birds are suspected of being a reservoir of, and serving as vectors for, a host of pathogens that may infect man, his crops or livestock. The ecology of disease transmission requires much more study, for the widespread occurrence of an organism in wild birds does not mean that these are necessarily implicated in its spread, while the risks of infection are usually circumscribed. Some pathogens have such a wide distribution that it would be surprising if they could not be identified in birds. Pigeon droppings constitute a potent source of the antigens causing interstitial pulmonary disease ("pigeon breeder's lung") and recently an enzyme which inhibits the hydrolytic activity of proteins and for which human blood serum has no inhibitors has been identified (Berrens and Maesen, 1971).

1. Bacterial and fungal infections

Salmonella gallinarum (Klein, 1889; Bergey *et al.*, 1925) was identified in rooks which were thought to be a reservoir of infection for outbreaks of salmonellosis among local domestic fowls (Harbourne, 1955); the organism has also been isolated from other species (e.g. Jennings, 1954). Outbreaks of salmonellosis occur in wild birds and are usually associated with crowded conditions, as round bird tables, where the ground can become heavily contaminated (Wilson and MacDonald, 1967; MacDonald and Cornelius, 1969). Pseudotuberculosis caused by *Pasteurella pseudotuberculosis* (Pfeiffer, 1889; Topley and Wilson, 1929) is common in wild birds and they could infect both livestock and perhaps man himself; more human cases are being reported (McDiarmid, 1960).

Migratory water birds frequenting rice fields in Italy were found to be infected with *Leptospira*, serogroup *bataviae* (Wolff and Broom, 1954) the area being one where human leptospirosis is common and birds were suspected to act as carriers (Babudieri, 1960).

Histoplasmosis is a pulmonary disease caused by a fungus *Histoplasma capsulatum* Darling. It is present in the faeces of many bird species and was isolated by Emmons (1961) in soil samples from under a starling roost. Men working in areas contaminated by starling faeces have been infected (Furcolow *et al.*, 1961). Four of 64 boy scouts who cleaned rubbish from a city park in Missouri, U.S.A. in 1959 later contracted the disease and it transpired that the area in which they worked had been the site of a starling roost (Murdock *et al.*, 1962). Another fungus (*Cryptococcus neoformans* (Sanfelice) Vuillemin) has been isolated from pigeon excreta in London (Randhawa *et al.*, 1965). It causes a skin disease cryptococcosis, and can also affect the lungs and central nervous system causing cryptococcal meningitis. Around 20 cases have been noted in Britain and deaths have been reported in the U.S.A. The authorities are concerned that the organism may be distributed in the air in dried faeces.

2. Virus infections

Birds may transmit plant diseases by physical contact in moving from infected to healthy plants. In an experiment, captive house sparrows transported tomato mosaic virus in this way (Broadbent, 1965).

The classic example of man being infected by disease from birds was that of the mortality among Faroese women in 1930 who contracted ornithosis (psittacosis) when they plucked and dressed infected fulmars (*Fulmaris glacialis* L.) for food (Rasmussen, 1938). Meyer (1959) provided a survey of psittacosis for a Joint Committee of the World Health Organisation. The virus occurs with a high incidence in some free-living feral pigeon populations, and up to 75 % of local populations in Paris have been shown to be infective (Lepine and Sautter, 1951). Fortunately, the strain seems to have a low infectivity for man being much less serious than the virulent strain found in psittacine birds, but the circumstances which lead to the emergence of new more virulent virus strains are not established. High rates of infection are also recorded in London (Andrewes and Mills, 1943) and Liverpool (Hughes, 1957). Ornithosis was confirmed in two pigeon fanciers and their flocks in Glasgow (Grist, 1960) and Ellenbogen and Miller (1952) give another example. Only one pigeon fancier of fourteen examined in 1950 showed indications of being infected (Grist, loc. cit.). Nevertheless, Meyer (1959) quotes evidence of transmission from feral pigeons to man in fifteen countries. A large outbreak of ornithosis in Chicago in 1944–5 was traced to town pigeons of which 45 % carried the virus. Haig and McDiarmid (1963) have also isolated the virus from rural wood pigeons. Of nineteen patients suffering from ornithosis over 11 years, two died, so although the risks of catching the disease from wild birds may be small it remains important to maintain constant supervision. Moreover, it is likely that many cases of ornithosis are mistakenly diagnosed as virus pneumonia. It would be interesting to learn how many working days are lost through short term infections resulting from bird transmission which are never diagnosed.

It has long been realized that strains of influenza virus which are closely related to those known to infect man occur in various domestic and wild animals. In a severe epizootic of influenza in April 1961 among European common terns (*Sterna hirundo* L.) wintering in South Africa (Rowan, 1962) the virus was found to be unrelated to all known influenza strains with the exception of Chicken/Scotland/1959 virus of which it was a variant (Becker, 1966). There is a possibility that infection can be spread between sea-birds and domestic poultry. This may have been the case in 1963 in Norfolk when turkeys contracted an influenza showing a cross-reaction with the above strain (Wells, 1963). Migratory waterfowl were found to carry antibodies to Influenza A virus and were suggested as having the potential to infect livestock (Easterday et al., 1968).

Many wild bird species can be infected with fowl pest or Newcastle disease virus (NDV), which exists as strains of varying virulence (Gustafson and Moses, 1953; Waterson et al., 1967). The disease has been isolated from several wild caught subjects including house sparrow (Gustafson and Moses, loc. cit.), pheasant (*Phasianus colchicus* L.)

(Gillespie, 1952), gannet [*Sula bassana* (L.)], cormorant [*Phalacrocorax carbo* (L.)], and shag [*P. aristotelis* (L.)] (Wilson, 1950) and more recently (since 1970) Ministry of Agriculture veterinarians have isolated the virus from kestrel (*Falco tinnunculus* L.), buzzard [*Buteo buteo* (L.)], barn owl [*Tyto alba* (Scopoli)] and other species in Britain (unpublished report).

Although sea birds were first implicated in the spread of the disease to poultry in the 1950's (Blaxland, 1951), a serious outbreak of a highly lethal strain among poultry in Britain in 1970–1971 stimulated a big interest in the rôle of wild birds in disseminating the disease, especially since many free-living pheasants were affected and died. The available evidence indicates that fowl pest is endemically a disease of poultry and that wild birds and game birds become secondarily infected. Evidently these free-living species do not easily transmit the virus, for infection is usually confined to within a kilometre of the poultry concentration; its presence in free-living birds is usually restricted to species like the pheasant which are artificially maintained at high densities. It is clearly not easy for wild birds to become infected and a house sparrow found dead on a site where poultry had died of Newcastle disease was uninfected (Keymer, 1958).

Arboviruses related to those causing Japanese B and West Nile encephalitises have been isolated from ticks [*Ixodes uriae* (White)] infesting guillemots [*Uria aalge* (Pontoppidan)] on opposite sides of the Pacific (Clifford *et al.*, 1971; Lvov *et al.*, 1971, see also for further references). Ticks (*Ornithodorus muesebecki* Hoogstraal) infesting cormorants in the Persian Gulf have also bitten petroleum workers and caused fever, headache and erythema. These clinical symptoms appear to be caused by an arbovirus in the Hughes group which has been isolated from the ticks (Hoogstraal *et al.*, 1970). A related tick (*O. amblus* Chamberlain) is a parasite of marine birds in Peru and it bites human guano diggers (Hoogstraal, 1969), while species of *Hyalomma*, well known vectors for agents of human disease, were isolated from 881 of 11 036 birds examined in Egypt (Hoogstraal, 1968). References to the possible part played by birds in the sub-clinical infection of man with Murray Valley Encephalitis or Australian X disease are given by McDiarmid (1960) and other sources worth consulting are: Clifford *et al.* (1969), Lord and Calisher (1970), Williams *et al.* (1972, 1974), and Main *et al.* (1973).

The possibility that migratory birds might be used as carriers of lethal virus into enemy territory has stimulated the U.S.A. army to give considerable financial support to studies of bird migration and animal pathology (e.g. McClure, 1969, 1971). The Russians have been no less interested and the results of a symposium on the part played by migrating birds in the distribution of arboviruses has been published containing abstracts of 151 papers (Acad. Nauk S.S.R., Siberian Branch, 1969).

It has been claimed that birds transmit foot and mouth disease from continental Europe to Britain. Outbreaks of unknown origin (that is, outbreaks that cannot be traced to infected swill or other identified cause) are concentrated on the south and east coast of England and this led Wilson and Matheson (1952) to suggest that migratory birds could be the vectors, because this is where they supposedly make their landfall; it was also pointed out that gulls associate with grazing cattle and sheep in coastal areas (Thompson, 1961). The idea became popular with many veterinarians, presumably because it absolved them from responsibility in dismissing incidents for which they could provide no other plausible explanation. Birds do not contract foot and mouth disease and only carry it mechanically. In laboratory experiments Eccles (1939) showed that starling ingesting the virus in contaminated food could excrete it for 10–26 h and it would persist for 91 h on the plumage. Murton (1964) analysed the distribution of foot and mouth outbreaks in Britain and produced strong evidence against the involvement of birds as important vectors. For one thing Wilson and Matheson's concept of North Sea bird migration was inaccurate as was well shown by radar studies (Lack, 1959a, b) while the pattern of bird migration within Europe was inconsistent with their theory. Perhaps the strongest arguments against the theory were that: (1) during the war years of 1940–44, a period when the level of continental infection was extremely high, there were very few outbreaks in Britain; (2) outbreaks during the 1951–2 epidemic showed a clockwise swing from the east to south coast and there was a marked tendency for outbreaks to be clustered round sea-ports. This suggested that the movement of goods and persons across the North Sea and English Channel was responsible for the transmission of disease from the Continent, in spite of the precautions taken to limit such movements. It remained uncertain whether birds might transmit foot and mouth disease locally, once it had arrived in Britain. Then during the 1967–8 outbreak Snow (1968) was able to correlate the main characteristics of the spread of the disease from an outbreak in the West Midlands with the prevailing strong winds. There was never any spread in a W or SW direction that could be correlated with the movements of winter migrants, while the presence of a large starling roost had no detectable influence on the spread of the disease, and farms within the catchment area of the roost were least affected.

IV. Bird Problems In Agriculture

A. ECOLOGICAL CONSIDERATIONS

1. *Species involved*

Cereals are the most important foods grown throughout the world for human consumption and birds which regularly eat wheat (*Triticum aestivum* L.), rice (*Oryza sativa* L.), millet (*Panicum mileaceum* L.), maize (*Zea mays* L.) and sorghum (*Sorghum* sp.) are the most significant pests of agriculture. Damage caused by grazing is of less importance. The species concerned naturally feed on wild weed and grass seeds and have been well fitted to take advantage of the increased supplies provided by man. Members of only five families, the pigeons (Columbidae), New World orioles (Icteridae), finches (Fringillidae), weaver-finches (Estrildidae) and true weavers and sparrows (Ploceidae), are almost entirely responsible for all the serious bird damage to cereal crops. In the main, passerines can perch and feed on standing crops, methods they employ to exploit their natural foods, while the pigeons or doves (the terms are synonymous) usually collect seeds they can reach from the ground for most do not perch easily. If a species has become a pest in one part of the world it is usually the case that the bird (a related or convergently similar species) occupying the same natural ecological niche elsewhere has also become a pest or can potentially do so. In other words, certain ecological niches have pre-adapted the species occupying them to benefit from agricultural development. In Africa, various *Streptopelia* doves feed on weed seeds and variably damage crops, and the group provides a good example of the ecological adaptations that make a potential bird pest.

The dusky turtle dove (*S. lugens* Rüppell) and pink-bellied turtle dove (*S. hypopyrrha* Reichenow) are essentially woodland species which have not adapted to open country. The red-eyed turtle dove (*S. semitorquata* Rüppell) (length 36 cm) favours fairly well wooded and well watered country, especially the dense thornveld and riverine forests, throughout Africa south of the Sahara. It feeds on the ground and also takes berries from trees; it takes some cultivated grain and peanuts. In dryer, more scrubby country, it is replaced by the mourning collared dove (*S. decipiens* Hartlaub and Finsch) (30 cm) with similar range and feeding habits. The African collared dove (*S. roseogrisea* Sundevall) and the white-winged collared dove (*S. reichenowi* Erlanger) are geographical replacements of this last in more limited areas of Africa. *S. decipiens* causes some damage to native crops, particularly sorghum in irrigated areas. The ring-necked dove (*S. capicola* Sundevall) (28 cm) is another dove that prefers trees but feeds chiefly on the ground. It takes a different size spectrum of food than the larger (*S. semitorquata* Rüppell) where their ranges overlap, and it also favours drier habitats. It occurs in the southern third of Africa where, in areas of irrigation and cultivation, provided tree cover is available, it is a pest of sorghum. The still smaller (25 cm) laughing or senegal dove (*S. senegalensis* L.) is adapted to arid scrub and thorn bush country and has adjusted to man-altered situations, including villages and town streets. It is a nuisance on millet and sorghum crops, causing serious damage for example to native crops in S.E. Botswana in the thornbush country bordering the Kalahari Desert. Another desert species, the masked dove (*Oena capensis* L.) is locally troublesome. In India, agricultural damage is done by the collared dove (32 cm) and laughing dove which here overlaps with the closely related and larger spotted dove (*S. chinensis* Scopoli; 28 cm) a bird that prefers closer proximity to the woodland edge. It is the dove of agriculture throughout most of S.E. Asia to Java and the Celebes, areas that are generally much less arid than parts of India and Africa.

In the New World the ecological niche of the *Streptopelia* doves is occupied by *Zenaida* and in South America the eared dove (*Z. auriculata* Des Murs) is the most important pest pigeon (see below). In Australia, three *Geopelia* doves, the bar-shouldered dove (*G. humeralis* Temminck; 29 cm), peaceful dove (*G. striata* L.; 20 cm) and diamond dove (*G. cuneata* Latham; 20 cm, but a long tail), partition the seeds occurring on the ground in open country but their ranges are primarily outside the areas developed for cereal cropping in the south west of the country. A parrot, the ubiquitous galah [*Eolophus roseicapillus* (Vieillot)] is responsible for causing serious damage to standing crops and stacks.

In North Temperate regions plant growth mostly stops in winter and seed stocks are not replenished so that the niche for specialist seed eating pigeons is consequently restricted: the turtle dove (*S. turtur* L.) is a summer migrant to Europe from Africa, the mourning dove (*Z. macruora* L.) of N. America migrates to the southern states, while the stock dove (*Columba oenas* L.), though resident in Europe south of latitude 65°N occurs at a low population density and does not cause economic harm. Instead, the wood pigeon has become the most serious bird pest of agriculture. It is essentially a woodland species whose natural foods are tree buds and shoots, and tree fruits such as acorns and beech nuts, supplemented by weed leaves and seeds collected in woodland glades (Murton *et al.*, 1964a). Agricultural development effectively enlarged the glades and provided cereal grains to replace wild seeds. However, these cultivated foods are not available in winter and the wood pigeon only started to increase in numbers when green winter forage crops were grown following the Agrarian Revolution of the 19th century (Murton, 1965a); at first turnips were grown for animal feed but these were later replaced by clover (*Trifolium* spp.). Cultivated clovers have a higher protein content than most weed leaves and pigeons can manage to collect sufficient during a short winter day (Murton *et al.*, 1963a). In parts of Paraguay and Argentina clover is being grown and the picazuro pigeon (*Columba picazuro* Temminck) is becoming a pest. Ecologically, this dove has a niche which approximates to that of the wood pigeon in Northern Europe. Similar ecological comparisons to those just drawn for the pigeons could be applied to the other pestiferous bird taxa.

A settled pastural economy first evolved amongst neolithic tribes in the Old World, particularly in the Middle East and Europe. Accordingly, Palaearctic birds have been exposed to agro-ecosystems for longer than species elsewhere and have, therefore, had a greater opportunity to adapt. Although attention is usually focused on the number of species successfully introduced to various parts of the world, the more interesting fact is the number of unsuccessful introductions attempted. Most European bird species introduced to Australia were unsuccessful at competing with the better adapted native species in natural habitats, but they fared better in man altered areas, presumably because birds like the house sparrow, starling, Indian myna [*Acridotheres tristis* (L.)] have had longer to adapt to man. New Zealand is faunistically impoverished compared with Australia and a higher percentage of introduced birds have been successful (about 27 species) many of which are pests, e.g. rook, starling, house sparrow (Williams, 1969). Sick (1968) discusses the situation in South America where the goldfinch [*Carduelis carduelis* (L.)], greenfinch [*C. chloris* (L.)], house sparrow from Europe, the Californian quail [*Lophortyx californicus* (Shaw)] from N. America and *Estrilda astrild* L. from Africa have become successfully established.

2. *Development of monocultures*

The historical development of cropping patterns is from local plots growing a variety of vegetables and sited in regions primarily supporting natural vegetation, to extensive monocultures in areas where only traces of natural vegetation can be found. In the early stages bird damage to the crops is incidental and is caused by those individuals which have territories adjacent to the field or by the chance arrival of nomadic flocks. The species concerned do not rely on the crop, that is, their populations are regulated in relation to natural resources, but any reproductive surplus may temporarily defer food shortage at the expense of the farmer. Many species, to varying degree, cause incidental damage of this kind. For example, in local areas linnet [*Acanthis cannabina* (L.)] peck the seeds from strawberries and ruin the fruit in consequence (Brown, 1961). The spatial distribution of the crop can be important, especially if edge effects are important. Thus bullfinch [*Pyrrhula pyrrhula* (L.)] damage to fruit buds was most intensive on the edge of orchards where they adjoined woodland, the natural habitat of the bird (Wright, 1959). With the development of extensive mono-cultures those species which can adapt must be able to obtain most of their ecological needs within the cropping system, and since in most cases cultivated crops must provide the bulk of their food throughout the year the successful species tend to be in competition with the farmer. These trends are illustrated in the sequence of species discussed in sections C to E below. The scheme is not perfect in that some species fall into more than one category—for instance, the wood pigeon is both a seed eater and grazer, but most of the economic damage it causes is in relation to its grazing habits.

The prime aim of agriculture is to channel as much of the available energy into human food as efficiently as possible, whereas in stable natural ecosystems energy is re-cycled by biological processes. Con-tinuous removal of energy would be a short term approach if new supplies were not made available. In the past this was achieved by appropriate rotations so that crops requiring different elements were grown in successive years while fallows and the growing of nitrogenous forage crops and grass in the rotation facilitated natural re-cycling processes. The modern trend is to use the same field continuously for a particular crop compensating for a loss of soil fertility by the use of inorganic fertilizer and using herbicides and insecticides to combat disease and pest risks. Primitive arable systems and those on marginal land are relatively diverse because they are composed of a variety of different crops, and these together with fallow fields, woodland frag-ments and hedges support wild weed plants and their associated inver-tebrates. They allow the escape of much energy in the complicated food chains of animals, because they are fluctuating systems, and this is reflected in the relatively rich avifaunas they may support. This was the case on a farm in eastern England sited on sandy infertile soil (Table I). At another fairly fertile site more intensive and efficient farming was associated with a decrease in the total bird population, but pest species now comprised a bigger percentage of the avifauna (Table I). It would be interesting to know how loss of energy due to birds differed in the two situations. On an acreage basis, the marginal site allowed wastage because parts were not cropped. Loss from the good site was reduced because of the lower overall density of birds but some of the most common components of the system were specialist feeders on the crops.

TABLE I. Proportion of breeding avifauna composed of pest species on some samples of farmland in Britain

	Total number of species per 100 acres (S)	Total number of individual birds per 100 acres (N)	% of total bird population composed of:				% total pest birds	Diversity index (α)
			Wood pigeon	Skylark	House Sparrow	Rook		
Dorset (pastural dairy farm with many hedges and copses)	54	320	7	3	5	1	16	18
Suffolk (mixed arable livestock on poor sandy soil with many waste areas)	61	571	8	2	12	0	22	17
Cambridge 1960 (intensive cereal arable on fertile boulder-clay)	52	302	14	10	11	12	47	17
Cambridge 1971 (as above but with some loss of leys, pastures and hedges)	56	218	9	10	11	9	39	24

Data for Dorset based on Williamson (1971) and for Suffolk on Benson and Williamson (1972) analysed by Murton and Westwood (1974). The diversity index α is derived from the formula of Fisher et al. (1943) in which $S = \alpha\log_e (1 + N/\alpha)$ where S = number of species and N = number of individuals.

Changes occurred at the Cambridgeshire locality between 1960 and 1970. These reflected more widescale trends on farms in northern Europe towards fewer and larger units dependent on increased mechanization and a reduced labour force. Stock rearing increasingly involves intensive factory production, with reliance on barley feeds rather than silage. There is much focus on profit margins and investment so that pest damage can be more severe in necessitating an alteration to programme schedules and marketing arrangements than in terms of the total crop consumed. This situation contrasts completely with primitive subsistence agricultures where crop damage is immediately reflected in a reduction in availability to the consumer.

The effect of such agricultural change on birds species diversity is discussed by Murton (1974b) and Murton and Westwood (1974). Many birds which adapt to the agro-ecosystem exhibit an increase in their food diversity and partition niches that would be occupied by separate species in more stable systems; this wider overlap in feeding preferences is well illustrated by the finches (Fringillidae) of farmland (Newton, 1967a). A shuffle of ecological rôles is also a phenomenon noted on impoverished islands (Keast, 1971). Potts and Vickerman (1974) have evidence that rotations which increase the diversity of invertebrate species, including predators, as do winter forage crops, reduce the frequency of outbreaks of aphid infestations. Their data for farmland support ideas originally propounded for forest by Voute (1946), that outbreaks of insect pests are commoner in pure than in mixed stands of trees. It is still debatable to what extent these observations are applicable to vertebrates, for it is probable that only a very inefficient agriculture could support an animal diversity sufficient to allow predator–prey interactions that could be effective in reducing damage by pest birds.

B. RED-BILLED QUELEA IN AFRICA

1. *Biology and distribution*

The red-billed quelea (*Q. quelea* L.) is a weaver-finch (Ploceidae) of the semi-arid grassland of Africa (Fig. 3). It is adapted to live in regions where a short rainy season stimulates a flush of annual grasses and enormous quantities of seed which fall to the ground and must last throughout a long dry season. The combination of rich alluvial soils and the rains which encourage a good growth of grass occur with a patchy distribution which varies from year to year. The habit of large scale communal roosting and nesting is characteristic of the granivorous ploceines but not the insectivorous forms and to a lesser extent in those of perennial grassland (Crook, 1964). It is an adaptation to facilitate the location of good feeding places for, in effect, social gatherings serve as information centres enabling birds which are unsuccessful in locating feeding grounds to follow the more successful flocks (Ward, 1965a; Ward and Zahavi, 1973). Once arrived at a feeding place flocking can still be advantageous in increasing feeding efficiency (Murton, 1971b).

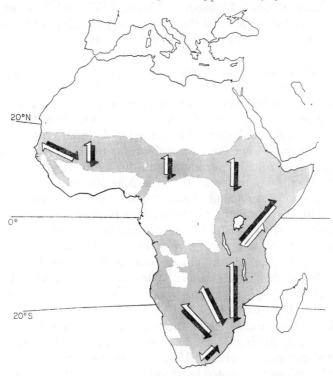

FIG. 3. Distribution of *Quelea quelea* (stippled) and known or suspected migration patterns in the areas covered. Dark arrows refer to the early rains migration and open arrows to the return breeding migration. (Compiled from Magor and Ward, 1972, and Ward, 1971).

Thus the social behaviour of these weaver birds is an adaptation to suit a nomadic life in a semi-arid environment where food supplies are unpredictable. The species was pre-adapted to take advantage of the crops of villagers scattered within its range, and for centuries native farmers have been trying to protect their crops from this "locust-bird" (Busnel and Grosmaire, 1955). The new large scale rice, millet and wheat growing schemes which are being developed throughout Africa provide even more attractive conditions for the birds and their depredations have stimulated international conferences, and intensive research and campaigns to mitigate the damage in East Africa (Williams, 1954; Disney and Haylock, 1956; Haylock, 1959), the Sudan (Wilson, 1947), Mauretania and Senegal (Morel and Bourlière, 1955, 1956,) and Nigeria (Ward, 1963, 1965a). Much literature is also in the form of mimeographed reports of the CCTA/CSA symposia on *Quelea* held at Dakar (Anon. 1955a), Livingstone (Anon. 1957) and Bamako (Anon. 1960a) under the auspices of the *Commission for Technical Co-operation in Africa South of the Sahara* and the *Scientific Council for Africa South of the Sahara*.

The main natural food plants of *Quelea* throughout Africa are such fast growing small seeded annuals as *Panicum, Echinochloa, Digitaria* and *Pennisetum*. A detailed study of the diet has only been made in the Lake Chad region of Nigeria (Ward, 1965a), but it is likely to be typical for other parts of Africa (Plowes, 1955; Morel *et al.*, 1957). With the decline of the seed supply after the end of the rains the birds congregate into bigger and bigger flocks, particularly favouring the large alluvial plains in the river valleys of the Senegal, Niger, Nile, Zambezi and the seasonal swamps round Lake Chad, Lake Rukwa and the Okovango Basin (Crook and Ward, 1968). In the feeding flocks males compete more successfully than do females for the diminishing food stocks (Crook and Butterfield, 1970) and the sex ratio changes in their favour (Ward, 1965b). The birds gradually change over to feeding on larger seeds as their preferred small seeds vanish. Wild rice (*Oryza barthii* (Chevalier), wild sorghum (*Sorghum purpureo-sericeum* Schweinf. and Aschers) were noted in the Lake Chad area and with *Echinochloa colonum* L. made up two-thirds of the total diet at this season. In years when wild seeds disappear early the birds include many cultivated seeds in their diet—cultivated rice and a cultivated sorghum of the natives called guinea-corn or Mazakwa were noted by Ward—and it is at this time that severe damage occurs.

At the beginning of the rains, the dry-season food supply is lost as a simultaneous germination occurs over large areas. The birds accumulate fat reserves and migrate to areas where rain has been falling for several weeks (Ward, 1971). The direction taken by the migrants, the distance they fly and the timing of the movement are dependent on the timing of the rains and the movement of the rain-front (Fig. 3). During the season of food shortage considerable mortality occurs and it appears that population size is naturally regulated at this stage. During this con-tranuptial sojourn the birds feed on the ripening seeds of grasses and also do damage to cultivated millet. The Lake Chad population moves around 200–300 km south during the early rains migration and returns after a few weeks to the new abundant supplies of seed. On the return "breeding migration" those individuals which have attained reproductive condition (see Ward, 1965c) stop to breed in sometimes large aggregations wherever they find conditions suitable. Nestlings are at first fed insect food, their diet gradually changing to one of seeds, mostly *Echinochloa pyramidalis* Hitchcock and Chase. Thus the location of colonies can vary considerably from year to year. Individual females can produce a succession of broods during the same breeding season at widely separated colonies, and probably with different mates.

2. Damage

Individual *Quelea* probably eat 2–2·5 g of food a day during the dry season. There is evidence that they prefer small wild seeds rather than the larger grained cultivated species. As Crook and Ward (1968) point out, cultivated cereals are available only for a few weeks and the birds are by no means dependent on them for all their food, even though they inflict heavy damage. Samples of birds were collected from a roost in Nigeria in 1961 in an area of intensive sorghum cultivation and at a time when damage to the crop was serious. Yet guinea corn comprised only 20% of the gizzard contents of all birds combined (the remainder was grass seed) and only 15 of 25 birds had taken any at all. In 1962, when damage was slight only 3% of the crop contents of 1350 birds sampled by Ward composed guinea corn. Hence damage to crops is incidental to the preferred feeding habits of *Quelea* and it is the enormous numbers involved, with flocks of up to a million birds, that can cause such devastating losses. The *Quelea* population of Africa may be in the order of 10^9–10^{11} birds (Crook and Ward, 1968). African farmers growing millet and sorghum are worst affected, though Crook and Ward comment that more attention has been focused on the birds' attacks on rice in Senegal and Mauritania and on wheat in Kenya, Tanzania, Rhodesia and South Africa.

Apart from the symposium and technical reports cited, good details of crop damage have been given by Fuggles-Couchman (1936), Wilson (1948), Plowes (1950), Crook (1957), Disney (1957), Naude (1959), Frade (1960) and Ward (1966). Disney (1964) lists the following estimates of damage to grain crops: central Tanganyika (1890)—famine caused and millet replaced by sorghum; Kenya (1952)—loss of wheat estimated at £250 000; Northern Transvaal (1953)—sorghum eaten in European areas valued at £500 000 and native crops a failure; Senegal (1954)—24 acres (9·72 ha) of rice eaten in 14 days. Other weaver bird species and their allies—for example, in India, the Baya weaver [*Ploceus philippinus* (L.)] and in South-east Asia, Java sparrow [*Padda oryzivora* (L.)] and chestnut munia [*Lonchura atricapilla* (Vieillot)] —inflict similar damage to that caused by *Quelea* but the scale of attack is much more restricted.

3. Control methods

(a) *Population reduction.* Knowledge of feeding ecology indicates the futility of indiscriminate slaughter campaigns, for money must be wasted on birds that do no or little damage. Even so, the literature abounds with references to uncosted widescale slaughter schemes. Since this deplorable situation applies to so many bird pests it is worth digressing to discuss why this should be. Often bird damage may appear to be serious when in reality it is not because of the recovery power of the plant and the temporal separation of damage and harvest. Examples of such "apparent" damage appear in Sections IV, D, 1; IV, E, 1 and V, A, 1. Both apparent and real damage give rise to intense reaction on the part of the sufferer whose livelihood or subsistence may be threatened and a variably powerful lobby is generated which pressures the appropriate authority for action. This usually occurs in a political context whereby any lack of action can be translated directly into lost votes or favour. If government departments and other agencies are pressed to spend money to tackle the problem it is not surprising that their administrators opt for control campaigns rather than scientific evaluations. Superficially this can seem to be the sensible approach, for tangible damage is witnessed and extrapolations are thereby made. Yet all too often this leads to a waste of money, because the killing effort is too small relative to the population at risk, or because control efforts become concentrated on those individuals which are the easiest to kill rather than those that do most damage: for these reasons control costs are often unrelated to damage costs either temporally or geographically (Murton, 1965b).

The above generalization has been applicable to some of the attempts to combat the *Quelea* problem, though several scientists have appealed for a more sensible approach. Crook and Ward (1968) emphasize that there is a risk of spending large sums on control measures aimed at reducing population size only to find that the campaign has coincided with a natural decline, after which the birds re-appear. This may have happened in South Africa where 400 million birds were killed by aerial spraying between 1956 and 1960 and by 1961 the problem appeared to have been solved. Then in 1962–3 the spraying programme had to be extended over a greater area than ever before because there was a massive invasion of farmland by immigrant *Quelea*; in 1966/7, over 6000 acres (2430 ha) were sprayed and 112 million birds killed. Crook and Ward refer to evidence that mass invasions periodically occur into S. Africa as in 1910, 1917, 1925 and 1929.

Because the range of *Quelea* in Africa is so great, and opportunist breeding soon allows the population to make good mortality losses, there must always be a reservoir population capable of re-infecting an area cleared at great expense. A worthwhile measure of population reduction has probably only ever been achieved in the Senegal Valley where conditions for control are particularly favourable. Instead, a policy of protecting important areas of cereal crops, such as large schemes of concentrated small holdings, by the planned destruction of all roosts and colonies within the main crop area is advocated but only so long as vulnerable crops exist (Ward, 1972, 1973). If no crops are at risk the killing of *Quelea* is deemed to be pointless. Exactly the same policy was earlier advocated for vertebrate pests in Britain (Murton, 1965b, 1968) but at the time the possibility existed that the scale of the *Quelea* problem and the fact that more lethal control techniques could be applied (aerial spraying of poisons) might make it exceptional.

(*b*) *Poison sprays*. References to control techniques are given in a valuable bibliography by Magor and Ward (1972). General control techniques are mentioned by Haylock (1959) and Anon. (1960b). The use of aerial sprays is treated in detail by Anon. (1956), Lourens (1957), Anon. (1968). Parathion, an organophorus insecticide which is very poisonous to mammals including man, was mostly used as the active ingredient. It inhibits the functioning of the enzyme cholinesterase and acts on the nervous system. It seems not to have resulted in significant damage to other wildlife where it has been used in Africa. The cost of killing *Quelea* by such means is about 0·05p Sterling per bird at an average rate of £300 Sterling per roost. Fenthion is a more recent organo-phosphorus compound, which when applied at low dosage acts to depress feeding activity. There is some hope that it will provide a means of reducing the quantity of poison needed to kill the birds (Pope and Ward, 1972). Efficient ground sprayers are also being developed which obviate the need for expensive aircraft. Fenthion is the most commonly used avicide for this purpose and is relatively cheap but it does have a high toxicity to mammals. Queletox, a formulation of fenthion, produced effective control at an average cost of £23·60 per ha. Phoxim (*o*-α-cyanobenzylideneamino *oo*-diethyl phosphorothionate) is marketed by Farbenfabriken Bayer A.G. and has the advantage of a low toxicity to mammals. However, when used at the rate of 60% active ingredient to produce effective control it proved to be more expensive than fenthion at £63·70 per ha; its use is justified if wild or domestic mammals are specially at risk (Pope and King, 1973). Wind tunnel experiments have been performed to determine the distribution of solution sprayed onto birds in flight (Ward and Pope, 1972) and penetration of spray droplets applied by helicopter has been discussed by Johnstone et al. (1974).

(c) Other. Compared with the spraying of toxic chemicals other methods of control seem of little avail. The traditional native methods involve a variety of labour intensive noise making contraptions, while acoustic scaring has been of limited value (Busnel and Gramet, 1955). Some trials have been undertaken with bird resistant varieties of sorghum (Anon. 1955a; Doggett, 1957; Plowes, 1957; see also p. 124).

C. EARED DOVE IN SOUTH AMERICA

1. Biology and feeding habits

The eared dove (24 cm) of South America forms a superspecies with the mourning dove of North America which is a more recent derivative. The latter is a much valued sporting bird and any damage it causes to agriculture is forgotten for the sake of the pleasure it brings to thousands of hunters. Research efforts are geared to improving its productivity to ensure bigger bags. In contrast, the eared dove occurs in regions of low human population density where the hunting pressure is totally inadequate to regulate numbers, although in some places it is a popular sporting bird (Johnson, 1967; Olivares, 1970). The eared dove exhibits many ecological parallels with *Quelea* for it is a seed eating species inhabiting semi-arid scrub and grasslands. Indeed, many of its natural food items are seeds related to those eaten by *Quelea* including the savanna grass (*Echinochloa colonum* L.) and wild sorghums (mostly *Sorghum almum* Parodi and *S. halepense* Pers. and their hybrids) and in addition seeds of *Amaranthus, Euphorbia, Croton* spp. (Murton *et al.*, 1974c). It readily eats cultivated sorghum, wheat, millet, maize, peanuts (*Arachis hypogaea* L.) and sunflower (*Helianthus annuus* L.) and has in consequence become a pest in many parts of Latin America (Aguirre, 1964; Bucher, 1970; De Grazio and Besser, 1970; Londõno *et al.*, 1972). In Nicaragua and Mexico the related white-winged dove (*Zenaida asiatica* L.) causes similar damage to standing sorghum and like the eared dove, but unlike the mourning dove, will perch on the heads of the standing grain (De Grazio and Besser, 1970; Cottam and Trefethen, 1968).

A natural habitat of the dove is the chaco region of Argentina, a thorn scrub ecotone which surrounds the fertile pampa and extends into

Brazil. Similar habitats occur in Venezuela, Colombia, Uruguay, Paraguay and Trinidad. Like *Quelea*, the eared dove has evolved behavioural adaptations to take advantage of patchily distributed food supplies, which may nevertheless provide a very abundant food source when they do occur. It feeds, roosts and breeds in large social congregations which serve as "information centres." A segment of the population is rapidly able to breed if it locates good feeding resources and so population size fluctuates drastically according to conditions. In contrast, the allopatric picui dove (*Columbina picui* Temminck; 22 cm) does not take advantage of these temporarily good food supplies and its small body size allows it to exploit tiny seeds which are always available in small amounts. It adopts a territorial strategy to exploit this more regular and predictable food source and its population fluctuates much less than that of *Zenaida*.

In the chaco inappropriate agriculture has created new food supplies for the eared dove. A farmer needs relatively little capital to begin business—he burns the scrub and can soon plant a sorghum crop. But unless considerable expenditure is then devoted to improving soil structure and fertility and humus is introduced, a "dust-bowl" agriculture is rapidly created. Agricultural advisors would prefer the land to be developed for cattle grazing in the long term but initially this involves more financial outlay. Wealthy land-owners farm the pampa and development of the poorer regions is by farmers in the lower socio-economic groups; again we should note that political and economic considerations cannot be divorced from the scientific assessment of bird pest problems. Today the chaco is a mosaic of natural scrub and cultivated plots. Throughout the region there exist large breeding/roosting concentrations of the eared dove about 90–100 km apart and containing between one and five million individuals; the birds radiate up to 40 km to their feeding grounds, sometimes further. A large segment of the roost can rapidly locate and devastate a particular field, when the grain is at the right stage of maturity. Analysis of the crop (here meaning the diverticulum of the oesophagous of pigeons used for food storage) contents of birds sampled at the roost show that a high proportion of the diet is of cultivated crops, unlike *Quelea* (Murton *et al.*, 1974c) but a wide spectrum of food items is taken. The problem is aggravated because some farmers may suffer almost complete crop losses, while others escape relatively unaffected, the time of ripening, varieties of crop grown, direction and distance from the roost being variables which affect the risk of damage.

Damage to soy beans (*Glycine max* L.) at the cotyledon stage has been noted in Colombia, in addition to attacks on rice and sorghum. Soy bean damage was simulated in trials in which no cotyledon was removed or 0·5 of one, 0·5 of both, 1 whole cotyledon or both whole cotyledons were removed: the average number of seeds later obtained from the plants was 93·1, 95·5, 88·7, 73·5, 67·5 respectively suggesting that slight damage may be unimportant (Woronecki et al., 1972).

2. Control methods

(a) *Scaring.* In Colombia and Venezuela attempts have been made to scare the birds by pajareros (bird scaring personnel), scarecrows, rockets, firecrackers and shot guns but to little effect (Woronecki et al., 1971). Avitrol (4-aminopyridine) ingested with a suitable bait causes the bird to suffer extreme convulsions and apparently pain. In other species the subjects emit distress calls which combine with the spasmodic movements to frighten other birds away (Goodhue and Baumgartner, 1965a, b). The unpleasant symptoms and indications of cruelty have rendered use of this agent illegal in Britain. Trials against eared doves in Colombia were unsuccessful, for affected birds failed to frighten other doves from the area, perhaps because pigeons do not have a distress call. Trials have also been made to test the effectiveness of the repellent methiocarb (4-methylthio-3,5-xylyl N-methylcarbamate) applied at 0·5% to soy beans (Thompson and Agudelo, 1969; see Schafer et al., 1967, 1971, for details of toxicity). Surface beans eaten by doves caused some deaths, but otherwise the results were inconclusive. This agent causes temporary paralysis in the subject by inhibiting cholinesterase activity and supposedly induces an aversion to the locality in both the recipients and those able to see its effects; the biological basis of this frightening effect needs more investigation. Methiocarb has been used with considerable success to reduce damage to corn sprouts by pheasants in South Dakota (West et al, 1969) and by Icteride (see p. 127).

(b) *Trapping.* In Argentina, a farmer has found it very easy to catch doves near to one of the roosts in cage traps sited over artificial drinking pools, although the proportion of the population at risk being caught was trivial (under 0·1%). The breast muscles are removed and cooked with spices and are then preserved in olive oil, and it has been argued that government financial support to create a bigger bottling industry would help solve the dove problem. The fallacy is in supposing that the return per unit of catching effort would remain constant with a decrease in population size or increase in number of predators.

(c) *Bird resistant crops.* Research is being directed by various agricultural institutes in South America (e.g. Instituto Nacional de Tecnologia

Agropecuaria, Argentina) into developing bird resistant varieties of sorghum. The doves avoid sorghums with a high tannin content but these are unpalatable for human consumption. There is an expectation that varieties can be produced in which the tannin is concentrated only in the husk of the seed to be removed during milling. Other varieties of sorghum which have a pendulous habit are not attacked for doves are unable to perch as they can on upright growing seed heads. These pendulous varieties presently have smaller yields but it is hoped that improved varieties will be bred combining all the features conducive to bird resistance without sacrificing yields. When birds have a choice of crops they can be dissuaded from attacking the "resistant" variety and there may be scope for a programme which involves the sacrifice of low value decoy crops.

(d) *Ecological approaches.* In the short term it is probable that the methods recommended against *Quelea* involving the aerial, and perhaps ground, spraying of roosts will be most successful. In the long term improvements in agriculture will probably solve the problem. In the fertile pampa cultivated crops are widespread and weed seeds relatively scarce. In this region the eared dove behaves more like the picui doves in the chaco. That is, with a predictable more evenly distributed food resource the optimum strategy for exploitation tends towards a territorial system. The birds are dispersed as isolated pairs and do not form the enormous gregarious assemblages. It is possible that the total loss of grain is similar in both situations, but in the second the loss is evenly partitioned and very few farmers suffer disproportionate damage or can even detect measurable yield reductions due to bird attack.

The relationship between flock size and the spatial distribution of food resources is depicted in Fig. 4 referring to different pigeon species for which details are available. A relationship must exist between the total area of country an individual bird can afford to search for food per day, the distribution of food within that area and the size of roosting population necessary to cover the whole area efficiently. Modifying influences include any tendency which cause searching birds to travel as flocks rather than as single individuals, for example, once a feeding place has been located it may require more than one bird to evaluate the appropriate object to eat (Murton, 1971b). Two factors perhaps contributed to the extinction of the passenger pigeon (*Ectopistes migratorius* L.) in North America (see Fig. 4). It used to travel in enormous flocks to locate the tree fruits on which it depended in winter. European immigrants chopped down forests and shot large numbers of doves. Instead of being able to have bigger flocks to counter the spatial restriction of food supplies fewer birds were available and we may surmise that the species then lacked the behavioural capacity to manage its food resources. Other, but different, evidence for "biological weakness" in the species is given by Brisbin (1968).

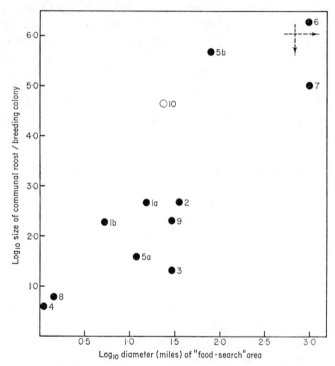

FIG. 4. Approximate relationship between the number of individual birds associating together in a communal roost/breeding colony and the diameter of the area of country covered by the assemblage in food searching. Note use of logarithmic scales. Data refer to different pigeon species (Columbidae) as follows: (1) *Columba palumbus*, (2) *Columba leucocephala*, (3) *Columba norfolciencis*, (4) *Columba squamosa*, (5) *Zenaida auriculata*, (6) *Ectopistes migratoria*, (7) *Phaps hystrionica*, (8) *Treron vernans*, (9) *Ducula spilorrhoa*. Data for *Quelea quelea* (10) are shown by an open point. The a and b suffixes refer to the same species experiencing different feeding conditions. (From work in progress by Murton and Bucher, unpublished observations.)

D. OTHER SEED EATERS

1. *Damage by Icteridae*

The adaptive radiation of this New World family shows a striking parallel with that of the Old World weaver finches (*Ploceidae*) for the two taxa provide many ecological counterparts. Two "blackbirds" are important pests in North America. The red-winged blackbird [*Agelaius phoeniceus* (L.)] has a wide distribution from Canada to the West Indies and though originally a marshland bird favouring reed and cattail swamps, finds cereal crops, including maize, a good substitute and it has prospered in areas of cultivation. Its feeding habits are well covered by Bird and Smith (1964) and Mott *et al.* (1972). The tricolor blackbird [*A. tricolor* (Audubon)] occurs in the South-west United States, especially the Sacramento and San Joaquin Valleys. It too is essentially a marsh bird where it feeds on the seeds of annual grasses and weeds, but it also eats many insects, especially locusts, and these may once have been an important food when breeding (Payne, 1969). The native haunts of both species in the southern states have been drained and then subsequently redeveloped for rice growing which depends on spring irrigation. Both these blackbirds have prospered by this cultivation (Neff and Meanley, 1957). This is well illustrated by tricolor blackbirds which have very large breeding colonies of over 10 000 individuals close to the flooded rice fields, whereas the colonies sited in dry grazing areas close to irrigated non-rice crops number in the order of 1000 individuals (Orians, 1961).

Prior to migration, red-winged blackbirds congregate in enormous roosting and feeding concentrations in marsh areas in late summer and autumn, often associating with starlings. The flocks range over the surrounding countryside and inflict severe losses to maize crops, the movements having been studied in detail by radar in Ontario, Canada (Dyer, 1964). Fields of sweet and field corn close to the roost were found to suffer most damage, with up to 96% of the ears affected, and the amount of damage declined and became sporadic 11 km or so from the roost (Dyer, 1967, 1969). It was found that birds did not feed randomly within each field and instead Dyer established a logarithmic relationship between the percentage of ears fed upon to some degree in each sample and the amount of damage per ear, thereby enabling losses to be estimated. Thus if 1% of ears were damaged, 0·0225 g were eaten per ear (0·89 kg per ha) while 96% of ears eaten was equivalent to 2845·4 kg per ha. An interesting experiment using this relationship has been performed using 4-aminopyridine (Avitrol) to scare red-winged blackbirds from corn crops in a 373 km^2 area in northern Ohio (Stickley *et al.*, in prep.). Damage in treated fields was found to be significantly lower than in nearby untreated fields within this experimental area. However, the birds intensified their attacks on the untreated fields, which in consequence suffered very heavy damage, and this nullified the gains obtained on the treated fields. In fact, the total amount of damage in the whole area was about the same as in a separate area of similar size in a nearby part of the state, where no treatment at all was performed (it was earlier established that the two areas would normally experience comparable blackbird damage). Thus, scaring simply pushed the birds onto other fields and the total amount of crop loss remained unaltered. Attempts have been made to construct simulation models of the impact of red-winged blackbirds on grain crops (Wiens and Dyer, 1975) using earlier models, developed by Wiens and Innis (1974), of energy flow in bird communities. Although, subject to limitations these procedures help in defining the scale of a problem and in delimiting appropriate methods of approach.

During 1968 and 1969 biologists of the Denver Wildlife Research Centre made surveys in six Latin American countries to obtain information on bird damage problems (De Grazio and Besser, 1970). Bird damage in the two sub-continents involves the same types of crops and genera of birds, with the Icterids featuring high on the list. For example, red-winged backbirds and, closer to marshes, yellow-headed blackbirds [*Xanthocephalus xanthocephalus* (Bonaparte)] are major pests of grain sorghum in Mexico. In Venezuela, wintering dickcissels [*Spiza americana* (Gmelin)] consumed nearly an entire sorghum planting, and flocks of around 75 000 birds were noted (De Grazio and Besser, 1970). Bobolinks [*Dolichonyx oryzivorus* (L.)] have also damaged sorghum and seem to be of increasing importance in rice culture (Slud, 1964; Woronecki *et al.*, 1971, 1972). In Colombia, the shiny cowbird [*Molothrus bonariensis* (Gmelin)] has caused serious damage to experimental and commercial plantings of rice, sorghum and maize. Brown-headed cowbirds [*M. ater* (Boddaert)] and boat-tailed grackles [*Cassidix mexicanus* (Gmelin)] in large numbers were eating sorghum in Mexico. The latter have also been noted damaging emerging corn seedlings in Honduras, Mexico and Guatemala (Skutch, 1960; Young and Zevallos, 1960; De Grazio and Besser, 1970).

A nationwide survey of bird damage to corn was instigated in the United States in 1970 using enumerators employed by the U.S. Department of Agriculture. The species involved were not identified but Icterids were presumably important. Two 15-foot (30·48 cm) units of two rows in a sample of fields ($n = 2854$) were examined and the ears checked for damage. In 1145 counties surveyed in 24 states, 15·6% of the fields examined had suffered some bird damage while an average of 1·8% of the ears within these fields had been attacked (Stone *et al.*, 1972). Birds accounted for $0·16 \pm 0·26\%$ of the total corn crop in the 24 states in 1970, equivalent to about \$U.S.9 $\pm$ 15 million (9% confidence limits). Bird feeding does not always result in damage because if only the tips of plants are eaten extra growth may be stimulated (Dyer, 1975).

2. Damage by sparrows

In temperate regions of the Old World, species of *Passer* parallel *Quelea* in causing damage to grain fields. Temperate seasonal climates restrict both winter resources and reproductive rates so population size never increases to the "locust proportions" noted for *Quelea*. Ecological conditions are most favourable in the southernmost parts of the range in the Middle East and this is where damage to field cereals is most serious. Here the spanish sparrow [*Passer hispaniolensis* (Temminck)] is the predominant species (Summers-Smith and Vernon, 1972), but the familiar house sparrow [*P. domesticus* (L.)] predominates throughout most of the Palaearctic. Throughout much of this range it is sympatric with the tree sparrow [*P. montanus* (L.)] which is much less directly associated with man and accordingly gives less cause for concern. One reason is that the tree sparrow eats around two-thirds less cereal grain than its congenor (Hammer, 1948). However, the house sparrow is absent from most of China and S.E. Asia and here its close commensal relationship with man is assumed by the tree sparrow in these areas (Summers-Smith, 1963). The house sparrow has been introduced to many other parts of the world (see Voous, 1960, and Summers-Smith, 1963, for maps). It has been rated an important agricultural pest in Northern Europe since mediaeval times (Murton, 1971a) with most attention focused on the large post-breeding flocks (well described by Summers-Smith) which resort like weaver birds to the fields of standing wheat and barley.

Locally, sparrows may be very troublesome but damage is usually patchy and when averaged for the whole crop of little significance. Costs may, however, be disproportionate at experimental stations where breeding trials are performed. Such sites deserve special measures to protect plots and Norris and Whitehouse (1970) have made appropriate suggestions, including the sowing of decoy crops of very early or late ripening cultivars planted in cage traps. In Britain, surveys by Ministry of Agriculture staff suggest that only few fields (less than 5%) are affected and then only a proportion of the crop is attacked (Murton, 1971a). In New Zealand, Dawson (1970) estimated the wheat and barley lost from standing crops by sampling 5 ears at 30 points within a crop just before harvest. The loss averaged 5% but was as high as 20% in a few fields. Some birds flew a mile from their nests to feed on grain, which was preferred at the milky stage. Dawson's paper is valuable in considering the best way of sampling to give the maximum efficiency. The most efficient sample gives the smallest standard error for a given expenditure of time so that:

$$\text{variance} = \frac{a}{P} + \frac{b}{PQ}$$

where P is the number of points sampled, Q the number of ears taken at each point, and a and b are coefficients varying from field to field and relating the variance to the number of points sampled and to the total number of ears taken, respectively (a sample of 30 points took 2 h to collect and the 150 ears about 2 h to examine). Use of the equation enabled Dawson to show that taking four ears at 34 points gave the same estimate of variance as five ears at 30 points. He gives graphs which would be of value in enabling other workers to undertake damage estimations in the most efficient manner. Judging from field counts of sparrows Dawson estimated that one bird day was equivalent to a loss of 30–240 g of mature wheat, but in fact sparrows probably eat closer to 10 g per day and the over-estimate was thought to result from a serious underestimate of the number of birds visiting the crop.

3. Damage by parrots

Strong beaks render some species particularly adept at dehusking the tougher cereals. In various parts of South America the monk parakeet [*Myiopsitta monacha* (Boddaert)] is destructive, flocks ranging from forest areas to raid adjacent fields. A research programme into the ecology of the bird has just been initiated in Argentina. Brown-throated parakeets [*Anatinga pertinax* (L.)] have been implicated in similar damage in Colombia as have parrotlets of the genus *Forpus* (Woronecki et al., 1972). In Nicaragua, orange-fronted parakeets [*A. canicularis* (L.)] were taking sorghum as were red-lored parrots [*Amazona autumnalis* (L.)] in Costa Rica (De Grazio and Besser, 1970). In Australia the galah does much damage to standing wheat in the south and also takes stored grain from silos, while in the Northern Territories the red-winged parrot [*Aporsmictus erythropterus* (Gmelin)] eats sorghum and has caused serious harm to experimental plots near Katherine (Ridpath, personal communication). Slight damage to sorghum has also been caused by the rainbow lorikeet [*Trichoglossus haematodus* (L.)] and scaly-breasted lorikeet [*T. chlorolepidotus* (Kuhl)] (Lavery and Blackman, 1970). The green parakeet (*Psittacula krameri* Scopoli) and Indian parakeet [*P. eupatria* (L.)] are troublesome in India.

4. Control methods

(a) *Chemical repellents.* Early trials with agents which were reputed to be distasteful to birds did not give satisfactory protection in situations where birds had a choice of feeding places. This applied when formulations containing anthraquinone and tetra methyl thiuram disulphide (thiram) were sprayed on fruit trees to prevent bullfinch damage to buds (see p. 148) by Duncan et al. (1960). Wright (1962) found these two agents ineffective in preventing rooks from digging up and eating newly planted maize, whereas Young and Zevallos (1960) considered that they reduced the incidence of similar damage in Mexico caused by boat-tailed grackles and brown-headed cowbirds. Early failures in Britain led to research into the sense of taste in birds and detailed experiments with captive subjects (Duncan, 1960). More recently success has been claimed for the agent methiocarb (see p. 124) which was effective in markedly reducing damage by grackles in Texas (West and Dunks, 1969) and in repelling blackbirds (Woronecki et al., 1967; Stickley and Guarino, 1972).

The stressing agent 4-aminopyridine (Avitrol) has been effective in reducing damage to maize, rice and sorghum by shiny cowbirds, but caused deaths among ruddy ground doves (*Columbigallina talpacoti* Temminck) (Woronecki et al., 1972) and in protecting ripening corn from blackbirds in North America (De Grazio et al., 1971, 1972; Stickley et al., 1972).

(b) *Surfactants.* Wetting agents or surfactants have been extensively used in the United States to produce mortality among roosting black-birds. Initially in 1958 ground application techniques were used but in 1966 high-volume aerial applications from tanker aircraft were employed to be followed by low-volume, high concentration aerial application just prior to expected rain (Lefebure and Seubert, 1970, and references cited therein). The exact mode of action of these agents is not known but it is thought that the destruction of the insulating properties of the feathers results in lethal hypothermia.

E. WOOD PIGEON IN EUROPE

1. *Biology and damage*

This is the major agricultural bird pest in Britain and Holland (van Troostwijk, 1965) but in France it is valued as a bird of "*La Chasse*". Reference has already been made to the effect of a developing agriculture on its status in Britain (p. 112), where in many areas it is almost entirely dependent on the arable monoculture. It feeds on the newly planted, ripening or ripe grains of wheat and barley when in season, the spilt grain on the post-harvest stubbles and resorts to grazing clover and some weed leaves for the remainder of the year (Murton et al., 1964a, b). For most individuals the breeding season corresponds with peak cereal availability in August and September and, with 70% of all young reared at this time (Murton, 1958; Murton et al., 1963b), population size increases about 2·5-fold. Nevertheless, the wood pigeon evolved as a bud feeding woodland species and individuals which begin breeding in March and April, when their physiological apparatus first becomes stimulated (Lofts *et al.*, 1967), are much more successful in rearing progeny that survive to become adult than those nesting later in the year (Murton, 1961). Late hatched young do not complete the moult before the winter season of limiting food reserves (Murton *et al.*, 1974a) and compete less successfully for places in the adult social hierarchy (Murton *et al.*, 1971). A proportion of the British population, primarily juveniles, emigrates to France for the winter months (Murton and Ridpath, 1962), as do most birds from northern Europe (van Troostwijk, 1964; Lebreton, 1969; Alerstam and Ulfstrand, 1974).

No damage is caused by the post-reproductive population during the autumn as the birds are able to feed on stubble grain. In the process juvenile, but not adult, numbers achieve a balance with the declining grain stocks (Murton, *et al.*, 1964b, 1974b). When grain is exhausted wood pigeons begin feeding on clover leaves, although if prevented by snow or frost they transfer to higher standing brassica crops and in these circumstances can cause serious damage. During January and February pigeons deplete the clover supply—which at this time of year grows very little—and both adult and juvenile numbers become adjusted in relation to stocks (Murton *et al.*, 1964b, 1966, 1974b). Birds which are displaced from the social hierarchy existing in the flocks feeding on clover (see Murton *et al.*, 1966, 1971 for the reasons) may resort to brassica fields and cause damage before eventually dying (see also Kenward, 1976). In addition, all birds may be forced to feed on brassicae during periods of snow or intense frost. In early spring, birds displaced from the social system may damage newly planted seedling crops. Pea, sugar beet, and brassica seedlings contain more protein and other nutrients than the mature plants and they sometimes offer more attractive food sources than depleted clover fields, depending on the season, district and relative availability of preferred alternatives. Thus if wild tree shoots and buds are readily available these will be eaten, whereas in tree-less country crop damage can be more severe. Some of the most expensive damage by wood pigeons is caused to seedling crops. By June, wild weed seeds are usually abundant and seedlings have grown sufficiently to obviate this risk (see Dunning, 1974).

Attempts have been made to quantify the national cost of wood pigeon damage in Britain. Assuming a breeding population of approximately 5 million rising to 10 million following reproduction, it was estimated that the total cost of the crops eaten would be in the order of £1–2 million (Murton, 1965a). This figure is lower than the value of the grain wasted at harvest as a result of spillage, which helps support the population during the early winter. Damage should not be simply extrapolated in these terms, although it does help to define the amount worth spending on control measures.

Studies have been concentrated on damage to Brussels sprouts (*Brassica oleracea* L.) and winter cabbage in the Vale of Evesham over three seasons (Murton and Jones, 1973; Jones, 1974). This area has favourable soils and climate which facilitate early maturation of the crop which can be sold when prices are high. Indeed, the whole economy of the local industry depends on achieving peak market prices, for later in the season the market becomes glutted with produce from other growers, who do not specialize in the crop and can afford to accept lower prices. Thus, although cabbages which are pecked by wood pigeons may well recover this can delay their harvest. Brussels sprout buttons were not damaged by pigeons and the tops were preferred to cabbages, hence the presence of the former helped to reduce damage to the latter. Brassica damage was not correlated with the growers estimates of what they suffered nor with their monetary outlay on crop protection (see also Kenward, 1976). At one time farmers claimed that pigeon grazing caused serious damage to clover. Since the birds can remove over 80% of the available leaves by February the loss is serious if the crop is needed for the immediate grazing of livestock. Mostly fields are not grazed in winter but are instead cut in June to provide silage that can be stored for later feeding to livestock kept under cover: the trend to battery husbandry gained momentum during the 1960's while favourable world prices have increasingly encouraged the use of barley feeds rather than silage. Clover like grass, recovers from intensive winter grazing so that by May yields are not reduced (Fig. 5). In fact, plots which were heavily grazed by pigeons, or where the leaves were artificially removed to simulate extreme damage, produced on average a bigger yield in May than areas where damage was prevented (Fig. 5). Since new growth is higher in nutritive content than old, it is possible, but not proven, that winter pigeon attack actually increased the nutritive value of the sward in spring (see also Greenwood and Titmanis, 1968).

2. *Natural and artificial control of population size*
(a) *Effect of shooting.* Intensive studies of the wood pigeon were instigated during the second world war, when it was considered that the bird might seriously reduce home food production (see Colquhoun, 1951 for summary). Following these investigations, the authorities in Britain designated the bird a ubiquitous pest and deemed it best to

prevent damage by a national slaughter campaign aimed at reducing
the total population (this policy was also applied to certain other
vertebrate pests including the Norway rat [*Rattus norvegicus* (Berken-
hout)], house mouse (*Mus musculus* L.) and grey squirrel (*Neosciurus
carolenensis* Gmelin). To this end reliance was placed on the traditional

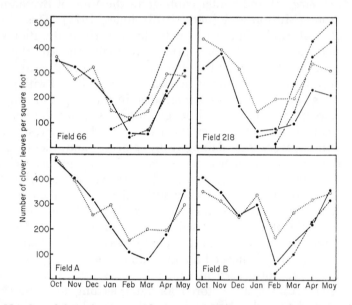

FIG. 5. Number of clover leaves per ft² on parts of fields where wood pigeons could graze
(solid symbols and solid lines) and exclosures where grazing was prevented (open
symbols and dotted line). Within these exclosures intensive grazing was sometimes
simulated by artificial cutting (solid symbol, dashed line). (From Murton *et al.*, 1966.)

love of British sportsmen to go shooting with double-barrelled 12-bore
guns and the Government encouraged these efforts by giving a 50%
subsidy on the cost of those cartridges used for killing pigeons and other
designated pests. Abuse of the scheme, intended or not, was considerable
and it was demonstrated that winter battue shooting merely removed a
population surplus which was doomed to die of food shortage during the
ensuing few weeks, and without effecting savings in damage (Murton
et al., 1964b; Murton, 1965a; Murton *et al.*, 1974b). Population size is
unaffected by shooting for it is compensated for by reductions in natural
mortality and is not additive to other losses (Fig. 6). The same applies
to the killing of young rooks as they leave their nests in April and May
(Dunnet *et al.*, 1969) for population size is determined a month later
by the availability of earthworms and other soil invertebrates (Murton

and Westwood, 1974). Marked inverse-density dependent effects resulted from the limitation that each gun could only shoot a theoretical maximum of two birds from each passing flock; more flocks passed when total population size increased but the proportion of birds killed declined (Fig. 7). No change could be detected from ringing recoveries

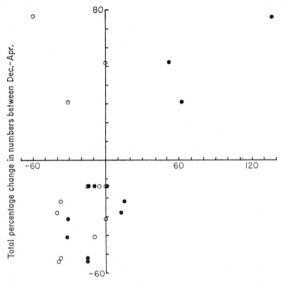

Percentage changes due to shooting o or other causes •

Fig. 6. Total percentage change in numbers of wood pigeons between December and April on a study area in England (y axis) plotted against the percentage of this change due to shooting (open symbols) and to natural changes (solid symbols). The total change in population size is not dependent on shooting but is strongly correlated with natural increases or decreases. (Based on data in Murton *et al.*, 1974.)

in the mortality rate of pigeons before or after introduction of the scheme (Murton, 1966). The studies led, therefore, to the removal of Government support for winter roost shooting in early 1965 and to the recognition that attempts to mitigate damage should be confined to the actual site of damage or other variables would cause the cost of control to exceed the cost of saved crops (Murton, 1965b). But decoy shooting over vulnerable crops could still be supported by a 50% grant obtainable through Rabbit Clearance Societies, provided shooting was confined to the site where pigeons actually caused damage. This was partly for political reasons but it remained possible that shooting could alter the seasonal pattern of mortality without affecting the absolute annual rate. Subsequently, it was shown experimentally that an intensive shooting scheme aimed at preventing pigeon attacks on cabbages did not reduce damage, although the movement of local inhabitants and farm workers near a village did bring benefits (Murton and Jones, 1973; Kenward, 1976). The effectiveness of decoy shooting

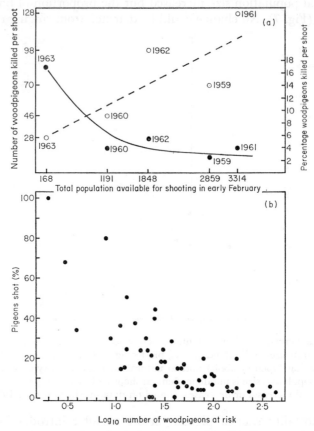

FIG. 7. Inverse density-dependent relationship between number of wood pigeons available for shooting and the proportion actually shot. (A) Number of birds in a study area of 2647 acres in early February and the number (dotted line, open symbols) and percentage (solid line, solid symbols) shot in February and early March. (From Murton *et al.*, 1964b.) (B) Percentage of pigeons shot by decoy gunners in relation to the $\log_{10}$ number passing within range of the decoys/hour. (From Murton *et al.*, 1974b.)

has also been studied in relation to the natural flocking behaviour of pigeons and their responses to artificial decoys (Murton, 1974a; Murton *et al.*, 1974b).

(*b*) *Stupefying baits.* Attempts to reduce the total population size of a pest might be economically sound given cheap and efficient killing agents, and the use of poison baits would seem an obvious procedure. However, the risks to other legally protected animals and to game birds is high and unacceptable in a country of high population density with a deep rooted concern for wildlife conservation and an abhorrence of cruelty to animals. Stupefying baits have the theoretical advantage that if protected species are caught they can be allowed to recover to be released unharmed. Early trials were conducted by Colquhoun (1943 and unpublished observations) with tribromoethanol while Mosby and Canter (1956) used Avertin (a mixture of 20 parts tribromoethanol and 1 part amyl alcohol) to catch wild turkeys. Daude (1942) first showed the value of alpha-chloralose (a substituted chloral hydrate) and it was used to catch birds, mainly corvids, in France (Danzel, 1949; Giban, 1950) and Sweden (Borg, 1955) and to catch feral pigeons in Britain (Ridpath et al., 1961; Thearle, 1969a, b). Its use was developed for catching wood pigeons (Murton et al., 1963c; Murton, 1965a; Murton et al., 1968). Alpha-chloralose proved a valuable research tool but continued to pose a small risk to game birds which some game hunters thought was unacceptable. Changes in the pest status of the wood pigeon have not stimulated a need for further work with these agents, although the cost of killing pigeons with them was well under half that needed to shoot the birds in trials that compared the performance of experts in the two techniques (Murton et al., 1974b). Improved formulations are now available which overcome some of the drawbacks of alpha-chloralose (Thearle et al., 1971).

(c) *Key-factor analysis.* Varley and Gradwell (1960) developed a technique of examining population data whereby the action of key-factors, that is, those components of the total annual mortality (K) which contribute most to year-to-year fluctuations in population size, can be readily identified. Strictly applied the method is most applicable when the various individual mortality factors k_0, k_1, k_2, . . . $k_n = K$ can be assumed to act successively on a single generation for which complete life table data are available, as is true for many insect populations where the different life stages show little overlap. Nevertheless, the technique has been successfully applied to birds (Blank et al., 1967; Southern, 1970; Krebs, 1970; Murton, 1974b). It provides a valuable means whereby wildlife managers can decide which components of the total mortality are most amenable to manipulation for the purposes of pest control or need attention for conservation purposes. Figure 8 sets out appropriate data for a wood pigeon population to demonstrate how mortality occurring between December and March (k_4) contributed most to the total annual mortality. That is, year to year fluctuations in population size in this species depend primarily on the losses that occur in winter when the birds are feeding on clover leaves. Variations in the reproduction rate (number of eggs produced, hatched or chicks fledged k_0, k_1, k_2) are not influential in spite of the fact that up to 80%

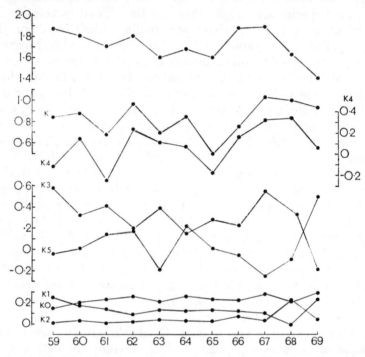

Fig. 8. Graphical key-factor analysis to show relationship of various mortalities ($k_0 \ldots k_5$) to total mortality (K) affecting a Wood Pigeon population. Top graph gives the logarithm of actual population per 100 acres. K is composed of: k_0, failure to achieve maximum egg production; k_1, egg loss; k_2, chick loss; k_3, autumn change in numbers; k_4, winter change in numbers; k_5, summer change in numbers. (From Murton, 1974b.)

of the eggs laid by pigeons may be eaten by predators and many game-keepers and others have argued that predators should be encouraged to help keep down the pigeon population. By plotting the individual k-values as the dependent variable against the $\log_{10}$ populations on which they act those mortalities which serve as density-dependent regulators of the population can supposedly be recognized. Actually, in the present example, k_3 and k_4 acting together provide the necessary density adjustment which serves to regulate population size (Murton *et al.*, 1974b). Figure 8 shows that the population declined in the late 1960's (note that logarithms are plotted). This depended on a loss of clover supplies which modified k_4 and which resulted from farming changes already outlined (p. 133). In effect, this has been a demonstration of the feasibility of adopting an ecological approach in dealing with bird problems.

F. WATERFOWL AND OTHER GRAZERS

1. Damage by swans and geese

Swans prefer to feed in shallow lakes and rivers where they pull up aquatic vegetation. They are sometimes attracted to flooded meadows and cereal fields adjacent to water and can then cause local damage by their habit of uprooting plants. Damage is frequently aggravated by excessive trampling and the mess made by droppings (Murton, 1971a). Grazing by mute swans has been reported to alter the vegetation composition in nature reserves (Gillham, 1956). There has been some increase in numbers of this species in Britain and North Europe, at least in the last twenty years (Rawcliffe, 1958; Campbell, 1960; Eltringham, 1963). The black swan [*C. atratus* (Latham)] in Australia and New Zealand causes similar problems (references in Scott *et al.*, 1972). Whooper swans [*C. cygnus* (L.)] and Bewick's swans (*C. bewickii* Yarrell) which winter in Britain and North Europe sometimes evoke farmer's complaints. In a few districts in Scotland, the former resorts to fields of swede–turnips and pecks at the unharvested plants. Similar damage is done to unharvested and harvested fields of potatoes, particularly in Perthshire and Angus. According to Pilcher and Kear (1966) the habit became established following the severe winters of the 1940's and is spreading to England. Wintering numbers may have increased between 1948 and 1952 (Boyd and Eltringham, 1962).

The magpie goose (*Anseranas semipalmata* Latham) of New Guinea and Australia is the most primitive living member of the family Anatidae. The bird feeds by immersing its head and neck in soft mud and dredging up the succulent roots of the bulkuru sedge (*Eleocharis dulcis* Henschel) and other water plants, and the heavy bill is equipped with a hooked upper mandible to facilitate this feeding technique. Attempts were made to develop a rice industry in the sub-coastal plain of the Northern Territory, two crops being grown per year.* Although the geese became very numerous during the wet season sowing time, they mostly fed on *Eleocharis* bulbs disturbed by the drill and did not

* Schemes to develop the Northern Territories have a political rather than economic motivation, for a Government and population isolated in the south has long felt a need to have a developed zone to serve as a clear boundary with South-East Asia.

seriously damage the rice (Frith and Davies, 1961). Broadcast rice sown during the dry-season was speedily eaten by the geese, especially in shallow water. Germinating rice was grazed but this may have encouraged tillering and therefore compensated for the grazing; the most significant damage was near harvest, when the geese knocked down the plants and stripped the heads. The rice scheme has now been abandoned so the conclusion reached by Frith and Davies that the geese would not be a continuing problem for various ecological reasons has not been further tested. In many respects the spur-winged goose [*Plectro-pterus gambensis* (L.)] of Africa has an ecological niche which is similar to that of the magpie goose and it has caused damage to rice growing schemes in Africa.

The large *Anser* and *Branta* geese cause some concern during their winter sojourn on arable farmland in Northern Europe. Greylag geese [*Anser anser* (L.)] and pink-footed geese [*A. brachyrhynchos* (Latham)] from Iceland and Greenland winter in Scotland and feed in large flocks on cultivated land. Here they frequent old potato fields and glean spilt grain from stubbles; when this supply is exhausted they turn to grazing grass and winter cereals. In hard weather they attack swede and kale fields while, in some areas, greylags have taken to using swedes (*Brassica napus* L.) as a regular diet (Kear, 1963a, 1964, 1967). This spoils the vegetable and encourages it to rot, and the problem is best avoided by earlier harvesting and storing the roots. Increase in the acreage of barley grown in Scotland has caused a larger number of pink-footed geese to winter there (Kear, 1965a), though with their more delicate bills they do less damage to the tougher foods than do greylags. In recent years, pinkfeet have taken to pecking unharvested carrot crops in the Ormskirk area of Lancashire, and stimulated a voluble demand for remedial action to be taken by the Government although it seems that the real damage is much less important than originally claimed. Canada geese [*Branta canadensis* (L.)] introduced into Britain during the Restoration, locally cause damage to pastures and cereals planted near the lakes they frequent (details in Murton, 1971a). There was a three-fold increase in numbers between 1953 and 1968 (Ogilvie, 1969). In South America, the sheldgeese (*Chloephaga* spp.) have a niche which is similar to that occupied by the true geese of the northern hemisphere. Migrant upland [*C. picta* (Gmelin)] and ashy-headed geese (*C. poliocephala* Sclater) from Patagonia winter further north in Argentina where they graze winter cereals and pastures and give rise to complaints comparable with those engendered by their north temperate equivalents; a race of the former also gives rise to complaints in the Falkland Islands.

As with pigeon damage to clover (Fig. 5), grass recovers from the effect of grazing by the following spring, and the sward may even be improved (Kear, 1965b, 1970; Kuyken, 1969). In intensive grazing in spring by barnacle geese [*Branta leucopsis* (Bechstein)] on the island of Gotland did not restrict the growth of the vegetation thereafter and the presence of geese was not harmful to sheep rearing (Bjärvall and Samuelsson, 1970). In fact the only serious damage occurs when geese single out fields of "early bite" grass in spring which are specially fertilized and prepared to provide a crop of nutritious young grass for lambing flocks of sheep. Similarly, winter grazing of cereals causes no permanent damage and may even improve the crop by inducing tillering. This was once purposely achieved by grazing sheep and it has been shown that provided the grazing is stopped by mid-April no reduction in grain yield occurs. Artificial clipping experiments also led to the same conclusion (Kear, 1970). If geese puddle the ground and reduce aeration in wet and frosty conditions the growth of plants may be checked but this can easily be countered by harrowing and top dressing in spring.

Many farmers consider that goose droppings repel sheep and cattle. Trials with sheep which were introduced to pasture strips on which fresh goose droppings were scattered at a density above that occurring in nature showed that contaminated areas were significantly avoided only on the first day (Rochard and Kear, 1968; 1970). It was concluded that the repellent factor must be rapidly volatilized and that there is unlikely to be any real crop loss to the farmer. Indeed, droppings may have some manurial value in terms of soil structure but the elements they contain have usually been removed from the same pasture (Kear, 1963b).

Recommendations to prevent goose damage are summarized by Kear (1963a). They include the use of various scaring devices, and some more recent field trials show that virtually any conspicuous unfamilar object, from a fertilizer bag to a man effigy scarecrow, placed in the field frequented by the birds will deter them for about a week (D.A.F.S. Advisory Leaflet, undated). Devices which produce noise or sudden movement, e.g. commercial "Red Man" scarers, captive hydrogen-filled balloons (Kimber, 1963), bangers and wind-rotated devices were rather more effective and give protection for up to three weeks. There is scope for more detailed work on what constitutes a good scarecrow, with expectation of greater success if biologically significant stimuli are employed. Thus red balloons have no significance for a wood pigeon apart from being a strange object, whereas the white wing patch does function as a sign stimulus in specific contexts, so that dead birds mounted as if flying evoked escape responses in conspecifics (Murton, 1974a; Hunter, 1974).

2. *Damage by other waterfowl*

Ducks in large concentrations may cause local problems by paddling waterside fields and eating ripening cereal crops and exceptionally they graze watercress beds (Murton, 1971a). Some of the rails (Rallidae) cause slightly more damage to waterside crops since they tend to uproot plants more than do ducks. Grass was found to be the main food of coots (*Fulica atra* L.) from December to March and an experimental field of autumn sown wheat and barley sited near open water suffered reduced yields due to grazing by this species (Hurter, 1972). Moorhens [*Gallinula chloropus* (L.)] have been found digging up and eating potatoes in the Isles of Scilly, and locally eating winter wheat or intensively grazing pasture (Murton, 1971a). These cases can be dismissed but the grazing of cultivated violets and the pecking of cultivated bulbs in Holland was more serious (van Koersveld, 1955) and similar damage has occurred in Lincolnshire, England (Murton, 1971a). The Tasmanian native hen (*Tribonyx mortierii* DuBus) gives rise to the same spectrum of complaints in man-altered parts of Tasmania as do the northern rails just mentioned, including the fouling of pastures and stock drinking places (Graham, 1954). Exclosure trials over $2\frac{1}{2}$ years showed that grazing of grass by native hens was fairly even throughout the year, but when it coincided with rabbit grazing there was a sharp check to spring growth and a subsequent decline in grass height: rabbits were apparently doing more damage than the rails (Ridpath and Meldrum, 1968a). Damage to cereals and suggested remedies are given by Ridpath and Meldrum (1968b).

3. *Damage by Larks*

Increasing attention has been focused on the skylark (*Alauda arvensis* L.) in England and there have been claims that its population has increased in some areas. Totally different trends have been recorded at different sites and on balance at a national level little change has occurred (Fig. 9) to account for the increase in damage (Fig. 10). Thus the acreage of sugar beet grown in Britain, mostly Eastern England, remained relatively constant from 1957 to 1972 (170 000 to 178 000 ha) but the incidence of grazing on young seedlings by small birds and wood pigeons, mostly in April and May, increased considerably (Dunning, 1974). This is shown by the reports of experienced fieldsmen of the British Sugar Corporation who complete a damage report form in a systematic manner (Fig. 10a based on Dunning, 1974). Most of the small bird damage was attributable to skylarks. During the period under review, and especially from the mid-1960's, the acreage of leys, a favoured habitat of the skylark, decreased (p. 133) as too did the availability of dicotyledonous weeds in cereal and other crops, consequent on increased herbicide usage (Fig. 10b). It seems possible, therefore, that decreases in natural food resources forced skylarks to make greater

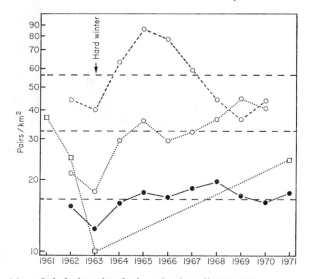

Fig. 9. Densities of skylark pairs during the breeding season at separate sites in Warwickshire (open symbol and dashed line), Westmorland (open symbol and dotted line), Cambridgeshire (open square and dotted line) and from a national census as monitored through the common bird census scheme of the British Trust for Ornithology. (From Hardman, 1974, with additional data from Murton and Westwood, 1974.)

use of cultivated seedling crops. An additional factor was probably the trend to precision space drilling so that the number of seedlings per acre was decreased by a third in six years thereby leaving a smaller wastage margin to absorb bird attack. Sugar beet seedlings show good powers of recovery from grazing attack (Edgar and Isaacson, 1974) and only severe defoliation of young plants appears to reduce sugar yield (Dunning, 1974). Artificial defoliation experiments involving the removal of half the leaf area did not affect yield; removing both cotyledons reduced yield by 6% and removal of both cotyledons plus first leaves decreased yield by 20% (Dunning and Winder, 1972). Tests of various supposed chemical repellents, applied to the seeds (dieldrin, Avi-test (Quassia), Morkit—which contains anthroguinone—and Cunitex, containing thiram) were without benefit and further trials, including one in which the new foliage was sprayed with 0·1 % methiocarb, had no significant effect on the extent of bird grazing (Dunning, 1974). These results contrast with reported experiences in the U.S.A (see p. 131). Various other species of lark, including the crested lark

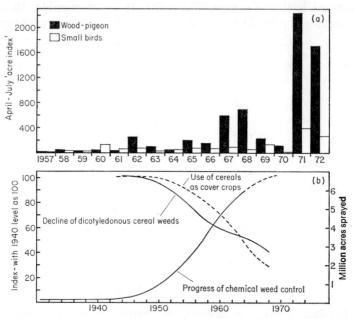

Fig. 10. (A) Index of damage to sugar beet seedlings by small birds and Wood Pigeons. (From Dunning, 1974.) (B) Decline of incidence of dicotyledonous weeds in cereal crops and use of cereals as a cover crop and the progress of chemical weed control as judged by the acreage of cereals treated with herbicides. (From Potts, 1970, and Woodford, 1964.)

[*Galerida cristata* (L.)], short-toed lark [*Calandrella cinerea* (Gmelin)], and calandra lark [*Melanocorypha calaadra* (L.)] damage seedling crops in the Middle Eastern countries, and are sometimes very troublesome on irrigation schemes as in Israel; horned larks [*Eremophila alpestris* (L.)] can be nuisance birds in N. America (Koehler, 1962).

G. BIRDS AND LIVESTOCK

1. *Direct losses to domestic animals*

Debate has centred on whether eagles cause important losses among sheep and lamb flocks, but the concensus is that they merely crop a doomed surplus. It is often forgotten that free-living sheep suffer much mortality during seasons of resource limitation, just as do wild mammals. Lockie (1964) was able to show that golden eagles [*Aquila chrysaëtos* (L.)] in Scotland take mostly carrion lambs, although he was unable to determine how many of the live ones eaten were already weak or sickly when captured and would have died in any case (Lockie and Stephen, 1959; also Brown, 1969); similar considerations apply to the wedge-tailed eagle [*A. audax* (Latham)] in Australia (Ridpath and Brooker, 1975). Some 70% of golden eagle nests in parts of Texas and New Mexico had remains of sheep and goats—mostly young—but in this case it was not known whether they had been taken alive (Moll-hagen *et al.*, 1972).

Ravens (*Corvus corax* L.) and carrion crows (*C. corone* L.) attend lambing sheep flocks to obtain after-births. Sometimes they become too venturesome and attack new born lambs, especially weak and ailing individuals, or one of a pair of twins when the ewe is occupied (Burgess, 1963). Lambs with their eyes picked-out rouse strong emotions in shepherds but in economic terms the problem is not serious affecting less than 0·6% of the lambs at risk and under 0·01% of the ewes at risk in Wales (K. Walton, *in litt.*); and affecting under 2% of the lamb crop in Australian studies (Smith, 1964). The widespread killing of corvid pairs in established territories is not recommended, for the damage is caused by surplus individuals which are displaced from the preferred habitat (Murton, 1971a, and for further details of damage estimation).

Many birds associate with feeding domestic animals and catch disturbed insects e.g. cattle egret [*Ardeola ibis* (L.)], jackdaw, magpie [*Pica pica* (L.)]. In addition, they sometimes search the fur of the animal for ticks. Less often they peck at wounds and may even enlarge these and prevent healing. Red-billed oxpeckers [*Buphagus erythrorhyn-chus* (Stanley)] were noted eating blood clots and skin fragments on cattle and sometimes purposely opened up a sore to eat the discharged serum and blood (Van Someren, 1951). Magpies learned to peck holes in the back of living sheep until they could eat the kidneys (Schorger, 1921; Berry, 1922). The kea (*Nestor notabilis* Gould) and kaka [*N. meridionalis* (Gmelin)] of New Zealand have unwholesome habits of this kind. Starlings inflicted wounds on cattle in Texas when pecking at warbles during a cold spell which rendered normal food inaccessible (McCoy, 1941).

2. *Loss of animal foods*

Starlings throughout their natural and introduced range frequent poultry farms, cattle rearing stations (feedlots), and other places where food is provided for domestic animals and they can remove large amounts. Starlings, which were eating cattle food at a feedlot near

Denver, Colorado, were estimated to have cost the equivalent of $U.S.84 per 1000 birds during the course of one winter, while red-winged black-birds consumed a total of food worth $U.S.2 per 1000 birds (Besser *et al.*, 1968). Red-winged blackbirds have been discouraged from using feedlots near Denver by baiting alleys with corn treated with methio-carb (Woronecki *et al.*, 1970). Quite apart from competing for food, it has been suggested that birds disturb the stock in some way that is detrimental to their growth. To test this, an experiment was designed in which bullocks were fed an *ad lib* diet of crushed barley and pelleted concentrate, in a 20-animal unit from which starlings were excluded by wire mesh, and in a similar unprotected unit. The protected cattle showed a higher growth rate and better food conversion efficiency, and over four months the gross profit margin was increased by £60 for an initial outlay of £10 on wire netting (Wright, 1973). At the same site experiments to control the birds by capturing them with crushed barley treated with alpha-chloralose were not worthwhile.

At a large commercial duck farm in eastern England, starlings were reckoned to be consuming £33 000 worth of animal food per year. The owner insisted that the authorities should kill the birds with narcotics or poisons. This was not recommended and instead, with such a high rate of loss, the capital cost of providing physical protection was con-sidered justified—only after much argument was this recommendation accepted and the problem solved.

V. Bird Problems In Horticulture And Forestry

The generalizations which were applicable to arable and pasture monocultures also apply to extensive planted forest and orchard cultures. Mature planted conifer forests, even of exotic species, are usually self-contained systems and their bird life, although impoverished in species variety, is representative of a climax system. Birds cause virtually no damage in mature conifer woodland and instead may be helpful in damping the population oscillations of some of their prey species, many of which are potential pests (Murton, 1971a). Orchards are temporary habitats and mostly only provide food when the crop is nearly ripe, for at other seasons a rigid regime of hygiene with insecti-cidal sprays render them unattractive feeding places.

A. BUD EATERS

1. *Bullfinches and fruit buds*
(a) *Damage.* For most of the year bullfinches live on the seeds of various woodland plants, particularly docks (*Rumex* spp.), nettle (*Urtica dioica*

L.) and bramble (*Rubus fruticosus* agg.) (Wright and Summers, 1960; Newton, 1967b). As supplies of these seeds become depleted in autumn the birds turn to those of birch (*Betula pendula* Roth and *B. pubescens* Ehrh.) and ash (*Fraxinus excelsior* L.) and then when these are exhausted they begin eating buds, usually in January. Buds remain an important food supply until April when weed seeds again become available. In natural habitats the buds of hawthorn (*Crataegus monogyna* Jacq) are eaten first, followed later in the season by those of blackthorn

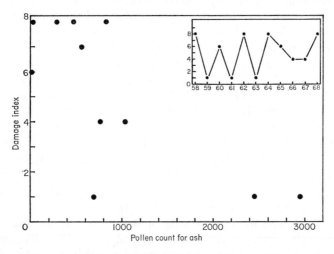

FIG. 11. Estimated seed crop of ash, judged by the spring pollen count, and an index of bullfinch damage to fruit buds in the following winter. Inset gives chronological sequence of damage. Data on pollen counts supplied by Dr H. A. Hyde, Asthma and Allergy Research Unit, St David's Hospital, Cardiff. Damage index based on information collated by D. D. B. Summers for S.E. England.

(*Prunus spinosa* L.). But if available, the buds of cultivated shrubs and trees may be an alternative diet, even a preferred one depending on their nutritive content, and losses can be severe (Fryer, 1939; Laflin and English, 1960). Ash, like other woodland trees, tends to alternate good with poor fruiting seasons. Wright and Summers (1960) first showed that damage to orchards also followed this biennial pattern, being moderate to severe in years when the ash crop failed and the birds had to turn to bud eating earlier in the winter and light or negligible in alternate seasons (see Fig. 11). Newton (1964, 1967b) later documented the same phenomenon from a study of the proportion of wild buds in the gizzard remains of shot birds. Thus the likelihood of damage can be predicted and protection measures applied.

Farmers and growers often have a psychological aversion to accepting that a pest is local and they seem to derive solace by attributing crop damage to immigrants—a "blame-the-foreigner" attitude. A disproportionate amount of propaganda was needed to convince farmers that Britain was not invaded by vast hordes of wood pigeons from continental Europe (Murton and Ridpath, 1962) and it similarly required much effort to persuade fruit growers in southern England that bullfinch damage resulted from locally reared birds (Wright and Summers, 1960); the same apparently applies in France (Aubry, 1970).

Bullfinch damage can appear spectacular and the birds may strip a gooseberry bush in an hour. Marked preferences are shown for certain fruit tree varieties, for example "Conference" pear is preferred to "Comice" pear (Wright, 1959; Wright and Summers, 1960) and some varieties, notably "Doyenne du Comice" are only exceptionally attacked (Becker and Gilbert, 1958). Newton has found in feeding trials that different wild buds have markedly different nutrient contents judged in terms of their capacity to maintain body weight in captive subjects and it seems reasonable to suppose that these fruit-bud preferences are also related to nutrient factors. In spite of heavy disbudding, it has proved difficult to demonstrate significant reductions in final crop yields because a host of variables intervene between damage and harvest, for example, frost and wind damage to flowers, summer-drop, and insect attack on buds and developing fruit. Wright and Summers measured the amount of bud loss on "Conference" pears by counting samples of 100 buds yet no relationship was found between the amount of bud loss in March and the final crop yield (Fig. 12). Damage can be more subtle in that selective pruning by the birds may alter the long term shape and development of a bush or tree and affect its yield in subsequent seasons (see details in Murton, 1971a).

(b) *Control techniques.* Various chemical repellents have been tried against bullfinches (see p. 130) but to no avail. Yellow distemper has been said to give protection to dormant buds but neither it nor gentian violet were effective when applied to plums and blackcurrents (English, 1953). Wright and Summers (1960) developed a modified "chardonneret" trap (see also Wright, 1961) to catch bullfinches which when used with a decoy was considered to be more effective than shooting (which results in much damage to trees). The technique is still in use and it has the advantage, as has shooting, that growers can actually handle bodies and this does help convince them that they are doing good. But it has yet to be shown that crop yields are increased as a result of killing bullfinches, and that it is an economically viable proposition. Sometimes extremely large numbers of birds are taken and it is evident that as each one is killed another moves in to take its place so that the grower effectively milks a much bigger population than the one causing damage; the effect was well demonstrated by Mewaldt (1964) when trapping passerines.

Fruit-growers used to trap in the spring at the time of damage. Newton (1968) pointed out that a more sensible policy would be to trap and kill in autumn and early winter for this would reduce intra-specific competition for the natural food supply and enable it to last longer, thereby reducing the likelihood of the birds having to switch to buds.

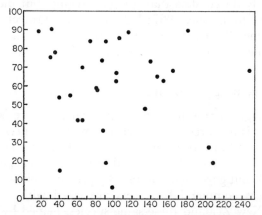

Fig. 12. Percentage of Conference pear buds eaten by bullfinches in winter on different trees in a uniform orchard stand, and the weight of fruit eventually harvested per tree. (From Murton, 1971, based on data supplied by E. N. Wright and D. D. B. Summers.)

2. Other bud feeders

In Europe various titmice (Paridae) and the goldfinch [*Carduelis carduelis* (L.)], greenfinch [*Carduelis chloris* (L.)], house sparrow and redpoll [*Acanthis flammea* (L.)] have been recorded eating pear buds in England (Newton, 1967c) while redpolls introduced to New Zealand do much damage to apricot flower buds in the Otago district (Stenhouse, 1962; Hawkins and Bull, 1962); introduced house sparrows, chaffinches (*Fringilla coelebs* L.) and greenfinches are also troublesome in New Zealand orchards. The house finch [*Carpodacus mexicanus* (Müller)] damages both buds and ripe fruit in the U.S.A. (Beal, 1904; Koehler, 1962) and its control is discussed by Palmer (1970).

Capercaillie (*Tetrao urogallus* L.) specialize on buds, shoots and cones of *Pinus* sp. and can sometimes do harm to young forestry plantations, especially nursery stock and newly planted out seedlings (Pennie, 1963;

Johnstone, 1967). Johnstone found that capercaillie had removed the leader from 44% of planted conifers but from only 14% of naturally regenerating trees. The former may have been more nutritive as a result of fertilizer treatment and it is well known that game birds, as well as other species, will select out plants of higher nutritive value than the average. Thus blue grouse [*Dendrogapus obscurus* (Say)] select needles of *Abies concolor* (Gord.) and *Pinus banksiana* Lamb which have the most protein (Hoffman, 1961; Gurchinoff and Robinson, 1972); the needles of trees infected with fungi and stunted trees may have a higher nutritive content (Lindroth and Lindgren, 1950). Black grouse [*Lyrurus tetrix* (L.)] feed less heavily on conifers than the capercaillie but they too can do much damage (Johnstone, 1967; Palmar, 1968). Protecting *Pinus* trees from black game allowed the trees to grow 50% more than unprotected trees during the first 10 years (Zehetmayr, 1954).

B. DAMAGE TO RIPE FRUIT AND VEGETABLES

Direct damage to ripe fruit is mostly real for there is no prospect of recovery. It is a source of concern to small gardeners who lose soft fruit, cherries or plums to starlings, blackbirds (*Turdus merula* L.), song thrushes (*Turdus philomelos* Brehm) and less often other species (Brough, 1962–3, 1967). But gardeners can usually protect their small areas with netting whereas commercial growers are faced with a more serious problem. In New Zealand these same species, helped by the common myna [*Acridotheres tristis* (L.)—introduced from India] and the indigenous white-eye [*Zosterops lateralis* (Latham)], plague orchards (Dawson and Bull, 1970). Starlings and common grackles (*Quiscalus quiscula* L.) were eating cherries in Canada (Virgo, 1971). In New Zealand, introduced goldfinches and redpolls removed the seeds from strawberries, just as linnets do in Britain (Brown, 1961). Gibb (1970) describes how the New Zealand Pigeon (*Hemiphaga novaeseelandiae* Gmelin) selected plums on the basis of their accessibility, ripeness and size.

Wright and Brough (1966) counted the number of apples and pears pecked by birds (mostly Parids) at harvest in three summers (1961–63) and found that between 1·0 and 4·1% of all varieties combined had been damaged. In 1957, damage to ripe pears and apples was particularly severe, individual trees had up to 25% of their fruit pecked (Wright, 1959). Pears and apples ripen at a season when birds have other food supplies and the populations have already suffered from post-breeding mortality (Murton, 1971a). But soft fruits ripen earlier so the population surplus from the many bird species that have just reproduced is able to raid the crop if unable to obtain diminishing natural food supplies. Thus starlings and thrush species are very harmful in dry summers, when their invertebrate foods are difficult to obtain. Native starlings do much damage to ripening grapes in European vineyards and so do introduced starlings in the Sunraysia district of the Murray River basin Australia (Thomas, 1957). Overwintering migrants, including herring gull, jay [*Garrulus glandarius* (L.)], song thrush, blackbird and hawfinch [*Coccothraustes coccothraustes* (L.)] damage cultivated olives in Yugoslavia (Tutman, 1969). Syrian woodpeckers have been reported eating ripening almonds in Germany (Schmidt, 1973b). Studies of the hairy woodpecker [*Dendrocopus villosus* (L.)] and downy woodpecker [*D. pubescens* (L.)] in apple orchards indicated that they were efficient predators of coddling moth larvae (MacLellan, 1970) so before a wide variety of birds are outlawed as pests more knowledge of their ecology in the damage situation is needed.

Pied wagtails (*Motacilla alba* L.) sometimes use greenhouses for roosting and as many as 600–800 birds may congregate together (Minton, 1960; Boswall, 1966) and do damage to such plants as tomato and carnation by fouling or breaking the blooms (Cohen, 1960). At some sites birds were captured by hand and with mist nets and transported 80 miles (128·7 km) where they were released (Mead, 1966a, b). Usually birds which are so released "home" to the place of capture so that it is usually better to kill them, but in this instance very few returned to the greenhouse. Wrens [*Trogladytes trogladytes* (L.)] were reported by Binns (1973) to have damaged developing cucumber fruitlets. This author also mentioned a grower in Hertfordshire who estimated he lost £1000 as a result of such damage between 1954 and 1958 but this estimate needs confirmation.

VI. Birds And Fisheries

Birds do not usually take large quantities of commercially important fish and they are more limited in their choice of feeding sites than are fishermen in the choice of places they can set their trawls. Many sea birds have increased in numbers this century, profiting from the increasing quantity of offal thrown overboard at sea by an expanding trawler industry, and examples include the *Larus* gulls (see p. 100), Kittiwake [*Rissa tridactyla* (L.)] (Coulson, 1963; Coulson and MacDonald, 1962) and fulmar [*Fulmarus glacialis* (L.)] (Fisher, 1966). Evans (1973) makes a tentative estimate of the biomass of birds utilizing the North Sea including shorebirds, wildfowl and seabirds at 390 000 kg (dry wt) in summer, 700 000 kg in autumn and 550 000 kg in winter with an average annual assimilation of food of $8·8 \times 10^{10}$ kcals.

A. BIRD PREDATION ON FISH

Cormorants in a large colony on the Ijsselmeer, Holland, had an average food intake per bird of 400 g per day comprising mostly eel (*Anguilla anguilla* L.), pike (*Esox lucius* L.) and other coarse fish (van Dobben, 1952). It was calculated that the cormorants removed around 7·5 million eels from the lake, mostly ones below the commercial size, while fishermen landed 55 million. The birds were thought to deplete a tenth of the pike-perch (*Perca fluviatilis* L.) fishery. Van Dobben found that 30% of the roach [*Rutilus rutilus* (L.)] eaten by cormorants were parasitized by *Ligula intestinalis* (L.) compared with only 6·5% of those left in the lake. In the lower Kattegat it was estimated that the Danish cormorant population of 300 pairs could potentially eat equivalent to about 1% of the total yield of the Danish eel fishery inside the Skaw (Madsen and Spärck, 1950) while cormorants in the North Caspian were calculated to eat 5000 tonnes of fish annually, representing 1·5% of the commercial catch (Sushkina, 1932). The diets of the shag and cormorant have been the subject of several early studies (Steven, 1933; Lack, 1945; Lumsden and Haddow, 1946). Both in Cornwall and the Clyde Sea area the most important food of the shag is the sand eel (*Ammodytes* sp.), with small fish such as sprat (*Clupea sprattus* L.), wrasse (*Ctenolabrus rupestris* L.) and gobies *Gobius* spp. of secondary importance. This was also true on the open coast of Angus and Kincardineshire (Rae, 1969) but not in the estuaries of the large rivers. Here gadoids and clupeoids were eaten, a prey spectrum partly overlapping that of the cormorant. The latter was found to feed more on flatfishes and salmonids in these estuaries though it was not considered a serious predator of salmon (*Salmo salar* L.) smolts, while the shag's predation pressure was negligible (Rae, 1969). Studies at another station on the east coast of Scotland where flatfish, especially dabs [*Limanda limanda* (L.)] were the most important food items, led to the conclusion that cormorants could have serious effects on fish stocks in more enclosed sea lochs (Mills, 1969). Earlier, Mills (1965) had found that cormorants on lochs and rivers ate mainly brown trout (*Salmo trutta* L.), perch and salmon, as distinct from the flatfish, gadoids and clupeoids favoured in estuaries, and, since trout of around 10 in. (25·4 cm) in length were eaten, the birds were in potential competition with anglers. District fishery boards offered bounty payments to encourage cormorant control on inland waters. Like all bounty schemes it was subject to abuse for people found it easier to shoot birds on the coast, where they do no harm, and then to claim the reward as if the birds had been shot inland (Mills, 1965).

The sawbill ducks, goosander (*Mergus merganser* L.) and red-breasted merganser (*M. serrator* L.), prey on sub-adult salmonid fish in rivers and lochs and are disliked by anglers. It is unlikely that they cause any harm to Scottish fisheries in general but they may do damage if they concentrate on hatchery reared fish (Mills, 1962). Elson (1962) released known numbers of salmon under-yearlings reared in hatcheries into the Pollett River, New Brunswick, and recorded their survival by recapture techniques, according to whether or not goosanders (the American merganser) and belted kingfishers [*Mergaceryle alcyon* (L.)] were killed. The number of goosanders and kingfishers killed depended on the availability of salmon parr and minnows, respectively. The average goosander density was one bird per 6–8 acres (2·4–3·2 ha) but the benefits of control were small until bird numbers were reduced to one per 18 acres (7·3 ha), and there were no further gains when bird numbers were below one per 55 acres (22·2 ha). It has yet to be shown convincingly that increasing the number of immature salmon which are reared in a river as a result of killing birds results in an increase in the number of adult salmon later returning to the river; Huntsman (1941) claimed a positive correlation between smolt output and size of the subsequent commercial fishery. No studies have been made of the impact of fish-eating birds, including herons and egrets (Ardeidae), on the fish-pond cultures which are initially stocked with small fish and which are such a feature of many parts of S.E. Asia.

Problems with birds and fisheries usually resolve into complex predator–prey relationships, with man and the bird being predators which compete for the same prey stocks. The difficulty of evaluating the significance of such interacting systems is well illustrated by the oystercatcher (*Haematopus ostralegus* L.) and its impact on the cockle industry.

B. OYSTERCATCHERS AND COCKLES

Cockles (*Cardium edule* L.) have been fished at four main stations in Britain by means of traditional local industries. For example in the Burry Inlet, Wales, where one-third of the country's total landings were made in the 1950's (Hancock and Urquhart, 1966), the industry has existed for 100 years giving part time employment to over 200 women. Since 1954, the landings at the Burry have declined so that by 1965 usually only 40–50 cockle gatherers took part in the industry each taking 2–3 cwt (102–152 kg) of cockles per tide during the four weekdays when most fishing was done. Davidson (1967, 1968) has calculated that over three winters oystercatchers removed between 557 and 1237 million second winter and older cockles compared with fishing catches of 46–128 million and total stocks of 1001–3232 million of the same age groups. A storm of protest from naturalists followed the decision of the Secretary of State for Wales and the Minister of Agriculture to improve fishing prospects by authorizing the South Wales Sea Fisheries Committee to cull half of the oystercatcher population over two years, this amounted to 11 000 birds. The cull started in August 1973 and a bounty of 25p was paid for each bird killed. The population at risk comprised 10% of the British and 4% of the West European population and the decision brought a letter of protest from the Norsk Ornitologisk Forening quite apart from much home reaction. In fact, the bulk of the Faeroese, Icelandic and British breeding populations of oystercatchers winter on the British coast, especially round the Irish Sea, while continental populations remain on the European mainland and winter in such areas as the Dutch Waddensea (Dare, 1966, 1970).

The population dynamics of the cockle have been intensively studied by D. A. Hancock and his colleagues and also to some extent by Dutch workers (Kristensen, 1957). Recruitment of young animals can be very variable from year to year depending much on the density of settled cockles. A hard winter in 1962–3 wiped-out cockle stocks in many places. Settlement in the following May and thereafter was so poor in the Morecambe Bay and Dee Estuary areas that the fisheries have never recovered, nor have oystercatcher numbers reached anything like their previous levels. In contrast, a spectacular settlement occurred in the Burry Inlet in 1963. This led to such a glut in 1964 that the market was unable to take immediate advantage of the extra yield and the birds were also unable to make much impression on the surplus. A processing plant was re-opened in 1966, while a deep-freezing plant took cockles in 1967 providing an outlet for 300 tons (270 tonnes) per month. Markets expanded as a result. Survival after settlement is also variable, for reasons that have nothing to do with oystercatchers, but the key-factor determining fluctuations in cockle numbers from year to year is clearly the settlement rate (see also analysis by Dempster, 1975).

Oystercatchers prefer second winter cockles as was well shown by Hancock and Urquhart (1965) when they erected exclosures on the Burry Sands (Fig. 13). If unable to obtain sufficient second year cockles, the birds will eat other age groups. Fishermen remove the largest cockles of the second-year category and those older when they reach the legal size for commercial fishing (this is about 23 mm in S. Wales). Few cockles reach a size of 30–35 mm by which age their shell is too tough for the birds to break. Bird predation on second-year cockles is density-dependent within any one season and the birds can feed successfully at densities of less than 20 per m^2 (Hancock, 1971). Predation by fishermen is less clearly related to density, partly because fishing is uneconomic at densities of less than 100 cockles per m^2.

Figure 14 from Hancock (1971) shows how oystercatcher numbers

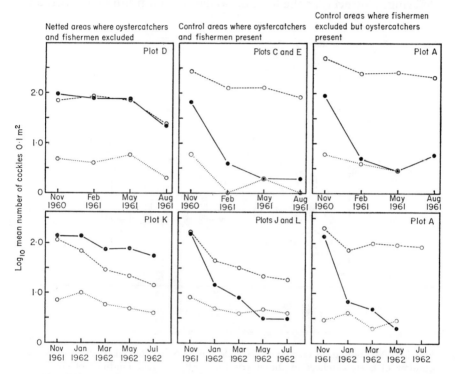

Fig. 13. Mean number of cockles per 0·1 m^2 in various experimental plots sited on the Llanrhidian Sands, Burry Inlet, South Wales. Age group of cockles designated as: 1st year (open symbols and dashed line), 2nd year (solid symbols, solid line) and older cockles (open symbols and dotted line). (Data simplified from Hancock and Urquhart, 1965.)

have varied in relation to stocks of first-year, second-year and older cockles in the Burry Inlet and the number and weight of cockles removed by fishermen. From 1958 to 1962 when oystercatchers consistently removed second-year cockles, the number of spawning cockles which survived the winter was low, but they reproduced well and recruitment was regularly good. However, only a low level of fishing could be supported during this phase. The severe 1962–3 winter initiated a new situation. Successful recruitment occurred only every second year. Numbers of the total stock became variable although differences in the age composition of the population reduced the variation in biomass. Oystercatchers could no longer specialize on second-year cockles and as these survived better through their second winter this allowed a much sounder fishery, at first without recruitment suffering. However, as the level of predation and fishing increased and

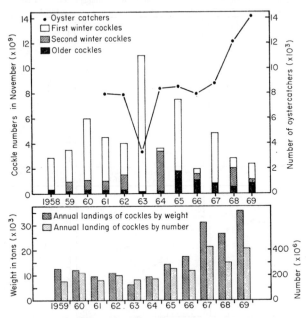

FIG. 14. (A) Population estimates of cockle numbers in November and the average number of oystercatchers in the Burry Inlet. (B) Annual landings of cockles by weight and by number. (Slightly modified from Hancock, 1971.)

the population became reduced, the recruitment rate declined. It was thought that 1971 might mark the return to the pre-1963 regular recruitment pattern allowing heavy predation of second-year cockles to occur with poor fishing prospects. But as the oystercatcher population has now risen above the pre-1963 level it is not clear what might happen in the future. The situation is complicated because oyster-catcher population size is probably regulated by events occurring immediately following breeding and the survivors can distribute themselves among different feeding grounds according to food availability. Thus there has been an increase in breeding oystercatchers in inland habitats in Scotland (Heppleston, 1972) and many birds feed inland on grass fields where they obtain earthworms (Lumbricidae) (Heppleston, 1971).

There might be grounds for altering the method of exploitation to compete more efficiently with oystercatchers. Two rather distinctive attitudes are possible depending on whether the need is (a) to maintain a traditional local industry and safeguard the fishing prospects of relatively few families or (b) expand the industry as efficiently as possible, without upsetting the livelihood of local fishermen, in order to take advantage of a growing market for cockles. In the first place, the fishermen are evidently in direct competition with the birds during the winter season. In the second situation (b) the number of cockles left at the end of the winter season assumes greater significance, as this stock will produce the next generation of spat, and the efficient exploitation of the fishery makes it undesirable to rely on a single-year class. At one time the fishermen of the Burry Inlet limited their catch to two bags (2 cwt) per day in order to conserve stocks, and because they needed to maintain a regular catch for fresh markets thereby ensuring stability in sales and prices. The alternative was to collect as many cockles as possible at the beginning of the winter, before oystercatchers or other agents could take their toll. But for this approach the whole structure of the industry, its fishing methods, means of storage, and presentation of the final product would have to be radically changed.

It was clear after virtual recruitment failure in 1968 and 1969 that the May 1970 cockle stock would not be adequate to support both predation and fishing at the level recorded in 1968 and 1969 and the choice was to refrain from fishing or to kill the birds. This was the background to the outcry against killing oystercatchers. We believe that the scale of kill relative to the European population to be too trivial to justify concern amongst conservationists. At the same time, it seems unlikely that enough animals will be killed to bring real benefits, because the limited cull must simply improve the feeding prospects for the remaining birds; immigration could also nullify this effort. We criticize the scheme on the grounds that it appears to be motivated more as a political gesture to the fishermen than as a serious scientific effort to improve the fishing industry. If birds must be killed, and factual experiments are needed, more efficient means than shooting might have been sought in view of experiences already gained about this method of control and the wisdom of making subsidy payments (p. 133).

Oystercatchers will eat other shellfish in the absence of cockles, including edible mussels (*Mytilus edulis* L.) and *Macoma baltica* L. Losses of experimentally grown mussels from rafts and floats in Argyll were attributable to eider ducks [*Somateria mollissima* (L.)]. The maximum loss due to the birds in one year was estimated at 3000 kg equivalent to 3–6% of the whole commercial crop (Dunthorn, 1971).

VII. Summary Of Control Techniques

References to the different kinds of control methods which have been applied to combat the harm caused by pestiferous birds are scattered in appropriate parts of the text. Some readers may find it convenient to have a classified summary of the methods in use and an index to the texts dealing with the particular topic (Table II).

TABLE II

Environmental Management

1. Ecological approaches. These cover situations where bird pest problems arise through the mis-use, or inappropriate management, of environmental resources and where alterations in land-use or resource management result in a lessening of bird damage. — Sections 1V, A, 2; 1V, C, 2, d; IV, E, 2, c; IV, F, 1; V, A, 1, a.

2. Habitat manipulation. Alterations of the habitat to reduce bird problems, not necessarily in accordance with best ecological procedures, and often particularly relevant in the environs of airfields. — Sections II, B, 2, a; II, D, 4; IV, E, 2, c.

Killing Methods

1. Trapping and netting — Sections II, C, 2, a; II, D, 4; IV, c, 2, b; V, A, i, b.

2. Poisons:
   Poison baits — Section II, C, 2, a.
   Poison sprays (ground and aerial) — Section IV, B, 3, b.
   Surfactants (wetting agents) — Section IV, D, 4, b.

3. Stupefying agents and baits — Sections II, C, 2, a; II, D, 4; IV, E, 2, b; IV, G, 2.

4. Shooting, also effect of — Sections IV, E, 2, a; IV, G, 1; VI, B.

5. Reproduction inhibitors — Section II, D, 4, d.

6. Destruction of eggs — Section II, C, 2, b.

7. Natural population regulation — Section IV, E, 2, c.

8. Artificial population control:
   Ecological assessment — Sections IV, B, 3, a; IV, E; IV, E, 2, a; IV, G, 1; VI, A.

   Bounty schemes — Sections IV, E, 2, a; VI, A; VI, B.

Scaring methods

1. Scarecrows:

Artificial	Section IV, F, 2.
Human personnel	Section IV, C, 2, a.
Birds of prey	Section II, B, 2, c.
Coloured lights	Section II, B, 2, c.
Pyrotechnics	Sections II, B, 2, c; IV, C, 2, a.

2. Chemical repellents — Sections IV, C, 2, a; IV, D, 4, a; IV, F, 3; IV, G, 2; V, A, 1, b.

Avitrol	Section IV, C, 2, a.

3. Auditory repellents:

Noise machines	Section IV, B, 3, c.
Recorded distress calls (bio-acoustics)	Sections II, B, 2, d; IV, B, 3, c.
Ultrasonics	Section LL, B, 2, d.

Physical protection

1. Proofing	Section V.
2. Protective Cages	Sections IV, D, 2; V, B.

Pest resistant crop varieties	Sections IV, B, 3, c; IV, C, 2, c.
Early warning	Sections II, B, 2, a; V.

The subject matter in this review is too diverse for convenient summary and Table II, locating text references to control methods, and the table of contents given at the beginning must suffice. There is no single conclusion that can be drawn about the problems posed by birds except to comment that in many instances it would have been wiser to adopt a policy of "laissez faire." Certainly, a pragmatic approach is desirable in dealing with most problem birds but there remain situations where, in the long term, appropriate widescale land management is likely to provide "ecological" solutions. The two most notorious "plague" birds are associated with subsistence agricultures in which cereal crops are grown on poor soils, intermixed with large areas of native vegetation; this applies to the weaver finch (*Quelea quelea*) in Africa and the eared dove (*Zenaida auriculata* Des Murs) in South America. P. Ward (pers. comm.) has expressed concern that a successful campaign which effectively removes *Quelea* could allow the widespread, and gregarious golden sparrow [*Passer luteus* (Licht.)] to expand to occupy the vacant niche. Whether this species would be able to exploit a patchy environment and whether, if it could, it would be so troublesome as *Quelea* it is interesting to speculate. It is to be noted that in extensive areas of fertile farming, as in the Argentinian pampa, where there is not a mosaic of both cultivated and natural habitat, the eared dove does not form the locust-like social gatherings which are so much a feature of scrublands, and which cause enormous crop losses. The distribution of the birds' food resources in the pampa does not encourage gregarious behaviour and similar ecological conditions apply in North America, where the closely related mourning dove (*Z. macruora* L.) is dispersed in small flocks and territorial pairs that do not cause intensive crop damage.

Why is the major gregarious bird pest of grain crops in Africa a passerine, with pigeons of secondary importance, whereas in South America a pigeon is the "locust" bird and grain eating passerines are of relatively little consequence? The answer presumably resides in the agricultural systems practised and the consequent pattern of resource dispersion. The "K" selection of MacArthur (1962) is relevant here. So too is the idea of Hamilton *et al.* (1967; also Hamilton and Gilbert, 1969) as applied to starlings, that dispersing birds behave to maximize the efficiency and rate of energy gain. These authors hypothesize that with increased distance from the central roost the number of individuals per unit area decreases, thereby relaxing intra-specific competition for resources. This supposedly compensates those individuals which have had to range further afield for their increased energy expenditure and flying time in reaching these more distant ranges. Pigeons and doves have advantages over passerines in terms of their energetics. They have a larger body size and lower metabolic rate (see Kendeigh, 1970) and so can make better relative use of food resources. Moreover, they have evolved some special adaptations which help to reduce and even cut their demands for energy; pigeons tend to avoid a need for marked peaks in environmental energy supplies, which passerines require to satisfy the demands of such seasonal body functions as a rapid moult, or the feeding of hungry poikilothermic nestlings. These adaptations of pigeons (see Murton *et al.*, 1974a) include: the possession of an oesophageal storage organ (crop), associated with which are two areas of glandular cells, which produce pigeon-milk; the ability to feed young from birth on a very nutritive food, in turn allowing the female to produce a small egg relative to her body size; a moulting season extended over about nine months so that little energy is needed for feather replacement at any one time. These adaptations enable pigeons to be independent of animal foods when breeding and to range long distances for food.

Reference to Fig. 4 indicates that the regression line relating food dispersion to flock size in pigeons has a shallower slope than might conceivably apply to passerines, although unfortunately few comparative data are available for the latter taxon to prove this point. Nevertheless, it is reasonable to suspect that flock size might become limiting in relation to food dispersion in passerines sooner than in pigeons. In absolute terms most passerines (according to body size) are able to subsist on a smaller quantity of food than can most pigeons so that agricultural niches that cannot be utilized by the latter will be available to them for exploitation. However, the capacity of passerines to establish themselves in an area of monoculture will depend on their ability to form a social gathering of appropriate size and to disperse. In North America, the social icterids, notably the red-winged blackbird, are markedly tied to extensive marshland areas and cattail swamps for breeding and their crop depredations are limited to the areas immediately surrounding these centres. Robertson (1973) suggests that the relative abundance of food for nestlings is the same in marshes or uplands but the higher absolute abundance of food in marshes allows the large, dense nesting colonies to be formed.

Future programmes aimed at mitigating the damage caused by the major pestiferous birds will clearly have to be based on a wider ecological assessment than is apparently demanded in the context of the actual problem situation.

References

Acad. Nauk. S.S.R. Siberian Branch (1969). Symposium on the study of role of migrating birds in distribution of Arboviruses (5th).

Aguirre, A. (1964). As avoantes do nordeste. *Estud. Técnico* No. 24. Ministry of Agric. Brasil. 47 p. Rio de Janeiro.

Alerstam, T. and Ulfstrand, S. (1974). A radar study of the autumn migration of Wood Pigeons *Columba palumbus* in southern Scandinavia. *Ibis*, **116**, 522–542.

Andrewes, C. H. and Mills, K. C. (1943). Psittacosis (ornithosis) virus in English pigeons. *Lancet* **1**, 292–4.

Anon. (1955a). Recommendations. (CCTA/CSA Africa (55) 129). CSA Réunion des Spécialistes du *Quelea*, Dakar 1955 Bukavu, Secrétariat Conjoint CCTA/CSA. 5 pp.

Anon. (1955b). Notes on bird-proof grain. (CCTA/CSA Africa (55) 111). Bukava, CCTA/CSA Joint Secretariat. 1 p.

Anon. (1956). Results of experimental spraying in Tanganyika with Parathion following the successful work done in South Africa. (CCTA/CSA Africa (56) 96). Bukavu, CCTA/CSA Joint Secretariat. 6 pp.

Anon. (1957). Report by the Field Officer (Bird Control) Moshi-Tanganyika. *Quelea*. 26.1.57 to 3.5.57. (CCTA/CSA Africa (57) QB7). CSA Symposium on *Quelea*, Livingstone, 1957. Bukavu, CCTA/CSA Joint Secretariat 4 pp.

Anon. (1960a). CCTA/FAO Symposium on *Quelea*, Bamako, 1960 Lagos, Nairobi and London CCTA/CSA Publ. No. 58.

Anon. (1960b). A critical assessment of control measures employed in West Africa by the Joint Organisation for Bird Control (OCLAV). (CCTA/CSA *Quelea* (60) 14). CCTA/FAO Symposium on *Quelea*, Bamako, 1960. Lagos, Nairobi and London, CCTA/CSA Publ. No. 58, 161–165.

Anon. (1968). *Quelea* control. 3. Farmer devises effective spraying technique. *Rhod. Fmr.*, 31 May 1968, 14–15.

Associate Committee on Bird Hazards to Aircraft. (1971–1972). Field notes. Ottawa Nat. Res. Council, Canada.

Aubry, J. (1970). Les déplacements du Bouvreuil pivoine, *Pyrrhula pyrrhula* (L.) en France. *Ann. Zool. Ecol. anim.* **2**, 509–522.

Austin-Smith, P. J. and Lewis, H. F. (1969). Alternative vegetative ground cover. "Proc. World Conf. Bird Hazards to Aircraft," Kingston, Ontario, September 1969, pp. 155–160.

Babudieri, B. (1960). Wild birds as carriers of pathogenic leptospira. *In* "Leptospirae and leptospirosis in man and animals." Polish Acad. Sci. Problem Ser. **19**, 88–92.

Beal, F. E. L. (1904). The relation of birds to fruit growing in California. Yearbook Agr. pp. 241–254.

Becker, K. (1968). Untersuchungen mit Sudanschwarz B zur Bestandsreglung verwilderter Haustauben. *Z. angew. Zool.* **55**, 427–446.

Becker, P. and Gilbert, E. G. (1958). Selective bird damage on pears in winter. *J. Roy. hort. Soc.* **83**, 509–515.

Becker, W. B. (1966). The isolation and classification of Tern virus; Influenza Virus A/Tern/South Africa/1961. *J. Hyg., Camb.* **64**, 309–320.

Beeker, W. J. (1953). Feeding adaptations and systematics in the avian order Piciformes. *J. Washington Acad. Sci.* **43**, 293–299.

Benson, G. B. G. and Williamson, K. (1972). Breeding birds of a mixed farm in Suffolk. *Bird Study* **19**, 35–50.

Berrens, L. and Maesen, F. (1971). An enzyme in pigeon droppings of possible relevance to pigeon breeder's disease. *Clin. exp. Immunol.* **9**, 383–389.

Berry, S. S. (1922). Magpies versus livestock: an unfortunate new chapter in avian depredations. *Condor* **24**, 13–17.

Besser, J. F., De Grazio, J. W. and Guarino, J. L. (1968). Costs of wintering Starlings and Red-winged Blackbirds at feedlots. *J. Wildl. Mgmt.* **32**, 179–180.

Binns, E. S. (1973). New or uncommon plant diseases and pests. *Pl. Path.* **22**, 197–198.

Bird, R. D. and Smith, L. B. (1964). The food habits of the Red-winged Blackbird *Agelaius phoeniceus* in Manitoba. *Canadian Field-Naturalist* **78** (3), 179–186.

Bird, W. H. (1965). Bird strike hazards can be reduced. Fifth National Conference on Environmental Effects on Aircraft and Propulsion Systems, Trenton, N.J. 15 September 1965. (mimeographed.)

Bird, W. H. (1966). Air Canada reported bird strikes/incidents. Air Canada, Montreal, December 1966 (mimeographed.)

Bjärvall, A. and Samuelsson, A. (1970). A study of grazing by Barnacle Geese *Branta leucopsis* on the island of Gotland. *Zool. Revy.* **32**, 26–33.

Blank, T. H., Southwood, T. R. E. and Cross, D. J. (1967). The ecology of the partridge. 1. Outline of population processes with particular reference to chick mortality and nest density. *J. Anim. Ecol.* **36**, 549–556.

Blaxland, J. D. (1951). Newcastle disease in shags and cormorants and its significance as a factor in the spread of this disease among domestic poultry. *Vet. Rec.* **63**, 731–733.

Blondel, J. and Isenmann, P. (1973). L'évolution de la structure des peuplements de laro-limicoles nicheurs de Camargue. *Terre Vie* **27**, 62–84.

Borg, K. (1955). On chloralose and its use in the capture of crows, gulls and pigeons (English Trans.) *Viltrevy-Jaktbiologisk Tidskrift* **1**, 88–121.

Boswall, J. (1966). The roosting of the Pied Wagtail in Dublin. *Bull. Br. Orn. Cl.* **86**, 131–140.

Boudreau, G. W. (1968). Alarm sounds and responses of birds and their application in controlling problem species. *The Living Bird* **7**, 27–46.

Bourne, W. R. P. (1969). Gulls and London's Airports. *B.T.O. News* **33**, 2–4.

Boyd, H. and Eltringham, S. K. (1962). The Whooper Swan in Great Britain. *Bird Study* **9**, 217–241.

Brémond, J.-C. (1963). Acoustic behaviour in birds. *In* "Acoustic Behaviour of Animals," pp. 709–750. Elsevier, Amsterdam.

Brémond, J.-C. (1965). Valeur réactogène de fréquences acoustiques dans le signal de défense territoriale du rouge-gorge (*Erithacus rubecula*). *C. r. hebd. Séanc. Acad. Sci., Paris.* **260**, 2910–2913.

Brémond, J.-C., Gramet, Ph., Brough, T. and Wright, E. N. (1968). A comparison of some broadcasting equipments and recorded distress calls for scaring birds. *J. appl. Ecol.* **5**, 521–529.

Bridgman, C. J. (1965). Seasonal variations in bird numbers on airfields. *In* "Colloque le Problème des Oiseaux sur les Aérodrome" (R. G. Busnel and J. Giban, eds), pp. 103–110. Institut National de la Recherche Agronomique, Paris.

Brink, B. W. (1969). Military aircraft command bird strike control program. "Proc. World Conf. Bird Hazards to Aircraft," Kingston, Ontario, September 1969, pp. 121–125.

Brisbin, I. L. (1968). The Passenger Pigeon. A study in the ecology of extinction. *Modern Game Breeding* **4**, 13–20.

Broadbent, L. (1965). The epidemiology of tomato mosaic. 9. Transmission of TMV by birds. *Ann. appl. Biol.* **55**, 67–69.

Brough, T. (1962–63). The problem of bird damage in horticulture. *Scient. Hort.* **16**, 35–41.

Brough, T. (1965). Field trials with the acoustical scaring apparatus in Britain. *In* "Colloque le Problème des Oiseaux sur les Aérodromes" (R. G. Busnel and J. Giban, eds), pp. 279–286. Institut National de la Recherche Agronomique, Paris.

Brough, T. (1967). The starling menace. *Grower*, **68**, 17.

Brough, T. (1968). Recent developments in bird scaring on airfields. *In* "The Problems of Birds as Pests" (R. K. Murton and E. N. Wright, eds.), pp. 29–38. Academic Press, London and New York.

Brough, T. (1969). The dispersal of Starlings from woodland roosts and the use of bio-acoustics. *J. appl. Ecol.* **6**, 403–410.

Brown, E. B. (1961). Linnet damage to strawberry fruit. *Pl. Path.* **10**, 41–42.

Brown, J. G. W. (1965). Birds on aerodromes the problems to the airline operator. *In* "Colloque le Problème des Oiseaux sur les Aérodromes" (R. G. Busnel and J. Giban, eds), pp. 31–32. Institut National de la Recherche Agromique, Paris.

Brown, L. H. (1969). Status and breeding success of Golden Eagles in northwest Sutherland in 1967. *Br. Birds* **62**, 345–363.

Brown, R. G. B. (1967). Breeding success and population growth in a colony of Herring and Lesser Black-backed Gulls *Larus argentatus* and *L. fuscus*. *Ibis* **109**, 502–515.

Bruyns, M. F. M. (1958). Gulls which are a menace to other species. The Herring Gull problem in the Netherlands. *Bull. Internat. Comm. Bird Pres.* **7**, 103–107.

Bucher, E. H. (1970). [Ecological considerations on the dove *Zenaida auriculata* as a pest of agricultural land in Córdoba, Argentine Republic.] Ministerio de Economia y Hacienda Dirección Provincial de Asuntos Agrarios. *Serie Ciencia y Tecnica* **1**, 1–11.

Burgess, D. (1963). Carrion crows in Northern England. *Agriculture* **70**, 126–129.

Busnel, R. G. and Giban, J. (1960). Colloque sur la protection acoustique des cultures. Institut National de la Recherche Agronomique, Paris.

Busnel, R. G. and Giban, J. (1965). Colloque sur le Problème des Oiseaux sur les Aérodromes. Nice 25–27 Novembre 1963. Institut National de la Recherche Agronomique, Paris.

Busnel, R. G. and Giban, J. (1968). Prospective considerations concerning bioacoustics in relation to bird-scaring techniques. *In* "The Problems of Birds as Pests" (R. K. Murton and E. N. Wright, eds), pp. 17–28. Academic Press, London and New York.

Busnel, R. G. and Gramet, P. (1955). Etudes préliminaires des réactions du *Quelea quelea quelea* Latham en captivité à des signaux acoustiques artificiels d'origines diverses. CSA Réunion des Spécialistes du *Quelea*, Dakar, 1955. Bukavu, Secrétariat Conjoint CCTA/CSA 10 pp.

Busnel, R. G. and Grosmaire, P. (1955). The traditional method of campaigning against *Quelea*. An enquiry among the people of the Senegal Valley. CCTA/CSA Africa (55). Joint Secretariat, Bukavu. Original report in French, partial translation by Crook (1956).

Caithness, T. A. (1968). Poisoning gulls with alpha-chloralose near a New Zealand airfield. *J. Wildl. Mgmt* **32**, 279–286.

Campbell, B. (1960). The Mute Swan census in England and Wales 1955–56. *Bird Study* **7**, 208–223.

Canadian Wildlife Service Report (1971). Series No. 14. Studies of bird hazards to aircraft. pp. 105.

Civil Aviation Authority (1973). Bird strikes to United Kingdom aircraft 1966–1971. Airworthiness technical note No. 106. pp. 50 (mimeographed). Civil Aviation Authority, Airworthiness Division, Brabazon House, Redhill, Surrey.

Clifford, C. M., Sonenshine, D. E., Atwood, E. L., Robbins, C. S. and Hughes, L. E. (1969). Tests on ticks from wild birds collected in the Eastern United States for Rickettsiae and viruses. *Am. J. Trop. Med. Hyg.* **18**, 1057–1061.

Clifford, C. M., Junker, C. E., Thomas, L. A., Easton, E. R. and Corwin, D. (1971). Isolation of a Group B arborivus from *Ixodes uriae* collected on Three Arch Rocks National Wildlife Refuge, Oregon. *Am. J. trop. Med. Hyg.* **20**, 461–468.

Cogswell, H. L. (1969). Gulls and solid waste disposal in the San Francisco Bay area, California. "Proc. World Conf. Bird Hazards to Aircraft," Kingston, Ontario, September 1969, pp. 131–134.

Cohen, E. (1960). Unusual roosting site of Pied Wagtails. *Br. Birds* **53**, 315.

Colquhoun, M. K. (1943). Preliminary trials with a narcotic bait for the control of Wood Pigeons. Report to the Agricultural Research Council (unpublished).

Colquhoun, M. K. (1951). "The Wood Pigeon in Britain." H.M.S.O., London.

Cook-Smith, R. A. W. (1965). The nature of bird strike incidents occurring at civil airfields in the United Kingdom. *In* "Colloque le Problème des Oiseaux sur les Aérodromes," Nice, 25–27 Novembre 1963 (R. G. Busnel and J. G. Giban, Eds), pp. 17–21. Institut National de la Recherche Agronomique, Paris.

Corkhill, P. (1970). Effect of egg puncturing on limiting chick production in Herring Gulls. *Bird Study* **17**, 340–342.

Cottam, C. and Trefethen, J. B. (Eds) (1968). "Whitewings." 348 pp. D. Van Nostrand Co., Inc.

Coulson, J. C. (1963). The status of the kittiwake in the British Isles. *Bird Study* **10**, 147–179.

Coulson, J. C. and Macdonald, A. (1962). Recent changes in the habits of the kitti-wake. *Br. Birds* **55**, 171–177.

Cramp, S., Pettet, A. and Sharrock, J. T. R. (1960). The irruption of tits in autumn 1957. *Br. Birds* **53**, 49–77; 99–117; 176–192.

Crook, J. H. (1964). The evolution of social organisation and visual communication in the weaver birds (Ploceinae). *Behaviour Suppl.* **10**, 178 pp.

Crook, J. H. (1957). Bird damage and crop protection in West Africa (CCTA/CSA Africa (57) QB4). CSA Symposium on *Quelea*, Livingstone, 1957. Bukavu, CCTA/CSA Joint Secretariat. 13 pp.

Crook, J. H. and Butterfield, P. A. (1970). Gender role in the social system of *Quelea*. *In* "Social Behaviour in Birds and Mammals" (J. H. Crook, Ed.), pp. 211–248. Academic Press, London and New York.

Crook, J. H. and Ward, P. (1968). The *Quelea* problem in Africa. *In* "The Problems of Birds as Pests" (R. K. Murton and E. N. Wright, Ed.), pp. 211–229. Academic Press, London and New York.

D.A.F.S. Advisory Leaflet (undated). Wild Geese and Agriculture.

Danzel, L. (1949). Contribution de la chloralose à la lutte contre les corbeaux. *Phytoma* **4**, 18.

Dare, P. J. (1966). The breeding and wintering populations of the Oystercatcher (*Haematopus ostralegus* L.) in the British Isles. *Fishery Invest., Lond.*, Ser. II, **15**(5), 69 pp.

Dare, P. J. (1970). The movements of Oystercatchers (*Haematopus ostralegus* L.) visiting or breeding in the British Isles. *Fishery Invest., Lond.* Ser. II **25**, 1–137.

Daude, J. L. (1942). Capture et destruction des corbeaux, pies et autres oiseaux nuisibles aux récoltes. *Bull. Acad. Med., Paris* **126**, 452–454.

Davidson, P. E. (1967). A study of the Oystercatcher (*Haematopus ostralegus* L.) in relation to the fishery for cockles (*Cardium edule* L.) in the Burry Inlet, South Wales. *Fishery Invest., Lond.* Ser. II, **15** (7), 28 pp.

Davidson, P. E. (1968). The Oystercatcher—a pest of shellfisheries. *In* "The Problems of Birds and Pests" (R. K. Murton and E. N. Wright, eds), pp. 144–155. Symp. Inst. of Biology. Academic Press, London and New York.

Davis, D. E. (1962). Gross effects of triethylenemelamine on the gonads of Starlings. *Anat. Rec.* **142**, 353–357.

Dawson, D. G. (1970). Estimation of grain loss due to Sparrows (*Passer domesticus*) in New Zealand. *N.Z. Jl. agric. Res.* **13**, 681–688.

Dawson, D. G. and Bull, P. C. (1970). A questionnaire survey of bird damage to fruit. *N.Z. Jl. agric. Res.* **13**, 362–371.

De Grazio, J. W. and Besser, J. F. (1970). Bird damage problems in Latin America. Proc. 4th Vert. Pest Control Conf. West Sacramento, Calif. March 3–5 1970, pp. 162–7.

De Grazio, J. W., Besser, J. F., De Cino, T. J., Guarino, J. L. and Starr, R. I. (1971). Use of 4-aminopyridine to protect ripening corn from blackbirds. *J. Wildl. Mgmt* **35**, 565–569.

De Grazio, J. W., Besser, J. F., De Cino, T. J., Guarino, J. L. and Schafer, E. W. (1972). Protecting ripening corn from blackbirds by broadcasting 4-amino-pyridine baits. *J. Wildl. Mgmt* **36**, 1316–1320.

Dempster, J. P. (1975). "Animal Population Ecology". Academic Press, London and New York.

Disney, H. J. de S. (1957). Annual Report on grain eating birds, 1956. (CCTA/CSA

Africa (57) QB5). CSA *Symposium on Quelea, Livingstone,* 1957 Bukavu, CCTA/CSA Joint Secretariat. 18 pp.

Disney, H. J. de S. (1964). *Quelea* Control. In "New Dictionary of Birds" (A. L. Thomson, ed.), pp. 673–674. Nelson: London and New York.

Disney, H. J. de S. and Haylock, J. W. (1956). The distribution and breeding behaviour of the Sudan Dioch (*Quelea q. aethiopica*) in Tanganyika. *E. Afr. agric. J.* **21,** 141–147.

Doggett, H. (1957). Bird-resistance in sorghum and the *Quelea* problem. *Fld. Crop Abstr.* **10,** 153–156.

Drost, R. (1958). The Herring Gull problem in Germany. *Bull. of ICBP, VII,* 108–111.

Drury, W. H. (1963). Results of a study of Herring Gull populations and movements in southeastern New England. In "Colloque le Problème des Oiseaux sur les Aérodromes" (R. G. Busnel and J. G. Giban, Eds), pp. 207–217. Institut. National de la Recherche Agronomique, Paris.

Drury, W. H. and Nisbet, I. C. T. (1972). The importance of movements in the biology of Herring Gulls in New England. In "Population Ecology of Migratory Birds": A Symposium 1969. U.S. Dept. of the Interior: Fish and Wildlife Service. Wild Life Research Report 2, pp. 173–212.

Duncan, C. J. (1960). Preference tests and the sense of taste in the feral pigeon. *Anim. Behav.* **8,** 54–60.

Duncan, C. J., Wright, E. N. and Ridpath, M. G. (1960). A review of the search for bird-repellent substances in Great Britain. *Annals des Epiphyties* **8,** 205–212.

Dunnet, G. M., Fordham, R. A. and Patterson, I. J. (1969). Ecological studies of the rook (*Corvus frugilegus* L.) in North-east Scotland. Proportion and distribution of young in the population. *J. appl. Ecol.* **6,** 459–473.

Dunning, R. A. (1974). Bird damage to sugar beet. *Ann. appl. Biol.* **76,** 325–335.

Dunning, R. A. and Winder, G. H. (1972). Some effects, especially on yield, of artificially defoliating sugar beet. *Ann. appl. Biol.* **70,** 89–98.

Dunthorn, A. A. (1971). The predation of cultivated mussels by Eiders. *Bird Study* **18,** 107–112.

Dunthorn, A. A. and Errington, F. P. (1964). Casualties among birds along a selected road in Wiltshire. *Bird Study* **11,** 168–182.

Dyer, M. I. (1964). Radar and morphometric studies on transient Red-winged Blackbird populations. Ph.D. Thesis, Univ. Minn.

Dyer, M. I. (1967). An analysis of blackbird flock feeding behaviour. *Can. J. Zool.* **45,** 765–772.

Dyer, M. I. (1969). Blackbird and Starling research program, 1964–1968. Publ. of the Ontario Dept. of Agric. and Food, 29 pp.

Dyer, M. I. (1975). The effects of Red-winged Blackbirds (*Agelaius phoeniceus* L.) on biomass production of corn grains (*Zea mays* L.). *J. Appl. Ecol.* **12,** 719–726

Easterday, B. C., Trainer, D. O., Tůmová, B. and Pereira, H. G. (1968). Evidence of infection with influenza viruses in migratory waterfowl. *Nature, Lond.* **219,** 523–524.

Eastwood, E. (1967). "Radar Ornithology". Methuen, London.

Eccles, M. A. (1939). Le role des oiseaux dans la propagation de la fievre aphteuse. *Bull. Int. Office of Epizootics.* **18,** 118.

Elder, W. H. (1964). Chemical inhibitors of ovulation in the pigeon. *J. Wildl. Mgmt.* **28,** 556–575.

Edgar, W. H. and Isaacson, A. J. (1974). Observations on skylark damage to sugar beet and lettuce seedlings in East Anglia. *Ann. appl. Biol.* **76**, 335–337.

Ellenbogen, B. K. and Miller, C. M. (1952). Psittacosis in a family. *Br. med. J.* **2**, 189–190.

Elson, P. F. (1962). Predator-prey relationships between fish eating birds and Atlantic Salmon. *Bull. Fish. Res. Bd Can. No.* 133.

Eltringham, S. K. (1963). The British population of the Mute Swan in 1961. *Bird Study* **10**, 10–28.

Emmons, C. W. (1961). Isolation of *Histoplasma capsulatum* from soil in Washington D.C. *Publ. Hlth. Rep., Wash.* **76**, 591–595.

English, W. S. (1953). Preventing bird damage to fruit tree buds. *Agriculture* **60**, 426–429.

Evans, P. R. (1973). Avian resources of the North Sea. *In* "North Sea Science" (E. D. Goldberg, Ed.), pp. 400–412. Cambridge, Mass. M.I.T. Press.

Finnis, R. G. (1960). Road casualties among birds. *Bird Study* **7**, 21–32.

Fisher, J. (1953). The Collared Turtle Dove in Europe. *Br. Birds* **46**, 153–181.

Fisher, J. (1966). The fulmar population of Britain and Ireland, 1959. *Bird Study*, **13**, 5–76.

Fisher, J and Hinde, R. A. (1949). The opening of milk bottles by birds. *Br. Birds* **42**, 347–357.

Fisher, R. A., Corbett, A. S. and Williams, C. B. (1943). The relation between the number of species and the number of individuals in a random sample of an animal population. *J. Anim. Ecol.* **12**, 42–58.

Fowler, H. S. (1967). Bird distribution and strike date. Associate Committee on Bird Hazards to Aircraft, National Research Council of Canada, Field Note No. 42.

Frade, F. (1960). *Quelea* in Guinea, Angola and Mozambique. (CCTA/CSA *Quelea* (60) 16). CCTA/FAO Symposium on Quelea, Bamako, 1960. Lagos, Nairobi and London. CCTA/CSA. Publ. No. 58, pp. 179–180.

Frings, H. (1954). Controlling pest birds with sound. "Proc. natn. Shade Tree Conf.", pp. 108–112.

Frings, H. (1962). Observations on acoustical control of Starlings. *Annals. Epiphyte.* **13**, 1st series, 87–94.

Frings, H. and Frings, M. (1962). Pest control with sound. Part I: Possibilities with invertebrates. *Sound* **1**(6), 13–20.

Frings, H. and Frings, M. (1963). Pest control with sound. Part II: The problem with vertebrates. *Sound* **2**(1), 39–45.

Frings, H. and Jumber, J. (1954). Preliminary studies on the use of a specific sound to repel Starlings (*Sturnus vulgaris*) from objectionable roosts. *Science N.Y.* **119**, 318–319.

Frith, H. J. and Davies, S. J. J. F. (1961). Ecology of the Magpie Goose, *Anseranas semipalmata* Latham (Anatidae). *CSIRO Wildl. Res.* **6**, 91–141.

Fryer, J. C. F. (1939). The destruction of buds of trees and shrubs by birds. *Br. Birds* **33**, 90–94.

Fuggles-Couchman, N. R. (1936). Some observations on birds raiding rice fields in Kilosa district, Tanganyika Territory. *E. Afr. agric. J.* **2**, 54–59.

Furcolow, M. L., Tosh, F. E., Larsh, H. W., Lynch, H. J. and Shaw, G. (1961). The emerging pattern of urban histoplasmosis. *New Engl. J. Med.* **264**, 1226–1230.

Giban, J. (1950). Recherches sur l'action du chloralose ou glucochloral chez les oiseaux. *Annals. Inst. natn. Rech. agron., Paris.* Ser. C. **1**, 337–366.

Gibb, J. A. (1970). A pigeon's choice of plums. *Notornis* **17**, 239.

Gillespie, A. C. (1952). *State vet. J.* **7**, p. 68.

Gillham, M. E. (1956). Feeding habits and seasonal movements of Mute Swans on two South Devon estuaries. *Bird Study* 3, 205–212.

Gloe, P. (1971). Besiedlung der Insel Helmsand durch die Lachmöwe (*Larus ridibundus*) und ihr Eindringen in die Brutplatze der Fluss-und Küstenseeschwalben (*Sterna hirundo* et *St. paradisaea*). *Corax* 3, 176–183.

Goethe, F. (1969). Zur Einwanderung der Lachmöwe (*Larus ridibundus*), in das Gebiet der deutschen Nordseeküste und ihrer Inseln. *Bonn. zool. Beitr.* 20, 164–170.

Goodhue, L. D. and Baumgartner, F. M. (1965a). The Avitrol method of bird control. *Pest Control* 33(7), 16–17, 46, 48.

Goodhue, L. D. and Baumgartner, F. M. (1965b). Applications of new bird control chemicals. *J. Wildl. Mgmt.* 29(4), 830–837.

Graham, F. H. (1954). Control of native hens in Tasmania. *Tas. J. Agric.* 25, 368–370.

Greenwood, E. A. N. and Titmanis, Z. U. (1968). The effect of defoliation on nitrogen stress, leaf nitrogen, growth rate, and soluble carbohydrates in young *Lolium rigidum* Gaud. *Aust. J. agric. Res.* 19, 9–14.

Grimes, L. G. (1972). The potential bird and bat hazards to aircraft in the vicinity of the international airport at Accra, Ghana. *Ghana J. Sci.* 13, 10–19.

Grist, N. R. (1960). Ornithosis and the railway guards (Letter). *Lancet* (ii) No. 7143, 207.

Gross, A. O. (1950). The Herring Gull–Cormorant control project. *Proc. Int. Orn. Cong.* 10, 532–536.

Gunn, W. W. H. and Solman, V. E. F. (1968). A bird-warning system for aircraft in flight. *In* "The Problems of Birds as Pests" (R. K. Murton and E N. Wright, Eds), pp. 87–96. Symp. Instit. of Biol. Academic Press, London and New York.

Gurchinoff, S. and Robinson, W. L. (1972). Chemical characteristics of jackpine needles selected by feeding Spruce Grouse. *J. Wildl. Mgmt.* 36, 80–87.

Gustafson, D. P. and Moses, H. E. (1953). The English sparrow as a natural carrier of Newcastle disease virus. *Am. J. vet. Res.* 14, 581–585.

Haig, D. A. and McDiarmid, A. (1963). Occurrence of ornithosis in the Wood Pigeon. *Nature, Lond.* 200, 381–382.

Hamilton, W.J. and Gilbert, W. M. (1969). Starling dispersal from a winter roost. *Ecology* 50, 886–898.

Hamilton, W. J., Gilbert, W. M., Heppner, F. H. and Planck, R. J. (1967). Starling roost dispersal and a hypothetical mechanism regulating rhythmical animal movement to and from dispersal centers. *Ecology* 48, 825–833.

Hammer, M. (1948). Investigations on the feeding-habits of the House Sparrow (*Passer domesticus*) and the Tree Sparrow (*Passer montanus*). *Danish Rev. Game Biol.* 1, 1–59.

Hancock, D. A. (1971). The role of predators and parasites in a fishery for the mollusc *Cardium edule* L. *In* "Dynamics of Populations." Proceedings of the NATO Advanced Study Institute, Oosterbeek, 1970 (P. J. den Boer and G. R. Gradwell, Eds), pp. 419–439. Wageningen Centre for Agricultural Publishing and Documentation.

Hancock, D. A. and Urquhart, A. E. (1965). The determination of natural mortality and its causes in an exploited population of cockles (*Cardium edule* L.) *Fishery Invest., Lond. Ser.* 2, 12(2). 40 pp.

Hancock, D. A. and Urquhart, A. E. (1966). The fishery for cockles (*Cardium edule* L.) in the Burry Inlet, South Wales. *Fishery Invest., Lond. Ser.* 2, 15(3), 32 pp.

Hansen, L. (1969). [Roadkill of Danish vertebrates.] *Dansk. orn. Foren. Tidsskr.* 63, 81–92.

Harbourne, J. F. (1955). The isolation of *Salmonella gallinarum* in wild birds. *J. comp. Path.* 65, 250–254.

Hardenberg, J. D. F. (1965). Clearance of birds on airfields. In "Colloque le problème des oiseaux sur les aérodromes," Nice. 25–27 Novembre 1963 (R. G. Busnel and J. Giban, Eds), pp. 121–126. Instit National de la Recherche Agronomique, Paris.

Hardman, J. A. (1974). Biology of the skylark. Ann. appl. Biol. 76, 337–341.

Harper, W. G. (1957). "Angels" on centimetric radars caused by birds. Nature, Lond. 180, 847–849.

Harris, M. P. (1964). Aspects of the breeding biology of the gulls Larus argentatus, L. fuscus and L. marinus. Ibis, 106, 432–456.

Harris, M. P. (1970). Rates and causes of increases of some British gull populations. Bird Study 17, 325–335.

Harris, R. D. (1965). The bird strike problem at Vancouver International Airport. Associate Committee on Bird Hazards to Aircraft, National Research Council of Canada, Field Note No. 27.

Hart, P. F. (1969). Military bird strikes in the United Kingdom. "Proc. World Conf. Bird Hazards to Aircraft," Kingston, Ontario, September 1969, pp. 21–30.

Hawkins, J. E. and Bull, P. C. (1962). Controlling redpolls in Otago orchards. The Orchardist New Zealand, May 1962.

Haylock, J. W. (1959). Investigations on the habits of Quelea birds and their control. Nairobi, Government Printers, 16 pp.

Heppleston, P. B. (1971). The feeding ecology of Oystercatchers (Haematopus ostralegus L.) in winter in northern Scotland. J. Anim. Ecol. 40, 651–672.

Heppleston, P. B. (1972). The comparative breeding ecology of Oystercatchers (Haematopus ostralegus L.) in inland and coastal habitats. J. Anim. Ecol. 41, 23–51.

Hickling, R. A. O. (1967). The inland wintering of gulls in England, 1963. Bird Study, 14, 104–113.

Hickling, R. A. O. (1969). The increase of gulls. Ibis 111, 445.

Hild, J. (1969a). Bird strikes in the German Air Force. "Proc. World Conf. Bird Hazards to Aircraft," Kingston, Ontario, September 1969, pp. 31–42.

Hild, J. (1969b). Methods of ecological research on airfields. "Proc. World Conf. Bird Hazards to Aircraft," Kingston, Ontario, September 1969, pp. 135–142.

Hinde, R. A. and Fisher, J. (1951). Further observations on the opening of milk bottles by birds. Br. Birds 44, 393–396.

Hodson, N. L. (1960). A survey of vertebrate road mortality 1959. Bird Study 7, 224–231.

Hodson, N. L. (1962). Some notes on the causes of bird road casualties. Bird Study 9, 168–173.

Hodson, N. L. and Snow, D. W. (1965). The road deaths enquiry 1960–61. Bird Study 12, 90–99.

Hoffman, R. S. (1961). The quality of the winter food of blue grouse. J. Wildl. Mgmt. 25, 209–210.

Hoogstraal, H. (1968). A brief history of the NAMRU-3 Medical Zoology Program. J. Egypt. Publ. Hlth. Ass. 43 (Special No.), 70–94.

Hoogstraal, H. (1969). Ornithodoros (Alectorobius) muesebecki, n.sp., a parasite of the blue-faced booby (Sula dactylatra melanops) on Hasikiya Island, Arabian Sea (Ixodoidea: Argasidae). Proc. Entomol. Soc. Washington 71(3), 368–374.

Hoogstraal, H., Oliver, R. M. and Guirgis, S. S. (1970). Larva, nymph, and life cycle of Ornithodoros (Alectorobius) muesebecki (Ixodoidea: Argasidae), a virus-infected parasite of birds and petroleum industry employees in the Arabian Gulf. Ann. Ent. Soc. Amer. 63, 1762–1768.

Hudson, R. (1965). The spread of the Collared Dove in Britain and Ireland. Br. Birds 58, 105–139.

Hudson, R. (1972). Collared Doves in Britain and Ireland during 1965–70. *Br. Birds* **65**, 139–155.

Hughes, D. L. (1957). Man and his animals. *Vet. Rec.* **69**, 1061–1065.

Hughes, W. M. (1965). Trapping and banding birds of prey on Vancouver International Airport, 1964–1965. Associate committee on Bird Hazards to Aircraft, National Research Council of Canada. Field Note No. 38.

Hughes, W. M. (1966). Birds trapped on Vancouver International Airport, banded and released, January 1964, May 15 1967. Associate Committee on Bird Hazards to Aircraft, National Research Council of Canada, Field Note No. 47.

Hunter, F. A. (1974). Preliminary practical assessments of some bird scaring methods against Wood Pigeons. *Ann. appl. Biol.* **76**, 351–353.

Huntsman, A. G. (1941). Cyclical abundance of birds versus salmon. *J. Fish. Res. Bd. Canada* **5**(3), 227–235.

Hurter, H.-U. (1972). Nahrung und Ernährungsweise des Blässhuhns *Fulica atra* am Sempachersee. *Orn. Beob.* **69**, 125–149.

Jennings, A. R. (1954). Diseases in wild birds. *J. comp. Path.* **64**, 356–359.

Johnson, A. W. (1967). "The birds of Chile". Platt Establecimientos Graficos S.A., Buenos Aires, Argentina. (2 Vols.)

Johnstone, D. R., Huntington, K. A. and Coutts, H. H. (1974). Penetration of spray droplets applied by helicopter into a riverine forest habitat of tsetse flies in West Africa. *Agric. Aviat.* **16**, 71–82.

Johnstone, G. W. (1967). Black game and capercaillie in relation to forestry in Britain. *In* "Wildlife in the Forest," pp. 68–77. Rep. of 7th Discussion Meeting, Cirencester 1967, Forestry Suppl. Oxford University Press.

Jones, B. E. (1974). Factors influencing Wood Pigeon (*Columba palumbus*) damage to brassica crops in the Vale of Evesham. *Ann. appl. Biol.* **76**, 345–350.

Jones, Pamela, Kominkova, Eva and Jackson, H. (1972). Effects of antifertility substances on male Japanese Quail. *J. Reprod. Fert.* **29**, 71–78.

Kadlec, J. A. and Drury, W. H. (1968). Structure of the New England Herring Gull population. *Ecology* **49**(4), 644–676.

Kear, J. (1963a). Wildfowl and agriculture. *In* "Wildfowl in Great Britain" (G. L. Atkinson-Willes, Ed.), pp. 315–328. Monog. No. 3 Nature Conservancy, London, H.M.S.O.

Kear, J. (1963b). The agricultural importance of wild goose droppings. *Wildfowl Trust Ann. Rep.* **14**, 72–77.

Kear, J. (1964). Wildfowl and agriculture in Britain. *In* "Proceedings of the M.A.R. Conference," I.U.C.N. Publication New Ser. 3, 321–331.

Kear, J. (1965a). Recent changes in Scottish barley acreages and the possible effect on wild geese. *Scot. Birds* **3**, 288–292.

Kear, J. (1965b). The assessment by grazing trial of goose damage to grass. *Wildfowl Trust Ann. Rep.* **16**, 46–47.

Kear, J. (1966). The food of geese. *Int. Zoo. Yb.* **6**, 98–103.

Kear, J. (1967). The feeding habits of the Greylag Goose *Anser anser* in Iceland, with reference to its interaction with agriculture. *Proc. VIIth Int. Cong. Game Biol.* **7**, 615–622.

Kear, J. (1970). The experimental assessment of goose damage to agricultural crops. *Biol. Conserv.* **2**, 206–212.

Keast, A. K. (1971). Adaptive evolution and shifts in niche occupation in island birds. *In* "Adaptive Aspects of Insular Evolution" (W. L. Stern, Ed.), pp. 39–53. Washington: Washington State University Press.

Kendeigh, S. C. (1970). Energy requirements for existance in relation to size of bird. *Condor* **72**, 60–65.

Kenward, R. E. (1976). The effect of predation by goshawks, *Accipiter gentilis,* on woodpigeon, *Columba palumbus,* populations. D. Phil. Thesis. University of Oxford.

Keymer, I. F. (1958). A survey and review of the causes of mortality in British birds and the significance of wild birds as disseminators of disease. *Vet. Rec.* **70**, 713–720; 736–740.

Kimber, D. S. (1963). Use of balloons as bird scares in field trials. *NAAS Quart. Rev.* **XV, 61,** 40–41.

Koehler, J. W. (1962). Linnets, horned larks, crowned sparrows and woodpeckers. "Proc. 2nd Vert. Pest Cont. Conf." pp. 174–185.

Krebs, J. R. (1970). Territory and beeding density in the Great Tit *Parus major* L. *Ecology* **52**, 2–22.

Kristensen, I. (1957). Differences in density and growth in a cockle population in the Dutch Wadden sea. *Archs néerl. Zool.* **12**, 351–453.

Krivenko, V. G., Lysenko, V. I. and Filonov, K. P. (1973). [Enlargement of the nest range of the Black-headed Gull *Larus melanocephalus.*] *Zool. Zh.* **52**, 618–619.

Kuyken, E. (1969). Grazing of wild geese on grasslands at Damme, Belgium. *Wildfowl* **20**, 47–54.

Kuhring, M. S. (1965). Equipment used in Canada for dispersing birds. *In* "Colloque le Problème des Oiseaux sur les Aérodromes" (R. G. Busnel and J. Giban, Eds), pp. 301–304. Institut National de la Recherche Agronomique, Paris.

Lack, D. (1945). The ecology of closely related species with special reference to cormorant (*Phalacrocorax carbo*) and shag (*P. aristotelis*). *J. anim. Ecol.* **14**, 12–16.

Lack, D. (1959a). Migration across the North Sea studied by radar. Part 1. Survey through the year. *Ibis* **101**, 209–234.

Lack, D. (1959b). Migration across the sea. *Ibis* **101**, 374–399.

Laflin, T. and English, W. S. (1960). Bird damage to buds of fruit trees and bushes. *Exp. Hort.* **3**, 13.

Langowski, D. J., Wight, H. M. and Jacobson, J. N. (1969). Responses of instrumentally conditioned Starlings to aversive acoustic stimuli. *J. Wildl. Mgmt.* **33,** 669–677.

Lavery, H. J. (1969). Collisions between aircraft and birds at Townsville, Queensland. *Qd J. agric. Sci.* **26**, 447–455.

Lavery, H. J. and Blackman, J. G. (1970). Sorghum damage by lorikeets. *Qd. agric. J.* 3 pp.

Lebreton, P. (1969). Sur le statut migratoire en France du Pigeon ramier *Columba palambus. Oiseau* **39**, 83–111.

Lefebure, P. W. and Seubert, J. L. (1970). Surfactants as blackbird stressing agents. Proc. Vertebrate Pest. Conf. 4th, 1970, pp. 156–161.

Lepine, M. P. and Sautter, V. (1951). Sur l'infection des pigeons parisiennes par le virus de l'ornithose. *Bull. Acad. natn. Md.* **135**, 332–338.

Lewis, M. F. (1967). Associate Committee on Bird Hazards to Aircraft. Bull. No. 5 National Research Council, Ottawa, Canada.

Lindroth, H. and Lindgren, L. (1950). [On the significance for forestry of the capercaillie, *Tetrao urogallus* L., feeding on pine-needles.] *Suomen. Riista* **5**, 60–81.

Lloyd-Evans, T. (1970). Bird strikes—low flying gull study. *B.T.O. News* **39**, 3.

Lockie, J. D. (1964). The breeding density of the Golden Eagle and fox in relation to food supply in Western Ross, Scotland. *Scot. Nat.* **71**, 67–77.

Lockie, J. D. and Stephen, D. (1959). Eagles, lambs and land management on Lewis. *J. Anim. Ecol.* **28**, 43–50.

Lofts, B., Murton, R. K. and Westwood, N. J. (1967). Photo-responses of the Wood Pigeon *Columba palumbus* in relation to the breeding season. *Ibis* **109**, 338–351.

Lofts, B., Murton, R. K. and Thearle, R. J. P. (1968). The effects of 22,25-diazacholesterol dihydrochloride on the pigeon testis and on reproductive behaviour. *J. Reprod. Fert.* **15**, 145–148.

Logan-Home, W. M. (1953). Paper tearing by birds. *Br. Birds* **46**, 16–21.

Londoño, V., Elias, D., Valencia, G. and Woronecki, P. W. (1972). Informe preliminar sobre la incidencia de torcaza naguiblanca (*Zenaida auriculata*) y su relación con problemas de daño a algunos cultivos en el valle del Cauca, Colombia. Inst. Colombiano Agropecuario, 11 pp.

Lord, R. D. and Calisher, C. H. (1970). Further evidence of southward transport of arboviruses by migratory birds. *Am. J. Epidemiology* **92**, 73–78.

Lourens, D. C. (1957). Parathion versus *Quelea* (CCTA/CSA Africa (57) QB11). CSA *Symposium on Quelea, Livingstone,* 1957. Bukavu, CCTA/CSA Joint Secretariat. 32 pp.

Lumsden, W. H. R. and Haddow, A. J. (1946). The food of the shag (*Phalacrocorax aristotelis*) in the Clyde sea area. *J. Anim. Ecol.* **15**, 35–42.

Lvov, D. K., Timopheeva, A. A., Chervonski, V. I., Gromashevski, V. L., Klisenko, G. A., Gostinshchikova, G. V. and Kostyrko, I. N. (1971). A new group B arbovirus isolated from *Ixodes (Ceratixodes) putus* Pick.-Camb. 1878 collected on Tuleniy Island, Sea of Okhotsk. *Am. J. Trop. Med. Hyg.* **20**, 456–460.

MacArthur, R. H. (1962). Some generalized theorems of natural selection. *Proc. Nat. Acad. Sci. U.S.A.* **48**, 1893–1897.

Macdonald, J. W. and Cornelius, L. W. (1969). Salmonellosis in wild birds. *Br. Birds* **62**, 28–30.

MacLellan, C. R. (1970). Woodpecker ecology in the apple orchard environment. "Proc. Tall Timbers Conf. on Ecological Animal Control by Habitat Management." Feb. 1970, pp. 273–284.

Madsen, J. and Spärck, R. (1950). On the feeding habits of the Southern cormorant. *Dan. Rev. Game Biol.* **1**, 45–75.

Magor, Joyce I. and Ward, P. (1972). Illustrated descriptions, distribution maps and bibliography of the species of *Quelea* (Weaver-birds: Ploceidae). Tropical Pest Bulletin 1. Centre for Overseas Pest Research.

Main, A. J., Downs, W. G., Shope, R. E. and Wallis, R. C. (1973). Great Island and Bauline: Two new Kemerovo group arboviruses from *Ixodes uriae* in Eastern Canada. *J. Med. Ent.* **10**, 229–235.

May, R. and Fisher, J. (1953). A Collared Turtle Dove in England. *Br. Birds* **46**, 51–55.

McClure, H. E. (1969). Migratory Animal Pathological Survey. Annual progress report 1968. U.S. Army Res. Devel. Group, Far East, Rep. No. FE-315-3.

McClure, H. E. (1971). Migratory Animal Pathological Survey. Annual Progress Report 1970. 18 pp.

McCoy, J. W. (1941). Injuries to Texas cattle caused by Starlings. *Vet. Med.* **36**, 432–433.

McDiarmid, A. (1960). Diseases of free-living wild mammals. F.A.O., Rome Anim. health monog. No. 1.

Mead, C. (1966a). B.T.O. to the rescue. *B.T.O. News* **19**, 2–3.

Mead, C. (1966b). Home Sweet Home. *B.T.O. News* **20**, 7.

Mewaldt, L. R. (1964). Effects of bird removal on a winter population of sparrows. *Bird-Banding*, **35**, 184–195.

Meyer, K. F. (1959). Some general remarks and new observations on psittacosis and ornithosis. *Bull. Wld. Hlth. Org.* **20**, 101–119.

Mills, D. H. (1962). The goosander and red-breasted merganser as predators of salmon in Scottish waters. D.A.F.S. Freshwater and Salmon Fisheries Research 29.

Mills, D. H. (1965). The distribution and food of the cormorant in Scottish inland waters. D.A.F.S. Freshwater and Salmon Fisheries Research 35, 1–16.

Mills, D. (1969). The food of the Cormorant at two breeding colonies on the east coast of Scotland. *Scot. Birds* 5, 268–276.

Minton, C. D. T. (1960). Unusual roosting site of pied wagtails. *Br. Birds* 53, 132–133.

Mollhagen, T. R., Wiley, R. W. and Packard, R. L. (1972). Prey remains in Golden Eagle nests: Texas and New Mexico. *J. Wildl. Mgmt.* 36, 784–792.

Mosby, H. S. and Cantner, D. E. (1956). The use of Avertin in capturing wild turkeys and as an oral-basal anaesthetic for other wild animals. *Southwestern Veterinarian* 9, 132.

Morel, G. and Bourliére, F. (1955). Recherches écologiques sur *Quelea quelea quelea* L. de la basse vallée du Sénégal. 1. Données quantitatives sur le cycle annuel. *Bull. Inst. fr. Afr. noire*, (A), 17, 617–663.

Morel, G. and Bourliére, F. (1956). Recherches écologiques sur les *Quelea quelea quelea* (L) de la basse vallée du Sénégal. II. La reproduction. *Alauda* 24, 97–122.

Morel, G., Morel, M. Y. and Bourlière, F. (1957). The blackfaced weaver bird or dioch in West Africa. *J. Bombay nat. Hist. Soc.* 54, 811–825.

Mott, D. F., West, R. R., De Grazio, J. W. and Guarino, J. L. (1972). Foods of the Red-winged Blackbird in Brown County, South Dakota. *J. Wildl. Mgmt.* 36, 983–987.

Munro, D. A. and Harris, R. D. (1963). Some aspects of the bird hazard at Canadian airports. *In* "Colloque le Problème des Oiseaux sur les Aérodromes" (R. G. Busnel and J. Giban, Eds), pp. 173–206. Institut National de la Recherche Agronomique, Paris.

Murdock, W. T., Travis, R. E., Sutcliff, W. D. and Ajollo, L. (1962). Acute pulmonary histoplasmosis after exposure to soil contaminated by Starling excreta. *J. Am. med. Ass.* 179, 73–75.

Murton, R. K. (1958). The breeding of Wood Pigeon populations. *Bird Study* 5, 157–183.

Murton, R. K. (1961). Some survival estimates for the Wood Pigeon. *Bird Study* 8, 165–173.

Murton, R. K. (1964). Do birds transmit foot and mouth disease? *Ibis* 106, 289–298.

Murton, R. K. (1965a). "The Wood Pigeon." New Naturalist Monog. Collins, London.

Murton, R. K. (1965b). Natural and artificial population control in the Wood Pigeon. *Ann. appl. Biol.* 55, 177–192.

Murton, R. K. (1966). A statistical evaluation of the effect of Wood Pigeon shooting as evidenced by the recoveries of ringed birds. *The Statistician* 16(2), 183–202.

Murton, R. K. (1968). Some predator-prey relationships in bird damage and population control. *In* "The Problems of Birds as Pests" (R. K. Murton and E. N. Wright, Eds), pp. 157–169. Academic Press, London and New York.

Murton, R. K. (1971a). "Man and Birds." New Naturalist, Collins, London.

Murton, R. K. (1971b). The significance of a specific search image in the feeding behaviour of the Wood Pigeon. *Behaviour* 40, 10–42.

Murton, R. K. (1974a). The use of biological methods in the control of vertebrate pests. *In* "Increasing the Biological Contribution to the Control of Pests and Diseases" (M. Price-Jones and M. E. Solomon, Eds). *Symp. Br. Ecol. Soc.*, pp. 211–232. Blackwell, Oxford.

Murton, R. K. (1974b). The impact of agriculture on birds. *Ann. appl. Biol.* 76, 34–42.

Murton, R. K. and Jones, B. E. (1973). The ecology and economics of damage to brassicae by wood pigeons *Columba palumbus*. *Ann. appl. Biol.* 75, 107–122.

Murton, R. K. and Ridpath, M. G. (1962). The autumn movements of the Wood Pigeon. *Bird Study* **9**, 7–41.

Murton, R. K. and Westwood, N. J. (1974). Some effects of agricultural change on the English avifauna. *Br. Birds* **67**, 41–69.

Murton, R. K. and Wright, E. N. (1968) (Ed.). "The Problems of Birds as Pests." Symp. Instit. of Biol. London, Academic Press, London and New York.

Murton, R. K., Isaacson, A. J. and Westwood, N. J. (1963a). The feeding ecology of the Wood Pigeon. *Br. Birds* **56**, 345–375.

Murton, R. K., Isaacson, A. J. and Westwood, N. J. (1963b). The food and growth of nestling Wood Pigeons in relation to the breeding season. *Proc. Zool. Soc. Lond.* **141**, 747–782.

Murton, R. K., Isaacson, A. J. and Westwood, N. J. (1963c). The use of baits treated with α-chloralose to catch Wood Pigeons. *Ann. appl. Biol.* **52**, 271–293.

Murton, R. K., Westwood, N. J. and Isaacson, A. J. (1964a). The feeding habits of the wood pigeon *Columba palumbus*, stock dove *C. oenas* and turtle dove *Streptopelia turtur*. *Ibis* **106**, 174–188.

Murton, R. K., Westwood, N. J. and Isaacson, A. J. (1964b). A preliminary investigation of the factors regulating population size in the wood-pigeon *Columba palambus*. *Ibis* **106**, 482–507.

Murton, R. K., Isaacson, A. J. and Westwood, N. J. (1966). The relationship between Wood Pigeons and their clover food supply and the mechanism of population control. *J. appl. Ecol.* **3**, 55–96.

Murton, R. K., Norris, J. D. and Thearle, R. J. P. (1968). Wood-pigeons. *Agriculture*, December 1968, pp. 587–592.

Murton, R. K., Isaacson, A. J. and Westwood, N. J. (1971). The significance of gregarious feeding behaviour and adrenal stress in a population of Wood Pigeons *Columba palumbus*. *J. Zool., Lond.* **165**, 53–84.

Murton, R. K., Thearle, R. J. P. and Thompson, J. (1972a). Ecological studies of the feral pigeon *Columba livia* var. I. Population, breeding biology and methods of control. *J. appl. Ecol.* **9**, 835–874.

Murton, R. K., Coombs, C. F. B. and Thearle, R. J. P. (1972b). Ecological studies of the feral pigeon *Columba livia* var. II. Flock behaviour and social organisation *J. appl. Ecol.* **9**, 875–889.

Murton, R. K., Westwood, N. J. and Thearle, R. J. P. (1973). Polymorphism and the evolution of a continuous breeding season in the pigeon, *Columba livia. J. Reprod. Fert. Suppl.* **19**, 561–575.

Murton, R. K., Westwood, N. J. and Isaacson, A. J. (1974a). Factors affecting egg-weight, body-weight and moult of the wood pigeon *Columba palumbus*. *Ibis* **116**, 1–22.

Murton, R. K., Westwood, N. J. and Isaacson, A. J. (1974b). A study of wood-pigeon shooting: the exploitation of a natural animal population. *J. Appl. Ecol.* **11**, 1–21.

Murton, R. K., Bucher, E. H., Nores, M., Gómez, E. and Reartes, J. (1974c). The ecology of the eared dove *Zenaidura auriculata* in Argentina. *Condor* **76**, 80–88.

Murton, R. K., Thearle, R. J. P. and Coombs, C. F. B. (1974d). Ecological studies of the feral pigeon *Columba livia* var. III. Reproduction and plumage polymorphism. *J. appl. Ecol.* **11**, 841–854.

Naude, T. J. (1959). The *Quelea* problem in Southern Africa. *Ostrich*, Suppl., No. 3, pp. 264–270.

Neff, J. A. and Meanley, B. (1957). Blackbirds and the Arkansas rice crop. *Univ. of Arkansas Agr. Expt. sta. Bull.* 584, 89 pp.

Newton, I. (1964). Bud-eating by bullfinches in relation to the natural food supply. *J. appl. Ecol.* **1**, 265–279.

Newton, I. (1967a). The adaptive radiation and feeding ecology of some British finches. *Ibis* **109**, 33–98.

Newton, I. (1967b). The feeding ecology of the bullfinch (*Pyrrhula pyrrhula* L.) in southern England. *J. Anim. Ecol.* **36**, 721–744.

Newton, I. (1967c). Attacks on fruit buds by redpolls *Carduelis flammea*. *Ibis* **109**, 440–441.

Newton, I. (1968). Bullfinches and fruit buds. *In* "The Problem of Birds as Pests," Symp. Instit. of Biol. (R. K. Murton and E. N. Wright, Eds). Academic Press, London and New York.

Nisbet, I.C.T. and Drury, W. H. (1971). Strategy of management of a natural population: the herring gull in New England. *In* "World Conf. Bird Hazards to Aircraft," Sept, 1969. pp. 441–454. National Research Council, Kingston, Ontario. 542 pp.

Norris, J. D. and Whitehouse, R. N. H. (1970). Decoy-crop trapping of House Sparrows. *Pl. Path.* **19**, 28–31.

Nottebohm, F. (1969). The song of the Chingolo, *Zonotrichia capensis*, in Argentina: description and evaluation of a system of dialects. *Condor* **71**, 299–315.

Nottebohm, F. (1970). Ontogeny of bird song. *Science N.Y.* **167**, 950–956.

Nowak, E. (1971). [The range expansion of animals and its causes.] *Zesz. Nauk.* **3**, pp. 255. (Polska Akad. Nauk; Inst. Ekol.)

Ogilvie, M. A. (1969). The status of the Canada Goose in Britain 1967–69. *Wildfowl* **20**, 79–85.

Olivares, A. (1970). Effects of the environmental changes on the avifauna of the Republic of Colombia. *In* "The Avifauna of Northern Latin America": A Symposium held at the Smithsonian Institution, Smithsonian Contributions to Zoology, Number 26.

Olney, P. J. S. (1965). Management of avocet habitats in Suffolk. *Bird Notes* **31**, 315–319.

Orians, G. H. (1961). The ecology of blackbird (*Agelaius*) social systems. *Ecol. Monogr.* **31**, 285–312.

Palmar, C. E. (1968). Blackgame. Forestry Commission: Forest Record No. 66, 23 pp.

Palmer, T. K. (1970). House finch (linnet) control in California. *Proc. Vertebeate Pest Conf.*, 4th, 1970, pp. 173–178.

Parslow, J. L. F. (1967). Changes in status among breeding birds in Britain and Ireland. *Br. Birds* **61**, 177–202.

Patterson, I. J. (1965). Timing and spacing of broods in the black-headed Gull *Larus ridibundus*. *Ibis* **107**, 433–459.

Payne, R. B. (1969). Breeding seasons and reproductive physiology of Tricolored blackbirds and Redwinged blackbirds. University of California Press, Berkeley and Los Angeles.

Pennie, I. D. (1963). Article on capercaillie. *In* "The Birds of the British Isles." Bannerman and Lodge, Vol. 12. Edinburgh: Oliver and Boyd.

Perrins, C. (1968). The purpose of the high-intensity alarm call in small passerines. *Ibis* **110**, 200–201.

Pilcher, R. E. M. and Kear, J. (1966). The spread of potato-eating in whooper swans. *Br. Birds* **59**, 160–161.

Plowes, D. C. H. (1950). The Red-billed *Quelea*. A problem for grain-sorghum growers. *Rhodesia agric. J.* **47**, 98–101.

Plowes, D. C. H. (1955). *Queleas* in Southern Rhodesia. (CCTA/CSA Africa (55) 121). CSA Réunion des Spécialistes du Quelea, Dakar, 1955. Bukavu, Secrétariat Conjoint CCTA/CSA. 13 pp.

Plowes, D. C. H. (1957). Bird-proof grains. (CCTA/CSA Africa (57) QB 28). CSA Symposium on Quelea, Livingstone, 1957. Bukavu, CCTA/CSA Joint Sécretariat, 2 pp.

Pope, G. G. and King, W. J. (1973). Spray trials against Red-billed Quelea (*Quelea quelea*) in Tanzania. Miscellaneous report No. 12 Centre for Overseas Pests Research.

Pope, G. G. and Ward, P. (1972). The effects of small applications of an organophosphorus poison, Fenthion, on the Weaver-bird *Quelea quelea*. *Pestic. Sci.* **3**, 197–205.

Potts, G. R. (1967). Urban starling roosts in the British Isles. *Bird Study* **14**, 25–42.

Potts, G. R. (1970). Recent changes in the farmland fauna with special reference to the decline of the Grey Partridge. *Bird Study* **17**, 145–166.

Potts, G. R. and Vickerman, G. P. (1974). Studies on the cereal ecosystem. *In* "Advances in Ecological Research" (A. Macfadyen, Ed.), pp. 107–197. Academic Press, London and New York.

Poulding, R. H. (1954). Some results of marking gulls on Steepholm. *Proc. Bristol Nat. Soc.* **29**, 49–56.

Rae, B. B. (1969). The food of Cormorants and Shags in Scottish estuaries and coastal waters. Dept. Agric. Fish., Scotland. Marine Research (1969) No. 1, pp. 1–16.

Randhawa H. S. Clayton, Y. M. and Riddell, R. W. (1965). Isolation of *Cryptococcus neoformans* from pigeon habitats in London. *Nature, Lond.* **208**, 801.

Rao, T. R. and Rajagopalan, P. K. (1970). Arthropod fauna of the nests of some common birds in Poona, India, with special reference to blood-sucking forms. *J. Bombay nat. Hist. Soc.* **67**, 414–429.

Rasmussen, R. K. (1938). Er primaer epidemisk alveolopneumoniog psittacosis samme sygdom? *Ugeskr Laeg.* **100**, 989–998.

Rawcliffe, C. P. (1958). The Scottish mute swan census 1955–56. *Bird Study* **5**, 45–55.

Ridpath, M. G. and Brooker, M. G. (In Press). The breeding of the Australian wedge-tailed eagle *Aquila audax* in semi-arid habitats. *Int. orn. Cong.* 16.

Ridpath, M. G. and Meldrum, G. K. (1968a). Damage to pastures by the Tasmanian native hen, *Tribonyx mortierii*. *CSIRO Wildl. Res.* **13**, 11–24.

Ridpath, M. G. and Meldrum, G. K. (1968b). Damage to oat crop by the Tasmanian native hen *Tribonyx mortierii*. *CSIRO Wildl. Res.* **13**, 25–43.

Ridpath, M. G. and Thearle, R. J. P., McCowan, D. and Jones, F. J. S. (1961). Experiments on the value of stupefying and lethal substances in the control of harmful birds. *Ann. appl. Biol.* **49**, 77–101.

Roberts, H. S. and Saul, E. K. (undated). Birds at Auckland International Airport— a statistical analysis. *N.Z. Math. Mag.* **5**, 44–50.

Robertson, R. J. (1973). Optimal niche space of the red-winged blackbird. III. Growth rate and food of nestlings in marsh and upland habitat. *Wilson Bull.* **85**, 209–222.

Rochard, J. B. A. and Kear, J. (1968). A trial to investigate the reactions of sheep to goose droppings on grass. *Wildfowl* **19**, 117–119.

Rochard, J. B. A. and Kear, J. (1970). Field trials of the reactions of sheep to goose droppings on pasture. *Wildfowl* **21**, 108–109.

Romer, J. D. (1969). Bird problems at Hong Kong Airport. "Proc. World Conf. Bird Hazards to Aircraft," Kingston, Ontario, September 1969, pp. 77–86.

Rooth, J. and Timmerman, A. (1962–66). Rivon MSS. Unpublished. 10 pp + tables.

Rowan, M. K. (1962). Mass mortality amongst European common terns in South Africa in April–May 1961. *Br. Birds* **55**, 103–114.

Sage, B. L. (1970). The winter population of gulls in the London area. *Lond. Bird Rep.* No. 33 (1968), pp. 67–80.

Saul, E. K. (1967). Birds and aircraft: a problem at Auckland's new international airport. *J. R. aeronaut. Soc.* **71** (677), 366–376.

Schaefer, G. W. (1968). Bird Recognition by Radar. A study in Quantitative Radar Ornithology. *In* "The Problems of Birds as Pests" (R. K. Murton and E. N. Wright, Eds), pp. 53–86. *Symp. Instit. of Biol.* Academic Press, London and New York.

Schafer, E. W. and Brunton, R. B. (1971). Chemicals as bird repellents: two promising agents. *J. Wildl. Mgmt.* **35**, 569–572.

Schafer, E. W., Starr, R. I., Cunningham, D. J. and DeCino, T. J. (1967). Substituted phenyl *N*-methylcarbamates as temporary immobilizing agents for birds. *J. Agr. Food Chem.* **15** (2), 287–289.

Schmidt, E. (1973a). Ökologische Auswirkungen von elektrischen Leitungen und Masten sowie deren Accessorien auf die Vögel. *Beitr. Vogelk.* **19**, 342–362.

Schmidt, E. (1973b). Über vom Blutspecht *Dendrocopos syriacus* verursachte Schäden an Mandelbäumen. *Beitr. Vogelk.* **19**, 175–178.

Schorger, A. W. (1921). An attack on livestock by magpies. *Auk* **38**, 276–277.

Schortemeyer, J. L. and Beckwith, S. L. (1970). Chemical control of pigeon reproduction. Trans. 35th N. American Wildl. and Nat. Resources Conf. March 1970, Wildl. Mgmt. Institute, Washington.

Scott, P. and The Wildfowl Trust (1972). "The Swans". Michael Joseph, London.

Seubert, J. L. (1968). Control of birds on and around airports. Final report. October 1968. Report No. RD-68-62, U.S. Department of the Interior, Bureau of Sport. Fisheries and Wildlife, Division of Wildlife Research, Washington D.C.

Sick, H. (1968). Über in Südamerika eingeführte Vogelarten. *Bonn. zool. Beitr.* **19**, 298–306.

Skutch, A. F. (1960). Life histories of Central American birds, 11, Cooper Ornith. Soc., Pacific Coast Avifauna No. 34, 593 pp.

Slud, P. (1964). The birds of Costa Rica, distribution and ecology. *Bull. Am. Mus. Nat. History* **128**, 430 pp.

Smith, I. D. (1964). Ovine neo-natal mortality in Western Queensland. *Proc. Aust. Soc. Anim. Prod.* **5**, 100.

Snow, D. W. (1968). Birds and the 1967–68 foot-and-mouth epidemic. *Bird Study* **15**, 184–190.

Solman, V. E. F. (1965). Use of falcons for airport bird control. Associate Committee on Bird Hazards to Aircraft, National Research Council, Canada, Field note 33.

Solman, V. E. F. (1966). The ecological control of bird hazards to aircraft. "Proc. Third Bird Control Seminar," Bowling Green State University, Bowling Green, Ohio. 13 September 1966, pp. 38–52.

Solman, V. E. F. (1970). Airport design and management to reduce bird problems. Trans. First World Conference on Bird Hazards to Aircraft, National Research Council of Canada, pp. 143–147.

Solman, V. E. F. (1973). Birds and aircraft. *Biol. Conserv.* **5**, 79–86.

Southern, H. N. (1970). The natural control of a population of Tawny owls (*Strix aluco*). *J. Zool., Lond.* **162**, 197–285.

Spaans, A. L. (1971). On the feeding ecology of the Herring Gull *Larus argentatus* in the northern part of the Netherlands. *Ardea* **59**, 73–188.

Stables, E. R. and New, N. D. (1968). Birds and Aircraft: The problems. In "The Problems of Birds and Pests" (R. K. Murton and E. N. Wright, Eds), pp. 3–16. Symp. Instit. of Biol., Academic Press, London and New York.

Stenhouse, D. (1962). A new habit of the redpoll *Carduelis flammea* in New Zealand. *Ibis* **104**, 250–252.

Stenman, O., Komu, R. and Ermala, A. (1972). [Finnish experience of poisoning Herring and Great Black-backed Gulls with α-chloralose]. *Suom. Riista* **24**, 107–116.

Steven, G. A. (1933). The food consumed by shags and cormorants around the shores of Cornwall (England). *J. Mar. Biol. Ass. U.K.* **19**, 277–292.

Stickley, A. R. and Guarino, J. L. (1972). A repellent for protecting corn seed from blackbirds and crows. *J. Wildl. Mmgt.* **36**, 150–152.

Stickley, A. R., Mitchell, R. T., Heath, R. G., Ingram, C. R. and Bradley, E. L. (1972). A method for appraising the bird repellency of 4-aminopyridine. *J. Wildl. Mgmt.* **36**, 1313–1316.

Stickley, A. R., Mitchell, R. T., Dyer, M. I., Seubert, J. L. and Ingram, C. R. Large-scale evaluation of blackbird frightening agent 4-aminopyridine in corn. (In prep.)

Stolt, B-O. and Risberg, E. L. (1971). [The Collared Turtle-dove *Streptopelia decaocto* in Uppsala 1959–69; occurrence and winter biology.] *Vår Fågelvärld* **30**, 194–200.

Stone, C. P., Mott, D. F., Besser, J. F. and De Grazio, J. W. (1972). Bird damage to corn in the United States in 1970. *Wilson Bull.* **84**, 101–105.

Sturtevant, J. and Wentworth, B. C. (1970). Effect on acceptability and fecundity to pigeons of coating SC 12937 bait with Zein or Ethocel. *J. Wildl. Mgmt.* **34**, 776–782.

Summers-Smith, D. (1963). "The House Sparrow". New Nat. Monog. Collins, London.

Summers-Smith, D. and Vernon, J. D. R. (1972). The distribution of *Passer* in Northwest Africa. *Ibis* **114**, 259–262.

Sushkina, A. P. (1932). Some data on the biology of the cormorant with reference to the harm it inflicts on fisheries. Aftrakhan.

Sutter, E. (1957). Radar als hilfmittel der vogelzugforschung. *Orn. Beob.* **54**, 70–96.

Tanner, J. A. (1965). The effects of microwave radiation on birds. Some observations and experiments. Associate Committee on Bird Hazards to Aircraft, National Research Council of Canada Field Note No. 31.

Tanner, J. A., Davie, S. J., Romero-Sierra, C. and Villa, F. (1969). Microwaves a potential solution to the bird hazard problem in aviation. "Proc. World Conf. Bird Hazards to Aircraft," Kingston, Ontario, September 1969, pp. 217–221.

Tanner, J. A., Romera-Sierra, C. and Davie, S. J. (1967). Non-thermal effects of microwave radiation in birds. *Nature, Lond.* **216**, 1139.

Thomas, G. J. (1972). A review of gull damage and management methods at nature reserves. *Biol. Conserv.* **4**, 117–127.

Thomas, H. F. (1957). The starling in the Sunraysia District, Victoria. *Emu* **57**, 31–48, 131–144, 151–180, 269–284, 325–337.

Thompson, H. V. (1961). Ecology of Diseases in Wild Mammals and Birds. *Vet. Rec.* **73**, 1334–1337.

Thompson, R. D., Grant, C. V., Pearson, E. W. and Corner, G. W. (1968). Differential heart rate response of Starlings to sound stimuli of biological origin. *J. Wildl. Mgmt.* **32**, 888–893.

Thompson, R. L. and Agudelo, F. (1969). Crop production program, subproject: bird control. Centro Internacional de Agricultura Tropical, Unpub. Rept.

Thearle, R. J. P. (1968). Urban bird problems. In "The Problems of Birds as Pests" (R. K. Murton and E. N. Wright, Eds), pp. 181–197. Symp. Instit. of Biol. Academic Press, London and New York.

Thearle, R. J. P. (1969a). Some problems involved in the use of stupefying baits to control birds. "Proc. 5th Br. Insectic. Fungic. Conf" pp. 458–464.

Thearle, R. J. P. (1969b). The use of stupefying baits to control birds. "The Humane Control of Animals living in the Wild" U.F.A.W. Symposium, 1969, pp. 10–16.

Thearle, R. J. P. (1970). Pigeons. Developments in control methods. In "Current Developments in Pest Control." Symposium R. Soc. Health, pp. 9–12.

Thearle, R. J. P., Murton, R. K., Senior, M. M. and Malam, D. S. (1971). Improved stupefying baits for the control of town pigeons. Int. Pest Control 13(2), 11–19.

Tŭrcek, F. J. (1954). The ringing of trees by some European woodpeckers. Ornis. Fenn., 31, 33–41.

Tŭrcek, F. J. (1960). On the damage by birds to power and communication lines. Bird Study 7, 231–236.

Tutman, I. (1969). Beobachtungen an olivenfressenden Vögeln. Vogelwelt 90, 1–8.

Van Dobben, W. H. (1952). The food of the Cormorant in the Netherlands. Ardea 40, 1–63.

Van Koersveld, E. (1955). Damage to crops by birds and mammals, and methods for the prevention of such damage. Wildlife Repellents, I.T.B.O.N. Arnhem 32, 9–76.

Van Someren, V. D. (1951). The red-billed oxpecker and its relation to stock in Kenya. E. Afr. Agric. J. 17, 1–11.

Van Tets, G. F., Vestjens, W. J. M. and Slater, E. (1969a). Orange runway lighting as a method for reducing bird strike damage to aircraft. CSIRO Wildl. Res. 14, 129–151.

Van Tets, G. F., Vestjens, W. J. M. and Slater, E. (1969b). Orange runway lighting may help reduce the bird hazard to aircraft on airfields. "Proc. World Conf. Bird Hazards to Aircraft, Kingston, Ontario," September 1969, p. 185.

Van Troostwijk, W. J. D. (1964). Some aspects of the wood-pigeon population in the Netherlands. Ardea 52, 13–29.

Van Troostwijk, W. J. D. (1965). On the wood-pigeon in the Netherlands. Trans. 6th Congr. Int. Union Game Biol., 1963, pp. 359–367. The Nature Conservancy, London.

Varley, G. C. and Gradwell, G. R. (1960). Key factors in population studies. J. Anim. Ecol. 29, 399–401.

Vernon, J. D. R. (1970). Food of the Common Gull on grassland in autumn and winter. Bird Study 17, 36–38.

Virgo, B. B. (1971). Bird damage to sweet cherries in the Niagara Peninsula, Ontario. Can. J. Plant Sci. 51, 415–423.

Voous, K. H. (1960). "Atlas of European Birds." London, Nelson.

Voute, A. D. (1946). Regulation of the density of the insect-populations in virgin-forests and cultivated woods. Arch. Néerl. Zool. 7, 435–470.

Ward, P. (1963). Lipid levels in birds preparing to cross the Sahara. Ibis 105, 109–111.

Ward, P. (1965a). Feeding ecology of the black-faced dioch Quelea quelea in Nigeria Ibis 107, 173–214.

Ward, P. (1965b). Seasonal changes in the sex ratio of Quelea quelea (Ploceinae). Ibis 107, 397–399.

Ward, P. (1965c). The breeding biology of the black-faced dioch *Quelea quelea* in Nigeria. *Ibis* 107, 326–349.

Ward, P. (1966). Distribution, systematics and polymorphism of the African weaverbird *Quelea quelea*. *Ibis* 108, 34–40.

Ward, P. (1971). The migration patterns of *Quelea quelea*. *Ibis* 113, 275–297.

Ward, P. (1972). New views on controlling Quelea. *Span* 15(3), 1–2.

Ward, P. (1973). A new strategy for the control of damage by Queleas. *Pans* 19, 97–106.

Ward, P. and Pope, G. G. (1972). Flight-tunnel experiments with Red-billed queleas to determine the distribution of a solution sprayed onto birds in flight. *Pestic. Sci.* 3, 709–714.

Ward, P. and Zahavi, A. (1973). The importance of certain assemblages of birds as "information-centres" for food-finding. *Ibis*, 115, 517–534.

Waterson, A. P., Pennington, T. H. and Allan, W. H. (1967). Virulence in Newcastle Disease virus. A preliminary study. *Br. med. Bull.* 23, 138–143.

Wells, R. J. H. (1963). An outbreak of fowl plague in turkeys. *Vet. Rec.* 75, 783–786.

Wentworth, B. C., Hendricks, B. G. and Sturtevant, J. (1968). Sterility induced in Japanese Quail by spray treatment of eggs with mestranol. *J. Wildl. Mgmt.* 32, 879–887.

West, R. R., Brunton, R. B. and Cunningham, D. J. (1969). Repelling pheasants from sprouting corn with a carbamate insecticide. *J. Wildl. Mgmt.* 33(1), 216–219.

West, R. R. and Dunks, J. H. (1969). Repelling boat-tailed grackles from sprouting corn with a carbamate compound. *Texas J. Sci.* 21(2), 231–233.

Wetherbee, D. K., Coppinger, R. P., Wentworth, B. C. and Walsh, R. E. (1964). Antifecundity effect of Sudan black B. Experimental Station Bull., Coll. of Agriculture, Univ. of Mass. 543, 1–16.

Wiens, J. A. and Innis, G. S. (1974). Estimation of energy flow in bird communities: A population bioenergetics model. *Ecology* 55, 730–746.

Williams, G. R. (1969). Introduced birds. *In* "The Natural History of Canterbury" (G. A. Knox, Ed.), pp. 435–451. A. H. and A. W. Reed, Wellington.

Williams, J. E., Watts, D. M., Young, O. P. and Reed, T. J. (1972). Transmission of Eastern and Western encephalitis to Bobwhite sentinels in relation to density of *Culiseta melanura* mosquitoes. *Mosquito News* 32, 188–192.

Williams, J. E., Young, O. P. and Watts, D. M. (1974). Relationship of density of *Culiseta melanura* mosquitoes to infection of wild birds with Eastern and Western encephalitis viruses. *J. Med. Ent.* 11, 352–354.

Williams, J. G. (1954). The quelea threat to Africa's grain crops. *E. Afr. Agric. J.* 19, 133–136.

Williamson, K. (1971). A bird census study of a Dorset dairy farm. *Bird Study* 18, 80–96.

Wilson, C. E. (1947). The Sudan Dioch in grain growing areas. *Sudan Notes Rec.* 28, 151–156.

Wilson, C. E. (1948). Birds causing crop damage in the Sudan. *Sudan Notes Rec.* 29, 161–172.

Wilson, J. E. (1950). Newcastle disease in a Gannet (*Sula bassana*). A preliminary note. *Vet. Rec.* 62, 33–34.

Wilson, J. E. and MacDonald, J. W. (1967). Salmonella infection in wild birds. *Br. vet. J.* 123, 212–219.

Wilson, W. W. and Matheson, R. C. (1952). Bird migration and foot and mouth disease. *J. Min. Agric.* 59, 213–228.

Wofford, J. E. and Elder, W. H. (1967). Field trials of the chemosterilant, SC-12937, in feral pigeon control. *J. Wildl. Mgmt.* **31**, 507–515.

Wolf, Y. (1973). Woodpecker damage to polyethylene irrigation pipes in orchards in Israel. *FAO Plant Protection Bulletin.* **21**, 54–55.

Woodford, E. K. (1964). Weed control in arable crops. 7th Brit. Weed Cont. Conf. **3**, 944–964.

Woodroffe, G. E. (1953). An ecological study of the insects and mites in the nests of certain birds in Britain. *Bull. ent. Res.* **44**, 739–772.

Woodroffe, G. E. and Southgate, B. J. (1951–2). Birds' nests as a source of domestic pests. *Proc. Zool. Soc. Lond.* **121**, 55–62.

Woronecki, P. P., Guarino, J. L. and De Grazio, J. W. (1967). Blackbird damage control with chemical frightening agents. Proc. Vert. Pest Cont. Conf. 3rd, pp. 54–56.

Woronecki, P. P., Guarino, J. L., Besser, J. F. and De Grazio, J. W. (1970). Carbamate baits discourage blackbirds from using feedlots. "Proc. Vertebrate Pest Conf.", 4th, 1970. pp. 171–172.

Woronecki, P. P., Londoño, V. J. F., Elias, D. J., Valencia, G. D., Vogel, E. and Bojorge, R. (1971). Vertebrate damage control research in agriculture. Cali, Colombia Field Station 1971 Annual Progress Report.

Woronecki, P. P., Londoño, V. J. F., Elias, D. J., Valencia, G. D., Vogel, E., Bojorge, R. and Sequira, F. J. (1972). Vertebrate damage control research in agriculture. Cali, Colombia Field Station 1972 Annual Progress Report.

Woulfe, M. R. (1970). Reproduction inhibitors for bird control. Proc. Fourth Vertebrate Pest Conf. West Sacramento, California, pp. 168–170.

Wright, E. N. (1959). Bird damage to horicultural crops. *J. R. hort. Soc.* **84**, 426–434.

Wright, E. N. (1961). Use of traps to control bullfinches. *Exp. Horticulture* **4**, 55–62.

Wright, E. N. (1962). Experiments with anthraquinone and thiram to protect germinating maize against damage by birds. *Ann. Epiphyties* **13**, 27–31.

Wright, E. N. (1965). A review of bird scaring methods used on British airfields. *In* "Colloque le Problème des Oiseaux sur les Aérodromes" (R. G. Busnel and J. Giban, Eds), pp. 113–119. Institut National de la Recherche Agronomique, Paris.

Wright, E. N. (1968). Modifications of the habitat as a means of bird control. *In* "The Problems of Birds as Pests" (R. K. Murton and E. N. Wright, Eds), pp. 97–105. Symp. Instit. of Biol. Academic Press, London and New York.

Wright, E. N. (1969). Bird dispersal techniques and their use in Britain. "Proc. World Conf. Bird Hazards to Aircraft," Kingston, Ontario, September 1969, pp. 209–214.

Wright, E. N. (1973). Experiments to control Starling damage at intensive animal husbandry units. OEPP/EPPO Bull. 9, 85–89.

Wright, E. N. and Brough, T. (1966). Bird damage to fruit. Fruit Present and Future. *Roy. Hort. Soc.* 1966, 168–180.

Wright, E. N. and Summers, D. D. B. (1960). The biology and economic importance of the bullfinch. *Ann. appl. Biol.* **48**, 415–418.

Young, W. R. and Zevallos, D. C. (1960). Studies with chemical seed treatments as bird repellents for the protection of germinating maize in the Mexican tropics. *FAO Plant Protection Bull.* **8**(4), 37–42.

Zehetmayr, J. W. L. (1954). Experiments on tree-planting on peat. *Bull. For. Comm. Lond.* **22**, 110 pp.

Zusi, R. L. and Marshall, J. T. (1970). A comparison of Asiatic and North American sapsuckers. *Siam Soc. nat. Hist. Bull.* **23**, 393–407.

Wildlife Management and the Dynamics of Ungulate Populations

GRAEME CAUGHLEY

*School of Biological Sciences, Zoology Building, University of Sydney,
New South Wales, Australia*

I. INTRODUCTION

A. SCOPE

Of galling necessity this paper is divided into three parts. The introduction discusses the relationship between population dynamics and management, arguing that efficient management necessitates an understanding of how the managed population works. The second part reviews our current knowledge of the demographic mechanisms underlying the dynamics of ungulate populations and their food supplies, and because that knowledge is scanty, offers models consistent with this knowledge that may capture a portion of the essence of how an ungulate population operates. The third part explores the ways in which these empirically derived facts and theoretically suspected mechanisms of ungulate dynamics are of use in managing these populations.

B. THE PROBLEMS OF WILDLIFE MANAGEMENT

There is no discipline of population management. Instead we have economic entomology, animal production, fisheries management and wildlife management, fields traditionally separated by barriers of custom, attitude and jargon. This presents a difficulty when writing about applied population dynamics. Since population management is split into fields defined largely by taxonomy rather than process, a discussion of ungulate population dynamics falls within the ethos of wildlife management. But that framework is too cramped for this purpose. Wildlife management will therefore be used only as a comfortable and familiar home base from which occasional raids will be made on the ideas and information provided by the other fields.

Wildlife management is fortunate in that its aims are few, specific, and circumscribed:

(a) the treatment of a population that is at low density or is declining, to increase density or halt the decline;

(b) the treatment of a population such that it provides an optimum or maximum sustained yield; and

(c) the treatment of a population that is too dense or which has an unacceptably high rate of increase, to reduce its density or rate of increase.

The first is commonly labelled "conservation." The second is called "game cropping" if carried out for profit, or "allocation of hunting permits" if sportsmen harvest the animals; here it will be called "sustained-yield harvesting." The third treatment is "control." Each of these three problems, and there is no other problem of wildlife management, is solved by a manipulation of the population's dynamics, either directly by changing animal numbers or indirectly by changing food supply and habitat. Wildlife management is, in fact, applied population dynamics directed at a specific sub-set of species. In practice, however, wildlife is usually managed pragmatically.

This is not to say that all problems of wildlife management require specific data on dynamics for their solution. Most recent successes in this field stem from manipulating habitat, a population's density being increased by changing habitat to its advantage or decreased by changing habitat to its detriment. At its most primitive, the success of this technique rests only on an accurate knowledge of habitat requirements. It is enough to know which changes generate a positive rate of increase and which a negative. The internal adjustments of age-specific fecundity and mortality that generate the new rate of increase need be known only when a fine tuning is sought. But this is an exception. Most management practices call for a more direct manipulation of dynamics and therefore require in the manager a feeling for and knowledge of how a population works. It is perhaps unnecessary, and certainly uncharitable, to remark that an integration of the concepts of population dynamics with the procedures of population management is, with a few important exceptions, conspicuously lacking from the main stream of wildlife management.

The first textbook of wildlife management was written in 1933 by Aldo Leopold. I have heard it argued, cogently and without malice, that no qualitative advance in the theory or practice of wildlife management has been made since then. This is an overstatement—one can point to advances in the understanding of prey–predator systems, of the effect of habitat on population density, and of the relevance of behaviour to the problem of manipulating a population—but the counter-attack lacks bite. These advances were foreshadowed if not launched by Leopold, a reflection more on the excellence of his book than on foot-dragging by his spiritual heirs. When all favourable facts and convenient rationalizations have been expended against it there is still enough left of the criticism to cause disquiet. Advances in wildlife management have not paralleled those in the other fields of population management. In relative terms the field has slipped behind.

Over the period that wildlife management has advanced with caution the closely related fields of fisheries biology and economic entomology have forged ahead. Their advances are traceable directly to the placing of population dynamics at the centre rather than the periphery of theory and practice. This contrast may well provide a clue to wildlife management's relative stagnation.

The principal theme of this paper is that a closer look at the dynamics of the populations we seek to manage will do wildlife management no harm. But that proposition leads only to further generalities unless it is brought into tighter focus by specific examples. To this end the discussion is focused on and limited to ungulates, both because they constitute one of the few groups of wildlife whose management spans the three categories of conservation, sustained yield and control, and because the little already known about their dynamics is sufficient to demonstrate how vital such knowledge is when we seek to manage these populations.

II. Statics and Dynamics

A. FECUNDITY PATTERNS

The fecundity pattern of a population, the trend of fecundity rate by age, is usually presented in terms of m_x which is defined as the number of female live births produced per female at age x. Figure 1 shows an

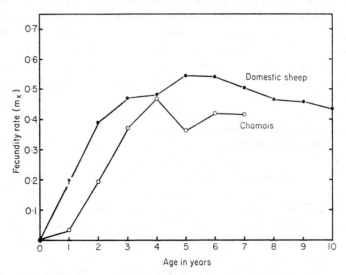

Fig. 1. Fecundity patterns of domestic sheep (Hickey, 1960) and chamois (Caughley, 1970a).

accurate trend for domestic sheep in the North Island of New Zealand, each value being a mean from several hundred ewes. The m_x for age one is missing because females were not mated in the first year of life. The second curve in Fig. 1 is the trend of m_x for a wild ungulate, chamois (*Rupicapra rupicapra* L.), in the Southern Alps of New Zealand. Minor irregularities reflect sampling variation rather than real effects, and the trend is truncated at an age beyond which any age-class frequency dropped below eight females. Both trends show the essential properties of an ungulate fecundity pattern: a steep rise over the first few years of life followed by a long plateau, often with a slight negative slope, that offers no hint of the sharp decrease of fecundity at old age that would signal menopause.

For purposes of population analysis, if not for a study of the physiology of aging, little precision is lost by calculating a single fecundity rate for adults as the weighted mean of plateau fecundity.

Figures 2 and 3 illustrate the malleability of fecundity patterns under the influence of different conditions of life. Figure 2 graphs fecundity by age for two populations of Himalayan thar [*Hemitragus jemlahicus* (H. Smith)], a goat-like bovid living in the Southern Alps of New Zealand. The Godley population had a rate of increase near zero whereas the Rangitata population was increasing at around 12% a year. The

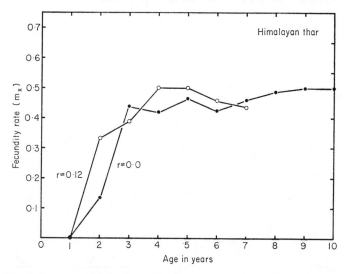

FIG. 2. Fecundity patterns of two populations of thar with differing rates of increase (data from Caughley, 1970b).

difference in rate of increase is reflected in a disparity of fecundity at two years of age indicating that fecundity of the Rangitata population climbs more steeply to reach plateau fecundity, or, put in another way, the mean age at puberty is lower in the Rangitata population. On the other hand the plateaus beginning at three years of age are similar in elevation and, on the available data, cannot be shown to differ significantly.

An interesting contrast to the thar data is provided by fecundity trends of red deer (*Cervus elaphus* L.) in New Zealand and Scotland, the lower two curves in Fig. 3. The Scottish data collected by Lowe (1969) have been reanalysed here to reflect an assumed sex ratio of parity amongst foetuses, thereby making it comparable with the New Zealand data. The trends differ both in mean age at puberty and in the elevation of the fecundity plateau, the New Zealand population having more favourable statistics in both cases. These differences in fecundity are unlikely to reflect differences in rate of increase. For the New Zealand population this rate was close to zero with density perhaps held a little below carrying capacity by sporadic hunting (Caughley, 1971b). The Scottish population was increasing (Lowe, 1969). Hence the Scottish red deer, although demographically more vigorous, had a lower rate of fecundity at all ages, the implication being that it had more favourable survival statistics than the New Zealand population.

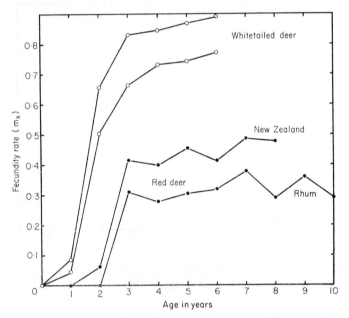

FIG. 3. Fecundity patterns of two white-tailed deer populations in Michigan (Eberhardt, 1960), and of two red deer populations, one on the Island of Rhum, Scotland (data from Lowe, 1969) and one in New Zealand (Caughley, 1971b).

The upper two fecundity curves of Fig. 3 are Eberhardt's (1960) estimates for two Michigan populations of white-tailed deer (*Odocoileus virginianus* Boddaert). The trends are truncated at six years of age because of low frequencies. This comparison demonstrates that both mean age at puberty and the elevation of the fecundity plateau can differ markedly between populations separated by a short distance.

The two pairs of curves in Fig. 3 indicate different mechanisms for increasing or decreasing fecundity. Red deer typically produce a single offspring per birth, a difference in plateau fecundity between populations therefore indicating a difference in frequency of pregnancy. It is at 90% for the New Zealand population and about 65% for the Scottish population, the difference reflecting pregnancy rates rather than size of litters.

In contrast, the difference in plateau fecundity for the two populations of white-tailed deer is ascribable largely to differences in mean litter size. The point is clearly made by Verme's (1965) experiment on two groups of white-tailed deer, one on a high plane of nutrition and the other on a low plane. Table I shows that a trivial difference in pregnancy rates was

TABLE I   Effect of nutrition on fecundity of white-tailed deer

	High nutrition	Low nutrition
Number of does	27	22
Percent of does pregnant	89	86
Fawns born per pregnant doe	1·96	1·11
Litter-size frequencies (1:2:3)	2:21:1	17:2:0

associated with a real difference in the frequency distribution of litter sizes.

Coop's (1966) researches on the reproductive physiology of domestic sheep indicate that both pregnancy rates and ovulation rates are influenced by a female's nutritional history as reflected in her current weight. More markedly, twinning rates are influenced by the plane of nutrition over the month prior to conception.

These examples illustrate the three ways in which an ungulate fecundity pattern can react to environmental change: (a) a raising or lowering of mean age at puberty; (b) a raising or lowering of the fecundity plateau by a shift in pregnancy rates; and (c) a raising or lowering of the fecundity plateau by a shift in mean litter size.

The first mechanism is common to all ungulate species. The second is used by those that typically produce one offspring per birth whereas the third characterizes species in which multiple births are common. The latter two mechanisms do not exclude each other. Multiple births are common for white-tailed deer in North America where change in litter size is probably the major way in which fecundity rates are changed. In New Zealand the same species typically produces one offspring per birth, the level of plateau fecundity there being set by pregnancy rates. Similarly, the Himalayan thar seldom produces twins in the wild (Caughley, 1970b), but when held on a high plane of nutrition in captivity twins are produced in 10% of births (Zuckerman, 1953).

B. MORTALITY PATTERNS

Producing a fecundity table for a population is relatively simple but producing a life table is not. The sample of animals required for a fecundity table need not comprise an unbiased sampling of the age distribution, nor need the population's rate of increase be known.

The life table requires more disciplined data. It is usually constructed from either the population's age distribution or from the distribution of ages at death. Age distributions are usually sampled by shooting, a technique that produces very inaccurate data unless great care is taken to control bias towards young and silly or large and conspicuous individuals. Distributions of ages at death are obtained by collecting skulls of animals that have died naturally, ageing each by tooth eruption, or tooth wear, or from a count of age lines in dental cementum or on the horns, and constructing from these data the frequency distribution of ages. Bias is again inevitable because the skulls of young animals break up faster than those of adults.

But the difficulty of sampling is only one of the problems faced in constructing a life table. The sample must be taken from a population with a stable age distribution and known rate of increase. In practice these restrictions tend to limit sampling to populations with a stationary age distribution, that special case of the stable age distribution generated by a zero rate of increase. As a consequence, although several life tables are available for stationary populations of ungulates, thereby allowing some commonplace generalization about the form of the mortality pattern, there is a dearth of information to answer the more important question of how a life table changes as rate of increase diverges from zero in either direction.

The previous comments on errors induced by bias are not relevant to the curve of mortality rate by age (q_x) in Fig. 4. It was constructed from ages at death of 83 000 female domestic sheep aged one year or older and the number of lambs dying before one year of age out of 85 000 of both sexes born alive. These data (Hickey, 1960 and 1963) from selected farms in the North Island of New Zealand can be accepted as an accurate representation of the mortality pattern.

Figure 5 gives q_x curves from populations of two races of the deer *Cervus elaphus* L., a ring species that circles the northern hemisphere (Caughley, 1971a). The population of *C.e. elaphus* (English park strain) derives from an introduction of this species into New Zealand in 1904. The population of *C.e. canadensis* (nannodes strain) was sampled on its natural range in the western United States. Both populations were judged stationary. In contrast to that of the sheep, the curves for *C.e.*

elaphus (Caughley, 1971b) and *C.e. canadensis* (McCullough, 1969) should be viewed with the scepticism appropriate to the claims of a second-hand car salesman, or to any mortality curve wrenched from field data. Sampling variation, sampling bias, smoothing errors, ageing errors and instability of age distributions all contribute to the shape of

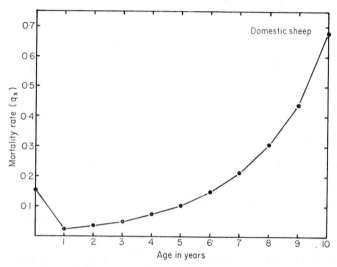

Fig. 4. Mortality pattern of domestic sheep (data from Hickey, 1960, 1963).

these curves. An obvious error can be seen in the curve for *C.e. elaphus* where q_x at one year of age is implausibly high. It probably reflects an oversampling of yearlings, an age group particularly vulnerable to a competent rifleman hunting in forest.

For all these inadequacies the two q_x curves are strikingly similar to the accurate q_x curve for sheep, perhaps indicating that the errors of estimation were not large enough to swamp the underlying pattern. Taken together the three reveal the basic mammalian mortality pattern, a robust configuration whose form is largely independent of taxon. The trend follows a U, a relatively high rate of mortality at infancy being followed by a low rate at puberty which increases progressively thereafter. This pattern is not restricted to ungulates but holds equally for mice and men (Caughley, 1966).

The pattern divides easily into two components, a juvenile phase and an adult phase. The rate of juvenile mortality decreases sharply with time from birth. Cook *et al.* (1971) investigated mortality of white-tailed deer by attaching transmitters to 81 fawns within twelve days of birth. Over the following two months 53 fawns died at a finite rate per month of

0·67 in the first and 0·15 in the second. An even more precise partitioning of juvenile mortality is allowed by Hight and Jury's (1969) figures on the fortunes of 7700 domestic sheep followed from birth to weaning in New Zealand. After rejecting records of those lambs that died at or before

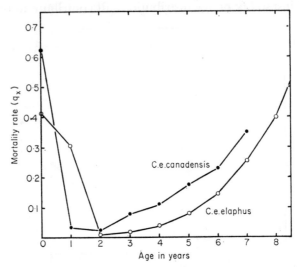

FIG. 5. Mortality patterns from two races of the deer *Cervus elephus* (data from McCullough, 1969 and Caughley, 1971b).

birth and of those that died at unknown ages the remaining records were re-analysed to give results in a form allowing comparison with the deer. Deaths were recorded in unequal intervals of age (1–3 days, 4–7 days and 8–82 days) and for each an instantaneous rate of mortality was calculated and then converted to a finite rate per month. Table II gives

TABLE II   Mortality of domestic lambs

Age interval (days)	Finite mortality rate per month	
	Single births	Multiple births
1–3	0·30	0·52
4–7	0·07	0·10
8–82	0·01	0·02

the results separately for lambs born singly and those born as twins or triplets. These data, and those from the white-tailed deer, clearly show the typically strong deceleration of the rate of mortality over the first few weeks of life.

The adult phase of mortality is more complex and its interpretation more controversial. Although attempts have been made to sub-divide adult mortality into two or more mortality regimes (e.g. Pearson, 1895; Bodenheimer, 1958) the smooth rise in rate of mortality from puberty onward argues against division. As Medawar (1951, p. 8) puts it, "there is no break or singularity to give evidence that at any later age development and maturation are at last completed and that deterioration then sets in."

The indivisibility of the adult phase of mortality is now largely accepted by demographers, if not by physiologists; but then those two groups still appear to be discussing different things when they talk of "ageing." To the demographer it connotes only a rise in rate of mortality with age whereas the physiologist equates it with irreversible changes in cells. Neither group has produced a completely satisfying explanation that makes biological sense of the adult pattern of mortality. Medawar (1951) comes closest. He pointed to the prevalence of genes whose phenotypic manifestation is a function of the animal's age. Natural selection does not act upon all age classes equally but, for a given age, as a function of survival and fecundity means at subsequent ages. This statistic is called the reproductive value of that age, its components being related formally by Fisher's (1930) equation. In ungulates and most other mammals, reproductive value peaks at puberty and declines progressively thereafter, the decline being preserved even when rates of fecundity and mortality are constant for all ages after puberty. Medawar argued that natural selection will affect the age at which a deleterious gene manifests, by pushing it away from the age of highest reproductive value. Concomitantly, the age of manifestation of an advantageous gene will proceed towards the age of peak reproductive value. By this model there is no age of potential longevity but a continuous increase in the probability of death as age increases. "The concept of senescence as an ordered curtailment of life, a destined fate at a definite age, is a consequence of a vitalist dogma" (Comfort, 1956, p. 190).

From the standpoint of population dynamics rather than genetics it is convenient to view the adult mortality pattern from a slightly different angle. If the q_x curves of Figs. 4 and 5 were redrawn as the frequency distributions of death by age, d_x, bimodal distributions similar to that of Fig. 6 would result. It illustrates the juvenile phase of mortality as a J-shaped distribution, and the adult phase as some modification of the normal distribution. The two intersect at puberty. The adult distribution can usually be described mathematically by the simple distributional statistics of mean or median, standard deviation and skew, and it can be described biologically as a dose–response relationship, a dose of age giving a response of mortality. Probit analysis (Finney, 1947) is the statistical treatment appropriate to this kind of problem.

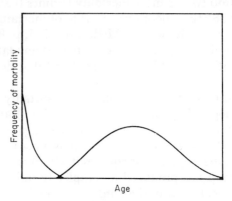

FIG. 6. A diagram of the typical dimodal distribution of mortality frequency with age.

The stable age distribution of an ungulate population can be related to the statistics of the frequency distribution of mortality after the first year of age by

$$\text{Probit } (kf_x e^{rx}) = a + bx^1$$

where f_x = frequency of age x in a sample, $k = f_x/f_1$, r = exponential rate of increase, a = regression intercept on the probit scale, b = regression slope, and i = a function of skew.

Having fitted this curve to all but the juvenile segment of the age distribution, the statistics of adult mortality can be calculated as

$$M = \left(\frac{5-a}{b}\right)^{1/i}$$

where M is the median age of adult death, and

$$s = \tfrac{1}{2}\left[\left(\frac{4-a}{b}\right)^{1/i} - \left(\frac{6-a}{b}\right)^{1/i}\right]$$

where s is the standard deviation of adult ages at death. The direction of skew and some idea of its magnitude is given by $-\log_e i$.

The juvenile rate of mortality as calculated from the stable age distribution is

$$q_0 = 1 - (f_1 e^r/f_0)$$

Hence a mortality pattern can be summarized by four statistics, one for the juvenile phase and three for the adult phase. Their use is demonstrated for the two populations of Himalayan thar whose q_x curves are graphed in Fig. 7. One population was stationary and the other in-

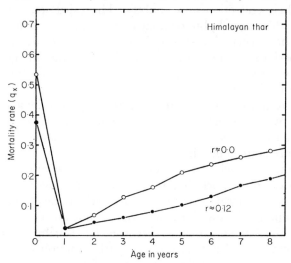

FIG. 7. Mortality patterns of two populations of thar with differing rates of increase (data from Caughley, 1970b).

creasing at around $r = 0.12$. Table III summarizes the mortality

TABLE III   Rate of increase and mortality pattern

Species	Rate of increase	First year mortality rate	Median age of adult deaths (yr)	Standard deviation of adult ages at death (yr)	Adult mortality index of skew
Thar	0·0	0·53	6·20	3·10	1·2
Thar	0·12	0·37	8·02	4·13	0·0
Sheep	0·20	0·16	7·85	2·35	−0·6

patterns of these two populations and the population of domestic sheep whose q_x is graphed in Fig. 4. The sheep had a stable rate of increase (latent rather than realized because of harvesting) of around 0·20 (Caughley, 1967). From Table III the differences in the mortality patterns of the thar populations are immediately obvious. The divergent trends of mortality rate with age (Fig. 7) result from a shift in the median, standard deviation and skew of ages at death.

Little can be concluded confidently from these results. The two sets of data from natural populations are flawed by the unknown errors inherent in their collection and analysis. The third set, from domestic sheep, is reliable enough, but comparing these data with those from thar confounds the effects of species and rate of increase. But it is possible, although perhaps ill-advised, to speculate on the inter-relationship between mortality pattern and rate of increase by using the statistics of Table III as talking points. No principle will be sought; only a hypothesis that can be tested when more appropriate data become available.

Rate of juvenile mortality is clearly correlated inversely with the population's rate of increase. Trends at the adult stage are less transparent but are consistent with these speculations:

(a) The major associate of rate of increase is the skew of the frequency distribution of adult mortality. It is positive at a low rate of increase, disappears at a moderate rate and reverses at a higher rate.

(b) The change in standard deviation is not an independent effect but reflects the change in skew. Because the distribution is bounded below and constricted above, the standard deviation is greatest when skew is zero, and it contracts with a change of skew in either direction.

(c) The statistic least affected by rate of increase is the median age at death.

This model of the change in the adult mortality distribution with rising rate of increase is shown diagrammatically in Fig. 8. It is offered only as a suggested starting point for further research.

C. GROWTH OF POPULATIONS

1. *Empirical*

When a population is relatively stable in size, its birth rate and death rate being closely balanced against each other, little can be learned about its internal workings or about the mechanisms by which it has accommodated itself to its environment. But when it is displaced from this comfortable position the forces that held it there immediately come into play. The population begins to exhibit dynamic behaviour. The most direct clues to the internal workings of a population, the potential and the limits of its reaction to environment, are provided at the point of maximum displacement, the system's point of maximum tension. This state is manifest at the initial stage of population growth when the ratio of resources to animals is at its maximum level. From this point the animal–resource system implodes towards some sort of accommodation between rate of production of animals and the rate at which resources, particularly food resources, are renewed. The manner and the speed of the implosion can teach us much about the nature of the vegetation–herbivore system.

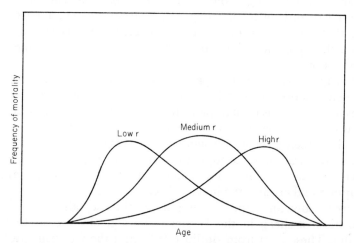

FIG. 8. Hypothesized change in the frequency distribution of adult mortality with age as rate of increase rises.

Most of the information on growth of wild ungulate populations comes from two places: from New Zealand where eight cervids and three bovids were liberated between 50 and 120 years ago, and from three islands in the Bering Sea where reindeer (*Rangifer tarandus* L.) were released this century. From these unlikely and heterogeneous sources emerges a revealing and remarkably consistent picture of population growth.

When ungulates are introduced into a previously unoccupied area they increase to a peak density and then crash steeply to a considerably lower level. Subsequent oscillations are heavily damped and density finally steadies well below the initial peak. The vegetation follows a reciprocal trajectory, first falling in density as the population rises, increasing again as the animals crash, and finally settling to a density and rate of production at equilibrium with a relatively constant pressure of grazing. In doing so its composition and structure are changed radically from those of its ungrazed state. Essentially it is a different vegetation. The animals have not simply consumed the interest on the capital supply of food, they have lowered the capital permanently and devalued the currency irrevocably.

This pattern of eruptive growth has been investigated in New Zealand by Riney *et al.* (1959), Riney (1964), Howard (1965) and Caughley (1970b). Scheffer (1951) and Klein (1968) provide the information on eruption of reindeer on the islands of the Bering Sea. Caughley (1970b) summarized the findings from these two regions and concluded, after examining records of further ungulate eruptions in other parts of the world, that the pattern of eruption and crash reflects an interaction between the dynamics of the animals and the dynamics of their food, the vegetation.

The eruption is the typical pattern of ungulate growth. It occurs in the presence of predators and in the absence of predators, on continents as on islands, in areas of high plant diversity and of low plant diversity, in areas that have never seen the invading species as in areas where the species has been present throughout the Pleistocene. Whenever an ungulate population is faced with a standing crop of vegetation in excess of that needed for maintenance and replacement of the animals, an eruption and crash is the inevitable consequence.

Figure 9 shows an eruption of ungulates, the rise, fall and subsequent stabilization of sheep in the Western Division of New South Wales, Australia. These data from Butlin (1962) and the Government Statistician of New South Wales (1956–1972) have not previously been interpreted as an ungulate eruption—the crash between 1894 and 1903 being traditionally ascribed to drought—but the pattern of growth is typical of wild ungulate populations. The initial overshoot to peak density is apparent, as is the subsequent crash. Dampened oscillations of the post-crash period are masked by fluctuations resulting from variations in weather, market forces and management techniques. But the eruptive pattern is clearly there and the overall trend may be interpreted confidently as reflecting a single process: the adjustment of sheep density to availability of food and the adjustment of the density and composition of the vegetation to the pressure of grazing.

Davidson (1938a, b) examined the records of sheep numbers in South Australia and Tasmania and concluded that both trajectories were adequately approximated by the logistic curve. But the original data through which he forced these curves exhibit the same sequence of overshoot (1852 in Tasmania and 1892 in South Australia) as does Fig. 9. Davidson interpreted these departures from expected as the effects of economic forces and of weather, but no special pleading is needed if they are accepted as integral to the ungulate pattern of population growth.

A more spectacular example of an ungulate eruption emerges from Klein's (1968) account of the population initiated by 29 reindeer on

St Matthew Island in the Bering Sea. Figure 10 is a copy of his inter-pretation of trend deduced from estimates of numbers in 1944, 1957, 1963 and 1966, and strong circumstantial evidence that the crash occurred during the 1963–1964 winter. By that time lichens, which earlier provided the main component of diet in winter, were all but

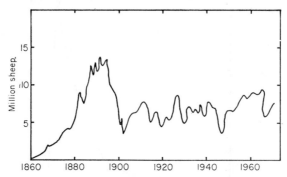

FIG. 9. Trend of sheep numbers in the Western Division of New South Wales between 1860 and 1972.

eliminated. Mean body weight fell dramatically as the population of reindeer built to a peak, at which time they were 40% lighter than when the population was climbing steeply. Concomitant with the massive mortality at the crash was a marked drop in conception and lactation rates. The most startling change during the crash was in population structure. Of the 42 surviving animals in 1966, after the crash, only one was male, and the females were grouped into an intermediate age class of 4–8 years.

Similar evidence of selective mortality during a crash comes from a massive die-off of Wildebeest [*Connochaetes taurinus* (Burchell)] in Botswana (Child, 1972). In most age classes the sex ratio was shifted in favour of females, and the age distributions of both sexes were compressed by differential mortality of younger and older animals. Similar selective mortality occurred among several species stranded on islands formed by the flooding of Lake Kariba (Child, 1968). These changes boost the reproductive value (Fisher, 1930) of the population, allowing it to increase more rapidly than if it had a stable age distribution.

Klein's (1968) study is of particular interest because it deals with the eruptive process at its violent extreme, and extreme cases tend to reveal mechanisms that lie hidden from view in less reactive systems. It will be discussed further in a subsequent section where its implications will be explored in greater detail. Here we need only note that, in terms of process if not necessarily in outcome, it conforms to the pattern of other ungulate eruptions: a population of herbivores and a vegetation reacting to each other as they seek a stable accommodation.

The only other account of the changes in population characteristics across an ungulate eruption comes from a study of Himalayan thar in

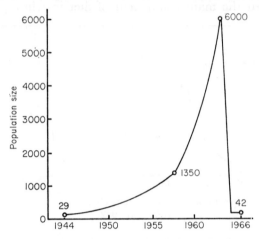

FIG. 10. The trend of reindeer numbers on St. Matthew Island (after Klein, 1968).

New Zealand (Caughley, 1970b). Although there were detectable trends in fat reserves, fecundity rates, mortality rates and generation length, the major determinant of rate of increase was traced to death rate. About 95% of the fall in rate of increase, from $r = 0.12$ halfway along the upward trend to $r = 0$ at peak density, was ascribable to a rise in death rate, the remaining 5% being related to a decline in fecundity. The drop from $r = 0$ at peak density to a rate of perhaps $r = -0.3$ or more during the crash was caused almost entirely by a further rise in mortality, the observed fall in fecundity over this period being sufficient in itself only to precipitate a decline of $r = -0.04$. The major component of changes in death rate across the eruption was isolated as a change in the rate of mortality over the first year of life.

Body weights of thar did not show the scale of change reported by Klein (1968) for reindeer, although such changes are standard during eruptions of red deer in New Zealand. There was a barely detectable decline in rate of growth of thar as rate of increase declined, and no apparent differences in adult size as the population rose and fell.

The vegetation was much more reactive. The tall snow tussocks (*Chionocloa* spp.) which, when ungrazed, form a continuous canopy, were almost entirely eliminated over wide areas, being replaced by turf forming grasses more resistant to grazing. Patches of alpine scrub were eliminated from some sites and severely modified on others. The structure and composition of the vegetation that developed to an equilibrium with the pressure of grazing thus differed in character from that of the vegetation before the thar arrived.

2. *Theoretical*

The observed trajectory of a growing population has two components, signal and noise. The signal comprises the broad sweep of the pattern of growth which results from basic mechanisms integral to the system. Disruption of this pattern, by random or trivial events that perturb the population's growth in an unpredictable manner, constitutes the noise. In any study of population growth it is convenient to strip the noise from the signal so that the essential character of the process can be viewed, freed from the extraneous effects of stochastic events, fluctuations in weather, and unbalanced age distributions.

The signal of the trajectory can then be described by an equation that summarizes the pattern of growth in the disciplined language of algebra and this can be done in two quite different ways. The first, easier but less useful, is to fit an arbitrary curve to the trajectory by the routine tricks of the mathematician's art. The constants of the equation describing this curve need have no necessary relationship to or correspondency with the actual mechanisms of growth. The equation reveals nothing about underlying mechanisms and may or may not be useful in predicting future growth. The second strategy is to start at the other end. The vegetation–herbivore system is studied to discover the determinants of growth and how they are related. The biological inter-relationships are then summarized as an equation which is used to generate a trajectory. Should the calculated pattern of growth differ in kind from the observed trajectory, it can safely be deduced that the assumed inter-relationships are incorrect. If it conforms there is a possibility that the growth mechanisms have been deduced correctly, but independent experimentation, with this possibility as the hypothesis, is needed for confirmation.

These two approaches, curve fitting and modelling, have spawned a hybrid offspring lacking the rough honesty of the first and the potential revelation of the second. A curve is fitted to a trajectory and the arbitrary constants of its descriptive equation are assigned *post-facto* and often fanciful biological meanings.

Two separate questions must be asked of the results of any of these exercises: does the curve fit the signal of the data, and does the equation describe the real attributes of the system.

(a) Logistic growth model. The tactics of modelling a growth pattern will be illustrated by a simple abstracted example. Suppose a population

of ungulates were grown in captivity, adequately housed, with as much water and space as needed. The food is supplied as hay, a fixed amount being shared out each day. Initially the population would grow at its intrinsic rate of increase, r_m, that rate set by its own genetically controlled capacity to survive and reproduce in the ambient circumstances of temperature, quality of food and quality of shelter. With the arrival of each new recruit the amount of food available per day to the rest of the population is reduced by that recruit's share, and this reduction in the plane of nutrition is reflected in a reduction by a constant amount in the population's rate of increase. Eventually rate of increase would fall to zero when the population had grown to a size where the amount of food available per head was sufficient only to allow each animal, on average, to replace itself.

This population's pattern of growth is determined by three factors only: the intrinsic rate of increase of the animals, the rate of production of food, and the rate of food intake an animal needs to replace itself. The system can be modelled by two equations, one describing the rate of change of the food and the other the rate of change of the population. The food, V, changes as

$$\frac{dV}{dt} = ge^{-\infty N} \tag{1}$$

where g is instantaneous food production and N is the number of animals; which is perhaps an over elaborate way of stating that food accumulates at an arithmetic rate in the absence of the animals, but if any animals are present they eat all the increment although they cannot get at the capital stock of food because it is locked away in a barn. If b is defined as the rate of food intake sufficient to maintain an animal and allow its replacement in the next generation, and N is the number of animals in the population, then the proportion of available food used for maintenance and replacement is bN/g and the proportion surplus to these demands that can be used to generate increase in numbers is $1 - bN/g$. Rate of change of animal numbers can therefore be written as

$$\frac{dN}{dt} = r_m N \left(1 - \frac{bN}{g}\right). \tag{2}$$

As N grows, the proportion of food used for increase must decline progressively until finally all food is used for maintenance and replacement (i.e. $bN/g = 1$). As bN/g approaches 1, dN/dt approaches zero. At this time the population has reached a maximum size of $g/b = K$. By substituting K for g/b, equation (2) contracts to a form containing no explicit term for rate of production of food:

$$\frac{dN}{dt} = r_m N \left(1 - \frac{N}{K}\right), \tag{3}$$

the equation for logistic growth. The term for food production is now hidden within the constant K which is defined as a number of animals.

Figure 11 illustrates the trajectory of a population growing in this way. The growth of the imaginary population of captive ungulates would not mirror this trend exactly because of time lags and instability of age distribution, but for present purposes these influences can be considered only as sources of noise, the underlying pattern of growth being logistic.

The fitting of a logistic curve to a trajectory of growth implies some very peculiar things about the resources, food in the example, utilized by the animals. The limiting resource in the logistic model is essentially an inert substrate. The amount of food the animals ate yesterday has no influence on how much is available to them today, and the amount of food a given animal eats today is influenced only by the rate of renewal of the food and how many animals are sharing it. Because food availability per head is an inverse function of N, the number of animals eating it, a term for food itself need not be included in the equation describing the population's growth. The amount of food available to an animal is represented precisely by the reciprocal of population size modified by a constant. This has led many writers to take the tacit substitution literally, and to miss the point of what logistic growth is all about. They describe it as the outcome of density itself acting on rate of increase, rather than as the outcome of a resource's rate of production being a constant uninfluenced either by the number of animals using it or by the capital level of the resource.

A further treatment of the relevance of the logistic curve to the growth of populations is provided by Andrewartha and Birch (1954, pp. 347–398) who arrived at similar conclusions by a different route.

Surprisingly, there actually are systems whose determinants of growth come close to approximating strict logistic assumptions. Plants have no influence on the rate of production of their resources, water and sunlight, and the growth of some plant populations might therefore be expected to approximate a logistic. An insect population whose larvae lives in stone fruit has no influence on the amount of food available to the next generation, and its growth might therefore be logistic. But for ungulates this model is not applicable. They affect both the capital and the interest of their food supply, the density as well as the species composition of the standing crop of plants. The amount of food available per head has only a tenuous relationship to the number of animals in the population at any given time. Food supply is influenced much more profoundly by the number of animals that modified it over a period stretching well back into the past. And the number of animals in the area now affects the amount of food available to the next generation, a direct violation of the principal logistic assumption. Natural populations of ungulates cannot grow logistically. The logistic curve is inadequate by both criteria: it does not fit and its biological assumptions are wrong.

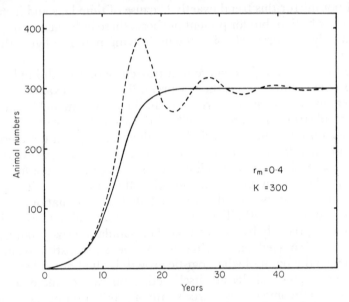

FIG. 11. A logistic curve of population growth (continuous line) and the same model incorporating a time delay of three years (dashed line).

(b) *Delayed logistic model.* The logistic equation can be modified to cope with the case where rate of increase is a function of population size sometime in the past rather than of the population now. The rationale for such a model is that the response in natality to a change in availability of a resource per head is lagged by an interval proportional to the product of the length of gestation and the time between breeding seasons.

The equation becomes

$$\frac{dN(t)}{dt} = r_m N(t) \left(1 - \frac{N(t - T)}{K}\right) \qquad (4)$$

indicating that rate of increase per head at time t is the intrinsic rate of increase multiplied by the complement of the proportion of carrying-capacity size K the population had reached by time (t − T), T being the time lag between a change in resources per head and the population's dynamic reaction to that change. But the logistic assumption still holds. The amount of food consumed by the population at either high or low density, over any short period of time, is a constant. The lag term cannot therefore be interpreted directly as a delay in the regenerative ability of the vegetation. Nor can it influence carrying capacity.

The form of the trajectory of a population obeying the rules of delayed logistic growth depends on the product of r_m and T. For $r_m T < 0.37$ (i.e. $1/e$) the population reaches a size of K without overshooting (R. M. May, pers. comm.), the curve of growth looking much like an unmodified logistic. Between $r_m T = 0.37$ and $r_m T = 1.57$ (i.e. $\pi/2$) the population overshoots K and reaches it through dampened oscillations as in Fig. 11. When $r_m T > \pi/2$ the population oscillates without ever reaching an equilibrium (footnote in Hutchinson, 1948, p. 237, giving an unpublished result by Lars Onsager; and Hayes, 1950). Thus by varying $r_m T$ three kinds of trajectories can be generated: monotonic approach to carrying capacity, approach through dampened oscillations, and stable limited cyclicity. One of these is almost certain to provide an empirical fit to any run of population estimates, and, in fact, the second is roughly what is observed for the growth of ungulate populations. But the act of fitting such a curve does not provide enlightenment on the mechanisms by which the population grows. It reveals only that the rate of production of the limiting resource may be a constant, and since this is about the one thing we can be certain is not true of an ungulate population's food supply we are no further ahead. In producing such a curve $r_m T$ becomes a mathematical constant of the fit, a magic number with no biological meaning that is juggled until the deviation between the data and the curve is minimized. Playing this game for a two-level system such as vegetation and herbivores is of dubious usefulness, but when it is tried with the terminal level of a three-tiered system—vegetation, herbivore, predator—as did Craske (1974) it degenerates to a mathematical exercise of no conceivable biological merit or relevance. The implication of this fitting is that the capital density of herbivores is uninfluenced by the density of predators, and the herbivores have no influence on the capital density of the vegetation. This is biological nonsense.

Not that a delayed logistic is always an inappropriate model in ecology. May (1973a) applied it successfully to Nicholson's (1954) runs of the size of a captive population of sheep–blowfly (*Lucilia cuprina* L.). The fit was close and it implied a time lag of nine days, two days less than the time for a larva to become an adult. Nicholson fed the blowflies a constant amount of ground liver each day and hence the principal logistic assumption is exactly met. Rate of production of the resource was constant. The amount fed to the flies was not influenced by the size of the population, nor by the amount of liver Nicholson stored in his refrigerator. Since the logistic assumption is true, May's analysis probably lays bare the biological essence of this artificial system.

The delayed logistic is not particularly useful as a model of the growth of ungulate populations, not because it cannot simulate the pattern of growth but because it hides the actual mechanisms of growth behind parameters to which it is difficult to assign biological meaning. There is, however, a special sense in which the delayed logistic does say something meaningful about the growth of herbivore populations, but this case will not be discussed until Section II, C, 2d.

(c) *Interactive model of growth.* The logistic and delayed logistic equations were rejected as a description of the growth of ungulate populations because they do not take account of an important attribute of the vegetation–herbivore system. Both models treat vegetation and other resources as inert. Only by this assumption can the dynamics of the herbivores be expressed by a single equation. In the real world each level of the system has its own dynamics which are modified by the dynamics of the other level.

For the remainder of this paper, unless explicitly qualified, all references to plant density or biomass refer only to that portion of the vegetation available to herbivores as food. Plant material out of reach, or poisonous, or tied up as wood, may well be important for shelter or shade, but in the following models this influence becomes a tacit component of the animals' intrinsic rate of increase and does not appear as a separate term.

The dynamics of a vegetation–herbivore system can be dissected into seven major components:

(a) In the absence of herbivores the vegetation would increase initially from low density at its intrinsic rate of increase, a_1.

(b) Because sunlight, water and minerals must be shared between the plants the initial rate of increase will be slowed down as more plants utilize these resources. This effect can be approximated by the logistic term

$$a_1 V \left(1 - \frac{V}{K} \right)$$

where V is the biomass of vegetation and K is the maximum sustainable biomass.

(c) The logistic rate of growth of vegetation will be slowed by an amount proportional to the number of animals eating it:

$$-c_1N$$

where N is the number or biomass of the animals and c_1 is the rate at which an animal eats.

(d) But the term c_1 will be a constant only when all animals eat as much as they want, i.e. when V is high. As V declines so also does the amount of vegetation eaten by each animal. This effect, equivalent to Holling's (1961) "functional response," can be approximated by multiplying c_1 by a saturating term that approaches unity at high V and zero at low V. Of the many offered, Ivlev's (1961) term is used here:

$$1 - e^{-d_1V}$$

where d_1 is the rate at which satiation is approached with increase in V.

(e) The animal population in the absence of vegetation will decline at a constant maximum rate per head, a_2.

(f) When vegetation is dense such that the animals each eat as much food as they want, the rate of decline is ameliorated by a constant c_2. The animals' intrinsic rate of increase can therefore be written c_2-a_2.

(g) At intermediate levels of vegetation density the degree to which maximum rate of decrease is ameliorated by food supply is symbolized by multiplying c_2 by a saturation term

$$1 - e^{-d_2V}$$

the equivalent of Holling's (1961) "numerical response," again in the Ivlev form. This term progressively reduces c_2 at a rate that is a function of d_2 as the vegetation is thinned out.

These terms can be strung together as a model of a vegetation–ungulate system:

$$\frac{dV}{dt} = a_1V\left(1 - \frac{V}{K}\right) - c_1N(1 - e^{-d_1V}) \tag{5a}$$

$$\frac{dN}{dt} = N\left[-a_2 + c_2(1 - e^{-d_2V})\right] \tag{5b}$$

The equations are essentially those of May (1973a, p. 84) who presented them as one of several possibilities for the interaction of two populations in different trophic levels. He introduced them primarily as a model for a prey–predator system whereas here they are slipped down one trophic level to represent a vegetation–herbivore system. At this level they are likely to be a little more appropriate, because a better biological case can be made for including a logistic term in the equation for vegetation than for ascribing logistic properties to the growth of herbivores.

The two equations are linked, neither being soluble without a solving of the other. Either equation could be elaborated further by introducing time lags, age distributions, and more complex numerical and functional responses, but for present purposes it is more convenient to investigate the qualitative behaviour of the system stripped of all but its bones. Figure 12 shows the trajectory of a population and its food supply

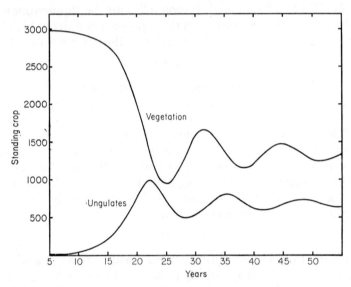

Fig. 12. Model of the trend of vegetation density and animal numbers during an ungulate eruption.

growing as directed by these equations. The system is parametered by

$$a_1 = 0{\cdot}8 \qquad\qquad a_2 = 1{\cdot}1$$
$$K = 3000$$
$$c_1 = 1{\cdot}2 \qquad\qquad c_2 = 1{\cdot}5$$
$$d_1 = 0{\cdot}001 \qquad\qquad d_2 = 0{\cdot}001$$

which are values close to what might be expected for a population of white-tailed deer released into a mosaic of grassland and forest. The animals erupt and approach an equilibrium with their food supply through dampened oscillations. The biomass of food plants crashes and then approaches an equilibrium with grazing pressure. The two sets of oscillations are displaced from each other, the vegetation trailing the animals by approximately a quarter of a wave length. Figure 13 is a phase diagram showing the changing ratio of animals to plants as the system implodes to its equilibrium point of N^*, V^*, a position that can be calculated (E. E. Robinson, personal communication) as

$$V^* = \frac{1}{d_2} \log_e \left(\frac{c_2}{c_2 - a_2} \right) \tag{6a}$$

$$N^* = \frac{V^* a_1 (1 - V^*/K)}{c_1 (1 - e^{-d_1 V^*})} \tag{6b}$$

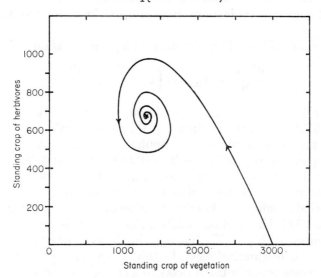

FIG. 13. Phase diagram of the relative densities of plants and animals during the eruption modelled in Fig. 12.

An interesting feature of the vegetative equilibrium is its complete independence of the parameters of plant growth, the animals alone determining its level. If the intrinsic rate of increase, a_1, or the maximum density of plants in the absence of grazing, K, were modified artificially by the application of fertilizer or water, the equilibrium level of vegetation is unaffected, the slack being taken up by an increase of herbivores.

By contrast, the equilibrium level of animals is determined by characteristics of both plants and animals. It is calculated as the instantaneous increment to equilibrium plant biomass, divided by the amount of plant biomass removed instantaneously by a single animal.

The interactive model provides a more informative simulation of ungulate population dynamics than does the logistic or delayed logistic. It generates the eruptive pattern of growth without the necessity of invoking arbitrary time lags, it treats plants and animals as equal partners in the vegetation–herbivore system, rather than declaring one inert with respect to the other, and its constants can each be assigned precise biological definition.

(d) *Another look at the delayed logistic.* Since the delayed logistic model provides a good empirical fit to an ungulate eruption, even though the assumptions on which it is based are biologically nonsensical, it is worth enquiring why. Could the biological meaning of its constants be redefined to provide some logical accommodation between assumptions and outcome? As it stands it gives the right answers for the wrong reasons.

The variable $N(t - T)$ in the delayed logistic equation

$$\frac{dN(t)}{dt} = r_m N(t) \left(1 - \frac{N(t - T)}{K}\right)$$

is usually interpreted (e.g. Hutchinson, 1948; Cunningham, 1954; Krebs, 1972) as a reaction time lag, the population's rate of increase taking T units of time to react to population density. Hence it responds to the population size of $N(t - T)$ rather than to $N(t)$. May (1973b) suggested that $N(t - T)$ could be considered more realistically as an average or integral of population size over past times stretching back over a period roughly equal to the characteristic regeneration time of the vegetation. This idea will be modified slightly here by accepting May's new definition of $N(t - T)$, but rejecting T as a time lag in anything but a trivial mathematical sense. By this interpretation the population's rate of increase reacts without delay to a change in vegetative biomass, the current level of which is a function of the average number of animals that have been eating it over a period extending back from the present (time t). $N(t - T)$ therefore becomes the average population size over this period, and $t - T$ becomes the time at which population size equalled that average. Thus the delayed logistic term

$$1 - \frac{N(t - T)}{K}$$

can be equated functionally with the numerical response term

$$1 - e^{-d_2 V}$$

of the interactive model, K and N^* being biological identities. Such a reconciliation between the two models may justify retention of the "delayed" logistic as a shorthand summary of the vegetation–herbivore system.

D. VEGETATION–HERBIVORE EQUILIBRIA

The interactive system of vegetation and herbivores modelled in equations (5) and (6) allows of three theoretical outcomes:

(a) Stable equilibrium: the system returns to equilibrium when displaced from it. This is the equilibrium of a marble in a basin.

(b) Stable limit cycle: instead of occupying a point equilibrium the two populations occupy a closed cyclic equilibrium trajectory, the densities of both plants and animals exhibiting well-defined periodic oscillations. When displaced from the equilibrium cycle, either inward or outward, the system reverts to its stable trajectory.

(c) Unstable equilibrium: when displaced from the equilibrium point the system oscillates with increasing amplitude until one of the components becomes extinct. This is the equilibrium of a marble balanced on top of an inverted basin.

Figure 14 diagrams the three outcomes in phase space. These disparate outcomes do not reflect differing processes; they reflect only differences in the ratios between constants in equation (5). One set of constant values will lead to stable equilibrium while a change in one or more of these values may trap the system in a stable limit cycle or push it into expanding oscillations. R. M. May (personal communication) has identified the boundary separating stable equilibrium from cycles and instability: defining

$$Y = d_1 K$$

and

$$X = \left(\frac{d_1}{d_2}\right) \log_e \frac{c_2}{c_2 - a_2},$$

the point N^*, V^* is stable if, and only if,

$$Y < \frac{X(2e^X - 2 - X)}{(e^X - 1 - X)}. \tag{7}$$

May's inequality can be expressed also in terms of K, d_1 and V^* as

$$K < \frac{V^*(2e^{d_1 V^*} - 2 - d_1 V^*)}{(e^{d_1 V^*} - 1 - d_1 V^*)} \tag{8}$$

which simplifies conveniently, for $d_1 V^* > 5$, to

$$K < 2V^*. \tag{9}$$

That relationship provides an ecological insight that can be pictured easily in terms of animals and plants, and which is likely to be relatively independent of the special characteristics of the model. A population of herbivores, the members of which are efficient at finding and utilizing food, will die out rapidly if they tend to hold the vegetation below half its ungrazed equilibrium biomass. Formally, and pedantically, the effect is to throw the system out of the parameter space characterized by stable equilibrium. Figure 15 shows, in terms of K, d_1 and V*, the boundary above which the system has a stable equilibrium point and below which is a region of cycles and instability.

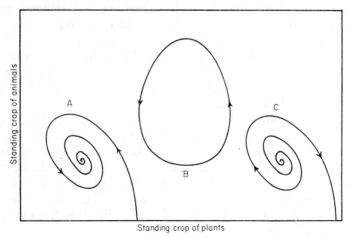

FIG. 14. Phase diagrams of the three possible outcomes of the ungulate–vegetation system: (A) stable equilibrium, (B) stable limit cycle, and (C) unstable equilibrium.

The last two outcomes are foreign to us. No cycling ungulate population has ever been recorded, and the idea of one oscillating with ever increasing amplitude is an affront to common sense. But it may be a mistake to dismiss these theoretically possible outcomes as algebraic aberrations reflecting the theological proclivities of mathematicians.

Although the stable limit cycle is unknown for ungulate populations it has been proposed to explain oscillations in a few other herbivores. Lack (1954) suggested that cycles of lemmings might be generated by the mutual interaction of the animals and their food supply, and May (1973c) subsequently formalized the suggestion in terms of the stable limit cycle. Caughley (1973) found evidence of long-term fluctuations in the density of elephants in Zambia and argued that it reflected a limit cycle between elephants and trees with a period of around 200 years.

The third outcome, oscillations of increasing amplitude, has not been reported for any herbivore in any area. But let us look again at Klein's (1968) eruption of reindeer on St Matthew Island. Figure 16 is a projection fitted by equation (5) to the estimates of numbers from 1944 to 1966. The values of some of the constants were approximated from Klein's data and the others were given plausible initial values and then juggled to achieve the fit:

$$a_1 = 0 \cdot 1 \qquad\qquad a_2 = 5 \cdot 8$$

$$K = 100\ 000$$

$$c_1 = 4 \qquad\qquad c_2 = 6 \cdot 105$$

$$d_1 = 0 \cdot 0002 \qquad\qquad d_2 = 0 \cdot 0002$$

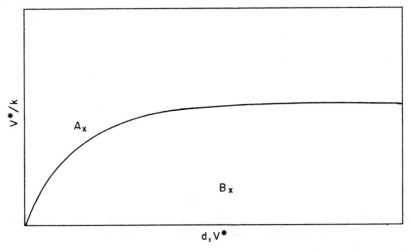

Fig. 15. Boundary separating stable equilibrium from cycles and instability. Crosses mark equilibrium points for (A) the white-tailed deer model and (B) the reindeer model. See text for definition of K, V^* and d_1.

The close fit achieved by the trajectory in Fig. 16 does not indicate that the constants have been assigned correct values, but the extremity of the eruptive pattern does not allow much reciprocal varying of the constants to achieve the trajectory by alternative pathways. The values are plausible, given the little known of the system, and their ranking at least is probably about right. By equation (6) the equilibrium point is estimated as a standing crop of 335 reindeer grazing 14 983 units of available vegetative biomass. But this point is highly unstable. A simulated shifting of the vegetation and the reindeer off the equilibrium by 0·001 % produced oscillations whose amplitude doubled with each successive cycle. After 18 cycles the reindeer were extinct. In biological terms this indicates that the system is unstable. Mathemetically, however, the system is characterized (E. E. Robinson, pers. comm.) by a stable limit cycle with maxima and minima of $V = 99\ 980$ and 2150, and $N = 6500$ and 10^{-12}, that takes around 160 years to complete

214	GRAEME CAUGHLEY

a cycle. Reverting again from mathematics to mammals, the model suggests that reindeer cannot survive indefinitely on St Matthew Island, and nor, for that matter, can they persist on any similar area of mainland.

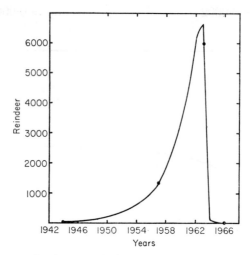

Fig. 16. A trajectory fitted by the interactive model to the population estimates (Klein, 1968) of reindeer on St. Matthew Island.

Too much can be made of this conclusion. The model is oversimplified grossly and the constant values are largely guesses, but the result allows the cautious speculation that the vegetation–herbivore system on St Matthew Island has parameters nor far removed from those leading to instability. At the last published count (1966) approximately 42 reindeer were present, all females. A critical test of the instability hypothesis would be to introduce a few males and observe the population's subsequent trajectory.

Having touched on two dubious examples of stable limit cycles in vegetation–herbivore systems, and an even more dubious amalgam of data and guesses that suggests the equilibrium point of one population of ungulates and its food supply is unstable, we are left with the bald fact that although limit cycles and unstable equilibria are theoretically possible, and may even have occurred in a few special instances, they are not a feature of ungulate population dynamics. The interaction of ungulates and vegetation typically leads to stable equilibrium through eruption and dampened oscillations. Why, of the three possible outcomes, does stable equilibrium occur commonly and the other two seldom or never? The question could be dismissed as a mathematical conundrum of no practical import, but here it will be treated as a real biological problem that should be faced, a hypothesis being offered to account for the anomaly.

Stable equilibrium is the least disruptive to both the plants and the animals. It is least likely to lead to extinction. Stable limit cycles are dynamically dangerous, particularly for the animals, because stochastic effects and environmental perturbations at the trough of the oscillation can lead to chance extinction. A local population locked into a stable limit cycle with its food supply, unless fuelled by immigration, would be at risk for about a quarter of each cycle. The third outcome is even more dangerous. Unstable equilibria provide maximum vulnerability: rapid extinction is guaranteed. In terms of evolution it is in the population's best interests that its parameters of intrinsic rate of increase, functional response and numerical response are adjusted relative to the vegetation's parameters of intrinsic rate of increase and K density such that the system keeps out of the parameter space leading to unstable equilibria or stable limit cycles. Systems that stray into this space will be selected against. This could be the reason that stable limit cycles and expanding oscillations are so rarely observed. First, they will be ephemeral because they lead to extinction, and consequently they will not be around long enough to attract attention. And secondly, they will not occur often because there will be heavy selection against the kind of population that has a predilection for getting itself into that difficulty.

If this hypothesis is true its implications are important ecologically and genetically. It implies that selection acts on ungulate populations as well as on individual ungulates, with all the theoretical problems of genetics following from that, and that selection acts less upon the population parameters individually than on the ratios between them and on these relative to those of the vegetation. Thus the concept of r and K selection (MacArthur and Wilson, 1967; Pianka, 1970; Roughgarden, 1971) would be such a gross oversimplification as to be almost meaningless, and certainly unhelpful, as a framework for considering the evolution of ungulate population dynamics.

May (1973a, p. 102) makes a similar point within the context of the delayed logistic model. He notes that the intrinsic rate of increase cannot be raised indefinitely by natural selection because the system will be precipitated into increasingly severe limit cycle oscillations. A similar argument can be made against unbounded increase in d_1, d_2 and $(c_2 - a_2)$ of the interactive model. To Birch's (1960) conclusion that "the tendency of natural selection is to increase r" we should perhaps add a rider that the tendency is reversed beyond a threshold level. Parameters are more likely optimized than maximized by natural selection.

E. CARRYING CAPACITY

A brief diversion is needed here for comment on the aims and methods of range management. These have profoundly influenced the wildlife manager's concept of the vegetation–ungulate equilibrium, a subject encapsuled in wildlife management jargon by the term "carrying capacity."

Stoddart and Smith (1955) defined range management as "the science and art of obtaining the maximum livestock production from range land consistent with conservation of the land resources". Stoddart (1967) subsequently expanded this definition by replacing "maximum livestock production" with "maximum livestock or game production". As the definition indicates, range management is the hand-maiden of the science of animal production. Its tools of research are surveys of plant density, vegetative composition, rates of growth, proportion of annual growth removed by animals, and time trends in these statistics. Its primary aim is the attainment of that equilibrium between plants and animals that provides the maximum sustained yield of wool, milk, meat or hides. A secondary aim of optimizing erosion rates and hydrological effects is pursued where appropriate.

The range manager has, through a long period of trial and error, learned what composition and density of vetetation provides a maximum sustained yield of sheep and cattle in most climatic zones. He characterizes this ideal vegetation in terms of the proportion of the standing crop of vegetation comprising species that increase under the action of grazing, those that decrease, and those that invade the grazed area. Table IV gives Sampson's (1952) evaluation of range condition according

TABLE IV   Percentage of plant groups characterizing condition of the range. (After Sampson, 1952)

Plant group	Range condition classes			
	Excellent	Good	Fair	Poor
Decreasers	55–80	35–55	10–30	0–10
Increasers	20–35	25–40	15–25	5–15
Invaders	0–10	10–45	45–75	75–100

to this classification. The range manager also measures the proportion of annual growth removed and compares it with the "proper use factor", the proportion that can be removed without displacing the equilibrium. Where the condition of the range departs from this optimum he initiates a trend towards it. "The principal and most universal method of control of vegetation of range lands is exercised by the manipulation of grazing pressure" (Harlan, 1956), that is, by taking stock off the area or putting more stock on it.

The density of stock at equilibrium with the range conditions providing maximum sustained offtake is described as the carrying capacity or grazing capacity of the land. This density is not the maximum standing crop of animals that can be maintained indefinitely but the standing crop yielding a maximum return. The two are not the same. The standing crop providing maximum sustained yield is lower than the maximum sustainable standing crop because food per head must be kept high enough to generate the yield.

To the wildlife manager, however, "carrying capacity" is something else. It is the maximum density of animals that can be sustained indefinitely without inducing trends in vegetation. The two meanings will be differentiated here by naming the wildlife management measure "ecological carrying capacity" and that of range management "economic carrying capacity". Both describe attainable equilibria between animals and vegetation but they are different equilibria, the first differing from the second in its higher standing crop of animals and lower standing crop of edible vegetation. The difference between the two is not widely recognized within either field of management.

A reason for the confusion lies in a persistent fallacy of wildlife management: that sustained-yield harvesting does not lower the density of a population below that at ecological carrying capacity. This notion is examined further in Section III, A, 2; here we need only note its prevalence. A similar and parallel fallacy pervades range management: that the economic carrying capacity density of animals and plants is the only combination of the two that does not induce changes in vegetation; and since this is the only attainable equilibrium it also represents ecological carrying capacity. Thus a wildlife manager can write that "every habitat, for wildlife as well as for domestic livestock, has its carrying capacity, which sets firm limits on population increase" (Dasmann, 1968, p. 238). This truism clearly refers to ecological carrying capacity, but it misses the point that the "carrying capacity" calculated by range managers with respect to livestock is a different measure from that applied to wildlife. Conversely, a range manager can write of wildlife that "where utilization checks are wanted on ranges that do not support livestock, no special problems are involved and these surveys can be made by the same methods used to determine livestock utilization" (Cook, 1962). The same methods perhaps, but the data may require a different interpretation.

The end result of this confusion is that criteria used by range managers to determine whether livestock are at economic carrying capacity are commonly used by both wildlife managers and range managers to determine whether wildlife are at ecological carrying capacity. With regularity the vegetation is judged to be in "poor" condition and the density of wildlife therefore judged above carrying capacity.

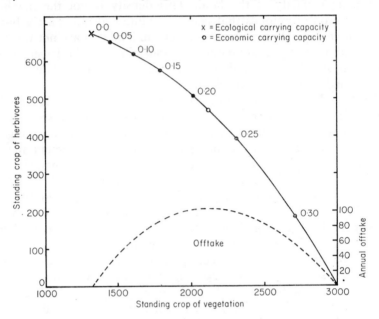

FIG. 17. The isocline (continuous line) of equilibrium between plant density and animal density, the rate of harvesting (dots) needed to impose the equilibrium, and the sustained-yield annual offtake accruing therefrom.

Figure 17 illustrates the difference between the two kinds of carrying capacity by use of the population modelled in Figs. 12 and 13. The continuous curve is an isocline where the density and composition of the vegetation is at equilibrium with the standing crop of animals. The dashed line is the annual sustained yield needed to impose that equilibrium. At ecological carrying capacity, the equilibrium in the absence of harvesting, the population contains 672 animals in balance with 1322 units of vegetation biomass. At economic carrying capacity a standing crop of 2120 units of vegetation is grazed by a standing crop of 470 animals harvested at an instantaneous rate of 0·22 per year.

Now suppose the unharvested equilibrium of this model represented a balance between deer and vegetation in a national park. A range manager called in to assess range conditions would find the proportion of increaser and invader plant species characteristic of "poor" range, and a proportion of annual growth removed in excess of the "proper use factor" for that climatic zone. He might well conclude that the area was "overgrazed" (vegetation is 40% below economic optimum) by a population 40% above carrying capacity. His professional reflex would be to recommend an immediate reduction of animals.

Or consider the commonly posed question of whether an area would yield more meat from wildlife than from livestock (Darling, 1960; Dasmann, 1964; Riney and Kettlitz, 1964; Roth, 1966; De Vos, 1969). This question deserves serious attention, but too often the evidence offered in favour of wildlife comprises measurements of wildlife biomass at (ecological) carrying capacity compared with livestock biomass at (economic) carrying capacity. The comparison is invalid both because the two densities are irrelative and because there is no close relationship between carrying-capacity density and sustained offtake. In stressing only those two points we can afford to ignore added complications: that an arithmetic error in converting square miles to hectares is responsible for several oft-quoted figures for wildlife biomass being too high by a factor of ten (Sharkey, 1970); that the biomass of wildlife living in the absence of stock is commonly compared with the biomass of cattle or sheep coexisting with wildlife; and, that a cursory inspection of the agricultural literature is sufficient to reveal that stock biomass on unimproved native pastures consistently tops that of wildlife in the same climatic zone, usually by at least a factor of three.

Much of the confusion over "carrying capacity" stems from a misunderstanding of vegetation–herbivore equilibria. Carrying capacity is, by definition, measured in units of animal density. Plants enter the definition only in the proviso that this density of animals does not cause trends in vegetation. The concept is often applied in a way that pictures the environment as an inert container of fixed size to be filled with animals, a view that probably reflects the logistic curve branded into each of our hind-brains. In reality plants and animals are equal partners in the vegetation–herbivore system. If we speak of the density of herbivores a vegetation can carry we must be prepared equally to consider the density and composition of vegetation the herbivores can "carry". Better still, the vegetation–herbivore equilibrium can be described by its coordinates of density, one dimension for the animals and one for the vegetation.

When the population is harvested the single equilibrium point representing ecological carrying capacity expands to an isoclinal curve as in Fig. 17, any point on which represents an equilibrium between vegetation density, animal density and rate of harvesting. Along this isocline there will be progressive changes in those attributes of the vegetation that range managers measure (plant density, composition and annual growth removed), and changes in what wildlife managers measure (animal density, condition, fecundity and survival): these changes are not temporal but coordinal. Wildlife managers have been as slow to appreciate that there is more than one vegetation–herbivore equilibrium for a given system as they have been to grasp that there is more than one sustained yield. Further, there is no "proper use factor" for a wildlife habitat but a range of them which, when balanced against the other variables of the system, can each reflect equilibrium grazing pressure.

Except in unusual circumstances only one equilibrium is of interest in livestock production, that of economic carrying capacity. But wildlife managers must contend with several equilibria: that appropriate to national parks (the ecological carrying-capacity equilibrium), those appropriate to various levels of sustained yield up to and including the maximum sustained yield, and equilibria between vegetation and herbivores when the latter are held by control measures, for one reason or another, at very low density. The wildlife manager's problem is in deciding which equilibrium is required and what action, if any, is needed to shift the system to that equilibrium and to hold it there.

III. Dynamics in Management

A. SUSTAINED YIELD

1. *Principles of harvesting*

To most people the harvesting of populations connotes whaling, sealing and commercial fishing, activities carried out by professionals for profit. But in terms of men and time these activities are only a minor branch of population harvesting; most harvesting effort is expended by sportsmen.

Whether a population is managed for commercial harvest or for recreational hunting the same principles apply. Management is aimed at providing a sustained yield (SY), a crop that can be taken year after year without forcing the population into decline. An SY is not a unique value for a given population. There will be a large number of SY values each corresponding to a different management treatment and population density. Efficient management aims at refining the treatment to provide a maximum sustained yield (MSY). Alternatively, since the MSY is not necessarily the harvest returning the greatest ratio of income to expenditure, and because uses of the land other than animal production may also be important, harvesting may be aimed at an optimum sustained yield (OSY).

The rate of harvesting that holds rate of increase to zero is that rate at which the population would increase initially if harvesting were terminated. Hence a population increasing at 20% a year, i.e. at a finite rate of $e^r = 1\cdot20$ and an exponential rate of $r = 0\cdot182$, can be harvested at an instantaneous rate of $H = 0\cdot182$ to hold it stable. The instantaneous rate of harvesting, H, requires some explanation. It is the rate at which the population could be harvested throughout the year. Symbolizing as $\bar{N}$ the mean number of individuals in the population over the year, the yield for the year totals $H\bar{N}$ animals. But when the population is harvested during only a small part of the year, the SY is calculated not from the instantaneous rate of harvesting but from the isolated rate of harvesting, h, where $h = 1 - e^{-H}$.

A couple of numerical examples will make this clear. Suppose a birth-pulse population increasing at $r = 0\cdot182$ contains 1000 animals immediately after the birth pulse, and that the severity of natural mortality is constant throughout the year at a finite rate of $\bar{n} = 0\cdot25$ per year (equivalent to $0\cdot0236$ per month). Numbers in successive months after the birth pulse will conform to the series for the unharvested population in Table V. By the end of the year the population is reduced by mortality to 750 individuals which give birth to $m = 0\cdot6$ offspring per head, upping numbers to $750 + 750\,m = 1200$ at the birth pulse. This paper population will now be harvested to hold its rate of increase to $r = 0$ by allowing sportsmen to crop it over a short hunting season. To calculate the appropriate rate of harvesting, and hence the number of animals that the hunters will be allowed to kill, the appropriate instantaneous rate of harvesting, $H = 0\cdot182$, is converted to the isolated rate of harvesting by

$$h = 1 - e^{-H} = 0\cdot167.$$

At any time of the year $0\cdot167$ of animals then alive can be harvested over a short period of time to hold rate of increase to zero. Although h is independent of the time of year the SY will differ according to when the hunting season is declared, because natural mortality progressively reduced between birth pulses the number of animals exposed to risk of death by hunting. Table V shows the effect of harvesting immediately after the birth pulse when 167 ($1000 \times 0\cdot167$) can be shot, and of harvesting in the 5th month when 151 ($908 \times 0\cdot167$) can be shot. Under either regime the numbers at the next birth pulse are held to 1000 and the population's rate of increase is therefore held to zero.

TABLE V Effect on numbers of harvesting a birth-pulse population once during the year (see text for further details)

Month	Unharvested numbers	Harvest in first month	Harvest in fifth month
1	1000	1000 h=0.167→	1000
2	976	833	976
3	953	813	953
4	930	794	930 h=0.167→
5	908	775	908
6	887	757	757
7	866	739	739
8	846	722	722
9	826	705	705
10	806	688	688
11	787	672	672
12	768	656	656
		640	640
1	750 + 750 m = 1200	625 + 625 m = 1000	625 + 625 m = 1000

$m = 0.6$	$m = 0.6$	$m = 0.6$
$r = 0.182$	$r = 0.0$	$r = 0.0$
$SY = 0$	$SY = 167$	$SY = 151$

If two hunting seasons per year are required, the appropriate rate of harvesting at each occasion is calculated by halving H and again calculating an isolated rate of hunting mortality:

$$_2h = 1 - e^{-H/2} = 0\cdot087.$$

Table VI shows the effect of harvesting on two occasions, firstly in

TABLE VI   Effect on numbers of harvesting a birth-pulse population on two occasions during the year

Month	Unharvested numbers	Harvests in 9th and 11th months	Harvests in 6th and 7th months
1	1000	1000	1000
2	976	976	976
3	953	953	953
4	930	930	930
5	908	908	908
6	887	887	887 $\xrightarrow{_2h=0\cdot087}$ 810
7	866	866	722 $_2h=0\cdot087$ 791 $\leftarrow$
8	846	846	705
9	826	826 $\xrightarrow{_2h=0\cdot087}$ 754	688
10	806	736	672
11	787	656 $\xleftarrow{_2h=0\cdot087}$ 719	656
12	768	640	640
1	750 + 750 m = 1200	625 + 625 m = 1000	625 + 625 m = 1000
	m = 0·6 r = 0·182 SY = 0	m = 0·6 r = 0·0 SY = 134	m = 0·6 r = 0·0 SY = 146

months 9 and 11, and secondly in months 6 and 7. The outcome is the same: population size at the next birth pulse is held to that at the previous birth pulse, i.e. r = 0.

By extension, the appropriate rate of harvesting can be calculated for any number of occasions throughout the year. Should the population be harvested at twelve equally-spaced occasions, the rate of harvesting appropriate to each occasion is

$$_{12}h = 1 - e^{-H/12} = 0.015$$

It produces an SY of 146 animals per year. But if animals are to be harvested with this frequency they might as well be harvested throughout the year. The effect is about the same. With continuous harvesting at the appropriate rate this population's size is $\overline{N} = 800$, and the yield is therefore

$$SY = H\overline{N} = 0.182 \times 800 = 146 \text{ animals.}$$

These numerical examples illustrate general rules of harvesting:

(1) An SY is calculated from the instantaneous rate of harvesting, H, which equals the potential rate of increase r_p which would become actual if the population were not harvested.

(2) When the year is divided into short intervals the population may be harvested during any one of these at a rate of $h = 1 - e^{-H}$ of animals surviving at that time.

(3) When harvesting is spread over more than one interval the appropriate rate of harvesting during each is $1 - e^{-H/y}$, where y is the number of short harvesting intervals.

(4) An SY accrues from harvesting in any short interval at any rate providing that these rates, expressed in instantaneous form, jointly total the appropriate overall instantaneous rate, H.

(5) As a close approximation, the above four rules hold whether rate of natural mortality is constant or variable throughout the year and whether the population has a birth-pulse, birth-flow or intermediate breeding system, providing that these aspects of the life history remain constant from year to year.

The numerical examples were of an imaginary population which, in the absence of harvesting, would increase. It was harvested on paper to reduce its rate of increase to zero by substituting a rate of harvesting for this rate of increase. It is an unlikely example because most populations, although fluctuating from year to year, have a rate of increase which, averaged over several years, is close to zero. If rate of harvesting depended solely on the population's actual rate of increase, as it does in the examples, a population with an average rate of increase of $r = 0$ has an appropriate instantaneous harvesting rate of $H = 0$ and therefore an SY of zero.

A population that is stable in the absence of harvesting can be harvested only after the vegetation–herbivore system has been manipulated to raise r above zero. In theory there are two ways of doing this: by treating the vegetation to raise its density or production, or by lowering the density of the animals. Both raise the amount of available food per head which, in turn, improves fecundity and survival to generate a positive rate of increase. In practice the second alternative is the universal choice. A positive rate of increase is generated by lowering density, and the population is then harvested at this rate to stabilize numbers at the lowered density.

Harvesting management uses the fact that, in general, the greater the availability of food and other resources per head, the greater is the population's rate of increase. Within limits, the farther a population is reduced below ecological carrying-capacity density the higher is its induced rate of increase; and the higher will be that rate of harvesting needed to hold numbers stable at the reduced density. Thus for each density there is a potential rate of increase, r_p, that would manifest if harvesting stopped. Put in another way, for each density there is a corresponding harvesting rate of $H = r_p$ that holds the population stable in size. Although H tends to increase as density is lowered the SY does not increase in parallel. H is small when density is reduced only a little and the appropriate SY is a small fraction of a comparatively large population. When density is reduced substantially the population, which is now comparatively small, will have a high r_p and hence a high H. The appropriate SY is a large fraction of a small population. The maximum unselective sustained yield is taken from a population of size N where HN is maximal. The task of estimating the MSY is therefore a complex dual operation. Estimates are required of both the density from which an MSY (or OSY) can be taken and the rate of harvesting that stabilizes density at that level. That sturdy work-horse of wildlife management, the technique of successive approximations, is unequal to this task. The probability of successfully approximating to the appropriate value of HN by varying H and N independently is low enough to make the search for the proverbial needle in the haystack a sure bet by comparison.

Figure 18 illustrates these points by a Ricker diagram. It represents an idealized relationship between numbers (or density) in one year and numbers a year later. The diagonal line gives all possible positions for $N_{t+1} = N_t$, i.e. when numbers do not change between one year and the next. A point falling to the left of the diagonal represents an increase in numbers between time t and t + 1; a point to the right records a decline. The curve in the same figure describes a relationship that might be expected between a population's size in two successive years. Its shape will differ between species and between populations within species. The level of N_t where the curve cuts the diagonal is the "steady density" the average size of the unharvested population at ecological carrying capacity.

No ungulate population is as neat as this. The environment fluctuates from year to year causing fluctuations in survival, fecundity, age distribution and the resultant rate of increase. The curve represents a relationship that might well underlie the fluctuations of a simple population in a simple environment. The actual trend would be blurred by environmental and stochastic effects but not obliterated.

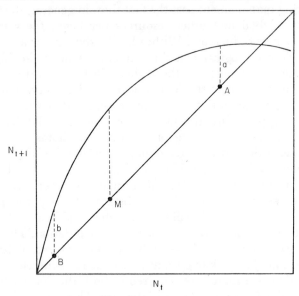

FIG. 18. Ricker diagram of the relationship between numbers in two successive years (see text).

Figure 18 shows three strategies whereby this idealized population could be harvested for sustained yield. In the first the population is harvested down from steady density to a size of $N_t = A$. The dashed line a, vertically linking the curve and the diagonal, represents the number that would be added to the population over the next year if harvesting were terminated. It is proportional to the number that must be harvested each year to hold the population stable at size $N_t = A$. This SY is a small proportion of a large population. Alternatively the population could be reduced to $N_t = B$ and an SY proportional to the length of line b could be harvested each year, the yield being a large proportion of a small population. The MSY is taken at the population size where the diagonal and the curve have maximum vertical separation, at $N_t = M$.

Figure 18, for all its abstraction, illustrates several points applicable to harvesting real populations.

(a) If a population is stable in numbers it must be reduced below steady density to generate a croppable surplus.

(b) For each density to which a population is reduced there is an appropriate SY.

(c) For each level of SY there are *two* levels of density from which this SY can be harvested.

(d) At only one density can an MSY be harvested.

(e) When a constant number is harvested from a population each year, the population will decline from steady density and finally stabilize at the upper population size for which that number is the SY. Should the number exceed the MSY, the population declines to extinction. It is not possible, by this harvesting system, to reach a stabilization at a density below that providing the MSY.

(f) If a constant percentage of the population is harvested each year, the percentage applying to the standing crop of that particular year, the population will decline to and stabilize at a level at equilibrium with the rate of harvesting. The level may be either above or below that generating the MSY.

2. *Harvesting theory in wildlife management*

Analyses for estimating sustained yield were pioneered by fisheries biologists, notably by Baranov (1926), by Hjort *et al.* (1933), and by Graham (1935). Beverton and Holt (1957) reviewed subsequent refinements up to 1954 and added several of their own. Thereafter further advances were made by Ricker (1954a, 1958), Chapman (1961), Gulland (1962, 1968), Ivlev (1966), Lefkovitch (1967), Schaefer(1967), and Allen (1971).

But this vast body of theory and practice has not penetrated the field of wildlife management, despite Ricker's (1954b) attempt to stimulate cross-communication with a paper in the *Journal of Wildlife Management*. Perhaps this journal's rotation of Ricker's explanatory diagrams through ninety degrees had something to do with the lack of response, but for whatever the reason wildlife management continued along its own line, unchanged and undaunted.

The theory of harvesting dynamics current in wildlife management is unique. It rests on the assumption that, at least after the first year of life, hunting mortality and natural mortality are exactly compensatory, the harvesting of one individual reducing natural mortality by one. From this assumption springs three corollaries forming the basis of harvesting theory in wildlife management.

(a) Maximum sustained yield of animals other than those in their first year of life is obtained by harvesting at a rate identical to the percentage of yearlings in the post-calf population.

(b) Harvesting of a population at ecological carrying-capacity density at a rate less than this will not lower density.

(c) The SY can therefore be calculated as the appropriate rate of harvesting multiplied by the size of the post-calf population at ecological carrying capacity.

That is the basic theory from which individual interpretations may diverge. Some writers recommend harvesting the entire population at that rate represented by the percentage of calves. Others take the percentage of yearlings in the total population as the appropriate rate applied to the post-calf population. But in each case the rate of harvesting is set as some proportion calculated from the age distribution.

Explicit examples of this reasoning behind recommended offtakes can be found in the publications of Pimlott (1959), Dasmann (1964), Bindernagel (1968), and Schladweiler and Stevens (1973). Although corollary (c) is the dangerous one because, if wrong, it would lead directly to massive overcropping, the corollaries will be ignored in favour of examining the basic assumption.

If hunting mortality and natural mortality exactly compensate, the resources made available by the death of one animal are released for use by another, the exchange being made without lag. Hence, if a rate of hunting mortality, equal to the rate of natural mortality in the absence of hunting, is imposed on a population, the only cause of post-calf death would be hunting. Similarly, if the unhunted population is below carrying capacity no adult dies until carrying capacity is reached. To a greater or lesser degree, according to the details of the particular interpretation, the curve of population growth therefore approximates an exponential truncated at carrying-capacity density.

These characteristics, which are necessarily implied by the assumption of exactly compensatory mortality, have not been recorded for any ungulate population; nor have they been postulated as characteristics that future research might uncover. The rate of natural mortality at densities below carrying capacity is certainly less than that at steady density, but it is not negligible. Figure 7 graphs mortality rate by age for a population of thar increasing at about $r = 0.12$ at a density considerably below carrying capacity. The weighted mean mortality rate is 10% per year, only a fraction of that being referrable to the effects of hunting. Similar examples can be drawn from life tables of captive small mammals kept in ideal conditions where food, space and other resources are superabundant (e.g. Wiesner and Sheard, 1935; Leslie and Ranson, 1940; Leslie *et al.*, 1955). They show that such treatment does not disrupt the U-shaped trend of mortality rate by age but simply lowers its elevation.

An interesting variant of the assumption that hunting mortality can be substituted for natural mortality is provided by Lobdell's *et al.* (1972) simulation of the effects of hunting on turkeys. They assume that when hunting mortality is less than about half the rate of natural mortality, the rate of total mortality, q, is unaffected by the hunting. Their calculation of the rate of natural mortality, n, in the presence of a given rate of hunting mortality, h, is therefore

$$n = (q - h)/(1 - h),$$

a formalization of the truism that the rate at which animals survive hunting, multiplied by the rate at which they survive other agents of mortality, equals the total rate of survival:

$$(1 - q) = (1 - h)(1 - n),$$

a contrast to the assumption of complete substitutability of mortality which, in the same terms, would imply

$$(1 - q) = (1 - h) = (1 - n).$$

That part of their model is unexceptionable but objection can be raised to their declaring q a constant, even within the imposed limits of variation in h. Although their estimated SY is lower than that calculated on the assumption of completely compensatory mortality, and is to that extent more realistic, the model is still constrained by the unnecessary and dynamically improbable assumption that a rise or fall in harvesting rate has no effect on population size. These remarks are addressed to the deterministic core of their equal-sexes stochastic model. Stochasticization does not affect the argument.

A third model of harvesting is provided by Davis (1967). It is, in fact, peripheral to the theme of his paper which is concerned with demonstrating the application of dynamic linear programming to optimizing harvesting strategies. It is mentioned here only because some wildlife managers have assumed that the results from analysis of his artificial examples provide real information on the harvesting rates appropriate to populations of large mammals.

Davis illustrated the method of optimization by use of a very simple and completely unreal population model in which rates of fecundity, natural mortality, population increase and food intake per head are independent of the level of available food. When the density reaches the level at which forage is consumed at its renewal rate, the population is harvested at the rate of increase generated by the arbitrary constant rates of fecundity and natural mortality. This paper is an excellent exposition of the uses of linear programming in wildlife management.

It is not, nor was it intended to be, a prescription for estimating sustained yield. The analysis is applicable to optimizing yield when levels of sustained yield, and the costs associated with each, have been estimated by more appropriate methods.

These models of harvesting constitute, in essence, the current state of harvesting theory in the field of wildlife management. The practice of harvesting is very much more pragmatic. Most populations of ungulates hunted by sportsmen are harvested without the administering agency having more than the haziest idea of either population size or current harvesting rate. The yield is usually known, however, and regulated by issue of hunting permits. Under this regime of relatively constant hunting pressure the population and its food supply will move to an equilibrium with the unknown rate of harvesting. The administering agency does not know what proportion of the MSY is represented by the SY resulting from this treatment. Most hunted ungulate populations in North America, Australia and Africa are managed in this way.

A quantitative refinement, applicable to a few populations in the above-mentioned regions, and more commonly to those in Europe, is introduced when the approximate size of the population is known. The administering agency then has estimates of the SY, the density from which the SY is taken, and the rate of harvesting determining the two. The information needed for further refinement is still lacking, however: the relationship between the arbitrary yield and the MSY is unknown.

These pragmatic approaches to harvesting are not to be scorned. Their greatest advantage lies in their relative safety: they seldom result in over-harvesting. If they are not very efficient at least they usually work, an accolade that cannot be directed towards the theoretical models in wildlife management reviewed previously.

Commonsense pragmatism will, for a long time, continue as the necessary grounding wire of ungulate management. It has already saved us from several unpublicised potential disasters. But the future lies in a cautious injection of population dynamics into wildlife management to allow a more efficient use of those wildlife resources that are currently underutilized.

3. Models for harvesting ungulate populations

An obvious approach to developing harvesting models for ungulates is to search through the models of fisheries management and adapt the more appropriate to the special characteristics of ungulate dynamics. This approach is not free of problems. Fisheries models tend to be anchored by an implicit assumption that the rate of production of food is not influenced profoundly by the fish themselves. In Section II, C, 1 we saw that ungulates affect both the capital of their food supply and its interest. This must be allowed for in any ungulate harvesting model.

As a first approximation the model of population growth exemplified by equations (5) and (6) will serve as a basis for a harvesting model. Figure 19 shows the SY, at several levels of standing crop, for the population simulated in Fig. 12. The curve of points cuts the x-axis at a standing crop of zero and at the ecological carrying capacity population size of 672, at which two points the SY is rather obviously zero. Between them the curve of SY arches asymmetrically, the peak being displaced to the right. For this example, and for others not given here, the curve can be made approximately symmetrical by square-transforming the standing crop. Over a wide range of parameter values the regression of SY on squared standing crop can be approximated by a parabola, the equation for which is written as

$$SY = bx^2 + cx^4$$

where x is the standing crop, and b and c are constants of the regression. If b and c can be estimated from field data the SY can be calculated for any equilibrium level of standing crop. This model has not strayed far from the methodology and concepts of fisheries harvesting. Fisheries biologists will recognize it as a variation on Graham's (1935) and Ricker's (1958) yield-parabola method.

The constants can be estimated in two ways.

(a) *First method.* Suppose a population has been harvested for some years by taking an SY of known size from a population of known size, the standing crop of animals being at equilibrium with the harvesting. Suppose further that the size of the population was also known before the harvesting programme was started, at which time the population was at ecological carrying-capacity density. We would then have a known value of K_2 (the subscript distinguishing this number of animals at carrying capacity from that of K representing ungrazed plant biomass), a known SY which will be labelled C, and a known population size N from which that C is taken. From the mathematical properties of a parabola on a square-transformed abscissa, the relationship between these statistics and those sought, the MSY and the population size from which it is taken, can be derived as

$$MSY = \frac{CK_2^4}{4N^2(K_2^2 - N^2)} \qquad (10)$$

taken from a population size of

$$N_{MSY} = 0.7K_2.$$

The calculation is demonstrated with figures from the example in Fig. 19, that model population having a K_2 of 672, and, at a harvesting rate of $H = 0.16$, an offtake of $C = 90$ taken from a standing crop of 565 animals:

$$\text{MSY} = \frac{90 \times 672^4}{4 \times 565^2(672^2 - 565^2)} = 109,$$

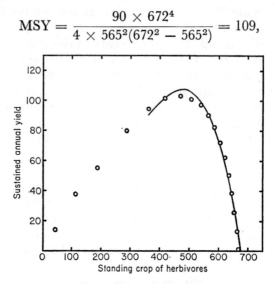

FIG. 19. Sustained annual yield (circles) against population size in equilibrium with this offtake, according to the interactive model. A curve of the form $y = bx^2 + cx^4$ is fitted to the right flank.

which compares well with the modelled $\text{MSY} = 104$. The population at equilibrium with this offtake contains

$$N_{\text{MSY}} = 0.7 \times 672 = 470 \text{ animals}$$

which is close to the modelled total of 469.

(b) *Second method.* When K_2 is unknown the MSY can still be calculated if C and N are known for two levels of harvesting. The two SY values might be obtained, for example, if a population had been hunted at a constant rate for many years, the population's size adjusting to this rate of offtake; and then the hunting pressure was increased to shift the standing crop to a second level at equilibrium with the higher yield. Such a set of data might reflect either good luck or good management.

Again data from Fig. 19 will be used as illustration. At harvesting rates of 0·1 and 0·2 respectively the offtakes and equilibrium standing crops are

$$C_1 = 62 \qquad\qquad N_1 = 621$$
$$C_2 = 102 \qquad\qquad N_2 = 508$$

First, two regression constants are estimated

$$b = \frac{C_2 N_1^4 - C_1 N_2^4}{N_1^2 N_2^2 (N_1^2 - N_2^2)} \qquad (11)$$

$$= \frac{(102 \times 621^4) - (62 \times 508^4)}{621^2 \times 508^2 \, (621^2 - 508^2)}$$

$$= 0.000864,$$

and

$$c = \frac{C_1 - b N_1^2}{N_1^4} = \frac{C_2 - b N_2^2}{N_2^4} \qquad (12)$$

$$= \frac{62 - (0.000864 \times 621^2)}{621^4} = \frac{102 - (0.000864 \times 508^2)}{508^4}$$

$$= -1.8 \times 10^{-9}.$$

The constants are related to the MSY and the standing crop at equilibrium with it by

$$MSY = -b^2/4c = 102 \qquad (13)$$

and

$$N_{MSY} = \sqrt{-b/2c} = 487 \qquad (14)$$

The SY appropriate to any given population size N can be calculated as

$$SY = bN^2 + cN^4, \qquad (15)$$

and the population size at ecological carrying capacity as

$$K_2 = \sqrt{-b/c}. \qquad (16)$$

The two methods yield approximations that must be treated as such. They allow a manager to estimate the vicinity of the MSY, or any OSY he desires, but he must fine tune to discover its precise location. The density yielding the MSY is, by these methods, always estimated as $0.7 \, K_2$, but by the model underlying the approximations it may lie anywhere between $0.6 \, K_2$ and $0.8 \, K_2$ for various combinations of biologically plausible parameter values. Creative caution rather than blind faith is the recommended approach to these recipes. To avoid the possibility of ending up on the wrong side of the MSY at the first tentative estimate of its level, harvesting rates should be held below that estimate.

After the standing crop has stabilized to an equilibrium with this lower rate it can be raised a notch and the population carefully monitored to ensure that standing crop again stabilizes. The cycle can then be repeated until the yield reaches the true MSY. This process of fine-tuning will take a number of years.

These two methods of estimating offtake operate on the trend of yield against equilibrium standing crop of animals. It is a strategy proven by fisheries management and has much to recommend it. However, Fig. 17 suggests that an alternative general method, radical but biologically more sensible, would repay investigation. In that figure offtake is graphed against standing crop of plants rather than of animals. That relationship is much more direct because it is the amount of resources available per head that determines the population's potential rate of increase and hence the rate of offtake required to hold that potential latent. The trend of sustained yield against standing crop of vegetation is not a parabola (see equation 6), but it is close enough to allow acceptance of the parabola as a good approximation. This leads to simplified calculations but to complex problems of interpretation. In equations (5) and (6) the vegetative variable V was introduced as simply a biomass of the vegetative standing crop. In reality it is the biomass of available food where each species of food plant is weighted by its nutritional value. V is therefore difficult to quantify because although the biomass of vegetation is easily measured its nutritional value is not. Further, as Bell's (1971) penetrating study shows, there is no simple relationship between the biomass of a particular food plant and the biomass of food from that plant available to a herbivore. The algebraic symbol V is hence a representation of a biologically complex variable but one which may be quantifiable, at least approximately, by a competent range manager. He could probably attach a figure to V^*, the value of the standing crop of available food at equilibrium with an unharvested population of ungulates, and by use of exclosure plots do the same for K, the equilibrium value of V when vegetation is ungrazed. Only one value of sustained yield and V would then be needed to estimate all possible sustained yields and the V levels from which each is taken.

This strategy, introduced here only as a suggestion that may open up interesting possibilities, could prove particularly appropriate to harvesting or control schemes whose major justification is the management of plant cover for hydrological purposes. If the required form of the vegetation can be summarized as a value of V, the sustained yield necessary to impose a vegetation equilibrium at that value can be calculated from the curve relating offtake to the vegetation's standing crop.

4. Game cropping in Africa

"Game cropping" as used here designates sustained-yield harvesting of wild mammals for profit. It has received much attention in Africa over the last decade and it will be examined here mainly in an African context. The literature is extensive (an incomplete bibliography of over 150 references was compiled by A. De Vos, personal communication, in 1971), but this section, which is aimed at providing only a cursory overview, quotes a highly selective subset.

From about the mid 1950's through the sixties wildlife biologists and conservationists were greatly taken with the idea that African wildlife could best be conserved by demonstrating its economic value. The movement was spurred by the then very real fear that, with independence, the lovingly constructed dam of interlocking game laws would be swept away and the wildlife slaughtered. It was hoped that the alien legalisms of the colonial game ordinances could be replaced by a rational economic motive for conserving wildlife. That events did not bear out the fears is another story, one for which the Africans themselves can take the credit, but here we are concerned only with the technical aspects of the game cropping projects that this period of tension generated.

The basis of these schemes was the belief that in many areas of Africa a sustained yield of game would be more profitable than a sustained yield of sheep or cattle. This proposition, put forward by Darling (1960, 1961), Huxley (1962), Dasmann (1962, 1964), Talbot (1963), Pollock (1969) and Linear (1970), to cite only a random sample, rests on an interlocking set of theoretical postulates. The argument goes something like this: African wildlife, having evolved with its habitat for millions of years, is uniquely adapted to the African environment. It will therefore utilize the vegetation more efficiently, be more productive, and attain a higher biomass than a cattle or sheep monoculture. Further, natural selection has ensured that the different species of game partition the resources of the environment such that competition is reduced. In comparison with cattle or sheep the multi-species complex would cause less overgrazing, be more resistant to disease, require less capital and recurrent expenditure, and less husbandry. It would provide a higher sustained yield and higher net revenue.

Two fair comments can be made on this theory. First, it is a theoretically sound and eminently reasonable expectation. Secondly, attempts to demonstrate its validity over the last fifteen years have been largely unsuccessful. That paradox cannot be resolved easily. On one hand the theory squares with modern concepts of ecology; on the other, I know of not one example where a sustained yield of game was shown to be more valuable than a sustained yield of livestock in a comparable area. Some projects lost money, others barely broke even; and others, which at first glance appeared to support the theory, proved on second glance to have extracted a short-term profit by capital reduction instead of by sustained yield. Those that came closest to success were mainly small-scale projects on private ranches in the Republic of South Africa. They were seldom more than lucrative side-lines of a cattle economy, a limited offtake of game products being sold to a luxury market. The game harvesting was not an alternative to cattle ranching.

The initial failure of game cropping in Africa may have several causes. The most likely is the short period over which it has been tried. The failures might reflect no more than teething problems. Certainly, fifteen years is not long enough to achieve an optimization that farmers reached through thousands of years of trial and error. But the attempts at sustained yield of game have also generated data throwing doubt on at least some of the basic assumptions.

The expectation that resources would be nicely partioned between species, thereby reducing competition, has been dented by Gwynne and Bell (1968), Casebeer and Koss (1970), Field (1970), Bell (1971) and Hvidberg-Hansen (1971). Diets overlap considerably between game species, and between game and livestock. Partitioning of food resources, when it occurs, is usually at the level of plant parts rather than plant species.

A more immediate reason for the failure to achieve expected returns was the often wildly optimistic predictions of sustained yield. The misunderstandings of the dynamics of harvested populations prevalent amongst wildlife managers, which are discussed in a previous section, combined and compounded to produce biological fantasies. Yield was assumed proportional to standing crop at ecological carrying capacity, a fallacy to which wildlife economists seem particularly prone (see for instance Pearse, 1968), productivity was equated with recruitment rate at ecological carrying capacity, and harvesting was expected to have no effect on the standing-crop density. An extreme outcome of these ideas can be seen in one project's advocacy of a 50% sustained annual offtake for warthog (*Phacochaerus aethiopicus* Pallas) on a Rhodesian ranch.

A less obvious reason for the general lack of success was consistent underestimation of the expense involved and level of expertise needed to harvest a multi-species complex. There may be sound historical and practical reasons for man's preference to farm only one or two domesticated species in a given area.

A particularly interesting perspective on the problems of game cropping versus livestock farming comes from standing the initial question on its head. Instead of asking why game cropping was not as successful as anticipated we could ask why cattle and sheep produce such high yields. One reason is the highly disparate sex-ratio fixed by sex-selective harvesting. It boosts sustained yield well above that accruing from across-the-board harvesting. Another is the tight control over fecundity, survival and density that can be exercised when the animals are tame enough to handle. These are bonuses induced by management practices. But there is enough evidence now to support a suspicion that sheep and cattle are intrinsically more efficient in providing a yield; that, by this criterion, they are better adapted than most game species to the African environment in tsetse free areas.

The attempts to produce a new domesticant as an alternative to cattle provide fuel for this suspicion. The eland (*Taurotragus oryx* Pallas), a huge antelope, appears to have all the talents needed to oust cattle as the premier domesticant in Africa. It tames well, is less dependent on water, has a higher reproductive rate, and has excellent carcase characteristics. Domesticated herds have been established in Kenya, South Africa, Rhodesia, Zambia and the U.S.S.R., the latter herd having been studied intensively since 1935 (Treus and Kravchenko, 1968). The Russians have investigated milk yield. Studies on grazing behaviour, meat production and conversion efficiency have been limited to Rhodesia (Posselt, 1963; Roth, 1970; Kerr *et al.*, 1970), South Africa (Skinner, 1966, 1967, 1972), and Kenya (Taylor and Lyman, 1967; Rogerson, 1968).

The main conclusion that can be drawn from these studies is that the eland is less efficient than cattle in converting plants to meat. If it could compete at all with cattle as a meat producing domesticant, it would be in arid regions. Results from such an experiment are not yet available. In a thoughtful paper on the ecological and economic basis of game ranching, Parker and Graham (1971) remark: "It has never been demonstrated that wildlife productivity at the lower end of the rainfall regime is higher than it is possible to achieve with domestic animals."

The reason for domestic livestock's success as an efficient converter of African plants, a vegetation to which, by theory, game species should be much better adapted, might be sought within the context of the interactive model in Section II, C and D. It emphasized the mutuality of the relationship between vegetation and herbivores, a mutuality that would hold in both the immediate dynamics of the system and in its evolutionary history. While game are adapting over evolutionary time to a vegetation, the vegetation is also adapting to the game. R. H. V. Bell (personal communication) has suggested to me a mechanism by which this interaction would lower the efficiency with which the animals convert plants to meat and energy. Plants produce defensive chemicals, the so-called secondary compounds, which affect the physiology of grazing animals. In defense the herbivores produce detoxifying microsomal enzymes. The role of these complementary compounds and enzymes has recently been examined by Freeland and Janzen (1974), Westoby (1974) and McKey (1974). In the evolution of the relationship between a plant species and the animal species that eats it, there might well be a selective pressure on the plant to maximize the toxicity of its secondary compounds towards that animal. The animal would counter by developing detoxifying enzymes specific to the offending compounds. The average effect would be a level of toxicity sufficient to reduce the animal's conversion efficiency. If a herbivore is introduced to a vegetation that has not previously been grazed by it, the vegetation will have no specific chemical defences against it. By chance, some secondary compounds developed against indigenous herbivores will act against the exotic, but others, which are crafted to reduce the conversion efficiency and hence standing crop of an indigene, will provide little or no protection. The average effect might be that the exotic is more efficient than the indigenous herbivore in converting plants to more animals. Is this the reason for the success of sheep and cattle? That question should be rated a top priority for research, but although the idea has a seductive simplicity, a number of theoretical objections can be arrayed against it and equally plausible alternatives advanced in its stead. Sinclair (1971 and personal communication), for example, blames a couple of initial failures in game cropping on the ability of cattle ranchers to restrict retail outlets for game meat, the unsympathetic attitude of the local veterinary department, and the high cost of refrigeration transport run over long distances. He considers that the apparent advantage of domestic stock over wildlife is referrable to modern animal husbandry. G. Child (personal communication) blames socio-economic rather than biological factors for a fair proportion of the early failures.

These comments on the utilization of wildlife could be construed as an argument against further experiments on game cropping. They are not so intended. Very much more experimenting is needed before the economics of game cropping and of new domestications can be evaluated in Africa. Rather, the argument is against theoretical postulates, untested predictions of sustainable yields, and enthusiastic "demonstrations of the commercial value of wildlife" substituting for carefully planned, necessarily long-term, disinterested research. The immediate need is for projects that combine investigations of economics, marketing and population dynamics. Marketing problems in particular rate a much closer look than they have received in the past. There is no parallel between the harvesting of game for a domestic market in Africa and the exploitation of deer in New Zealand for a luxury market in Germany.

Wildlife has a demonstrable economic value in Africa, if not necessarily as a source of cheap meat. As a generalization, an aggregation of African game provides maximum revenue when photographed by tourists (national parks) and rather less when harvested by elderly businessmen (safari hunting). The profitability of game cropping at present comes a distant third.

B. CONSERVATION

Many problems of conservation turn out to be, on close examination, not technical problems but problems of economics and sociology. In most instances no great insight is needed to discover why a population is declining, and countermeasures, if not immediately practicable, are at least theoretically specifiable. The main difficulty lies in persuading people to take appropriate action.

The technical part of tackling a conservation problem—discovering why the population is declining and deciding what can be done about it—can range from very simple to very difficult, with the majority of problems clustering towards the easy end of the gradient. Since there is little point in launching a five-year study when the answer might be found in the first week, the investigation is best carried out in two stages. If no answer is forthcoming from the simple investigation of the first stage a more detailed investigation can begin.

During an initial investigation the details of a population's dynamics are best ignored, the main effort being channelled into an appraisal of food supply, water supply, shelter, disease, and hunting pressure. The study is made immeasurably more simple if the researcher has access to a population of the same species in healthy condition, whose habitat and resources can be compared with those of the threatened population. Any difference between the two environments can be viewed as a possible cause of one population's decline, and the habitat can be manipulated accordingly. This method carries its own safety device in that the result of the treatment prescribed to halt the decline is the test of the hypothesis explaining the cause of the decline.

If the initial investigation fails to locate the cause of the problem we then know that it is neither simple nor obvious. Tactics must be changed from assault to siege with the emphasis being moved to an investigation of population dynamics.

First, fecundity rates should be measured to find whether the decline is a consequence of breeding impairment. If it is, a further search is required to isolate the cause. Breeding impairment is an uncommon cause of decline amongst ungulate populations. Its discovery would suggest that breeding physiology is affected by either disease (e.g. foot-and-mouth, contagious abortion) or by a metabolic poison, but the possibility of massive food shortage should also be kept in mind.

Since a decline can result only from reduced fecundity or increased mortality, if fecundity rates are found to be at healthy levels the problem is unambiguously one of excessive mortality. Should mortality be excessive at the adult stage but early juvenile mortality is at a normal level for the species, this is *prima facie* evidence that the decline is caused by excessive hunting. Most other agents of mortality act more heavily on juveniles. Should the decline reflect inadequate food or habitat, the diagnostic feature is a rise in early juvenile mortality usually coupled with a decline in late juvenile fecundity.

C. CONTROL

The control of populations divides into two distinct categories. The first contains that set of problems relating to displaced equilibria, the treatment being aimed at moving the vegetation–herbivore system back to equilibrium with a minimum of trauma. The second category comprises problems of unwanted equilibria where the task of control is to impose an alternative equilibrium appropriate to human requirements. These might include a denser vegetation for control of run-off, or a reduced standing crop of wild ungulates to permit a higher stocking of domesticated ungulates.

1. *Establishment of equilibria*

At any given time the biomass of ungulates and the biomass of their food supply are unlikely to be at equilibrium with each other. Under the influence of environmental fluctuation the system is moved around in the vicinity of the equilibrium point and may on occasions be perturbed well away from it. Unless the displacement is large, more than 30% or so, little is gained by instigating management procedures to hasten re-establishment of the equilibrium. The most practical route back to equilibrium is usually that traced by the unaided system itself. Attempts to help it on its way by lowering animal density can lead to oscillations, thereby creating a problem where no real problem existed before.

But when displacement from equilibrium is extreme, as in an ungulate eruption, appropriate management can minimize the unwanted effects of violent oscillations. Figure 20 gives the trajectory of ungulate density and vegetative density for the system modelled previously in Fig. 12.

The vegetation plunges to a deep trough as ungulate density moves to a peak. Irreversible changes in floral composition and soil cover can occur at this stage. Management should therefore be aimed at lowering the vegetation more gently onto its equilibrium, thereby eliminating the trauma of the vegetative crash.

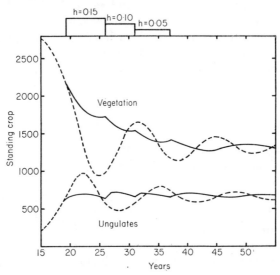

FIG. 20. Trajectory of a modelled ungulate eruption (dashed lines) and the trajectory it would follow (continuous lines) if animals were harvested over the intervals and at the rates per year diagrammed by the rectangles above.

The unbroken lines in Fig. 20 are the trajectories of ungulates and plants under the management regime diagrammed at the top of the figure. The ungulate population is harvested at a rate that is reduced in steps of 0·05 from 0·15 to zero. As a result the fluctuations in animal density and plant density are reduced as the system moves to equilibrium. There are two rules of thumb to keep in mind when using this metho.d First, harvesting must be initiated at a rate of about half the population's intrinsic rate of increase when animal density is well below its peak. Many control schemes are mounted when the population is at or near peak density, at which time the chance to achieve any significant benefit has been lost. Secondly, the imposed rate of harvesting must be maintained until plant density bottoms out and begins to rebound, the trend in animal number being irrelevant. The harvesting rate is then reduced and maintained at this lower level as plant density falls again to a second level of rebound. A harvesting regime of two or three steps will be adequate to flatten out most ungulate eruptions.

2. *Imposing an equilibrium*

When the carrying-capacity equilibrium level of ungulates is considered too high according to whatever is envisaged as the optimum level, the system can be shifted to a more convenient equilibrium by killing a quota of animals each year. Control by hunting, trapping or poisoning is an exercise in sustained yield harvesting, whether or not the yield is utilized, and the analyses and techniques appropriate to its planning are precisely those used in a harvesting programme. Direct control and harvesting are operationally identical. The efficiency of the first is determined by the prevailing level of technical competence in the techniques of the second.

D. RECOMMENDATIONS FOR RESEARCH

A secondary theme of this paper is that the requirements of ungulate management call not so much for more data as for different kinds of data, and for a different perspective or theoretical framework within which these data can be collated and interpreted. At present we have some knowledge of the dynamic characteristics of ungulate populations and some knowledge of plant succession and dynamics. Of the ungulate–vegetation system's core, the process by which the dynamics of the two components interact to achieve an equilibrium, we are almost totally ignorant.

This huge gap in our knowledge stems historically from a reluctance to consider ungulates and vegetation as forming an interacting system. Wildlife managers tend to view ungulate populations as closed systems generating their own dynamics while feeding on a dynamically inert substrate. Range managers are well aware that the vegetation is shaped by dynamic processes, but the dynamics of ungulate populations enter their calculations only as unfortunate properties that may lead to problems. Because they are used to dealing with domesticants whose dynamics are imposed upon them by man, range managers tend to view natural populations from the same perspective, equating the dynamic initiatives of these populations with annoying misdemeanours that should be suppressed in the same way as are those of livestock. Both views are limited by a self-imposed bias towards one or other component of the ungulate–vegetation system.

For the efficient management of the system we need data on the vegetation, on the ungulates, and on the interaction between them. Specifically, we must measure the vegetation's intrinsic rate of increase, its ungrazed K density, the rate at which an animal removes vegetation at different levels of vegetative density (the functional response), the maximum rate at which the animals can decrease, the rate at which they increase at different levels of vegetative density (the numerical response), and the time between effect and response. These parameters have not been estimated for any ungulate–vegetation system. Until they are, and until we have models of their relationships more real than the caricature presented as equation (5), the management of ungulate populations will remain a process of trial and error.

Two recent studies serve as sign posts: Bell's (1971) investigation of the Serengeti ungulate–vegetation system, and May's (1973a, Ch. 4–5) exploration of the theoretical consequences of interaction between two trophic levels. Despite the complexity of the first and the simplicity of the second, these two approaches are convergent. When they finally meet, the problems of wildlife management may differ in appearance from our image of them today.

IV. Summary

Over the last thirty years advances in wildlife management have not paralleled those of the other fields of population management, particularly fisheries biology and economic entomology. The reason seems to lie in the paradox that wildlife management is essentially applied population dynamics but the principles of population dynamics are seldom applied when wildlife populations are managed.

The relevance of population dynamics to the three problems of wildlife management—conservation, sustained yield and control—is outlined with respect to the ungulate–vegetation system. Current knowledge of ungulate fecundity patterns and mortality patterns is summarized briefly, and the pattern of population growth is pictured as a complex resultant of the intrinsic dynamics of an ungulate population interacting with those of its food supply. The typical outcome is an eruption followed by a population crash and dampened oscillations leading to an equilibrium density. Ungulates appear to determine both the capital level of vegetative biomass at equilibrium and the rate at which the interest is produced and consumed.

Prevalent notions of "carrying-capacity" are examined critically against this background. It is argued that these have led directly to confusion over the nature of ungulate–vegetation equilibria and indirectly to overestimates of sustained yield.

A model of the ungulate–vegetation system is manipulated to study the reaction of this system to exploitation. From these simulations come suggestions for estimating sustained yield and for managing an ungulate eruption to minimize trauma to the vegetation.

Acknowledgements

I am grateful to the following people who criticized a previous draft of this paper:
R. H. V. Bell, G. Child, N. Dankers, R. W. Day, J. J. R. Grimsdell, R. M. May,
T. Riney, E. E. Robinson, A. R. E. Sinclair and A. J. Underwood.

References

Allen, K. R. (1971). *J. Fish. Res. Bd. Can.* **28**, 1573–1581.
Andrewartha, H. G. and Birch, L. C. (1954). "The Distribution and Abundance of
Animals." Chicago University Press, Chicago.
Baranov, F. I. (1926). *Biull. Rybnovo Khoziaistva* **8**, 7–11.
Bell, R. H. V. (1971). *Scientific American* **225**, 86–93.
Beverton, R. J. H. and Holt, S. J. (1957). *Min. Agr. Fish. and Food, Fisheries Investi-
gations* Ser. 2, 19, 1–533.
Bindernagel, J. A. (1968). Game cropping in Uganda. Uganda Game Dept., Kampala.
Birch, L. C. (1960). *Amer. Natur.* **94**, 5–24.
Bodenheimer, F. S. (1958). *Monog. Biol.* 6.
Butlin, N. G. (1962). *In* "The Simple Fleece" (A. Barnard, Ed.), pp. 281–307. Mel-
bourne University Press, Melbourne.
Casebeer, R. L. and Koss, G. G. (1970). *E. Afr. Wildl. J.* **8**, 25–36.
Caughley, G. (1966). *Ecology* **47**, 906–918.
Caughley, G. (1967). *Ecology* **48**, 834–839.
Caughley, G. (1970a). *Mammalia* **34**, 194–199.
Caughley, G. (1970b). *Ecology* **51**, 53–72.
Caughley, G. (1971a). *New Zeal. J. Sci.* **14**, 993–1008.
Caughley, G. (1971b). *Mammalia* **35**, 369–383.
Caughley, G. (1973). *In* "Luangwa Valley Conservation and Development Project,
Zambia: Game Management and Habitat Manipulation," pp. 50–157. F.A.O.,
Rome.
Chapman, D. G. (1961). *Univ. Calif. Publns Statist.* **4**, 153–168.
Child, G. (1968). "Behaviour of Large Mammals during the Formation of Lake
Kariba." Nat. Museum Rhodesia, Salisbury.
Child, G. (1972). *Arnoldia (Rhodesia)* **5**, No. 31, 13 pp.
Comfort, A. (1956). "The Biology of Senescence." Routledge, London.
Cook, C. W. (ed.) (1962). "Basic Problems and Techniques in Range Management."
National Academy of Sciences—National Research Council, Washington D.C.
Cook, R. S., White, W., Trainer, D. O. and Glazener, W. C. (1971). *J. Wildl. Manage.*
35, 47–56.
Coop, I. E. (1966). *J. agric Sci., Camb.* **67**, 305–323.
Craske, N. G. (1974). *Search* **5**, 261–263.
Cunningham, W. J. (1954). *Proc. Nat. Acad. U.S.A.* **40**, 708–713.
Darling, F. F. (1960). "Wildlife in an African Territory." Oxford University Press,
Oxford.
Darling, F. F. (1961). *Span* (Shell Magazine, London) **4**, 100–103.
Dasmann, R. F. (1962). *Pacific Discovery* **15**, 3–9.
Dasmann, R. F. (1964). "African Game Ranching." Pergamon Press, Oxford.
Dasmann, R. F. (1968). "Environmental Conservation," 2nd Edition. John Wiley
and Sons, New York.
Davidson, J. (1938a). *Trans. Roy. Soc. South Australia* **62**, 342–346.

Davidson, J. (1938b). *Trans. Roy. Soc. South Australia* **62**, 141–148.
Davis, L. S. (1967). *J. Wildl. Manage.* **31**, 667–678.
De Vos, A. (1969). *Adv. Ecol. Res.* **6**, 137–183.
Eberhardt, L. (1960). *Michigan Dept. Conservation, Game Div. Report*, No. 2282.
Field, C. R. (1970). *Zool. Africana*, **5**, 71–86.
Finney, D. J. (1947). "Probit Analysis: a Statistical Treatment of the Sigmoidal Response Curve." C.U.P., Cambridge.
Fisher, R. A. (1930). "The Genetical Theory of Natural Selection." Clarendon Press, Oxford.
Freeland, W. F. and Janzen, D. H. (1974). *Amer. Natur.* **108**, 269–289.
Government Statistician of N.S.W. (1956–1972). "Official Year Book of N.S.W". No. 46–62.
Graham, M. (1935). *J. Conseil Expl. Mer.* **10**, 264–274.
Gulland, J. A. (1962). In "The Exploitation of Natural Annual Populations" (E. D. LeCren and M. W. Holdgate, Eds), pp. 204–217. Blackwell, Oxford.
Gulland, J. A. (1968). *FAO Fish. Tech. Paper* No. 40, Revision 2.
Gwynne, M. D. and Bell, R. H. V. (1968). *Nature, Lond.* **220**, 390–393.
Harlan, J. R. (1956). "Theory and Dynamics of Grassland Agriculture." van Nostrand Coy., Princeton.
Hayes, N. D. (1950). *J. London Math. Soc.* **25**, 226–232.
Hickey, F. (1960). *N.Z. J. agric. Res.* **3**, 332–344.
Hickey, F. (1963). *N.Z. Agriculturalist* **15**, 1–3.
Hight, G. K. and Jury, K. E. (1969). *Proc. N.Z. Soc. Anim. Prod.* **29**, 219–232.
Hjort, J., Jahn, G. and Ottestad, P. (1933). *Hvalr. Skrif.* **7**, 92–127.
Holling, C. S. (1961). *Ann. Rev. Entomol.* **6**, 163–182.
Howard, W. E. (1965). *N.Z. Dept. Sci. Industr. Res. Inf. Ser.* **45**, 1–95.
Hutchinson, G. E. (1948). *Ann. N.Y. Acad. Sci.* **50**, 221–246.
Huxley, J. S. (1962). *Endeavour* **21**, 98–107.
Hvidberg-Hansen, H. (1971). *E. Afr. Agr. For. J.* **36**, 322–33.
Ivlev, V. S. (1961). "Experimental Ecology of the Feeding of Fishes." Yale University Press, New Haven.
Ivlev, V. S. (1966). *J. Fish. Res. Bd. Can.* **23**, 1727–1759.
Kerr, M. A., Wilson, V. J. and Roth, H. H. (1970). *Rhod. J. Agric. Res.* **8**, 71–77.
Klein, D. R. (1968). *J. Wildl. Manage* **32**, 350–367.
Krebs, C. J. (1972). "Ecology: the Experimental Analysis of Distribution and Abundance." Harper and Row, New York.
Lack, D. (1954). "The Natural Regulation of Animal Numbers." Clarendon Press, Oxford.
Lefkovitch, L. P. (1967). *Bull. Ent. Res.* **57**, 437–445.
Leopold, A. (1933). "Game Management." Charles Scribner's Sons, New York.
Leslie, P. H. and Ranson, R. M. (1940). *J. Anim. Ecol.* **9**, 27–52.
Leslie, P. H., Tener, T. S., Vizoso, M. and Chitty, H. (1955). *Proc. Zool. Soc. Lond.* **125**, 115–125.
Linear, M. (1970). *Ceres* **3**, 51–54.
Lobdell, C. H., Case, K. E. and Mosby, H. S. (1972). *J. Wildl. Manage.* **36**, 493–497.
Lowe, V. P. W. (1969). *J. anim. Ecol.* **38**, 425–457.
MacArthur, R. H. and Wilson, E. O. (1967). "The Theory of Island Biogeography." Princeton University Press, Princeton.
McCullough, D. R. (1969). *Univ. Calif. Pubs. Zool.* **88**, 1–191.
McKey, D. (1974). *Amer. Natur.* **108**, 305–320.

May, R. M. (1973a). "Stability and Complexity in Model Ecosystems." Princeton University Press, Princeton.

May, R. M. (1973b). *Ecology* 54, 315–325.

May, R. M. (1973c). *Science* 177, 900–902.

Medawar, P. B. (1951). "An Unsolved Problem of Biology." H. K. Lewis Coy, London.

Nicholson, A. J. (1954). *Aust. J. Zool.* 2, 9–65.

Parker, I. S. C. and Graham, A. D. (1971). *Symp. Brit. Ecol. Soc.* 11, 393–404.

Pearse, P. H. (1968). *E. Afr. Agr. For. J.* 33 (special issue), 84–89.

Pearson, K. (1895). *Phil. Trans. roy. Soc.* A186, 343–414.

Pianka, E. R. (1970). *Amer. Natur.* 104, 592–597.

Pimlott, D. H. (1959). *J. Wildl. Manage.* 23, 381–401.

Pollock, N. C. (1969). *Biol. Cons.* 2, 18–24.

Posselt, J. (1963). *Rhod. J. Agric. Res.* 1, 81–87.

Ricker, W. E. (1954a). *J. Fish. Res. Bd. Can.* 11, 559–623.

Ricker, W. E. (1954b). *J. Wildl. Manage.* 18, 45–51.

Ricker, W. E. (1958). *Fish. Res. Bd. Canada Bull.* 119, 1–300.

Riney, T. (1964). *IUCN Publ. New Ser.* No. 4, 261–273.

Riney, T., Watson, J. S., Bassett, C., Turbott, E. G. and Howard, W. E. (1959). *N.Z. Dept. Sci. Industr. Res. Bull.* 135, 1–75.

Riney, T. and Kettlitz, W. L. (1964). *Mammalia* 28, 188–248.

Rogerson, A. (1968). *Symp. Zool. Soc. Lond.* 21, 153–161.

Roth, H. H. (1966). *Mammalia* 30, 397–423.

Roth, H. H. (1970). *Rhod. J. Agric. Res.* 8, 67–70.

Roughgarden, J. (1971). *Ecology* 52, 453–468.

Sampson, A. W. (1952). "Range Management Principles and Practices." John Wiley and Sons, New York, and Chapman and Hall, London.

Schaefer, M. B. (1967). *Bull. inter-Am. trop. Tuna Comm.* 12, 87–136.

Scheffer, V. B. (1951). *Sci. Monthly* 75, 356–62.

Schladweiler, P. and Stevens, D. R. (1973). *J. Wildl. Manage.* 37, 535–544.

Sharkey, M. J. (1970). *Mammalia* 34, 564–572.

Sinclair, A. R. E. (1971). *Outlook on Agric.* 6, 261–266.

Skinner, J. (1966). *Afr. Wild Life* 20, 29–40.

Skinner, J. (1967). *Anim. Breed. Abstr.* 35, 177–186.

Skinner, J. (1972). *Afr. Wild Life* 26, 4–9.

Stoddart, L. A. (1967). *J. Range Manage.* 20, 304–307.

Stoddart, L. A. and Smith, A. D. (1955). "Range Management." McGraw-Hill Book Co., New York. 2nd edit.

Talbot, L. M. (1963). *IUCN Publ. New Ser.* No. 1, 320–335.

Taylor, C. R. and Lyman, C. P. (1967). *Physiol. Zool.* 40, 280–295.

Treus, V. and Kravchenko, D. (1968). *Symp. Zool. Soc. Lond.* 21, 395–411.

Verme, L. J. (1965). *J. Wildl. Manage.* 29, 74–79.

Westoby, M. (1974). *Amer. Natur.* 108, 290–304.

Wiesner, P. B. and Sheard, N. M. (1935). *Proc. Roy. Soc. Edinb.* 55, 1–22.

Zuckerman, S. (1953). *Proc. Zool. Soc. Lond.* 122, 827–950.

Population Biology and the Management of Whales

Whale Research Unit, Institute of Oceanographic Sciences,
c/o British Museum (Natural History), Cromwell Road,
London, England

I. INTRODUCTION

A dozen species of large whales have been hunted over the centuries. Eleven of these are baleen (whalebone) whales, which are filter-feeders bearing baleen plates in their mouth instead of teeth:

* Present address: International Whaling Commission, The Red House, Histon, Station Road, Cambridge CB4 4NP.

Greenland right whale, or	
bowhead	*Balaena mysticetus* L.
North Atlantic right whale	*Eubalaena glacialis* Müller.
North Pacific right whale	*Eubalaena sieboldii* Gray.
Southern right whale	*Eubalaena australis* Desmoulins.
gray whale	*Eschrichtius robustus* Lillejeborg.
blue whale	*Balaenoptera musculus* L.
fin whale	*Balaenoptera physalus* L.
sei whale	*Balaenoptera borealis* Lessen.
Bryde's whale	*Balaenoptera edeni* Anderson.
minke whale	*Balaenoptera acuto-rostrata* Lacepede.
humpback whale	*Megaptera novaengliae* Borowski.

The twelfth species is the sperm whale, *Physeter catodon* L., the largest of the toothed whales.

These species, illustrated in Fig. 1, are the largest members of the Order Cetacea, which comprises the whales, dolphins and porpoises. Although the smaller cetacea have been the object of various fisheries at different times, whaling is generally reckoned to be concerned with the larger species listed above. Of these, only the blue, fin, sei, minke, humpback and sperm whales have been of major importance in recent years and it is these six species which will be considered in the following discussion.

A. OUTLINE OF WHALING HISTORY

Whale hunting has a long history, dating back perhaps to the Stone Age when man hunted the smaller whales and dolphins. This was a subsistence fishery, and the remnants of it are still present today in the Alaskan Eskimo and Soviet Aleut catches of bowheads and gray whales in the North Pacific, Bering and Chukotsk Seas (International Whaling Statistics, 1973).

The beginning of commercial whaling, where the animal is a cash crop to be marketed for local or more distant utilization, can be dated to the 12th century or even earlier. Then the Basques began hunting the North Atlantic right whale from the shores of the Bay of Biscay. This fishery was extended by whaling voyages right across the North Atlantic as the coastal stocks were depleted. This led on to the Northern Whale Fishery for the Greenland right whale which began in 1611 and lasted in the Arctic until the last Dundee whaler returned empty in 1913. This fishery was carried out by British, German, French and Dutch vessels. At first the whales were hunted in the bays around Spitsbergen and then along the ice edge to Greenland. The blubber was flensed off the carcases and boiled out to obtain the oil, used for lighting and lubricants, and the long baleen plates were cut out for use as stiffeners in corsets, as umbrella stays and springs.

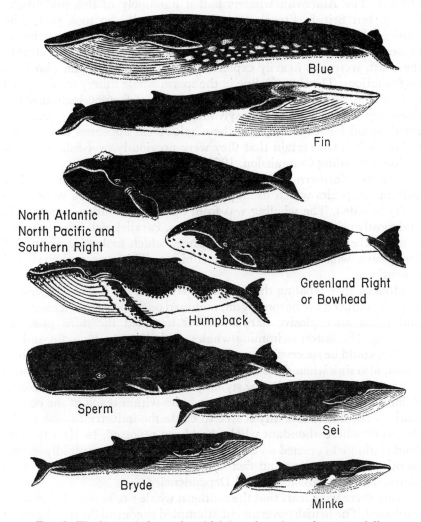

FIG. 1. The large whale species which have been hunted commercially.

The New England colonies began hunting the sperm whale in 1712, when a shore whaler blown off course in a gale caught a sperm whale. Sperm oil is a better illuminant than that from right whales, and the spermaceti from the head was used to make the finest candles. From this developed the second main phase of commercial whaling, the Southern Whale Fishery. In addition to sperm whales, this fishery also took right whales and humpback whales, in the Atlantic, Indian and Pacific Oceans. The American whalers had a monopoly of this world-wide fishery, but British, French and German vessels also took part. The southern right whales and the northern bowheads were both seriously depleted by the early 1900's. The Pacific gray whales, which stay close to the coast, were also heavily exploited by the whaleships and also from shore stations. The slow decline in the sperm whale fishery until the last voyage ended in 1925 was due to a number of factors, including the discovery of petroleum in Pennsylvania in 1859. This discovery reduced the demand for sperm oil, and the whale stocks appeared to increase, although it is not certain that they were previously over-fished (International Whaling Commission, 1969a).

Both the Northern and Southern Whale Fisheries were for the slow swimming species which usually float when killed, and so were more easily handled. The whaling was from open boats under oars or sail, and mostly using hand harpoons and lances. Parallel with this European whaling there was also a Japanese fishery which took gray, right and humpback whales by a netting technique. This was a shore-based operation.

Modern style whaling dates from 1864, when the Norwegian Svend Foyn introduced the harpoon gun, mounted on a powered catching boat and firing an explosive harpoon. This heralded the third phase of whaling. The fastest swimming whales, including the blue, fin and sei whales, could be successfully pursued. These whales, in addition to their speed, also sink when dead and have to be inflated with compressed air to keep them afloat. This new style whaling spread widely in the North Atlantic and North Pacific, and the whales within reach of the coastal stations became sufficiently scarce to cause the industry to look to the Antarctic where abundant whales had been reported. In 1904 the first land station was opened on South Georgia, and whaling rapidly spread to other shore stations and factory ships moored in suitable harbours throughout the Falkland Island Dependencies.

Soon there were fears that the southern whale stocks were being over-exploited. The British government attempted to control the development of the industry by issuing licences for the factories, which were all within its territorial waters. The idea of unrestricted pelagic whaling from a factory ship which could operate wherever the catcher boats found whales became increasingly attractive. This aim was achieved in 1925 when the steamship *Lancing* was fitted with a slipway in the stern so that whale carcases could be hauled up on deck for dismemberment and processing. Previously the whales had been worked up in the water alongside the moored factory ship. Within five years there were forty-one Norwegian and British factory ships working in the Antarctic zone with 205 catcher boats. In the 1930/31 season they caught so many whales that the world whale oil market collapsed. In the following seasons the whaling companies agreed to limit whale oil production by setting quotas for the individual whaling expeditions. These voluntary agreements were only partially successful in stabilizing the industry however, because Germany and Japan also started whaling in the Antarctic in the late 1930's. By this time it was clear that humpbacks and blue whales were being over-fished, and the whaling industry's oil production was only maintained by catching more and more fin whales.

After the brief respite given to the whales by the 1939–45 war, the Antarctic industry rapidly grew again until twenty expeditions were operating each season. The fin whale stocks could not withstand this level of hunting, and the industry declined as the whales were depleted. In an attempt to boost their production in the 1960's, the expeditions started taking large numbers of sei whales, which had previously been considered too small to bother with. Now, in the most recent seasons, the even smaller minke whales have been hunted extensively. The rise and fall of the catches of these species in the Antarctic is illustrated in Fig. 2.

It appears almost always to have been the case that the catching power of the whaling industry, right from the earliest times, has been greater than the reproductive potential of the various whale species and stocks. Thus the history of whaling seems to have been a repeated story of discovery, over-exploitation and collapse, with the possible exception of the 18–19th century sperm whale fishery. Certainly the future of whaling today depends on a rational scheme of management, agreed and implemented on a global and international scale.

B. REGULATION OF WHALING

Coastal whaling from land stations in Norway and the Falkland Island Dependencies was regulated by national legislation at the beginning of the 20th century. In 1929 the Bureau of International Whaling Statistics was set up in Norway to collect and publish statistics of catches from all over the world, as a basic source of information for checking on the state of the stocks and the industry.

The League of Nations introduced an International Convention for the Regulation of Whaling in 1931. This came into operation in 1935, and gave total protection to right whales, which had been severely reduced in numbers by earlier whaling, and also prohibited the catching of female whales which were accompanied by calves.

A further international agreement signed in 1937 gave protection to another depleted species, the gray whale. This also laid down minimum length regulations for blue, fin, humpback and sperm whales. The duration of the Antarctic whaling season was limited to three months, and pelagic whaling was banned in all oceans north of 40°S except in the North Pacific. A sanctuary for whales, in which no hunting was permitted, was established in the Pacific sector of the Antarctic in 1938.

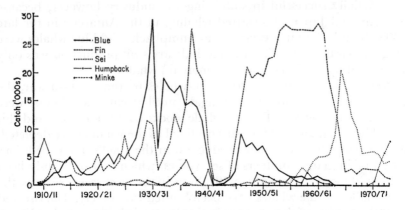

Fig. 2. Annual catches of humpback, blue, fin, sei and minke whales in the Antarctic (data from the International Whaling Statistics).

In 1946 another International Convention for the Regulation of Whaling was agreed which led to the formation of the International Whaling Commission (IWC). This organization regulates most of the world's whaling, and has as its stated aim the conservation, development and optimum utilization of the whale resources. Its regulations are based on scientific recommendations, but it also has to take into account the interests of the consumer of whale products and of the whaling industry itself. It is this latter aspect which has caused the IWC to be less effective than many would wish. Despite warnings from scientists that the catches were much greater than the various stocks could reasonably withstand, the whaling nations permitted their industries to take nearly as many whales as they wanted. Until recent years, the economic argument that the industry could not survive without a large catch always carried more weight than the scientific advice urging reductions in catches.

The regulations governing the whaling activities of the member nations of the IWC are embodied in a Schedule which can be amended at the annual meeting of the Commission. These regulations set total catch quotas for each management stock of the different whale species in various areas of the southern hemisphere, and for the same species in the North Atlantic and North Pacific. The length of the whaling seasons, minimum size limits and full utilization of the carcases are specified. The most depleted whale species, the right, blue and humpback whales, together with the gray whale, are given total protection from commercial hunting, as are females of all other species accompanied by calves. Inspectors appointed by the flag nation of each whaling operation record the species, length, sex, and if a pregnant female, the length and sex of the foetus of each whale processed. They also see that the regulations are obeyed and report any infractions. In addition, there is an exchange of observers between nations who report to the IWC on the manner in which the whaling activities are carried out.

Amendments to the Schedule are not binding on a signatory government if that country lodges an objection to the decision within a period of ninety days. Whilst it is likely that the Convention would not have been signed at all without this let-out, it does mean that any decision of the Commission has in effect to be unanimous in order to be implemented.

The present (1976) members of the IWC are Argentina, Australia, Brazil, Canada, Denmark, France, Iceland, Japan, Mexico, New Zealand, Norway, Panama, South Africa, U.S.S.R., U.K. and U.S.A.

Whaling from the west coast of South America is regulated by a separate organization, the Permanent Commission for the Exploitation and Conservation of the Marine Resources of the South Pacific. This was set up by Chile, Peru and Ecuador in 1952.

Other countries catching whales independently of any international control include China, South Korea, Somalia, Spain and Portugal.

C. SCIENTIFIC ASSESSMENT OF WHALE STOCKS

The large catches of whales taken during the early years of the Antarctic fishery led the British government to set up the Discovery Committee in 1924 to investigate the whale stocks in the region. Norway also played an important part in furthering knowledge of the large whale species hunted by the whaling industry. After the war, much of the basic biology and related studies necessary for conservation and management of the whale resource were investigated by scientists involved in the work of the Scientific Committee of the IWC. The lack of a firm quantitative assessment of the stocks gave their advice less weight than it needed to counter the industry's economic arguments. The stocks were therefore depleted despite persistent but not unequivocal evidence of the decline. It was only when the situation had reached a critical point in 1960 that the IWC decided to set up an independent group to assess the situation and advise on catch levels.

Thus the Committee of Three, experts in population dynamics and from countries not engaged in Antarctic whaling, was created. The work of this committee in analysing the biological and catch data according to the methodology and techniques then developed for fisheries assessment laid the foundations for the present lines of whale stock analysis. The final report of the Committee of Three (Chapman *et al.*, 1964) was addressed to the problems of estimating the sizes of the Antarctic whale stocks, determining the level of yield which these stocks could sustain, and advising on conservation measures that would increase this sustainable yield.

Development of the initial methods of assessment and the introduction of new techniques have taken place during the ensuing years to the present time. The most important aspects of whale biology currently taken into account in the scientific appraisal and management of the stocks are the distribution, migration and identity of the various unit stocks; reproduction and subsequent recruitment into the exploitable stocks; age, growth and mortality. These matters will be discussed in the following pages. In addition, features such as the influence of interspecific relationships and competition, the social organization of the whales, and the concept of biomass rather than numbers as a more fundamental measure of whale stock size have been raised recently. Many of these ideas are still being developed, so that they are not yet incorporated into the population models which presently form the basis of advice for the regulation of the whaling industry. There is no doubt, though, that they will be important additions to the population parameters considered in the future.

One result leading to, and arising from, the work of the Committee of Three has been the focusing of research attention on the baleen whales in the southern hemisphere, and particularly the fin whale. The other species and the whales in other areas have been of rather less economic importance. This has meant that they have been more poorly sampled and studied, and this emphasis will be reflected in the following account.

II. MIGRATION

A. BALEEN WHALES

The large baleen whales, humpback, blue, fin and sei whales, frequent the warm waters of tropical and sub-tropical latitudes to mate and calve during the winter months. In the summer they migrate to the feeding grounds in the cold polar waters of both the northern and southern hemispheres. The presence of the whales in these regions at these seasons, and their migrations between the winter and summer grounds is known from such evidence as the times and places of whaling, direct observations of the seasonal population densities, and the recoveries of marked whales.

For example, whaling operations in the Antarctic have been largely confined to the months from October to April, with the greatest catches in the period from December to March. In the low latitudes of the southern hemisphere, at shore stations in South Africa and Australia for instance, the main catches have been made in the months from May to October. This suggests that the greater part of the baleen whale population spends the summer in the Antarctic and the winter months in the warmer water. However, there was whaling throughout the winters of 1914/15 to 1918/19 at South Georgia (Harmer, 1931), and a number of blue and fin whales were taken. Thus not all the whales can migrate north in the autumn from the Antarctic.

The main trend of migrations to and from the Antarctic feeding grounds was illustrated by Mackintosh and Brown (1956) in an analysis of whale sightings by RRS *Discovery II*. An organized look-out was kept during nearly 47 000 miles steaming in the Antarctic from 1933 to 1939, and a curve showing the variation in the estimated number of all species of whales combined is shown in Fig. 3. The numbers showed a gradual rise from about August to February, and then a fall to July. This pattern suggests a long stream of arrivals in the first period and of departures in the latter. Fin whales were thought to make up 75% of the total, blue whales 15% and humpbacks 10% on the evidence of the identified animals.

It can be noted that some whales were seen even in the winter months, although there may be some overlap between the latest departures and earliest arrivals. Evidence from the sightings of whales at sea by merchant ships and other vessels led Brown (1957, 1958) to conclude for both the Indian Ocean and the North Atlantic Ocean areas that some animals also miss or get out of step with the main migrations from the warm waters to the polar seas in their respective spring seasons.

The fact that the seasons are opposite in the two hemsipheres means that the northern and southern populations do not converge towards the equator at the same time. When it is summer in the north and winter in the south the baleen whales are at the northern ends of their ranges, feeding in the northern hemisphere and breeding in the southern. The whales then migrate south for the northern winter and southern summer, to breed in the warm waters of the North Atlantic and North Pacific, and to feed in the Antarctic. It is possible that the few whales which may get out of step with the great majority of their kind at the equatorial ends of these extensive migrations could cross into the opposite hemisphere.

However, the northern whales of all the baleen whale species tend to be slightly smaller, both in average length and the lengths at which they become sexually and physically mature, than their southern counterparts. It is therefore unlikely that there is any significant interchange across the equator.

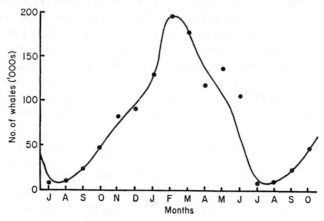

FIG. 3. Estimated seasonal variation in the numbers of large baleen whales in the ice-free waters of the Antarctic, from sightings by RRS Discovery II, 1933–39 (after Mackintosh and Brown, 1956).

1. *Segregation by species*

Within the stream of migrating whales entering the Antarctic, the blue whales tend to arrive before the fin whales. Mackintosh (1942) showed that both on the pelagic grounds and at South Georgia, comparatively few fin whales appeared in the catches in the early part of the summer, and comparatively few blue whales in the later part. Blue whales were most abundant from November to February (to January at South Georgia), with peak numbers caught in December. Fin whales were most frequent in the pelagic catches from January to March, and at South Georgia in December and January. Humpback whales were also most frequent in December and January. Sei whales are later still in arriving, with high catch densities in January–March at South Georgia in recent seasons, when they were not a less preferred species (Gambell, 1968).

At the other end of the migration route, the succession of baleen whales through the Durban whaling grounds was analysed by Bannister and Gambell (1965). Using catch data per unit of effort corrected for increased catcher size and power by a tonnage factor, and aircraft sightings per unit distance flown by a spotter plane, they plotted the

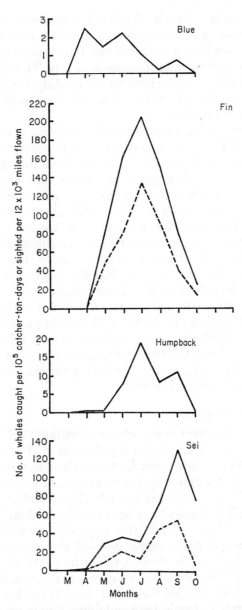

Fig. 4. Average monthly catches (solid line) and aircraft sightings (broken line) per unit effort of baleen whales off Durban, 1954–63 (from Bannister and Gambell, 1965).

monthly variations in the species density. The results are shown in Fig. 4. Blue whales were early arrivals, being most common from April to June, but with a few occurring up to September. Fin whales were present from April to October, and were most common in July. The humpbacks were similar to the fin whales, with a peak number in July. Sei whales were also present in small numbers from April onwards, but reached their greatest concentrations in September.

Thus the pattern of species migration is consistent in the records from the Antarctic and the warm waters of the south western Indian Ocean. This is strong evidence that the differences in timing of migration between species persist throughout the whole migratory cycle of the whales. In addition to the succession of species, there are also differences in their degree of penetration into the high latitudes. Blue whales were hunted right up to the ice-edge in the pre-war Antarctic pelagic fishery. Fin whales do not seem to go quite so far, and sei whales can be considered more as sub-Antarctic in their summer distribution. It seems in all these species in the southern hemisphere that the bigger, older animals go further towards the pole than the younger whales.

Comparable evidence from the northern hemisphere is not so clear. It seems that the blue whales in the North Pacific do not cross the Aleutian chain into more northerly waters in their summer migration, but fin whales migrate through the Bering Sea and on into the Arctic Ocean. Sei whales sometimes migrate into the Bering Sea but do not go through the Bering Strait (Nishiwaki, 1966).

2. Segregation within species

Humpback whales tend to stay close to coastlines during their regular migrations between the tropical and polar waters. The main stream of humpback whales migrating past Australian land stations passed within ten miles of the coast and very few were seen or captured more than twenty miles off shore, in spite of a much wider searching zone (Chittleborough, 1965). The whales have been caught by shore-based whaling operations over a large part of this migration route. Thus data are available for analysing the segregation of the migrating streams of animals on the basis of the timings of the first arrival, mean and last departure dates of the various sexual classes at different latitudes.

Dawbin (1966) has studied the records from 24 000 humpback whales caught in the southern hemisphere and found that in general the sexual classes all travel in the same sequence past each land station north of 41°S. On the northbound migration from the Antarctic feeding grounds to the breeding grounds, the females at the end of lactation are the earliest group to arrive. The mean date of arrival is about one month after the first catches were taken. These animals are followed successively by the immature whales of both sexes, mature males, resting females and females in late pregnancy. The mean dates of arrival for these various categories are twelve, twenty, twenty-three and thirty-one days after the lactating females. There is considerable overlapping between the different classes, as shown by the diagrammatic representation in Fig. 5.

The migrating stream of whales can therefore be thought of as a procession, with the sexual classes concentrated at particular points but not exclusively separated from one another. The fact that the intervals between the dates of arrival for each class are nearly the same at the various land stations situated between 41°S and the equator indicates that the whales all migrate at the same speed, but must leave the Antarctic at different times.

On the southbound migration from the breeding grounds, the first arrivals are a mixture of females classified as resting and in early pregnancy. These represent the first arrivals from the south, the lactating whales, which have just weaned their calves and then mate on the breeding grounds. They have such small foetuses on the return journey that they are often overlooked by non-biologists. Following these whales at mean successive intervals of three, thirteen and nineteen days are respectively the immature whales, mature males, and females in early lactation which calved on the breeding grounds. The latter group at the end of the migrating stream are the same whales which brought up the rear of the northbound movement as pregnant females.

There appears to be a random aggregation of the humpback whales on the Antarctic feeding grounds once they have all arrived. However, the pregnant females seem to have a prolonged stay in the Antarctic waters compared with the other classes, while the lactating females are there for the shortest time.

A sequence in the composition of the humpback whales migrating in the North Pacific from the tropical breeding grounds past the south of Japan has been observed. Immature whales, mostly males, pass the area first, and are followed about a month later by the main body of animals. These comprise the mature males and females not in late pregnancy, and the migration is ended by the lactating females and their calves (Nishiwaki, 1966).

In fin whales the evidence for segregation of the sexual classes is not so firm. This is largely due to the much wider spread of the species away from continental coasts, so they have not been so well sampled as the humpbacks. However, Mackintosh (1942) suggested that the composition of the catches at South Georgia made it likely that the fin whale migration to the south is headed by the males, with the females pre-

dominating towards the end. In addition, the earlier arrivals are generally older whales than the later, since the average age of the catch as
determined by the sexual and physical maturity of the whales declined
throughout the season (Wheeler, 1934). The proportion of adult females
in the catch which were pregnant also fell during the season from 85%
in October to 27% in April (Mackintosh, 1942). On the evidence of
blubber thickness data, Ash (1956) has suggested that fin whales arrive

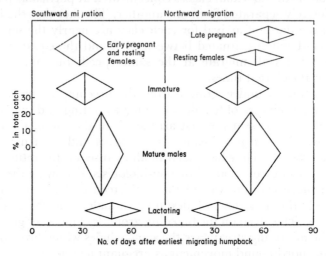

Fig. 5. Means and standard deviations of the dates of arrival of the various sexual
classes of migrating humpback whales in the southern hemisphere (after Dawbin,
1966).

in the Antarctic in groups which are made up of males, pregnant females
and non-pregnant females, which maintain their identity during the
summer feeding season. Laws (1961) concluded from all this evidence
that the older animals and pregnant females migrate in advance of the
other classes, and that the sexually immature whales are at the rear of
the stream.

An analysis of the sexual classes of the female sei whales sampled at
South Georgia and Durban gave evidence of segregation in this species
(Gambell, 1968). At South Georgia the pregnant females are the first
arrivals, and they leave the Durban area in advance of the other females.
Age segregation also occurs in the distribution of sei whales. Both in the
North Pacific and the Antarctic pelagic catches there is a greater proportion of older and bigger whales in the higher latitudes. In the Antarctic the catches between 40°–45°S have a markedly greater number of
smaller and younger whales than those further south (Doi *et al.*, 1967).

B. SPERM WHALES

The seasonal distribution and migrations of sperm whales are funda-
mentally different from those of the baleen whales. The females and
younger males usually remain in tropical and warm temperate waters
between the latitudes of 45°N and 45°S. Only the big bulls penetrate
into the cold polar waters. The widespread distribution and seasonal
migrations of sperm whales were demonstrated in monthly charts prepared by Townsend (1935) of the catch positions recorded in the log-
books of 19th-century American whalers. With the addition of modern
whaling data (Gilmore, 1959), the catch positions illustrated in Fig. 6
show the more northerly distribution of the sperm whales in both
northern and southern hemispheres during the northern summer and
southern winter, and the southward shift of the populations in the
opposite seasons.

Short term recoveries of whale marks have provided confirmation of
the northward migration of sperm whales in the autumn in the western
Indian Ocean. A small male and female marked south of Durban in
February 1963 and a small male marked in November 1963 were
recaptured in more northerly positions in the following March and April,
one and five months later respectively. Another male marked in the
Antarctic south of South Africa at 62°S in December 1967 was recovered
at Durban the next May (Best, 1969b).

Two Soviet marks found at the Donkergat whaling station on the
Atlantic coast of South Africa demonstrate even longer migrations than
the shortest route distance of 1800 miles (2900 km) of the last record.
These were marked off the Congo (6°S) and Cap Blanc (21°33'N),
involving minimum movements of 2000 and 4000 miles (3200 and
6400 km). The connection between the sperm whales in the northern
and southern hemispheres shown by the latter movement is especially
interesting, but the fact that the breeding seasons in the two hemispheres
are about six months apart probably prevents any significant inter-
breeding taking place (Best, 1974b).

Further evidence of the migrations of male sperm whales between the
Antarctic and southern temperate waters is given by the incidence of the
Antarctic diatom *Cocconeis ceticola*. This organism can form a yellowish
skin film on a whale in about a month, but only in the Antarctic (Hart,
1935). Some medium and large male sperm whales are found carrying
the diatom in the autumn off the west coast of South Africa (Best, 1969b)
and in early to mid-summer off Western Australia (Bannister, 1969).
This implies that these whales have recently arrived from the Antarctic.
Diatom film is absent or slight on the sperm whales at South Georgia

from October to February, but is fully developed in the following months. This suggests that the whales have newly arrived from lower latitudes in the earlier period (Matthews, 1938a).

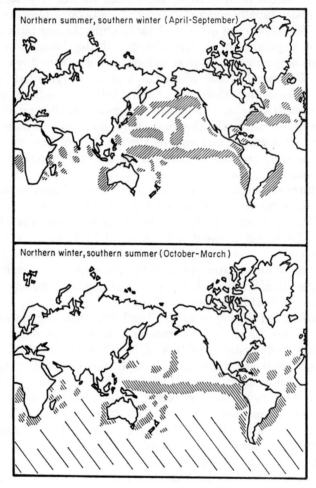

FIG. 6. Main whaling grounds and concentrations of sperm whales by season (after Gilmore, 1959).

Sperm whales are present in the coastal waters of Japan from the beginning of the year. The main groups migrate northwards after July, and include males, females and calves. Some of the males separate north of about 45°N in the western North Pacific and continue into the Aleutian waters and Bering Sea. The females and calves return south, and many females appear in the late season catches off Japan (Nishiwaki, 1966).

Sperm whales are most abundant off central California in May and September. Three whales marked off southern California in January were recovered off northern California in June, off Washington in June and in the western gulf of Alaska in April. It seems from this evidence that sperm whales move north along the Californian coast in the spring and return south again in the autumn (Rice, 1974).

1. Segregation

a. Seasonal abundance. The movement of only the bigger male sperm whales into the cold polar seas has already been mentioned, so segregation of this component of the population is obvious at certain seasons. Within the temperate waters there is also evidence of distinct groupings of the whales according to sex and size. This is shown by the seasonal movements of sperm whales through coastal whaling grounds, and has been demonstrated in the catches taken off Western Australia (Bannister, 1969) and the Atlantic and Indian Ocean coasts of South Africa (Best, 1969b; Gambell, 1972).

The densities of the various sex and size groups of sperm whales in the Durban area are plotted in Fig. 7. Two independent series of estimates are available, from the catches by the whaling boats and the sightings by the spotter aircraft. Both of these series of data, expressed on a unit of effort basis, show similar trends. The females and small males (less than 39 ft (11·9 m) in length) are most abundant in the catches at the start of the whaling season. They reach a peak in April, and minima in August before increasing again at the end of the season. The sightings of small whales, in which the sexes cannot be distinguished, follow a similar pattern. The medium sized (39–45 ft; 11·9–13·7 m) and big sperm whales (over 45 ft; 14 m), which are all males, show density fluctuations similar to one another but opposite to that of the small whales. They are poorly represented at the beginning and end of the whaling season, but reach winter maxima from May to July or August. These variations in density indicate that the sperm whales pass through the whaling grounds in waves, the small whales preceding the medium and big bulls in the northward autumn migration.

Similar analyses of catches and sightings data from Dongergat on the west coast of South Africa (Best, 1969b) indicated that all four sex and size groups follow the same patterns of abundance. The peak densities occur roughly one month earlier than off Durban, which is about 200 miles (320 km) further north on the east coast. The density of the medium and big bulls increases again in the spring as they migrate south at the end of the whaling season on the west coast, but there is no comparable increase in the females and small males before the end of whaling.

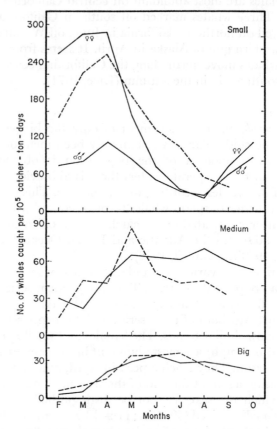

Fig. 7. Average monthly catches (solid line) 1954–69 and aircraft sightings (broken line) 1961–69 per unit effort of various sex and size classes of sperm whales off Durban (from Gambell, 1972).

b. Social grouping. The social organization of sperm whales, with their polygynous habit and the grouping of animals of particular size and sex, has been known since the days of the 18th- and 19th-century fishery. More recent studies by observations at sea and analyses of catch compositions have confirmed the various units of the populations along the following lines (Clarke, 1956; Caldwell *et al.*, 1966; Gambell, 1967; Gaskin, 1970; Ohsumi, 1971).

The prime grouping is the nursery herd, consisting of females, calves and immature males. When joined by one or more big bulls, particularly during the mating season, this grouping is often termed a harem school. The number of animals present can range as high as 200 whales, but generally the size is of the order of 10–30 whales. Nursery schools appear to have a very stable composition. Females marked together in schools in the North Pacific have been caught together after 6 and 10 days, and up to 5, 8 and 10 years from the date of marking (Ohsumi, 1971). As the calves grow they become the young immature females and males still found in this basic grouping, or they can form temporary aggregations on their own.

Soon after the young males start to become sexually mature at about 32–33 ft (9·8 m–10·1 m) in length they begin to leave the female schools and migrate to higher latitudes. This behaviour gives rise to the formation of bachelor schools. Ohsumi (1966) compared the age distribution curves for male and female sperm whales in Japanese coastal waters, and found that the difference between them corresponded very closely to the age composition of the male sperm whales in Aleutian waters. He took this as confirmation of the segregation of the males to the higher latitudes, and calculated that the segregation rate increases from ages 12 to 25 years and then becomes constant. Half the males have segregated themselves in this way by age 18 years, when they are nearly 40 ft (12·2 m) long.

Further confirmation for this process is given by the cyamid infestation oj sperm whales off the west coast of South Africa (Best, 1969a). The females and small males are infested almost exclusively by the species *Neocyamus physeteris*, but an increasing proportion of the males over 37 ft (11·3 m) are infested with a second species, *Cyamus catodontis*. The proportion of bigger whales carrying *N. physeteris* falls rapidly, so that it is absent in animals of 42 ft (12·8 m) or longer. The change over in infestation corresponds with the segregation of the males from the females, and at a length of 39–40 ft (11·9 m–12·2 m) equal proportions of the males carry either cyamid species. The entry of the males into the Antarctic waters at this stage in their development appears to clean them of one cyamid species, which presumably cannot tolerate the conditions in the higher latitudes, and the males then become reinfested by another species which can.

Bachelor schools of medium sized sperm whales comprise an average of half a dozen males between 39 (11·9 m) and 45 ft (13·7 m) long. These groups break up as the animals grow to full breeding maturity, and the biggest bulls have a strong tendency to be solitary. There is some evidence from tooth scars that the big bulls compete with one another to gain possession of a nursery school during the mating season. It is these harem masters who are the principal breeding force in the population, but the fate of the males who are unsuccessful in this social selection is uncertain. They may compete again in another season for the chance to breed, or they may remain in the polar waters as outcasts.

It has been suggested (Clarke, 1956) that the mature female sperm whales around the Azores segregate according to their reproductive condition. Unexpectedly high proportions of resting females were sampled in the catches, and it was proposed that the pregnant and nursing females might be sequestered further offshore to account for this feature. Off Durban, mixed groups of females in all stages of the reproductive cycle are normal, and the composition of the female stock sampled is representative of the total population (Gambell, 1972). The latter situation also appears to be the case in the other sperm whale stocks sampled throughout the world.

III. STOCK UNITS

Although the large baleen whales and sperm whales are widespread in occurrence throughout the waters of the northern and southern hemispheres, the various species are not considered to be composed each of single stocks. Initially there is a division between the whales in the two hemispheres. The whales in the North Atlantic and North Pacific are geographically isolated, and the warm water breeding grounds in the southern hemisphere are also separated by continental land masses.

There is further evidence for even greater sub-division which will be considered now for each species. In the case of baleen whales it is evident that more information is available for the whales in the southern hemisphere than those in the north. This is largely the result of the greater whaling activity which has taken place in the south this century, providing both the whale carcases needed for scientific study and the incentive to assess the effects of the heavy exploitation on the stocks. Whaling in the North Atlantic has been conducted on a very reduced scale by comparison, so the information here is less abundant. The North Pacific has been extensively hunted since the Second World War, and the basic data available from this region have allowed rather more detailed analyses to be made. Important results for sperm whale stocks in particular have been obtained, although the conclusions drawn on the baleen whales are not always so firm as in the south.

A. BLUE WHALES

1. *Northern hemisphere*

Blue whales were fished extensively in the North Atlantic by land stations on the Canadian coast and by pelagic expeditions in the Davis

Strait in the 1920's and 1930's. The catches fell markedly, and the catches from Iceland at this time were also low by comparison with those in 1896. The catching history of the eastern stock formerly hunted from the Faroe Islands and Norway was different. From this evidence, Jonsgård (1955) concluded that the blue whales in the western and eastern parts of the North Atlantic follow different migration routes and are different stocks.

There is some evidence, though, that blue whales can cross the North Atlantic. Harpoons of American origin were found in blue whales caught at Iceland and north Norway last century and an explosive harpoon fired off north Norway was recovered at Iceland (Jonsgård, 1955). It may be that blue whales range widely through their northern feeding grounds in the Barents Sea, so that the eastern and western components of the North Atlantic population mix during the summer before separating to migrate south again.

In the northern North Pacific there are three main summer concentrations of blue whales in the eastern Gulf of Alaska, south of the Aleutian Islands and towards Kamchatka. Whale mark recoveries have demonstrated movements between all these areas (Ivashin and Rovnin, 1967; Whales Research Institute, Tokyo, 1967). This main group of blue whales was reduced in numbers by pelagic whaling in the post-war years.

Another stock of blue whales congregates from February to early July each year along the west coast of Baja California. It probably migrates north to the vicinity of Vancouver Island or the Gulf of Alaska for the summer feeding season. This eastern North Pacific stock appears to have remained stable under the light catching which took place from land stations, and so is considered a separate stock unit (Rice, 1974).

2. *Southern hemisphere*
a. *Antarctic catches*. Blue whales were the prime species hunted in the Antarctic during the early years of the industry's expansion in that area. Particularly when pelagic whaling was newly developed, the catchers attached to the floating factories concentrated chiefly on the capture of blue whales. Hjort *et al.* (1932a) analysed the geographical distribution of the blue whale catches and the smaller catches of fin whales by Norwegian vessels, and proposed a sub-division of the Antarctic zone occupied by the whalers into five Areas. Area I was the small region hunted by the catchers operating from the land stations in the Falkland Islands' Dependencies. The remaining Areas II–V represented extensive stretches of 60°–70° of longitude from 60°W eastwards to 170°W, which appeared each to contain a concentration of blue whales. These concentrations were not totally separated from one another, but similar

analyses of the catches made in subsequent seasons indicated that they were reasonably evident and constant from year to year (Hjort *et al.*, 1933–1938; Bergersen *et al.*, 1939; Bergersen and Ruud, 1941).

Thus it was concluded that since the factory ships and their catchers regularly became segregated on four more or less distinct whaling grounds (Areas II–V), the blue whales, and to a lesser extent the fin whales, which were the object of hunting must also be segregated into at least four corresponding stocks.

Mackintosh (1942) examined the distribution of blue whales, along with fin and humpback whales, around the Antarctic continent. In addition to the catch data, he presented sightings observations made during the course of whale marking and oceanographic cruises. The sightings indicated concentrations of whales in Areas II–IV, and also to the west of 60°W. Mackintosh therefore proposed that Area I should be re-allocated to encompass the south-eastern part of the Pacific from 60°–120°W. Areas I–V each contained a concentration of blue whales considered as separate stocks. The rather empty region between 120°– 170°W was designated Area VI to complete the circle of Antarctic whaling areas now generally adopted (Fig. 8).

b. Whaling marking. The numbers of blue whales marked and re- covered in the Antarctic zone are small. Brown (1962b) reviewed the evidence provided by 77 returns from 889 blue whales marked up to the 1957/58 season. This marking was carried out by the Discovery Com- mittee, and under the international marking scheme in post-war years.

There is evidence of considerable longitudinal movement taking place during the whaling season, including some whales which crossed between Areas II and III, and Areas III and IV. One blue whale marked in Area III was recovered in Area VI two years later, a longitudinal shift of 170°, but the majority of recoveries were made within 90° of the marking position. Because of the small numbers involved it is not possible to know if the range of longitudinal movement increases with time elapsed since marking. Brown (1962b) concluded that the Antarctic Areas division has some reality for blue whales, reflecting a basic separation of the total population into groups. However, the exact status of these divisions is not clear from this evidence.

3. *Pygmy blue whales*

Whalers in the Antarctic have for long spoken of *Myrbjönner*, a small blue whale with many pale spots, particularly found east of the Green- wich meridian (Mackintosh, 1942). In the early 1960's a separate sub- species of pygmy blue whale was identified as *Balaenoptera musculu brevicauda* (Zemsky and Boronin, 1964). This sub-species had been proposed and described by Ichihara (1961, 1963, 1966a) on the evidence of Japanese catches mainly around Kerguelen, Marion and Crozet Islands. This whale is characterized by a generally paler colour than the

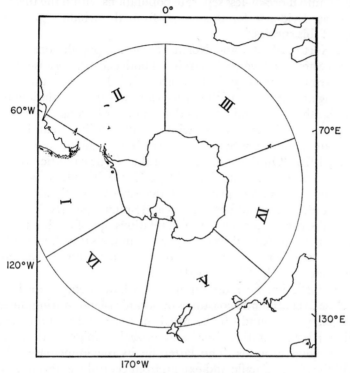

FIG. 8. The Antarctic whaling Areas.

ordinary blue whale; a shorter tail region and longer trunk; relatively shorter baleen plates. The pygmy sub-species reaches sexual and physical maturity at smaller sizes than normal, and no pygmy whale longer than 80 ft (24·4 m) appears to have been caught.

The pygmy blue whales were thought to inhabit a restricted zone of the Antarctic during the summer months, broadly north of 54°S and between 0°–80°E. In the winter they must migrate and breed in the temperate Indian Ocean, for specimens have been identified in the catches off Western Australia (Vervoort and Tranter, 1961) and at Durbna (Gambell, 1964). There is also a record from the west coast of South Africa (Bannister and Grindley, 1966). However, pygmy blue whales have also been found in the catches off Chile (Aguayo, 1974), so their distribution must be more wide ranging than at first proposed.

1. Northern hemisphere

Although humpback whales are found world-wide, they tend to be segregated into more-or-less separate populations within the three major ocean areas. Evidence for this comes from the whaling grounds and sightings of this species.

In the North Atlantic and North Pacific the populations are found along the eastern and western margins of both oceans. Because the water masses narrow to the north in both areas, it is likely that there is some overlapping and mingling of the eastern and western populations of each ocean when the whales migrate to their summer feeding grounds.

Humpback whales which over-winter in the Caribbean and Bermuda area migrate to the Davis Strait by way of Newfoundland and Labrador (Mitchell, 1973). On the eastern side of the North Atlantic, humpback whales were observed around the Cape Verde Islands in winter, and migrated northwards in spring past the Azores, Shetland and Faroe Islands to the seas around Bear Island and Spitzbergen (Kellogg, 1929). However, the precise movements and relationships of the humpbacks in the northern North Atlantic is not clear, for animals travelling westwards from the eastern Arctic have been observed off Finmark in January, February and March (Risting, 1912).

In the North Pacific most humpback whales congregate in warm waters close to continental coastlines or oceanic islands during the winter months. They are found off the Mexican coast and around the main Hawaiian Islands, at this time, and probably migrate north to the summer feeding grounds. The latter lie in the immediate off-shore waters of the North Pacific and extend from central California to Japan (Rice, 1974). Recovered Japanese whale marks have shown the migration of humpback whales between the winter grounds of the western North Pacific in the Ryuku and Bonin Island areas and the summer grounds to the east of the Aleutians. These movements are plotted in Fig. 9, together with others suggesting a migration path on the North American side (Whales Research Institute, Tokyo, 1967).

2. Southern hemisphere

The distribution of humpback whales in the southern hemisphere has been summarized by Mackintosh (1965). Catches indicated a high degree of segregation of local stocks, both on the winter breeding grounds north of 40°S and the summer feeding grounds in the Antarctic. Coastal whaling operations took appreciable numbers of this species on (1) the west coast of South America, (2) the coast of Brazil, (3) the west coast of

Africa, (4) the east coast of Africa and Madagascar, (5) the west coast of Australia, and (6) New Zealand, the east coast of Australia and some South Pacific island groups.

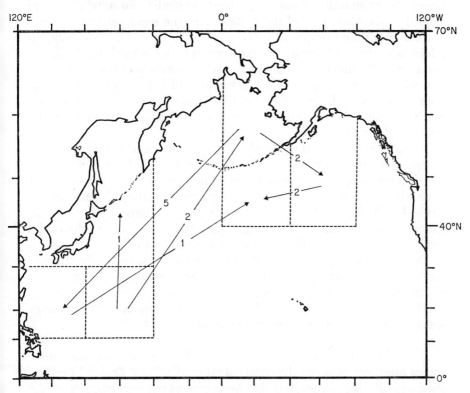

FIG. 9. Movements of marked humpback whales in the North Pacific, shown by numbers of whales moving between areas indicated (after Whales Research Institute, Tokyo, 1967).

Antarctic catches of humpbacks showed that there were five nearly separate concentrations of these whales on the feeding grounds during the summer. These concentrations were centred (1) 70–80°W, the Bellinghausen Sea area, (2) 10–35°W, in the eastern Scotia Sea, (3) 10–40°E, off Queen Maud Land, (4) 80–100°E, off Queen Mary Land, and (5) 150–180°E, around the Balleny Islands and the Ross Sea. The species is not entirely absent in the regions between these main centres of abundance, but the existence of the concentrations was also confirmed by sightings from research vessels during the course of whale marking cruises.

Pre-war recoveries of whales marked in the Antarctic were given by Raynor (1940). Twenty-two humpback whales marked between 75°E and 102°E and south of 60°S were recovered in the three successive seasons after marking from north west Australia. Four whales were caught in the same part of the Antarctic in the season after they were marked, and one humpback three years later from the same area. In addition to this evidence for the connection between the humpbacks off Western Australia and those in the Antarctic somewhat to the south west, two whales were caught off Madagascar which had been marked at approximately 11°E and 54°E. Another whale marked in the Antarctic south of South Africa was recovered the following year close to the position of marking.

These features led Mackintosh (1942) to propose the existence of independent stocks of humpback whales in the southern hemisphere. These came to be called "Groups" identified by the Antarctic statistical Area which they occupied, for one of these groups fell neatly into each of Areas I to V in the Antarctic. The whales in Group II, the Atlantic sector, probably include two breeding stocks from opposite sides of the ocean, so that there are thought to be six breeding stocks.

The humpback groups are certainly isolated from each other during the breeding season by the land masses and unoccupied water masses which separate them. However, in the Antarctic there may be some overlapping of adjacent stocks, although the great majority of the whales seem to return to their own breeding areas.

a. Australian and New Zealand stocks. The best known migration routes are those between the coasts of Australia, New Zealand and the southwest Pacific islands and the Antarctic waters immediately to the south of these regions. With large scale post-war marking carried out on or near the breeding grounds, some 3000 humpback whales have been marked in this sector.

The Group IV population had 56 recoveries taken more than six months after marking. Only two of these came from outside the Group IV area, having moved into the Group V area. The comparable figures for the Group V population were 84 recaptures after six months or more, with 10 whales taken in the Group IV area and one in Group I (Chittleborough, 1965). Thus 97% of the Group IV whales and 87% of the Group V humpbacks were recovered in their original population territory. Dawbin (1966) has suggested that a degree of segregation exists between the east Australian and the New Zealand/Pacific islands components of the Group V population on the evidence of the small interchange of whales between these breeding grounds. The recoveries of marked humpback whales from Groups IV and V are summarized in Fig. 10 to show the range of movements.

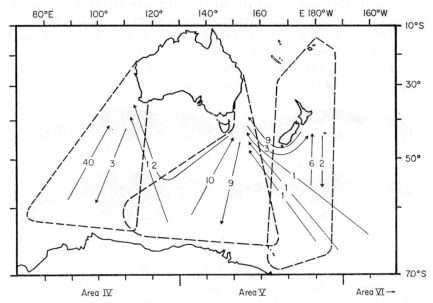

FIG. 10. Movements of marked humpback whales in the region around Australia and New Zealand, shown by numbers of whales moving between areas indicated (after Dawbin, 1966).

There seems little doubt that as the humpbacks migrate southwards from their restricted breeding areas they fan out to some extent so that there is a slight crossing of tracks on the southern feeding grounds. The great majority of whales return to their own breeding ground, but there is probably sufficient interchange from one stock to another to prevent genetic isolation developing.

b. Colour patterns. One piece of evidence bearing on the degree of homogenity of the breeding groups comes from a study of the colour patterns of humpback whales. Seven different patterns were distinguished by Lillie (1915). The four main types are illustrated in Fig. 11, ranging from animals with extensive white skin on the ventral and lateral surfaces to completely black individuals. Three intermediate forms were recognized between these four main patterns. This classification was used subsequently by workers studying humpbacks at various locations in the southern hemisphere, and their results are summarized in Fig. 12.

Humpbacks from New Zealand examined by Lillie (1915) were mainly in the middle colour range, with few at the two extremes. By contrast, Matthews (1937) found that the whales off South Georgia and South Africa, which he combined, were predominantly at the darker end of the scale. Omura (1953) gave further evidence of a decrease in the degree of dark pigmentation from west to east in the Antarctic, comparing an Area IV sample (Matsuura, 1940) with two from Area V. All three samples showed a predominance of middle colour range whales.

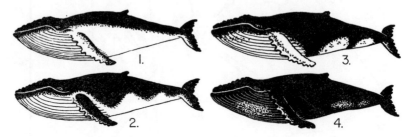

Fig. 11. Humpback whale colour patterns (after Lillie, 1915).

Because observers differed in their interpretation of the intermediate patterns, only the four main colour groups were used by Chittleborough (1965) in a comparison of the humpback whales sampled on the west and east Australian coasts. His results are shown in Fig. 13. Although the whole range of patterns was represented in both groups, the west coast (Area IV) whales tended to be darker than the east coast (Area V) animals.

Thus the evidence from the colour patterns suggests that there must be sufficient interchange between the breeding stocks to prevent genetic differences from reaching significant levels.

C. FIN WHALES

1. *North Atlantic*

There appear to be a number of small independent stocks of fin whales within the North Atlantic area. On the eastern side Jonsgård (1958) compared catch data from the west coast of Norway and the Faroe Islands, which both showed a decline in catch per unit of effort from 1951, and suggested a connection between the fin whales in the two areas. Analysis of catch statistics and reproductive data from the fin whales caught off the west and north coasts of Norway gave evidence that they are two distinct stocks (Jonsgård, 1966). The north Norway stock has been relatively stable under exploitation, and so has that off

Iceland, and it is possible that the whales in these two areas are linked. They may also have a connection with the fin whales off southeast Greenland, for two whales marked in this area were recovered at the Icelandic whaling station on the west coast (Jonsgård, 1974).

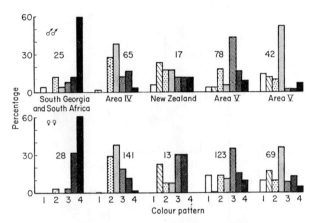

Fig. 12. Incidence of humpback whale colour patterns in the southern hemisphere, (data from Lillie, 1915; Matthews, 1937; Matsuura, 1940; Omura, 1953).

Two more fin whale stocks apparently occur off eastern Canada and the northeastern U.S.A. One of these has its main concentration off Nova Scotia and the other is found off northern Newfoundland and Labrador. Differences in the length distributions of the catches in these areas due to differences in growth, and changes in abundance under exploitation suggest a degree of separation between the two stocks (Allen, 1971). Marking data and stranding records indicate that these two stocks migrate over a fairly limited range along the coastline between winter and summer, but the grounds they occupy overlap to some extent within this range (Mitchell, 1974).

It is possible that all the fin whales in the North Atlantic make relatively small seasonal migrations, for whales are found in almost all the area between 30° N and the ice-edge in summer. This led Kellogg (1929) to the idea that the stocks are stratified, the summer feeding grounds of some fin whales being occupied during the winter by whales which had spent the summer further north.

2. North Pacific

There is some evidence that possibly three different stocks of fin whales exist in the North Pacific basin, but their degree of isolation from each other is not clear. The main lines of study leading to this conclusion are the recoveries of marked whales, blood typing and morphological analyses.

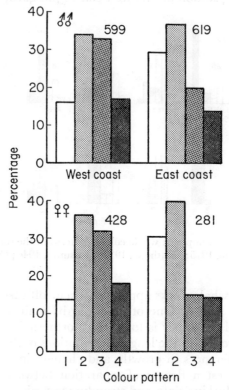

Fig. 13. Incidence of humpback whale colour patterns off the east and west Australian coasts (after Chittleborough, 1965).

The movements of marked whales are plotted in Fig. 14. They suggest that the whales which feed in the Aleutian area during the summer months come from both the eastern and western sides of the North Pacific. There appears to be a certain amount of mixing of the whales in the northern waters but the evidence is not inconsistent with the view that there are two separate stocks on the Asian and American sides which overlap in the northern ends of their ranges (Fujino, 1960).

Investigations into the blood types of fin whales by Fujino (1960) led him to propose a three allele system to account for the Ju blood types found in the North Pacific. On the evidence of non-random geographic distribution in the frequency of occurrence of these blood types he proposed the existence of three stocks. One in the East China Sea is isolated from two others which occupy the eastern and western sides of the Aleutian area and overlap to varying extents from year to year.

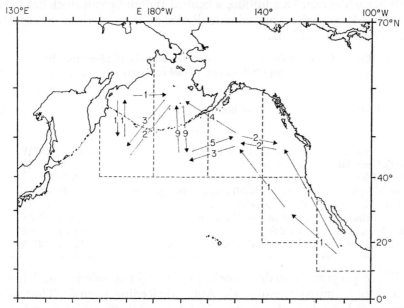

Fig. 14. Movements of marked fin whales in the North Pacific, shown by numbers of whales moving between areas indicated (after Whales Research Institute, Tokyo, 1967).

The distinction between the fin whales in the East China Sea and those in the northern North Pacific is also apparent in their general body form. Those in the East China Sea have longer head and shorter tail regions than the others, as determined by linear discriminant function analysis of external measurements of the whales (Ichihara, 1957). There are also indications that the whales in the northern North Pacific reach sexual maturity at a larger body length and have longer baleen plates than the animals in the East China Sea (Fujino, 1960).

It is possible that the main northern North Pacific population contains more than the two stocks suggested, but there is no firm evidence by which to draw dividing lines separating these components other than the rather arbitrary one at 180° longitude generally adopted (Omura and Ohsumi, 1974).

3. Southern hemisphere

The fin whale population in the southern hemisphere is considered to be composed of a number of separate stocks. The identification and delineation of these stocks is by no means complete, but the broad conclusions suggested in published analyses point to the existence of separate breeding stocks either in each southern ocean, or sub-divided within each ocean. In addition, a central Indian Ocean stock has been postulated, and the approximate limits of these various stocks are summarized in Table I.

TABLE I   A suggested division of the southern hemisphere fin whale populations (after Ivashin, 1969)

Stock	Wintering area	Summer distribution
Chile–Peruvian	West of N. Chile and Peru	100/110°W–60°W
South Georgian	East of Brazil	60°W–25°W
West African	West coast of Africa	25°W–0°
East African	East coast of Africa and Madagascar	0°–40°E
Crozet–Kerguelen	East of Madagascar	40°E–80°E
West Australian	Northwest of W. Australia	80°E–110/120°E
East Australian	Coral Sea	140°E–170°E
New Zealand	Fiji Sea and adjacent waters	170°E–145°W

These proposed breeding stocks are thought to overlap and inter-mingle to a limited extent on the Antarctic feeding grounds. The stocks correspond closely to the six statistical Areas (Fig. 8), which were based primarily on the feeding concentrations of blue whales, with the additional sub-division of Areas II and III into eastern and western components. The evidence for the stocks and their discreteness comes from a number of sources.

a. Whale marking. The most direct evidence of the link between the breeding and feeding grounds of fin whales comes from recovered whale marks. Relevant marking and finding positions are plotted in Fig. 15, from data given by Brown (1962a, c; 1964, 1972, 1973). Fin whales marked off both coasts of South America have been caught in the western half of Area II, and whales marked in Area III have been caught off both coasts of South Africa. In addition, one whale marked off Durban on the east coast of South Africa has been caught further south and east in Area III, and another marked just north of the western part of Area IV has been recovered at Durban.

The movements eastwards or westwards of fin whales marked and recaptured in the Antarctic indicate that relatively few were found in an Area different from that in which they were marked. Under the international whale marking scheme, only 82 (17·6%) of 466 marks recovered up to 1970 had moved to an adjacent Area (Brown, 1962b, updated in Chapman, 1974a). A similar result can be derived from the Soviet marking data (Ivashin, 1973), which show that 8 (18·6%) of 43 fin whales recovered had moved into the next Area.

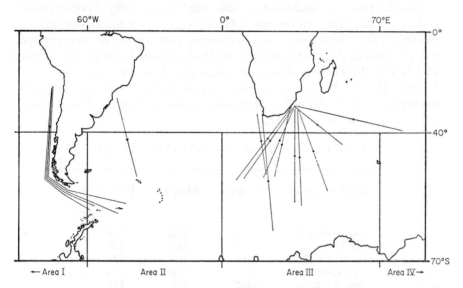

Fig. 15. Movements of marked fin whales between the breeding and feeding grounds in the southern hemisphere (data from Brown, 1962–1973).

Movement eastwards has taken place between all of the Areas, and movement westwards has been recorded between all except Areas VI–V. It appears that movements between Areas II and III, III and IV and I and VI are about equal, but there may be rather more movement between Areas I and II, at least in an eastward direction. It may be noted that the location of firing and finding the marks was very close in many cases, and over a period of time extending up to 37 years (Brown, 1973). Only a few degrees of longitude separated the positions even when these fell on either side of an Area boundary. It seems from these results that many fin whales return to the same feeding place in the Antarctic year after year. The whales are segregated in their separate breeding areas, but disperse and associate on the feeding grounds.

b. Iodine values of whale oil. During the feeding period whales build up reserves of fat, chiefly in the sub-cutaneous blubber but also in and around the internal body organs. The composition of the constituent oils varies according to the food supply, migrations and environmental factors, and these are reflected in the iodine value of the oil. Norwegian work has shown some evidence of regional segregation of the fin whales in the Antarctic using iodine values as a means of comparison between regions (Lund, 1950a, b, 1951).

Samples taken on board factory ships working around the polar region and at the land stations on South Georgia gave four distinct groups of iodine values. These were taken to indicate more or less discrete groups of fin whales feeding in the regions 50°W–0°, 0°–70°E, 70°E–130°E and 160°E–170°W. These regions correspond closely to the Antarctic Areas II, III, IV and V. The iodine values rose uniformly in all the areas during the course of the whaling season by some 8–11 units. The average values are shown in Table II.

TABLE II   Average iodine values for whale oil samples

Whaling ground	1948/49	1949/50	1950/51
South Georgia	125	125	130
50°W–0°	123	125	130
0°–70°E	118	122	124
70°E–130°E	114	116	116
160°E–170°W	(107)	112	111

These results, whilst not conclusive in themselves, do suggest that there is little interchange of whales between the areas indicated during the whaling season. However, the small variations demonstrated make it impossible to determine to what extent whales may move between areas outside the Antarctic whaling season and grounds.

c. *Length compositon.* The length distributions of the catches between 50°–60°S and 60°–70°S over a long period of years both pre-war. and post-war were plotted by Laws (1960a) by 10° sectors of longitude The mean lengths of females caught between 60°–70°S are shown in Fig. 16, and illustrate a striking segregation by longitude. Four main groups are represented, roughly corresponding to South Atlantic, South Indian, West Pacific and East Pacific Oceans.

An analysis of mean length data by Antarctic Areas (International Whaling Commission, 1971a) showed that fin whales aged 25 years and over, broadly representing the size at physical maturity, were largest in Area II and smallest in Area VI. There is a decreasing mean size east-wards through Areas III, IV and V, and Area I is intermediate between Areas II and VI. Although the mean lengths for neighbouring Areas are not statistically significantly different, their gradation does suggest that more than one stock is present within the circumpolar feeding grounds.

d. Serological studies. Three major Ju blood groups were identified in Antarctic fin whales by Fujino (1964), and they were considered to be produced by two main and equal allelic systems. On the basis of the non-random geographical distributions of the incidence of the blood types, it

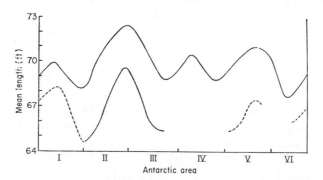

FIG. 16. Range of mean lengths of female fin whales caught between 60°–70°S, by 10° sectors of longitude (after Laws, 1960a).

was proposed that four different breeding stocks enter the Antarctic in Areas II, III (north of 50°S), III (south of 50°S) and IV. Adjacent stocks overlap to a certain degree on the feeding grounds and intermingle to the extent of some 10% between Areas II and III.

These results agree well with the evidence of stock units derived from the mark recovery data, with the addition of the low latitude ground proposed in Area III. This suggests the possibility of a latitudinal segregation of stocks similar to that proposed in the North Atlantic (p. 275), but no other evidence has yet been put forward to support this idea in the southern hemisphere.

Variations in a number of other features of the southern fin whales were also suggested by Fujino (1964) to be associated with the blood types described. These included the school size, pregnancy rate, age composition and rate of ovarian corpora accumulation. Whilst it is possible that the observed variations in all these features around the Antarctic zone could be associated with genetic variations reflected in the blood types, they could also result from the status of the separate stocks after their varying histories of exploitation. Thus they may not be direct indicators of stock units as such.

D. SEI WHALES

Much less is known about the movements and stocks of sei whales than those of the larger baleen whales. In part this is the result of their relatively lower value to the whaling industry until recent years, so that fewer records and animals have been available for study. In addition, they do seem to be less regular in their migrations in many parts of the world, so that whalers have often spoken of "sei whale years" when they have appeared in numbers in a certain area.

A complicating factor in analysing the distribution and catch data on sei whales is the confusion which has occurred in past years with Bryde's whales. The Bryde's whale (Olsen, 1913) is very similar to the sei whale in appearance, so that whalers have not always recognized the two animals as separate species. The most conspicuous external difference is the presence of three longitudinal ridges on the head of Bryde's whale, compared with one median ridge on the sei whale. In addition, the ventral grooves extend as far as the umbilicus in the Bryde's whale, but end more anteriorly in the sei whale. The Bryde's whale also has courser baleen bristles than the sei whale (Omura, 1966).

Particularly in the North Pacific, sei and Bryde's whales were not recognized or reported separately until 1955, so earlier records of sei whales around the Bonin Islands and the south and west coasts of Japan are probably wrongly identified as to species (Omura, 1959). The species is now known to have a wide distribution around the world, chiefly in temperate waters, and there also appear to be distinct inshore and offshore forms (Best, 1974a).

In the North Atlantic, sei whales have been caught from land stations on both eastern and western seaboards and at Iceland. There is little or no evidence to show what separate stocks may exist, although Mitchell (1973) has suggested that there may be two stocks in the northwest Atlantic, presumably by analogy with the fin whale situation.

Information on possible North Pacific sei whale stocks is similarly scarce in that catches from eastern and western coastal stations and the pelagic operations in the Aleutian area have yielded little direct evidence for stock units. By analogy with the fin whales, the population has been arbitrarily divided into two groups on either side of longitude 180° (Omura and Ohsumi, 1974). None of the 49 marks recovered up to 1965 had come from whales which had crossed this line (Whales Research Institute, Tokyo, 1967), but there is little other evidence.

The paucity of relevant data from sei whales in the southern hemisphere has made stock identification extremely tenuous in this part of the world too. Since the southern sei whales do not penetrate very far into the

Antarctic zone, the centre of their abundance is likely to be in the temperate waters. The breeding stocks must therefore number at least three, one in each southern ocean.

The pattern of exploitation in the Antarctic fishery when it began to concentrate on sei whales in the early 1960's, and the resulting changes in stock density, suggested the need to sub-divide Area II into eastern and western halves (FAO, 1966, 1967). These could correspond to breeding stocks off the east coast of South America and the west coast of South Africa.

Few sei whales have been marked in the southern hemisphere, because of their less preferred status until recent years. Recoveries from 64 marked whales (Brown, 1968a, c; 1973; Ivashin, 1973) suggest that the movements of sei whales are similar to those of blue and fin whales in the same region. They return to the same feeding grounds year after year, and also disperse longitudinally in the Antarctic zone. The main movements shown by marked whales are plotted in Fig. 17. In the South Atlantic there is a link between the whales off the coast of Brazil and those in the western half of Area II. The sei whales in the eastern part of Area II, the western part of Area III and the west coast of South Africa seem to be associated. On the east coast of South Africa there is a connection with the eastern half of Area III and the western half of Area IV. Whales off both west and east coasts of Australia have been found in the eastern half of Area IV, and movements from New Zealand have been into both Areas V and VI.

Nevertheless, the traditional six whaling Areas seem to reflect the sei whale groupings reasonably accurately, although possible sub-divisions may be confirmed by additional information.

E. SPERM WHALES

A number of attempts have been made to find distinguishing features by which the sperm whales frequenting various parts of the world may be recognized. Studies of some of the external characters of the sperm whales sampled off the east and west coasts of South Africa, in the Antarctic, the southeast Pacific, the North Pacific and around the Azores have shown the whales to be remarkably similar (Clarke et al., 1968; Best and Gambell, 1968). The external characters studied included colour patterns, tooth eruption, numbers of mandibular teeth and dorsal humps, the incidence of deformed lower jaws and double teeth. Some slight colour variations noted may be due only to the difficulty of standardizing recording of these markings.

Measurements and body proportions have also been compared for the sperm whales in these regions. Some differences have appeared in the analyses by Clarke and Paliza (1972) and Machin (1974), which will be described in the relevant sections below.

There are also indications of differences between the internal parasites, notably the helminths, found in sperm whales inhabiting the North Atlantic and North Pacific Oceans, as well as between the northern and

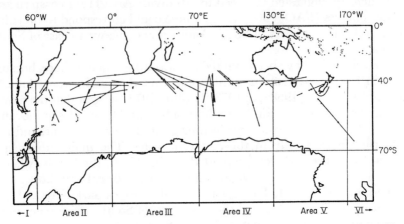

FIG. 17. Main movements of marked sei whales in the southern hemisphere (data from Brown, 1968a, c; 1973; Ivashin, 1973).

southern hemispheres (Berzin, 1971). However, insufficient sampling has been done to date to use these parasites as definite indicators of separate sperm whale stocks.

1. *North Atlantic*

Although sperm whales were fished heavily in the North Atlantic during the American whale fishery of the 18th and 19th centuries, the numbers caught in modern whaling from land stations around the ocean have been small. The main evidence for stock identification in the area is derived from the sightings by merchant vessels (Brown, 1958; Slijper *et al.*, 1964). These suggest concentrations of whales off the northwest African coast, in a band right across the ocean between 30° and 60°N, and in the Caribbean area. Studies in the relict Azores fishery (Clarke, 1956) provided no firm data for linking or separating the whales in this and other areas of the North Atlantic. For the present the sperm whales in this ocean therefore are regarded as one stock.

2. *North Pacific*

There is more information on stock identities of sperm whales in the North Pacific than anywhere else in the world. The evidence from whale marking, blood typing and the density distribution of the whales suggests that there are three possible stocks. These are located on the western side of the ocean, west of 170°E; on the eastern side, east of 150°W; and in a central position between 170°E and 150°W. There is probably considerable overlapping of the stocks at these boundaries, and also much intermingling north of 40°N.

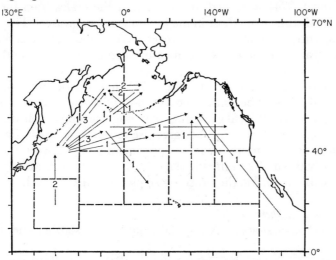

Fig. 18. Movements of marked sperm whales in the North Pacific, shown by numbers of whales moving between areas indicated (after Whales Research Institute, Tokyo, 1967).

Whale mark recoveries have shown migration routes north and south on both sides of the North Pacific. These are illustrated in Fig. 18, where the mixing of sperm whales in the higher latitudes is also obvious. The latter whales are predominantly males.

Blood typing of North Pacific sperm whales has been carried out only in the eastern part of the area. Ju-2 positive cells were detected in 52 out of 123 whales sampled in Japanese coastal waters, but none at all in 198 whales sampled in the Aleutian area (Fujino, 1963). This significant geographical difference in the incidence of the blood types suggests the existence of two different breeding populations which distribute themselves in these two areas. Seasonal changes in the incidence of the Ju-2 positive type, as well as the results from whale marking, indicate the movement of whales between the two areas.

Sperm whale density distributions derived from catches and sightings per unit of effort, coupled with differences in the seasonal size compositions of the catches, lead to the conclusion that there are three centres of abundance (Masaki, reported in Best, 1974b). These are equated with three stocks along the Asian side, including the area around the Bonin Islands, the Japanese coastal area and around Kamchatka; the American side, including the Bay of Alaska; and a central stock area around the Aleutian Islands.

A multivariate analysis of the external body measurements carried out by Machin (1974) suggested, however, that the males from the Bonin Islands are distinct from those in the Japanese coastal waters. The females are apparently similar, and both sexes were found not to differ in an allometric analysis of the same measurements by Clarke and Paliza (1972).

It has also been suggested (Berzin, 1971) that the sperm whales in the North Pacific should be considered as sub-divided into the much smaller units of herds. These local groupings may migrate along their individual routes which considered together give rise to the three stocks previously outlined. However, there is likely to be some mixing between the herds, particularly the males in the more northerly waters, so that it would be impracticable to define the breeding stock units at this level.

3. *Southern hemisphere*

Information on stock units of sperm whales in the southern hemisphere is sparse.

A morphometric analysis by Clarke and Paliza (1972) suggested that the whales caught around South Georgia and on the pelagic grounds between 95° and 150°E are similar. They have a narrower insertion of the flukes into the tail stock, and flippers which are longer in the free part and shorter at the insertion into the body than sperm whales from the southeast Pacific, Japan, the Bonin Islands and off Durban. There is a skew in the allometric growth curve for the measurement of the distance from the dorsal fin to the flukes in the Antarctic samples. This prompted the suggestion that these Antarctic whales comprise a mixed population containing a component similar in morphometry to whales in the other localities studied, and another component, strongest at South Georgia, which is different and presumably comes from the Atlantic area which has not been investigated so far.

The canonical analysis of the same data by Machin (1974) gave rather similar results. This indicated that the females from three localities in the southeast Pacific are similar to each other but different from those off Durban. The males off Durban are also different from those at South Georgia.

Blood typing has been carried out on only a very limited scale in the southern hemisphere. The preliminary results from rather small samples suggested that whales caught in 40°–55°E and 58°–92°E may differ in their blood types (Cushing *et al.*, 1963).

The whale marking data already discussed (p. 261) indicate a strong north–south component of movement. Other recoveries (Best, 1969b; Brown, 1972, 1973; Ivashin, 1973) suggest a certain discreteness in the sperm whale distribution in the southern hemisphere. Most marking of sperm whales has been carried out in the vicinity of Durban. Seventeen whales marked on or near the whaling grounds have been recovered at Durban, together with five whales marked outside the whaling grounds but within the longitudes of 26° and 51°E. Two other whales have been marked and caught by pelagic fleets in the temperate waters in longitudes 54° and 33°E after intervals of two and twenty-two years respectively. Two whales marked in the Antarctic at 55° and 88°E have also been recovered within this general region.

In other parts of the southern hemisphere, a sperm whale marked off Chile was recovered two years later in the same area, and two whales marked off Western Australia were also caught not far away after three months and two years. Whale marks fired and recovered in the Antarctic also suggest that sperm whales remain or return to the same area year after year.

Since the breeding grounds and concentrations of female sperm whales in the southern oceans are separated by the continental land masses, separate stocks in each ocean are likely to exist. This does not preclude the possibility of some genetic exchange occurring which would prevent the total isolation of the stocks, through the movements of the males into the higher latitudes. In this connection, the density of sperm whales as determined from catch per unit of effort data and whale sightings have been plotted and discussed by Best (1974b). Certain regions of high density can be detected and together with the other evidence available which is outlined above, this led to the proposal of the following nine stocks (International Whaling Commission, 1973):

West Atlantic	60°–30°W
East Atlantic	30°W–20°E
West Indian	20°–60°E
Central Indian	60°–90°E
East Indian	90°–130°E
East Australian	130°–160°E
New Zealand	160°E–170°W
Central Pacific	170°–100°W
East Pacific	100°–60°W

IV. Reproduction, Age and Growth

A. REPRODUCTIVE CYCLE

Whales are mammals and their reproduction is typically mammalian in most essentials (Laws, 1961; Best, 1967; Gambell, 1968, 1972). The two ovaries of an immature female contain many oocytes. These develop, each within a fluid filled follicle, as the whale matures. At sexual maturity there is considerable enlargement of a number of the follicles, which appear rather like blisters in the surface layer of the ovary. At ovulation one of these follicles swells and ruptures to release the contained ovum, and the remainder of the follicles shrink back into the tissue of the ovary. This cycle of development and regression takes place at each subsequent oestrus.

Ovulation appears to be spontaneous in most whale species, and generally only a single follicle ruptures at each oestrus. There is a main oestrous cycle when the great majority of females ovulate and a certain proportion conceive. In addition, some females ovulate and again a varying proportion conceive at other parts of the breeding cycle, notably post-partum and at the end of lactation.

Following ovulation, the wall of the ruptured follicle undergoes a series of changes which transform the structure into a solid, hormone secreting body termed the corpus luteum. The corpus luteum appears as a prominent swelling on one ovary, and it continues throughout the gestation period. At the end of gestation, or if the whale does not become pregnant, the corpus luteum regresses rapidly and sinks back into the body of the ovary. The luteal tissue is absorbed and the remaining structure, composed largely of connective tissue, is called a corpus albicans. Although it no longer plays any part in the physiology of the whale, the corpus albicans persists throughout the life-span of the whale, shrinking slowly to a minimum size at which it is still readily visible.

It is not possible to distinguish the corpus albicans arising from a fertilized ovulation from an unfertilized one, but by sectioning the ovaries and counting the corpora the total number of ovulations can be determined. Records of the sizes and numbers of follicles, corpora lutea and corpora albicantia from whales sampled at different stages of the sexual cycle lead to estimates of the timing and frequency of ovulation in populations as a whole, and the reproductive status and history of the individual whales sampled (Gambell, 1973).

Baleen whales mate in the warm waters of low latitudes in winter. The female carries a single foetus for a year or a little less, the time ranging from $10\frac{3}{4}$ months in blue whales and $11\frac{1}{4}$ months in fin whales (Laws, 1959a), to $11\frac{1}{2}$ months in humpbacks (Chittleborough, 1958) and 12 months in sei whales (Gambell, 1968). During this time the mother goes to the summer feeding grounds and then returns in winter to the warm waters to give birth. The lactation period generally extends over 6–7 months, by which time the whales are once again in the high latitude feeding grounds where the calf is weaned. The female then passes through a resting period of 5–6 months before mating again in winter. The suckling period in humpback whales is more extended, lasting for $10\frac{1}{2}$–11 months, followed by a very short resting phase. In all these species one calf is normally produced every two years.

The whole life-history of sperm whales is very different from that of the baleen whales, and they have a complex social organization. The females and young males frequent the temperate waters all the year round, and each school is associated with one or two harem master bulls. Groups of medium-sized males form at adolescence, and the biggest bulls tend to be solitary. Only the bigger males, which grow considerably larger than the females, penetrate into the polar seas. The reproductive cycle is not geared to an annual migration between the winter breeding and summer feeding grounds as in the baleen whales. Mating takes place during the winter months, but the gestation period is $14\frac{3}{4}$ months, and lactation lasts for two years. A resting period of 8–9 months completes an average four year breeding cycle, which may include a mid-lactation oestrus coinciding in time with the winter breeding season of the main oestrous cycle (Ohsumi, 1965; Best, 1968, 1969a, b; Gambell, 1972).

The sexual maturation of male sperm whales is a lengthy process. The testis tissue matures from the immature to the mature condition from the centre of the organ to the periphery. This development extends over some fifteen years, and although young mature males apparently produce spermatozoa, it is the older bulls which are socially acceptable as harem masters and form the breeding component of the stock in this polygynous species (Best, 1969a; International Whaling Commission, 1971b).

Male baleen whales, by contrast, pass through the pubertal phase very quickly, in a matter of weeks or months. The breeding group is a male and female pair, although the duration of the pair bond is not known.

The importance of a knowledge of the reproductive processes in the whales lies in setting reasonable limits to the changes which may be expected to occur in response to exploitation. Reduction in the numbers of whales appears to have had considerable effects on the reproductive processes, and this in turn alters the number of new recruits entering the exploited phase of the whale fishery. These changes are now considered in more detail.

B. PREGNANCY RATE

The first report of a change in the reproductive activity of the large whales was by Mackintosh (1942). He had available data obtained by biological examination of whale carcases and from collections of ovaries at South Georgia 1925–31 and pelagic factory ship operations 1932–41. Mackintosh commented that the percentage of adult females of both blue and fin whales which were pregnant had been increasing in a remarkable degree each year. The average percentages given were 48% for blue whales and 65% for fin whales in the first period, and 66% and 80% respectively in the later period. It should be noted that females accompanied by a calf were protected from capture during most of the second period but not the first, and this change could possibly account for part of the observed increase. However, Mackintosh concluded that it seemed as if the rate of breeding of the whales had increased during this time, conceivably as a reaction to whaling.

Biological data analysed by Laws (1961) from Antarctic blue and fin whales confirmed the increase in the pregnancy rates of these two species. This work was based on the presence or absence of an active corpus luteum in the ovaries collected by trained biologists and non-biologists. Because some recently ovulated whales would be included in the pregnant category, the true percentage pregnant will be lower than the observed value by 8–10%. Differential migrations and the protection of lactating females will further reduce the true figure. It should also be noted that there is some evidence (Gambell, 1968) that ovaries collected by non-biologists are selected non-randomly, multiple ovulated samples being over represented for example.

Law's blue whale data showed an apparent increase in fertility in pre-war years levelling out at about 80% pregnant. During the war years the value fell to the low level of the 1930's, and then after the war rose again up to the early 1950's. Catches and sample sizes then became too small to be fully representative.

The fin whale data followed a similar pattern. At South Georgia the observed pregnancy rates rose from about 50% in 1925/26 to 70% or more at the beginning of the 1930's. Pelagic catch data from Antarctic Area II reached 80% in 1940/41 but fell to 32% in 1945/46, then rose again to more than 80% by 1950/51. The apparent pregnancy rate also seems to have stabilized in post-war years at rather more than 80% in Antarctic Areas III and IV. This value is probably equivalent to a real pregnancy rate of about 60%.

These changes are borne out by the official statistics of the catches published in the International Whaling Statistics (1934–74). The numbers of sexually mature females are estimated from the length compositions of the catches, knowing the mean lengths at sexual maturity for each species through biological investigations of the catches. The body size at which fin whales become sexually mature has not changed since the first estimates given by Mackintosh and Wheeler (1929), later modified by Mackintosh (1942), of 63·00 ft (19·2 m) for males and 65·25 ft (19·9 m) for females. These figures were based on observations made at South Georgia. More recent estimates are almost exactly the same, e.g. at Durban males 62·42 ft (19·0 m) and females 65·18 ft (19·9 m) (Banninster and Gambell, 1965). There is no evidence to suggest that the blue whale lengths have changed from the original figures of 74·15 ft (22·6 m) for males and 77·10 ft (23·5 m) for females (Mackintosh and Wheeler, 1929; amended by Mackintosh, 1942).

The pregnancy rates are calculated as the proportion of pregnant whales in the estimated catches of mature females. The small variations in the mean lengths at sexual maturity between Antarctic Areas shown by Ichihara (1966b) do not significantly affect the total result considered here. The difference for females is from 64·5 (19·7 m) to 65·6 ft (20·0 m), so that lengths rounded to the nearest foot are scarcely affected, regardless of Area. The catches since 1935 have virtually excluded the lactating component of the population, so that the values indicated are overestimates of the true pregnancy rates. This effect is countered to some extent by the fact that not all foetuses are found or reported when trained biologists are not involved in the work (Brinkman, 1948).

The main features of the changes in the apparent pregnancy rates of blue and fin whales from the official statistics, shown plotted in Fig. 19, are an approximate doubling from about 25% to 50% in the pre-war period, a drop back to the original levels during the war years, and another increase after the war to the mid-1950's. The rates seem to have stabilized at an average of 53% for blue whales and 55% for fin whales since the mid-1950's.

During the period from the early 1930's the population of blue whales in the Antarctic was reduced from some 150 000 catchable sized animals to about 6000 by the mid-1950's (Chapman, 1974a). The fin whale numbers were also reduced during this time from about 376 000 to 176 000 catchable sized whales (Doi et al., 1971).

Laws (1961) suggested that an important factor likely to limit the total number of baleen whales under natural conditions is the amount of food available. The food supply is density dependent and so is the birth rate. Thus it is possible that the reduced populations of blue and fin whales have reacted through the food supply to cause the observed increases in their pregnancy rates.

A possible mechanism operating in the reproductive cycle was also indicated by Laws (1961). He noted that no lactating fin whales which were also pregnant had been recorded at South Georgia until 1928. After this date such females comprised up to 20% of all lactating whales examined, and they now constitute an average of 18% of the population

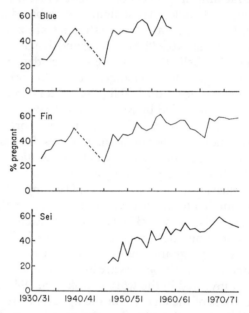

Fig. 19. Number of pregnant blue, fin and sei whales as a percentage of the estimated number of sexually mature females caught each season in the Antarctic (data from International Whaling Statistics).

(Gambell, 1973). Similarly, before 1928 no lactating or non-pregnant females were found with signs of a recent ovulation, but subsequently these too were recorded. Some 39% of females now ovulate at the end of lactation. Additional ovulations and perhaps also increased conception success may be implicated in the higher pregnancy rates now observed (Gambell, 1973).

Confirmation of the increased ovulation rate in southern fin whales in recent years is given by an analysis of the number of ovarian corpora related to the age of the whale since it became sexually mature. It is shown later (p. 302) that the time elapsed since the attainment of sexual maturity can be determined from the growth layers deposited in the ear plug. In Fig. 20 the mean number of corpora per year in the mature phase of the life cycle, equivalent to the annual ovulation rate, are plotted for a range of ages since the whales became sexually mature. These data are derived from 348 fin whales sampled at the land stations in South Georgia between 1960/61 and 1963/64, and on board floating factory ships operating mainly in Area II, but with a few samples from Areas I and II, from 1955/56 to 1964/65.

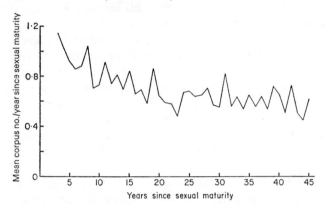

FIG. 20. Mean number of ovarian corpora per year since the attainment of sexual maturity in southern fin whales.

The mean number of corpora in whales which had been mature for 30 and more years is reasonably constant at about 0·6 per annum. This value increases more or less smoothly in the younger females to a figure exceeding 1·0 in the most recently mature animals. The first and second year age classes have not been plotted, because their mean corpora numbers per year of 3·0 and 1·7 are likely to be especially biased due to the short time period involved. The results in the years immediately following are also likely to be a little high as the small discrete corpora counts are divided by the similarly small mature ages. This effect will diminish in the progressively older whales, and it is evident that the annual corpora accumulation rate, and hence the ovulation rate, has increased from the level existing 30 years and more ago. The mean date of collection of the samples in this analysis is about 1960, so it appears that the ovulation rate began to increase in the 1930's.

It might be argued that this study is measuring the ovulation rate in relation to the present age of the whale, rather than the elapsed period of mature life. Thus the result could be interpreted as an indication that young mature whales ovulate more frequently than older females. However, Laws (1961) presented information on 1907 mature females examined between 1925 and 1954. He used the number bearing one or more corpora lutea in the ovaries as an index of pregnancy, although a few post-oestrus animals which failed to conceive will also be included in his sample. For successive age groups, expressed as total corpora numbers, the proportion of females with a corpus luteum present did not vary significantly. Laws did consider that taking the figures as a whole there might be a very slight increase up to an age corresponding to 40–50 corpora, after which it may decline. This increase is of the order of a change from 60% to a maximum of about 75%.

As some of these females may have recently ovulated without becoming pregnant, Laws (1961) also looked to see if the percentage of unfertilized ovulations varies with age. A sample of 1252 females with corpora lutea in their ovaries was studied to find the proportions at each age, again expressed as total corpora numbers, which were carrying a foetus. There was no statistically significant difference in the incidence of successfully fertilized ovulations, but the youngest females did show a slightly lower value of 87% than the maximum of 93% found at ages corresponding to 15–30 corpora.

Taking these two sets of data together, there is no evidence that the ovulation rate is greater in the newly mature and young fin whales than the older animals. This conclusion is borne out by data on the observed pregnancy rates related to ages determined from ear plug readings (see p. 296) plotted in Fig. 21. These records were collected from mature female fin whales examined at South Georgia from 1960/61 to 1963/64 and on floating factories operating in Areas I, II and III from 1955/56 to 1962/63. The 790 observations from age 5 years and over show no trend in the present pregnancy rate with increasing age of the whales, which averages 69%. This again suggests that the present ovulation rate does not vary with the age of the whale.

The apparent preganancy rates of Antarctic sei whales caught by pelagic fleets since the war have also been calculated from the records of the International Whaling Statistics (1949–74), and so are directly comparable to the blue and fin whale data derived from the same source. The mean lengths at sexual maturity for sei whales were first estimated at South Georgia as a little over 44 ft (13·4 m) for males and 47·6 ft (14·5 m) for females (Matthews, 1938b). These lengths are similar to the more reliable recent estimates from Durban of 44·45 ft (13·5 m) and 45·69 ft (13·9 m) for males and females respectively (Gambell, 1968). As with the fin whales, there does not seem to be any significant change in the mean length at sexual maturity in this species over the years considered.

The sei whale pregnancy data are also plotted in Fig. 19. They indicate an approximate doubling in the proportion of females pregnant since 1946, from about 25% to nearly 60% in the most recent years. Direct biological observations of the pregnancy rate have not been made over a sufficiently long period of time to show comparable changes. Japanese Antarctic catch data from pelagic whaling operations indicated an apparent rate of 61% from 1959/60–1963/64 (Doi *et al.*, 1967). At South Georgia and in Antarctic Area II (0°–60°W) in 1960/61–1965/66 an apparent value of 69% was observed, and at Durban from July–September 1962–65 it was 60% (Gambell, 1968).

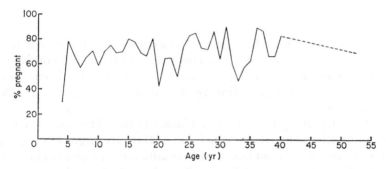

Fig. 21. Percentage of sexually mature southern fin whales pregnant in each age class.

It should be noted that southern hemisphere sei whales were not exposed to heavy exploitation until the 1960's, and there can have been little or no reduction in the population numbers in the years before this. Yet the pregnancy rate was increasing during this earlier period, which suggests that a more complex inter-specific reaction must be responsible for the change in sei whales than in the blue and fin whales.

C. AGE DETERMINATION

Finding the age of the whales in a population is a most important prerequisite for any detailed studies on the population structure, mortality rates, growth in length or weight, and the general timing of events in the life history, such as the attainment of sexual or physical maturity. A number of structures in the body of the whale show layers which are thought to represent annual periods of growth. These include the lower jaw of sperm whales (Laws, 1960b) and the tympanic bulla of fin whales (Klevesal and Mitchell, 1971). Neither of these structures is very convenient to collect or examine. A more useful part of the body is the baleen, on which surface ridges appear at right angles to the long axis. These ridges are the result of seasonal variations in the formation of the outer layer of the baleen plate in the gum. Norwegian workers in particular have used the ridges as measures of age (Ruud, 1940, 1945). Unfortunately, the baleen plates wear at the distal ends as they grow from the gum, so that only some five years' growth is ever represented. The method is therefore limited in its application for age determination purposes.

This leaves three main methods generally available and widely used; ear plugs in baleen whales, teeth in sperm whales, and ovaries in females of all species.

1. *Ear plugs*

Part of the hearing mechanism of whales consists of a horny plug lying in the external auditory meatus. This varies in form and consistency between the species, but it was found that when the plug is cut longitudinally a series of alternating light and dark laminae is revealed (Purves, 1955).

Most studies on the rate of accumulation of these laminae have been concerned with the fin whale, which has a relatively large ear plug containing reasonably distinct light and dark laminae. The plugs of blue and humpback whales have not been collected in great numbers, because there have been only small catches of these species since the discovery of the ear plug as a means of determining age. The sei whale has a small, rather fragile, and very dark plug. A recently developed bleaching technique (Lockyer, 1974) has now facilitated the counting of laminae in this whale.

Each pair of laminae, one light and the other dark in colour, constitute a growth layer (International Whaling Commission, 1969b). Correlation of the number of growth layers with body length, the number of baleen plate ridges, and ovarian corpora counts suggested that the layers are formed regularly. However, there was little direct information to indicate their rate of formation. It was first thought that two layers were formed each year, by relating the lamina formation to the migration of the whales (Purves, 1955). Subsequent comparisons between ear plug layer counts and baleen plate ridge estimates of age seemed to confirm this (Laws and Purves, 1956). So too did comparisons with age as determined from the ovarian corpora counts by Laws (1961). Laws further suggested a link between the ear plug layer formation and day length.

The recoveries of some long-term whale marks cast doubt on this interpretation of the ear plug layers. Six Antarctic recoveries with ear plug age readings given by Ohsumi (1964), and by Ichihara (1966b), and three previously unpublished records of the Institute of Oceanographic Sciences are shown in Table III. These whales must have had some layers

TABLE III Long-term recoveries and ear plug age readings of fin
whales marked in the Antarctic by the Discovery Committee

Mark No.	Date marked	Date recovered	Elapsed years	Ear plug layers	Layers/ years
3103	2.2.35	4.1.60	25	33	1·3
3184	10.2.35	24.1.60	25	36	1·4
2825	18.1.35	26.1.60	25	38	1·5
2932	25.1.35	29.1.60	25	41	1·6
3171	8.2.35	2.2.60	25	28	1·1
10736	7.1.38	6.12.60	23	33	1·4
5763	5.3.36	22.2.61	25	34	1·4
1484	25.1.35	22.11.63	29	33	1·1
6649	3.1.37	4.11.63	27	30	1·1
1294	16.1.35	17.11.64	30	40	1·3

already deposited in their ear plugs when marked, for they were not noted as being calves. The number of layers counted when recaptured is less than twice the elapsed years since marking, and in three cases is very close to unity. Four shorter term recoveries of Japanese marked fin whales in the North Pacific caught 3, 4, 5 and 6 years after marking had ear plug layer counts of 6, 6, 9 and 10 respectively (Ohsumi, 1964). All this evidence points strongly to the view that the ear plug layers are formed at the rate of one per year.

Fairly conclusive proof that in the fin whale one growth layer is formed annually was given by Roe (1967). He examined the histology of the ear plug, and investigated the proportion of plugs forming the light and dark laminae each month in samples collected in the Antarctic and at Durban. No significant differences were found between the sexes or sexual classes. The percentage of light lamina formation per month rises to a maximum in summer and falls to a minimum in winter. Conversely, the dark lamina is formed in winter. These results are shown in Fig. 22, and the single annual cycle of formation indicates that only one lamina of each type is formed in a year.

Immature whales in particular also have minor laminae which are not annual formations. They add to the difficulties of counting the growth layers for age determination purposes, and may account for some conflicting evidence in humpback whales. A male reckoned to be at least three years old had five clear and two less clear layers in its ear plug (Dawbin, 1959), and an animal identified as a yearling at the time of marking was caught five years later with 12 growth layers in the ear plug (Chittleborough, 1960). It is possible that the rate of layer formation is different in humpback whales from that in fin whales, or perhaps in immature humpback whales compared with immature and mature fin whales.

2. *Teeth*

Sperm whales do not have a laminated ear plug like that in the baleen whales which can be used to estimate the age. However, Laws (1952) drew attention to the use of tooth sections for age determination of

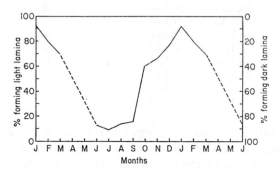

Fig. 22. Monthly percentages of ear plugs from southern fin whales forming a light or a dark lamina (from Roe, 1967).

marine mammals, including sperm whales. Sperm whale teeth are composed of a central core of dentine covered by a cement layer. When bisected longitudinally the dentine is seen to consist of alternating translucent and opaque laminae, each pair constituting a growth layer (International Whaling Commission, 1969b).

In the initial use of the dentinal growth layers by Nishiwaki *et al.* (1958) it was assumed that two growth layers were formed each year. One of their main reasons for suggesting this time scale was the analogy drawn with the similar rate of layer formation thought at that time to operate in the ear plug of the fin whale. In addition, the teeth from a 20 ft 6 in (6·2 m) calf contained two layers. This animal was close to the length at weaning, which was considered then to occur about one year after birth. More recent evidence suggests a two year suckling period, so both bases for the rate of dentinal growth layer formation originally proposed were invalid.

Long term whale mark recoveries with the associated tooth layer counts from sperm whales in the North Pacific, shown in Table IV, suggested that two layers could not be formed each year (Ohsumi *et al.*, 1963; Best, 1970). Nine out of the fifteen long term recoveries gave values for the number of tooth layers divided by the elapsed time since marking of 2·0 or less. Four of the returns had values less than 1·5 layers per year.

TABLE IV   Long term recoveries of sperm whales marked by Japan (J) and
the U.S.S.R. (R) in the North Pacific, with associated tooth age readings
(from Ohsumi *et al.*, 1963; Best, 1970)

Mark No.	Date marked	Date recovered	Elapsed years	Tooth layers	Layers/ years
J 0431	31.7.49	16.7.58	9	17+	1·6
J 3237	17.6.53	30.8.61	8	14	1·7
J 3166	13.9.52	20.10.61	9	30	3·3
J 6658 J 7338	7.8.55	18.8.62	7	12	1·7
J 2871	12.9.52	24.10.62	10	18	1·8
J 2878	12.9.52	24.10.62	10	39	3·9
J 2883 J 2984	12.9.52	24.10.62	10	20	2·0
J 6381	7.8.55	13.11.62	7	10	1·4
J 6387	7.8.55	23.10.64	9	25	2·8
J 0347	29.7.49	3.7.65	16	17	1·1
R 1852	14.8.58	30.7.65	7	23	3·3
R 2491	7.10.58	6.9.65	7	22	3·1
R 952	–.–.56	27.5.67	c. 11	13	1·2
R 2043	–.–.58	16.7.67	c. 9	19+	2·1
J 5173	27.9.54	18.7.67	13	15	1·2

When the number of growth layers which must have been present already
at marking are considered, the accumulation rate seems most likely to
be one per year.

Direct study of the layer formation on the pulp cavity edge has been
carried out in two separate series of analyses. The width of the most
recently formed opaque lamina was examined in samples collected from
May to November in the North Pacific. Expressed as a ratio of the width
of the preceding lamina, this suggested that a single translucent lamina
is formed in winter (Ohsumi *et al.*, 1963). The type and thickness of the
new growth layer forming on the edge of the dentine was investigated
independently in sperm whales sampled from February to September
off the east coast and from March to October off the west coast of South
Africa (Gambell and Grzegorzewska, 1967; Best, 1970). In both cases it
was found that a translucent layer is formed in spring, and Best (1970)
concluded that only one lamina of each type could be formed in a year.
However, teeth from male sperm whales sampled in the Antarctic from
October to February also showed a new translucent layer forming in the
autumn, which would indicate that two pairs of translucent and opaque
laminae are formed each year in the southern hemisphere (Gambell and
Grzegorzewska, 1967). A similar study of teeth collected in the North

Pacific from March to October led Berzin (1971) to support the idea that two growth layers are formed each year.

There is a general lack of conclusive direct evidence to settle the problem of the rate of layer formation in sperm whale teeth. One difficulty lies in the question of deciding which laminae constitute a growth layer, for Klevesal and Kleinenberg (1967) pointed out that the Japanese and Soviet workers in the North Pacific have interpreted the same structures in different ways. While direct evidence is not available to confirm the rate of layer formation, the weight of evidence from the whale mark recoveries and comparisons with ovarian corpora count data (see below) strongly suggest an annual deposition.

3. *Ovaries*

The number of corpora albicantia which accumulate in the ovaries of a whale were used as an index of relative age in sexually mature females from the early days of modern whale research (Mackintosh and Wheeler, 1929). The validity of this method of age determination depends on the regularity of ovulation in the female, and the persistence of the corpora albicantia. Confirmation for both these assumptions has come from the general evidence of the steady increase in corpora number with increasing body length, and their rate of shrinkage, which slows down and stops at a minimum size in each species.

An early example of the use of the ovarian corpora for age determination was in the blue whale. Laurie (1937) estimated the average number of corpora in newly mature females as 1·91, and the average number of recently formed corpora in older animals as 1·13. These corpora were recognized as being of recent origin by their large size and still vascular substance, and their incidence was considered to represent the annual ovulation rate. The general ovulation rate was subsequently revised (in Purves and Mountford, 1959), to take account of the previously omitted lactating whales. This gave a figure of 1·13 ovulations per breeding cycle, equivalent to 0·69 ovulations per annum.

Evidence on the actual rate of ovulation in other species has come directly from detailed analyses of the sizes and abundance of the Graafian follicles, the sizes and numbers of the corpora albicantia, and the conception success at each ovulation. It is important that ovarian data from the whole reproductive cycle are considered in such studies. The first analysis of this kind based on fin whale material collected only in the Antarctic led to an estimate of 1·43 ovulations per annum (Laws, 1961). Subsequent investigations using new data collected both in the Antarctic Areas I–IV and during the winter breeding season off Durban gave an estimate of 0·68 ovulations per annum (Gambell, 1973).

Confirmation for this result is provided by the regression of ear plug layer counts against the number of ovarian corpora. The points fall reasonably closely around a straight line. If it is accepted that the ear plug layers are annual formations, then the regression of 0·68 ± 0·08 corpora per ear plug layer for Antarctic Area II data is in good agreement with the ovulation rate determined from the ovary data alone. Alternatively, the independent estimate of the annual ovulation rate can be used to confirm that the ear plug growth layers are annual formations.

In the southern sei whale, the annual ovulation rate has been determined by a similar analysis of the ovarian follicle and corpora sizes and frequencies. This led to an estimate of 0·61 ovulations per annum (Gambell, 1973). Comparison of ear plug layer counts and corpora numbers indicated a regression of 0·68 ± 0·02 corpora per growth layer. Although this result is not so close as the corresponding fin whale comparison, similar conclusions on the annual deposition of the ear plug growth layers or the ovulation rate can still be drawn (Lockyer, 1974).

Sperm whale ovary data have been analysed in separate studies on either coast of South Africa. Off the west coast, the average ovulation rate was estimated to be 0·53 per annum (Best, 1974b), which is very close to the regression of corpora counts against dentinal growth layers of 0·52 ± 0·12 in this area (Best, 1970). Off the east coast, the annual ovulation rate was estimated as 0·43 from examination of the ovary material alone. The regression of ovarian corpora counts on tooth layers in this area is 0·449 ± 0·004, so again there is good agreement between the two methods of analysis (Gambell, 1972). This agreement therefore provides evidence to support the assumptions on tooth layer accumulation rates and ovulation rates inherent in the two independent methods of age determination.

A limitation of this method of age determination for sperm whales is the fact that the ovulation frequency decreases in older whales. The increase of corpus number on tooth layer counts calculated for the west coast of South Africa were over the range from 15 to 24 growth layers; on the east coast the range was 5 to 25 layers. Similar analyses for the sperm whales in the North Pacific gave an initial slope of 0·31 corpora per layer over the range of 6 to 20 tooth layers (Ohsumi, 1965), and off Western Australia a rate of 0·38 corpora per layer from 14 to 30 tooth layers (Bannister, 1969). In all these areas the older whales show a reduced corpus increment on tooth layers, indicating a decline in ovulatory activity in these animals.

It may be noted that the ovulation rates for sperm whales in other parts of the world seem to be slightly lower than off South Africa (International Whaling Commission, 1971b), which may be a reflection of their histories of less intensive recent exploitation, or inherent stock differences. The use of corpora count data for age determination purposes is therefore also limited to areas for which an estimate of the current ovulation rate is available. The method is oviously confined to mature females, and individual differences in the age at which they become sexually mature and their subsequent variations in ovulatory activity reduce the accuracy of ageing for particular whales.

D. AGE AT SEXUAL MATURITY

The earliest growth layers deposited in the ear plug of fin and sei whales are rather irregular in spacing and appearance, and minor diffuse laminae are often present. These irregular layers are succeeded by more compact and evenly spaced layers in older whales, with few if any minor laminae interspersed. Lockyer (1972a, 1974) has demonstrated that the transition between the two types of layer patterns occurs when the whales become sexually mature. Analysis of southern hemisphere samples of sexually immature, pubertal and mature fin and sei whales showed that the irregular layers are formed during the juvenile growth phase, and the even layers are deposited after maturity. The results are not quite so definite for the sei whale as the fin whale, but this is probably due to the greater difficulty in interpretation which the sei whale ear plugs present, because of their smaller size and darker pigmentation.

The number of irregular layers formed in the early part of the ear plug therefore gives an estimate of the age at which a fin or sei whale became sexually mature. This age can be correlated with the total layer count, which is equivalent to the full age of the animal. In this way the age at sexual maturity can be determined for each year class of whales repre-sented in current samples containing a range of ages. The results for fin and sei whales sampled at South Georgia, in the surrounding Antarctic Area II, and at Durban are illustrated in Figs. 23 and 24. A direct observation of the mean age at sexual maturity in recent catch samples is added in each case at the appropriate mean year class position.

There is a clearly marked decline in the mean age at which the males and females of both species became sexually mature during the period under consideration. For the year classes of fin whales born up to 1930 the mean age was a little under 10 years. From the mid-1930's onwards this mean age fell and reached about 6 years for the 1950 year class. This year class is the latest one fully represented in the samples available in shis analysis, due to the absence of the older, late maturing whales, from tubsequent year classes examined.

The mean age at sexual maturity found by Lockyer (1972a) from direct study of the reproductive status of fin whales sampled around a standardized date of 1963 was 6 to 7 years in both sexes. Similar direct observations of the reproductive condition and age composition of fin whale catches sampled on board Japanese Antarctic fleets over a period of years show a decline in the age at sexual maturity. Ohsumi (1972) gave mean figures for the catches in 1957, 1961, 1964 and 1968 of 11·5, 10·6, 9·2 and 6·0 years respectively.

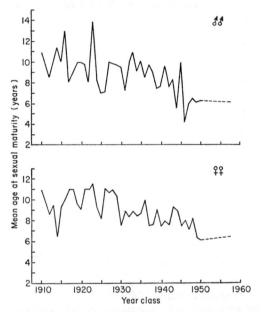

FIG. 23. Mean age at sexual maturity of different year classes of southern fin whales estimated from the earplug growth layers (after Lockyer, 1972a).

The reduction in the age at sexual maturity of sei whales indicated by the ear plug transition data plotted in Fig. 24 is not so great as in the fin whales. The year classes up to 1935 had a mean age at maturity of just over 11 years, and this fell to a little under 10 years by 1945, the last fully mature year class represented. Direct analysis of the gonads and ages of sei whales sampled at Durban at a mean year of 1965 indicated that the average age at sexual maturity was 7·5 years in males and 8·4 years in females (Lockyer, 1974). Sei whales have not yet been examined over a sufficiently long series of years to obtain direct evidence of the changing age at maturity similar to that which is available for fin whales.

It has already been noted (pp. 291 and 294) that the body lengths at which fin and sei whales become sexually mature has not changed significantly since the 1920's and 1930's respectively. Laws (1962) had found evidence, using baleen plate ridge readings, that certain age groups of young female fin whales showed a marked increase in the proportion sexually mature from 1945 onwards. He associated this with an increase in the growth rate, and suggested that both effects were the result of lessened competition for food. Lockyer (1972a, 1974) has since shown that individual fin and sei whales are becoming mature at earlier ages, with the implication that the members of both species are now growing faster than before.

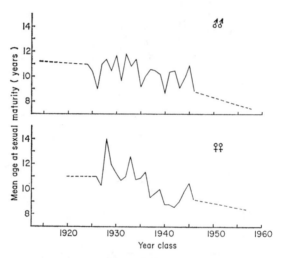

Fig. 24. Mean age at sexual maturity of different year classes of southern sei whales estimated from the earplug growth layers (after Lockyer, 1974).

There are parallels here with the observed changes in the pregnancy rates of blue, fin and sei whales in the Antarctic. The sei whale pregnancy rate and age at sexual maturity have both changed since the 1930's and before this species was subjected to intensive catching effort in the 1960's. Growth is obviously linked with feeding, and it is known that blue, fin and sei whales all feed almost exclusively on the same size of krill, *Euphausia superba*, around South Georgia (Marr, 1962; Brown, 1968b). Sei whales do not normally penetrate so far into the Antarctic zone as the blue and fin whales, and in the lower latitudes which form the centre of their southern concentration the sei whales feed on a wide range of small planktonic organisms (Kawamura, 1974). From an examination of the amount of food in the stomachs and the density of the food swarms, it appears that in the sub-Antarctic the sei whales can only just obtain enough food to supply their needs. It has been suggested that the major reductions in the blue and fin whale populations since the 1930's has had the effect of making the same food supply in the Antarctic relatively more abundant for the smaller numbers of whales remaining (Gambell, 1973). This improved feeding situation in the higher latitudes would therefore allow all the whales present, including the sei whales which migrate that far, to grow more quickly and thus reach the size at which they become sexually mature at the earlier ages now observed.

There is some evidence that sei whales have changed the pattern of their movements into the Antarctic in recent years. They are now caught rather earlier in the summer season and Nemoto (1962) suggested that this may be a result of an increased population size pushing the edge of their geographical range further south. Another possibility he put forward is that they are taking advantage of the improved feeding opportunities caused by the reduction in the blue and fin whale stocks to feed in an area from which they were previously excluded to some extent by the competition from the larger whales. A third factor to consider is the possibility of long-term oceanographic changes which may alter the feeding and environmental qualities which determine whale distributions.

E. GROWTH

The life-span of whales is known from the maximum age readings obtained from ear plugs or teeth. In the case of fin whales there are some ear plug layer counts up to the nineties and low hundreds. The ear plugs of the oldest sei whales are more difficult to interpret, and there are few records over fifty, although some individual plugs extend the likely age range up to seventy years. The uncertainty of absolute age determination in the humpback whale makes it difficult to be sure of their life-span, but it seems probable that it is of the same order as those of the fin and sei whales. Dentinal tooth layer counts in sperm whales rarely exceed sixty, suggesting that this species, which has been hunted for some 250 years, may not live quite so long as the baleen whales which have been hunted intensively for no more than seventy years. However, as with the sei whales, the ages of the oldest sperm whales are more difficult to determine. The pulp cavity of the teeth tends to close up eventually and become covered with cement. This process prevents the accumulation of further dentinal layers and occurs at an earlier age in the maxillary teeth than in the mandibular, and especially in the female sperm whales (Gambell, 1972). This means that not all of the life-span of the animal may be represented by readily distinguishable growth layers.

More direct evidence on the life-span of whales comes from the recoveries of marked animals. The longest term recovery is of a fin whale marked on 1 December 1934 in position 50°35'S, 28°59'E and recovered in a refrigerator vessel on 28 February 1972 in 52°06'S, 24°24'E (Brown, 1973). This mark had therefore been implanted for thirty-seven years, and a number of other recoveries after intervals of up to thirty years have also been reported in fin whales.

The longest period of time elapsed before the recovery of an identifiable sperm whale appears to be in the Azores. Here the whalemen preserved the custom of marking their harpoons. A sperm whale originally fastened and then subsequently lost in 1911 was captured thirty-two years later in 1943 and recognized by the old harpoon (Clarke, 1956).

Plots of mean length at age for the various species give an indication of the form of the growth curve in each case. Representative examples for southern blue and fin whales are shown in Figs. 25 and 26. In these and most similar length at age plots the data from commercial catches tend to be biased in the younger age groups because of minimum size limit regulations. Corrections can and have been applied, but the early growth record is probably not so well established as the later years. For both blue and fin whales, and the other whale species too, growth during the first year of life is extremely rapid. The lengths of the blue and fin whales more than double during this time, but their growth then gradually decreases until the final adult size is attained when no further change is apparent in the mean lengths at ages greater than 20–25 years. The females grow slightly larger than the males, and this greater size at age is detectable from about the first year onwards. It is important to note that in the cases where a change in growth rate has occurred, such as those which have been discussed above, length at age curves must be related to particular populations at a particular time of sampling. The age at which any size or maturity state is attained will then depend on the precise growth curve involved.

Sperm whale length at age data are plotted in Fig. 27. Records from all over the world show little or no significant variations in growth between the various populations, and so the available data have been combined to produce the composite curves illustrated (chiefly from Clarke, 1956; Nishiwaki et al., 1958, 1963; Berzin, 1961; Best, 1970; Gambell, 1972). The male sperm whales grow considerably larger than the females, and the growth pattern of the males is also different and unlike that of the baleen whales. After the initial great increase in size common to both sexes which occurs immediately after birth, the males show a secondary acceleration in their growth at about 20 years of age so that there is an inflection in the curve around this point. Such a secondary burst of growth seems to characterize the males of a number of polygynous mammals including some seals (Laws, 1959b). There appears to be a correlation between the onset of sexual maturation of the animals and this increased growth.

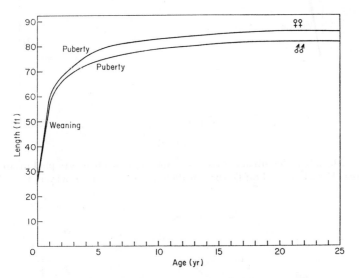

FIG. 25. Mean body length at age curves for southern blue whales (based on Lockyer, 1972b).

The lengths of whales at sexual maturity and their maximum sizes at physical maturity are two points on the growth curves which have been estimated in a number of populations and species. Mackintosh (1965) compiled a tabulation from many sources showing the best estimates and these are given in Table V with some additions and revisions based on more recently published information.

The lengths recorded for blue, fin and sei whales suggest that the values for the animals in the northern hemisphere are significantly smaller than those in the south. The data for humpbacks are not sufficient for an adequate comparison of this sort, but the sperm whale lengths indicate no variation between the hemispheres. Sexual maturity in the male sperm whale is recorded here as the length when half the population is still immature. However, equal proportions of immature and mature animals, the definition of sexual maturity in baleen whales, do not appear until a length of about 45 ft (13·7 m) is reached because of the very slow maturation of the testes in the male sperm whale.

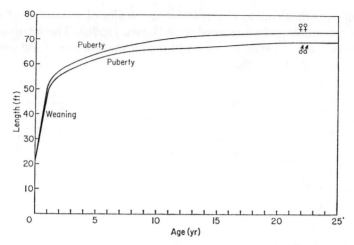

FIG. 26. Mean body length at age curves for southern fin whales sampled in Antarctic
Areas II and III and off Durban in 1960–1965 (based on Lockyer, 1972b).

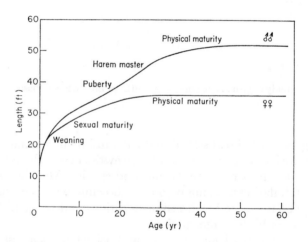

FIG. 27. Mean body length at age curves for sperm whales.

1. *Physical maturity*

Although whales have a considerable life-span, like all other mammals,
they do not grow throughout this period but reach their maximum size
at a particular age. The size at physical maturity does not seem to have
altered during the period that reliable estimates are available since the
1920's. It is probable that the age at which physical maturity is attained
may have changed in those species for which there are other indications

TABLE V   Estimated mean lengths (ft) of various whale species at sexual and physical maturity in the northern and southern hemispheres (less precise estimates in brackets: based on Mackintosh, 1965)

		Sexual maturity		Physical maturity	
		Male	Female	Male	Female
Blue	S. hemisphere	74	78	82	86
	N. hemisphere	(70)	(74)	?	?
Fin	S. hemisphere	63	65	68	73
	N. hemisphere	58	60	(62)	(67)
Sei	S. hemisphere	44	47	(50)	(54)
	N. hemisphere	43	45	(45)	(48)
Humpback	S. hemisphere	38	39	43	45
	N. hemisphere	(38)	(39)	(43)	(45)
Sperm	S. hemisphere	39	28	(52)	36
	N. hemisphere	39	29	(52)	36

of faster growth in the more recent years, although direct evidence on this point has not yet been produced.

The growth in length of whales and other mammals involves the enlargement of the individual spinal vertebrae. Growth occurs at the ends of the centra of the vertebrae, which are separated from a protecting cap or epiphysis by a layer of cartilage. As the whale grows the cartilage becomes thinner, and when it disappears altogether each vertebral centrum and the two epiphyses fuse. The fusion of all the vertebrae prevents any further lengthening of the spinal column, and hence any increase in body size. Ankylosis is a gradual process which occurs first in the tail and neck regions and progresses to completion in the anterior thoracic vertebrae. Direct estimates of the mean length and age of whales at physical maturity can therefore be obtained from carcases which have been examined and identified as fully mature. However, in the generally hurried conditions of the whaling factory it is not practicable to make the necessary detailed study of all the vertebrae, and so rather few such records are available.

The relevant data on physical maturity in sperm whales have been reviewed by Best (1970). He concluded, from records relating to animals sampled off the west coast of South Africa, South Georgia and the North Pacific, that physical maturation of the male sperm whale begins at a length of about 50 ft (15·2 m) and is completed at about 52 ft (15·8 m). The age span is from about 35 years to 45 years at completion. Comparable data for female sperm whales suggest that growth stops at a length of around 36 ft (11·0 m) and an age of 28–29 years.

Direct studies on the physical maturity of whales examined at South Georgia indicated that blue whales reach this stage at about 82 ft (25·0 m) in males and 85 ft (25·9 m) in females; the corresponding sizes for fin whales are 69 ft (21·0 m) in males and 72 ft (21·9 m) in females (Mackintosh and Wheeler, 1929). These estimates were supported by further studies which showed that female blue whales reach physical maturity at 86 ft (26·2 m) and at an age corresponding to the accumulation of 11 ovarian corpora (Laurie, 1937). Similarly, female fin whales attaining physical maturity at 69 ft (21·0 m) contained 15 or more corpora in their ovaries (Wheeler, 1930). Without knowing the precise ovulation rates applying at that time, these ages can only be said to approximate 25–30 years.

North Pacific fin whale data show that physical maturity is attained by some individuals at 57 ft (17·4 m) in males and 58 ft (17·7 m) in females (Ohsumi et al., 1958). The ages corresponding to the estimated lengths at full physical maturity of 61 ft (18·6 m) and 66 ft (20·1 m) in males and females respectively are quoted as 40–45 years from ear plug layer counts in both sexes, but 14–15 ovarian corpora in the female. The ages from the ear plugs in particular are very high by comparison with the southern hemisphere data, but the ovarian age probably corresponds to about 30 years. It may be that the North Pacific fin whales were not so much changed in their growth patterns as the southern populations when these samples were obtained. They may therefore represent the situation before major stock reductions had altered the growth curves, but this needs confirmation.

Humpback whales examined off Western Australia (Chittleborough, 1955) also appeared to be relatively old at physical maturity, for they contained some 30 corpora in their ovaries. It is possible that the heavy fishing mortality and selection of the larger individuals which this stock had experienced had removed many of the physically mature animals sampled in 1951–1954. Less than 3% of the catch of sexually mature females was physically mature, compared with 20–40% of sexually mature blue and fin whales in Antarctic catches taken in Areas II–IV in 1939–1940 (Brinkmann, 1948). Another possibility is that humpback whales do not reach physical maturity until a later age than the blue and fin whales.

2. Weight

The great whales are of such a size that the easiest measure of that size is the length of the animal. This is recorded as the distance in a straight line from the tip of the snout, or the front of the head in sperm whales, to the notch between the tail flukes (International Whaling Commission,

1974). In many cases it would be more useful to have the weight of the whale for commercial use in connection with the yield of products, and for stock assessment purposes involving considerations of biomass.

Rather few whales have been weighed, and various formulae have been proposed to convert length data to weight. Lockyer (in press) has compiled body weight data for the large whale species from all available sources, and used these to develop body weight/length relationships. These formulations, shown in Table VI, have been adjusted to allow for

TABLE VI   Formulae for converting whale lengths (L, in ft) to weights (W, in tonnes), including body fluids (from Lockyer, in press)

Species	$W = aL^b$	
	a	b
Blue	0·000061	3·25
Fin	0·000255	2·90
Sei	0·001436	2·43
Minke	0·003188	2·31
Humpback	0·000495	2·95
Sperm	0·000152	3·18

blood and fluid losses during flensing. Most large whales have been weighed piecemeal during normal whaling operations, and there have been few opportunities to weigh large animals whole. The largest whale weighed whole and in parts was a 44 ft (13·4 m) sperm whale (Gambell, 1970). This and a 38 ft (11·6 m) sperm whale also weighed on a railway weighbridge before flensing at Durban in 1973 indicated weight differences of 12 and 15 % respectively due to the loss of blood and other tissue fluids during flensing. A 36 ft (11·0 m) minke whale weighed whole in the Antarctic in 1958 suggested a weight loss of 5 %, and baleen whales in general may have less blood to lose than sperm whales (Lockyer, 1976).

Corrected weight/length formulae can be used to convert length at age curves into weight at age curves. Because weight is a more or less cubic function of length, the early rapid growth of whales in their first year or two of life is accentuated when considered in weight terms. Southern blue and fin whales increase in weight by a factor of about ×10 in the first year after birth, and the blue whales go on to reach about 120 tonnes in the females and 100 tonnes in the males at physical maturity. Comparable sizes for southern fin whales are 65 tonnes in females and 55 tonnes in males. These are all average figures for the Antarctic summer season, when weight gains of at least 50% in blue whales and 100% in humpback whales have been estimated to result from the intensive feeding which takes place at this time (Lockyer, 1972b). There is obviously scope for considerable variation in individual body weights, depending on the age, and feeding condition of the whales. Their sexual status is also important, for pregnant females have thicker blubber and weigh more than average, while lactating females are leaner and weigh less. The sexually immature members of both sexes also tend to have slightly thicker blubber and to be heavier than the adults relative to their body length.

V. POPULATION ASSESSMENT

The Committee of Three (later Four) Scientists set up by the International Whaling Commission in 1960 introduced the techniques and methodology then developed in fisheries research into the field of whale investigations (Chapman *et al.*, 1964). These methods were further extended and modified by the Committee and subsequent workers to give the range of assessment models now commonly employed.

A number of the methods of analysis depend to a greater or lesser extent on catch and effort data. The whale catch records are reasonably reliable, given the long series of data on numbers, lengths and sex of each species caught which is held by the Bureau of International Whaling Statistics. The effort statistics are much less firmly based, because the measurement of fishing effort in the mixed species whale fishery in the Antarctic is not easy. Over the years the whale catcher boats have become more powerful, they have been fitted with more sophisticated equipment for tracking whales, finding their own and the whales' positions, communicating with the rest of the whaling fleet, and overcoming the difficulties and dangers of poor weather conditions and ice. In addition, the skill of the gunners varies, and the different national fleets have differing modes of operation which affect their relative efficiencies. All of these factors are hard to quantify precisely, but Holt and Gulland (1964) suggested that many or all of them are reflected in a tonnage correction which had been shown to give a better adjustment than horsepower (Hylen, 1964). The use of Asdic for tracking sperm whales underwater increases the catching efficiency by a factor of $\times 2 \cdot 3$ (Best, 1973; Gambell, 1975a).

Other factors which should be taken into account include weather, for which corrections can be calculated (Gulland and Kesteven, 1964), and day length. However, it has been generally assumed that weather is a random factor when considered over a number of seasons, even though long-term changes in the whaling grounds related to varying species interest have occurred during the years. Similarly, day length varies with latitude and the time of year, so that the unit of catching effort commonly adopted, catcher-day's-work, is not necessarily constant. Stop-catch days, when the whaling factory can process no more carcases, shorten that day's catching effort, while the introduction and increasing use of scouting vessels and spotter aircraft tend to increase the hunting efficiency. There are also very considerable problems in trying to allocate the catching effort to the various species in a multispecies fishery. This, and the other difficulties mentioned, have not been sufficiently studied so far to allow proper corrections to be applied in making calculations. Rather, the problems have been circumvented to a greater or lesser extent by examining in detail only data from years or parts of years when there was roughly constant interest in one species; by looking at areas frequented more by one species than another; or by dealing with areas and periods of more or less equal whaling intensity.

Ideally, all assessments should be calculated for individual unit stocks of whales. But these are not always fully known and delineated. Separate biological stocks may overlap and intermingle at certain times of the year and over parts of their migrational range. Thus, although independent breeding stocks may be identifiable when they are isolated from other stocks of the same species by obvious barriers such as continental land masses, they may not be separable when they mix together on common feeding grounds. In these cases the most convenient units to consider are the ones which can be most easily managed, in terms of collecting catch, effort and biological data, and in controlling the activities of the whaling operations. There is a distinction between these two kinds of stock unit, for the management variety may contain one or more biological stocks. Since the biological stock is the breeding unit, it is important that this is considered as the ultimate basis for assessment and management, even though it may be through the intermediary stage of the more easily handled management stock.

A. METHODS OF ASSESSMENT

Most methods of population assessment currently employed for whales contain some biological input. Age composition data are used for recruitment and mortality estimates, reproductive data for estimates of recruitment, and behavioural information is utilized especially in sperm whale models and sightings estimates. The main techniques of assessment which have been used for whale populations are now described.

1. *DeLury method*

The size of a declining population can be estimated from catch and effort data alone using the DeLury method (DeLury, 1947). In this, the accumulated catch is plotted against the catch-per-unit-of-effort in successive years. An extrapolation to the intercept with the zero catch-per-unit-of-effort axis gives an estimate of the stock size in the first year of the series. This simple model assumes that the population under study is a closed one. In practice, modifications have to be introduced to take account of the fact that recruitment and mortality occur within a whale population during the time period covered by the data.

One modification developed by Chapman (1970) uses the relationship:

$$X_i = k[N_0(1 + (r - M)i) - cc] \qquad (1)$$

where X_i = catch-per-unit-of-effort in season i; N_0 = population size at start of study period; $r - M$ = net recruitment rate (gross recruitment − natural mortality); and cc = cumulative catch to midpoint of season i.

This is an approximation, since gross recruitment is derived from the parent population, while natural mortality applies to the actual population.

If cc = di + f then equation (1) can be rewritten as

$$X_i = [N_0(1 + (r - M)i) - di - f]$$
$$= (N_0 - f) + k[N_0(r - M) - di]$$

d and f can be calculated from cumulative catch data, and the regression of catch-per-unit-of-effort on season derived using:

$$X_i = a + bi$$

Then with

$$k(N_0 - f) = a$$

and

$$k(N_0(r - M) - d) = b$$

$$\frac{N_0 - f}{N_0(r - M) - d} = \frac{a}{b} = h$$

or

$$N_0 = \frac{f - dh}{1 - (r - M)h}$$

Clearly this procedure relies on an accurate independent estimate of the net recruitment rate $r - M$ being available, and the assumption that it is constant during the study period.

Another form of this method of analysis, but which is concerned with shorter term time series, assumes that any decrease in catch or sightings per unit of effort in successive seasons is proportional to the change in population abundance (FAO, 1967; Jones, 1973). Thus, the decrease in the population is equal to the average catch in the two seasons, less the net annual recruitment in that period.

2. *Least squares method*

This method, developed by Allen (1966, 1968), is based on the approximation:

$$N_{t+1} = (N_t - C_t)e^{-M} + R_t \qquad (2)$$

where C_t = catch in season t; N_t = population at the beginning of season t; R_t = recruitment in year t; M = natural mortality coefficient.

This assumes that the natural mortality occurs after the fishing season. The Antarctic whaling season is only some three or four months in duration, so this is probably a reasonable approximation in this case, but it may make the method less useful in other areas with longer whaling seasons.

Estimates of recruitment are obtained from age composition data. The ratio of the catches from a partially recruited year class to a fully recruited year class is compared in successive seasons:

$$\frac{C_{it}}{C_{i-1,t}} = r_i \frac{N_{it}}{N_{i-1,t}}$$

where r_i = fraction of the year class i which is recruited in season t.

It is assumed that the year class i — 1, one year older, is fully recruited, so that for the catches in the next season:

$$\frac{C_{i,t+1}}{C_{i-1,t+1}} = \frac{r_i N_{it} e^{-Zt} + R_{i,t+1}}{N_{i-1,t} e^{-Zt}}$$

where $R_{i,t+1}$ = recruits from year class i in season t + 1. Z = total mortality coefficient (natural + fishing mortalities)

with

$$A_{i,t+1} = \frac{R_{i,t+1}}{r_i N_{it} e^{-Zt} + R_{i,t+1}}$$

the proportion of new recruits in the population $N_{i,t+1}$ (and also in the catch $C_{i,t+1}$ if this is now a fully recruited year class),

then
$$\frac{C_{i,t+1}}{C_{i-1,t+1}} = \frac{r_i N_{it}}{N_{i-1,t}} \frac{1}{1 - A_{i,t+1}}.$$

With
$$B_{i,t+1} = \frac{C_{it}}{C_{i-1,t}} \frac{C_{i-1,t+1}}{C_{i,t+1}}$$

then
$$A_{i,t+1} = 1 - B_{i,t+1}.$$

This estimates the proportion of new recruits in the year class fully recruited for the first time, and by working backwards in time it can be extended to estimate the proportions of new recruits in all the catches.

Using this calculated recruitment, the population size is estimated from equation (2) by computing the value for the population which minimizes the sum of the squares of the differences between actual catches and the catches expected from the population.

3. *Mortality and catchability coefficient methods*

The basic relationship assumed in fisheries analysis is:

$$C = qf\bar{N} \tag{3}$$

where C = catch; q = catchability coefficient; f = unit of effort; and $\bar{N}$ = mean population during the fishing season.

The size of a year class in year t is related to its size a year later $t + 1$ by

$$N_{i,t+1} = N_{it}e^{-Zt}$$

where N_{it} = size of year class i at beginning of season t; $N_{i,t+1}$ = size of year class i at beginning of season $t + 1$; and Z_t = total instantaneous mortality coefficient.

The total mortality coefficient can be derived from the ratio of the catch-per-unit-of-effort (C/f) in two successive years of a fully recruited year class, thus:

$$Z_t = \log \frac{(C/f)_{i,t+1}}{(C/f)_{it}}$$

Estimates are usually calculated by month, comparing similar months a year apart, and by sex and suitable sub-areas. In this way a number of estimates can be derived which may be pooled to give an average for a particular season, sex and area. Even so, the estimates often differ quite widely, due to variable migration patterns of the whales, fluctuations in catching effort from place to place and season to season, and variations in the catches resulting from weather and other environmental factors.

In an effort to reduce this variability, the Committee of Three averaged their total mortality estimates over four seasons, and these smoothed results were considered satisfactory (Chapman *et al.*, 1964). Subsequently, Doi *et al.* (1970) developed another smoothing technique. After calculating the total mortality coefficients by area and season, they estimated the corresponding natural mortality coefficients from the numbers of the year classes which were fully recruited before heavy exploitation took place. These year classes are represented in recent catches as the oldest whales, and obviously the method depends on having good samples of accurately aged whales. The difference between the abundance of successive year classes of these old animals recruited before exploitation and which have subsequently experienced the same history of exploitation is a measure of their natural mortality rate.

Now since $$Z_t = M + F_t = M + qf_t$$

where M = natural mortality coefficient; F_t = fishing mortality coefficient in season t; and f_t = fishing effort in season t, the fishing mortality coefficient can be calculated by simple subtraction of the natural mortality coefficient from the total mortality coefficient. This makes the assumption that the natural mortality remains unchanged throughout the period, and this may not be true when there have been very large changes in stock size.

For each estimate of the fishing mortality coefficient F_t there is a corresponding value for f_t, the fishing effort applied, and for q, the catchability coefficient. The estimates of q are combined to give a smoothed value, particularly for periods of more or less uniform effort, and the smoothed estimate can then be applied in formula (3) to find the population size.

It should be noted that this method gives an estimate of the population size during the whaling season, whereas most of the other methods employed give estimates for the start of the season.

4. *Recruitment curve methods*

a. Baleen whales. Using mathematical models, Japanese scientists have used the best available estimates of the relevant parameters to calculate population sizes and sustainable yields in a number of different formulations (e.g. Doi *et al.*, 1967, 1970; Doi and Ohsumi, 1970; Ohsumi *et al.*, 1971; Ohsumi, 1972, 1973).

These are all based ultimately on the equation (2) model, with the approximation:
$$N_{t+1} = (N_t - C_t)e^{-M} + R_{t+1}$$

where N = catchable stock size; C = catch; R = recruits; t = season; and M = coefficient of natural mortality. One example of the model is as follows:

Notation: tm = age at sexual maturity
Ro = number of whales of age tm
tc = age at recruitment
R = number of whales of age tc i.e. recruits
N = number of catchable whales
A = number of sexually mature whales
M' = natural mortality, immature whales
M = natural mortality, mature whales
F = fishing mortality
So = survival rate from tm to tc
S = survival rate after tc
P = pregnancy rate
E = exploitation rate
C = sustainable yield
K = reproduction rate
T = catching period
sex ratio, male:female = 1:1.

The following relationships are then derived:

$$K = \frac{P}{2} e^{-tmM'}$$

$$Ro = KA$$
$$R = Roe^{-(tc-tm)M}$$
$$So = e^{-M}$$
$$S = e^{-(M+F)}$$

$$E = \frac{F}{F + TM} (1 - e^{(-F+TM)})$$

$$N = \frac{R}{1 - S}$$

$$C = EN$$

$$A = Ro\left(\frac{1 - So^{(tc-tm)}}{1 - So} + \frac{So^{(tc-tm)}}{1 - S}\right)$$

The values and fluctuations in the key parameters of pregnancy rate, age at sexual maturity in females, age at recruitment and the natural mortality rate after sexual maturity are a mixture of observations and expected changes related to the stock size.

Pregnancy rates can be obtained from the official records in the Bureau of International Whaling Statistics data, and from biological observations. In both cases a correction must be calculated to compensate for the absence of the lactating females from the catches.

The natural mortality coefficient in the immature whales is not known directly, but can be calculated from the equation:

$$1 - e^{-M} = \frac{P}{2} e^{-tcM'} e^{\ (tm-tc)}$$

With this technique, population assessments are developed from an assumed starting population using the known catches and a range of biological parameters. These assumed values can be modified until the model fits with the observations on the actual population under consideration.

b. Sperm whales. An essentially similar approach of using models with variable parameters in the basic population equations has been used for assessing sperm whale populations (Ohsumi and Fukuda, 1972; Allen, 1973). Because of the polygynous nature of this species, the two sexes can be treated separately, although not of course independently, and the underlying equations involved in the calculations are as follows (International Whaling Commission, 1969a).

For the females, a stable population will be maintained when the number of female calves surviving to maturity balances the number of mature females dying each year:

$$\frac{Nf \cdot p}{2} e^{-tmf \cdot Mf} = Nf (1 - e^{-Mf})$$

where Nf = number of mature females; p = pregnancy rate; tmf = age at sexual maturity in females; and Mf = natural mortality coefficient of mature females.

When such a stable population is fished, parameter changes may be expected which will increase the recruitment by an increase in the pregnancy rate, a reduction in the age at maturity and reduced natural mortality. These changes, analogous to some of those which have been observed in Antarctic fin whales, will provide a sustainable yield for harvesting. Calculations based on these assumptions and the known catches then lead to assessments of the female sperm whale population.

Comparable equations and calculations for the male sperm whales have to take into account the fact that the breeding component of the population is that part which reaches social maturity, or harem master status. The number of females which a harem bull can control is also an important feature. A number of estimates from school sizes and compositions suggest that an average of 1·5 big bulls are found with 15 females

(Gambell, 1972), and 10–16 females have been given as average school numbers in a review by Best (1974b). The number of females per bull is therefore about 7–11, and might be expected to change in response to a decrease in population size.

It has been generally assumed that the socially mature males over and above the number required for breeding can be harvested. It is possible that these surplus males may play a role in breeding by stimulating the harem bulls through their competition for the females. If they are not necessary to provide this kind of facilitation, then this carries with it the corollary that there is a surplus of males which can be caught on a sustainable basis, even in previously unexploited populations. The mathematical derivation of this is:

$$\text{Number of males born} = \frac{Nf \cdot p}{2}$$

$$\text{Number of males reaching social maturity} = \frac{Nf \cdot p}{2} e^{-tmmM_1}$$

$$\text{Number of males required for breeding} = \frac{Nf}{n}$$

Number of males in breeding stock dying from natural causes each year = annual replacement required $= \dfrac{Nf}{n} (1 - e^{-M_2})$

Thus the surplus, equal to the potential harvest is:

$$\frac{Nf \cdot p}{2} e^{-tmmM_1} - \frac{1}{n}(1 - e^{-M_2})$$

where Nf = number of mature females; p = pregnancy rate; tmm = age at social maturity in males; M_1 = natural mortality coefficient of males before maturity; M_2 = natural mortality coefficient of males after maturity; and n = harem size.

5. *Whale marking methods*

The proportion of recovered marks in a catch to the number of effectively marked whales gives a factor by which the size of the catch can be related to the total population being fished. This direct use of whale marking returns should incorporate a factor to correct for the less than complete recovery and reporting of whale marks. Whale mark recoveries from the Antarctic have shown a remarkable increase in the efficiencies of returns in the post-war years (International Whaling Commission, 1967). The efficiency rose from 9% in 1945/46–1948/49 to 46% in 1959/60–1963/64. This probably resulted from the increasing use of carcases for meat rather than oil, so that the marks were more likely to be found when the whales were cut up. Also, Japanese fleets took a larger proportion of the catch in the later years, and they have the highest mark recovery rate of the pelagic whaling nations. Even the Japanese fleets are not fully efficient, for of 101 marks fired into baleen whale carcases during pelagic operations, only 70 (70%) were found during cutting up, and only 15 (65%) of 23 marks thrown into sperm whale cookers were later recovered (Doi *et al.*, 1970). Similar seeding experiments carried out at the land station at Durban in 1969 (Gambell, 1972) and in 1971, when sixteen marks were concealed in carcases, gave 100% returns.

An alternative approach is to use Seber's (1962) method of analysis. This makes a comparison of the number of marks recovered in the same season from different marking experiments. It eliminates the problems of varying efficiencies of recovery between expeditions and years, since these factors are common to the different experiments. Zero year recoveries are often disregarded because they may introduce a bias due to incomplete mixing. The ratio of the recoveries from the various marking experiments in a period after the last is then a measure of the total mortality operating during the period between the experiments. The mortality is calculated as:

$$1 - \frac{t_1 S_{02}}{t_0 (S_{12} + 1)}$$

where t_0 = number marked less zero year recoveries; t_1 = number marked in following season, less zero year recoveries; S_{02} = number of marks recovered in second season and later; and S_{12} = number of marks from following season's marking in first or later seasons.

The mortality rates so obtained consist of fishing (F) and natural (M) components. By subtraction of a known or assumed natural mortality figure, the fishing mortality can be obtained and used to estimate the total population size (N) from the catch (C) thus:

$$N = \frac{C}{F}$$

The analyses presented here make no use of biological information as such. In practice, the usefulness of whale marking data have often been extended by calculating the number of marked whales likely to be at liberty in successive seasons after the first. This involves the use of an estimate of the natural mortality rate obtained from some other source.

6. *Whale sightings*

The whale species which are protected from hunting cannot be assessed by any of the foregoing methods, which rely on catch data of some sort. Their numbers can only be estimated by sightings. Such observations also provide useful additional estimates for the non-protected species, and comparison with results from other methods of analysis gives a means of checking and calibrating the sightings methodology.

One of the first quantitative assessments of the Antarctic baleen whale stocks was based on sightings from RRS *Discovery* analysed by Mackintosh and Brown (1956). They assumed that the whales seen on either side of the ship's track represented a proportion of the total number present, which they calculated to be approximately 27 % on the evidence of the number of sightings recorded at varying distances from the ship. The estimated number of whales within the track width was then raised to the total area of the region surveyed to give the total population size.

$$N = \frac{An}{LDp}$$

where N = total population; A = total area; n = whales seen; L = distance steamed; D = sighting range; and p = sighting probability.

Sightings of whales by the scouting boats operating with the Japanese pelagic fleets have been used extensively in more recent years for estimating population numbers. Conversion of the observations made into total population numbers was based initially on similar formulations to the above, involving a sightings probability factor (Doi *et al.*, 1967). The estimates of sightings range and probability were considered in a theoretical study by Nasu and Shimadzu (1970), taking an effective visual field forward of the ship rather than at right angles to its course. They found that most whales were sighted at a range of three miles from the ship, with smaller numbers seen at greater and lesser distances.

A new and more detailed theoretical model for converting sightings into total population estimates was then developed by Doi (1974). This incorporated modifications to allow for the speed of the vessel and the visual angle of observation, and applied a correction for the whales missed due to the angular velocity of eye-scanning. The diving time of the various species of whales and the duration of their blows was also taken into account, as well as the number of observers on the ship. However, actual sightings data did not match the theoretical model. The differences were attributed to the difficulty of seeing whales at long distances, the observers concentrating their attention immediately ahead of the ship instead of to one side, and the fact that no allowances had been made for sea and weather conditions. A modifying factor was therefore calculated which had the effect of reducing the population estimates by nearly two-thirds. This model could be improved still more if data were incorporated on the diving and swimming behaviour of whales, and their reaction to ships, as well as the psychophysiology of eye scanning.

Sightings by commercial scouting vessels are inevitably concentrated in areas of relatively high whale density, and this will bias the results for the species being hunted. It may not affect the results for the protected species so much, unless they also concentrate in those same areas which are made particularly favourable by hydrographic or other environmental factors.

B. SUSTAINABLE YIELD

A simplified model of a natural animal population can be constructed in which the population is treated as a single unit. Variations between individuals such as size or age are ignored, and it is assumed that the population number is steady at the carrying capacity of the environment. In this equilibrium situation the rate of reproduction is exactly balanced by the rate of natural mortality so that the population neither increases nor decreases. If such a population is reduced in numbers by catching some of the animals, it will increase again to the limiting abundance. The rate of increase depends only on the abundance of the population, and is brought about by an increase in the rate of reproduction, or a decrease in the natural mortality rate, or both. Either of these processes cause the production of a surplus of new recruits over the number of animals dying from natural causes, and the extra animals are added on to the depleted population to rebuild its numbers. However, if they are removed by catching, the size of the population will remain unaltered and such a catch can be sustained indefinitely.

The *sustainable yield* is defined as the net recruitment, that is, the excess of the gross recruitment over natural deaths. Each population size has a certain capacity for reproduction and a certain rate of natural mortality. The net recruitment rate tends to increase with decreasing population size, and the product of these two parameters is the sustainable yield at each particular population level. The natural increase giving rise to this yield is small for very small populations, at least in terms of absolute value even if not as a proportion of the population size. It is also small for large populations near the limiting population size. At some intermediate level of population it reaches a peak value which is termed the *maximum sustainable yield* (MSY).

Catching the sustainable yield will, by definition, cause no change in the population size at the end of the whaling season. Catching less than the sustainable yield will allow an addition of recruits to the population which will thus increase in abundance. For a population which is smaller than the level giving the MSY, this will allow some rebuilding towards that level, and hence a larger sustainable yield in the following seasons. If the population is less than the MSY level, catches greater than the sustainable yield will decrease the population size by an amount equal to the difference between the catch and the sustainable yield. Each lower population level will have successively smaller sustainable yields and so be less productive. Constant catches maintained by increasing fishing effort in this situation will lead to progressively faster depletion of the population.

Populations which are above the MSY level can support catches greater than the sustainable yield indefinitely, provided that they are no greater than the MSY. This is due to the fact that as the population is reduced by the catches, so its sustainable yield increases. Eventually, when the population is reduced to the level at which the sustainable yield is equal to the catch, that catch can be maintained without any further changes occurring in the population size.

The simple model so far considered differs from real whale populations in a number of ways. One of the most important factors in the whale situation is the effect of time-lags in the system. The number of whales lost from the exploitable phase by natural mortality is a fairly constant proportion of the current population. The recruitment to this phase will be related to the number of mature animals alive some years earlier. This means that the concept of a sustainable yield becomes very complicated in a population which is changing in abundance. For example, a population which has decreased recently will have a parent population larger than the present one providing the recruitment, but the natural deaths will be related to the current smaller population. This may then allow a sizeable catch to be taken without changing the over-all population size, but it will only be available for the one season. Conversely, a population which is increasing will have recruitment from a smaller parent population but current natural mortalities, so that the available catch to maintain the population level is relatively small. These problems have been discussed by Gulland and Boerema (1973), and they proposed a number of terms to clarify the situation in a dynamic model.

The *replacement yield* (RY) is that catch which will leave the abundance of the population at the end of the year the same as it was in the beginning.

This is specific to a particular year and includes no concept of continuity, unless the population has remained around the same abundance for at least as long as the age to recruitment.

The *equivalent sustainable yield* from a given population is the sustainable yield from an equilibrium population of the same abundance.

The *maintainable yield* is the yield which can be taken from the population indefinitely over a long period. It may cause some changes in the population initially. In the case where the population is above the level giving the maximum sustainable yield, the maintainable yield will be equal to the maximum sustainable yield. For smaller populations which are changing in abundance, the maintainable yield lies between the equivalent sustainable yields of the parent and present populations.

1. *Recruitment curve*

The exact shape of the sustainable yield curve, and especially the position of the level providing the maximum sustainable yield, depend on the form of the recruitment curve in any particular whale population. If the recruitment rate increases linearly as the population size decreases, the MSY level is 50 % of the initial population number. The precise form of the recruitment curve in the various species and stocks is still under study, and there are few direct observations of the recruitment rates over a sufficiently wide range of population sizes. Mathematical models incorporating the observed and expected changes in the governing parameters of the pregnancy rate, ages at sexual maturity and recruitment into the exploited phase of the population, and assumed changes in the natural mortality rates at different ages suggest that the recruitment curve may be of a curvilinear form, and convex upwards. Such a shape would have the effect of moving the MSY level to a higher population number (International Whaling Commission, 1976).

It is also important to specify the way in which the parent population providing the recruitment is measured. Strictly, the sexually mature whales are the parents. It is often easier, however, to consider the total exploited population as the parent unit because it can be estimated more directly. If the age at sexual maturity is higher than the age at recruitment, and providing that the proportion of immature whales in the catches does not vary significantly over a period of time, the effect of this approximation is only to insert a constant which reduces the value of the recruitment rate. In some exploited whale populations, notably the Antarctic sei whales, only part of the total number of whales enters the whaling grounds during the summer season. These animals are mainly from the older and mature range of the population. If these whales are taken to represent the parent population, the recruitment rate appears artificially inflated. Allowance should be made for the mature whales which are outside the exploited phase but which do contribute to the recruitment (Chapman, 1974b). The population level at MSY is naturally a lower proportion of the total mature population than of the exploited mature population.

Also in connection with the Antarctic sei whales, the evidence of changes in pregnancy rates and age at maturity (pp. 294 and 304) before the population was heavily exploited suggests that the recruitment is not necessarily related directly to the sei whale population abundance. A proposal has been put forward that the total Antarctic baleen whale biomass may be a better base line parameter than the individual species abundance or biomass (Gambell, 1975). The evidence for this comes from the closer agreement of blue, fin and sei whale pregnancy rate changes when related to total biomass reductions than to individual species populations. There is comparable better accord between the fin and sei whale age at sexual maturity data when considered on a total biomass scale.

An increase in recruitment before the Antarctic sei whales were hunted extensively also implies that the sei whale population must have been increasing in numbers during the earlier period. This makes it even less likely that the recruitment curve for the sei whales is primarily dependent on the abundance of this species alone. The recruitment curve and sustainable yield models must then be related to a much more complex population base-line. The full ramifications of the concept of inter-specific dependence amongst the whales, even without involving a wider environmental web of organisms, is only now beginning to be considered.

2. *Weight*

To date, whale population assessments and yields have been calculated almost entirely in terms of numbers of whales. Since it is the individual animals which reproduce and die, this emphasis is perhaps not un-expected, coupled with the difficulties of actually weighing the catches. But when ecosystem concepts are involved, it is probably better to make use of weight or biomass units, for the role of the whales within their environment can be better gauged in these terms. The fact that whales are hunted commercially for the value of the products which can be derived from the carcases also suggests that the weight of the whales is a more useful index than the numbers of whales alone.

By applying the appropriate conversion factors for whale weights to lengths (p. 311), the sustainable yield curve can be drawn on a popula-tion weight scale instead of population number. This has the general effect of skewing the curve to the right, so that the MSY population level is at a higher proportion of the original population size than on the number scale. The magnitude of the change varies between species. It will be relatively small in those whales where there is rather little growth potential remaining after recruitment into the fishery, and this includes most of the baleen whales which are or have been exploited in recent years. A greater change will occur in those species, such as the sperm whale, in which much more growth can still take place after the whale reaches catchable size.

The fact that the MSY level by weight is at a greater population size and density than by number has the advantage for the whaling industry of making it also a relatively more economical yield. The optimum yield in terms of cost is obtained from a population with a high density, although it has not proved practicable so far to quantify this result precisely, due to the lack of relevant economic data and the varying national interests involved (Allen *et al.*, 1966).

C. POPULATION ESTIMATES

The various methods of estimating whale population sizes and yields have been used to assess the status of the different species and stocks for the purpose of advising the IWC in its management decisions. The stock estimates are under constant review, and the addition of new data and analyses necessitate up-dating and revision of the results from time to time. The estimates given in Table VII of population numbers are therefore liable to amendment, but represent a personal evaluation of our present state of knowledge based on published evidence.

Most of the estimates represent the numbers of catchable sized animals, that is, of a length greater than the minimum size limits which are or have been applied in the various whale fisheries. Estimates of right and gray whales are for total populations, because these figures are derived only from sightings observations, as are the values for the minke whales in the newly developed fishery for this species in the Antarctic. Total populations are greater than the exploited numbers by factors depending on the natural mortality rate before recruitment, and the age at recruitment to the exploited phase. The increases range from 50% in the case of Antarctic fin whales to 150% in the case of male sperm whales.

The introduction of the concept of inter-specific density dependent reproduction parameters, discussed above, has raised serious doubts recently about the population model for Antarctic sei whales. For this reason, the estimates of the original and MSY population levels must be viewed as very tentative. It is possible that the original population cal-

TABLE VII Estimates (and ranges) of the exploitable stock sizes and sustainable yields of the great whales ($\times 10^{-3}$) (after Gambell, 1976)

Species	Initial stock	MSY level	Present stock	MSY	RY
Southern Hemisphere					
Fin	400(375–425)	234(209–248)	84(83–97)	7.7(6.8–8.6)	3.4(3.4–4.9)
Sei	[150(125–150)]	[54(51–56)]	53(52–54)	[4.5(4.1–5.0)]	5.0(4.0–5.2)
Minke	260(220–299)[a]	122–158	251(211–291)	5.0–12.2	0.3
Blue	180(210–150)	100–125	5	6	v. small
Pygmy blue	10	5	5	0.2	v. small
Humpback	100	50	3[a]	2–4	v. small
Right	?	?	3[a]	?	v. small
Sperm ♂	257	112	128	8.5	8.2
Sperm ♀	330[b]	231[b]	259[b]	4.5	1.8
North Pacific					
Fin	43.5(42–45)	27(26–28)	16(14–19)	1.2(1.2–1.3)	0.83(0.76–0.90)
Sei	45	ca. 26	21	ca. 1.9	2.5
Blue	4.9	2.4	1.6(1.4–1.9)	0.09	0.08
Humpback	?	?	1.4(1.2–1.6)[a]	?	v. small
Right	?	?	0.15(0.1–0.2)[a]	?	v. small
Grey	?	?	11(7.5–13)[a]	?	?0.16
Sperm ♂	195	58(53–62)	91	5.7(5.5–5.9)	5.8
Sperm ♀	152	79	125	3.4	1.6
North Atlantic					
Sperm (Canadian coastal area)	?	?	22[a]	?	?
Fin	4.7	?	2.4	0.3	0.14
Sei	1.6+	?	1.6	0.08	?
Blue	1.1–1.5	?	0.1	0.1	?
Humpback	1.0–1.5	?	1.0	0.1	?
Fin (Iceland)	?	?	4–8	?	?0.24

[a] Sightings estimate of total population.   [b] Mature females.

culated is the number after a population increase due to the decrease of the blue and fin whale abundance. The MSY level would therefore relate to a new situation which was not based on the original, in the sense of pre-1904 Antarctic whaling, population.

Ideally, the population estimates shown should be sub-divided into separate stocks. There are various estimates available, but all tend to be based on the assumptions either that the population parameters of each stock are the same, or that the various stocks can be proportioned according to cumulative catches or present sightings densities of the total population. Neither of these approximations, which have to be made because of lack of better information, are likely to be completely reliable. It seems better to await the results of current assessments before setting out such stock estimates in detail.

VI. MANAGEMENT

Before the start of the Second World War the British and Norwegian governments had taken an initiative in attempting to limit the Antarctic catches. This had stemmed from the whaling companies' own desire to regulate the production of oil by the industry to stabilize the market. Limits to oil production were set, along with minimum size regulations and various other protective measures concerning the length of the whaling season, and the species and areas for hunting.

Immediately after the war all the whaling nations agreed to limit the catches to about two-thirds of the pre-war level. The catch limit was expressed in terms of Blue Whale Units (BWU), broadly a measure of the oil yield of each species, where 1 blue whale equalled 2 fin whales, $2\frac{1}{2}$ humpback whales or 6 sei whales. The limit of 16 000 BWU set for the 1945/46 and 1946/47 Antarctic seasons was taken over by the newly created International Whaling Commission for the following seasons. Evidence produced by the IWC's Scientific Committee of declining catch per unit effort data and decreasing mean lengths of the catches soon warned the Commission that the stocks were being depleted. However, the competition between the whaling fleets to gain as large a share of the total quota as possible involved considerable capital investment in ships and machinery, so there was strong economic pressure to keep the catches high.

The economic arguments for maintaining the catches at levels which the stocks clearly could not sustain prevented any real management policy as such from being formulated or implemented by the IWC at this time. Faced with the signs of falling whale stocks they did reduce the catch quota to 15 500 BWU in 1953/54, to 15 000 BWU in 1955/56, and to 14 500 BWU in 1956/57. But these were little more than token adjustments because the quota was increased to 15 000 BWU again in 1958/59, largely because the Netherlands was not convinced that the blue and fin whale stocks were really declining.

The pelagic whaling operations were very much a free for all. Restrictions on the length of the whaling season for fin whales, an even shorter season for blue whales, and only four days in which to take humpback whales, meant that there was a great emphasis on each expedition catching as many whales as it could before the total catch limit was achieved, but at the expense of less than full utilization of the carcases. It was more profitable to catch another whale for its oil-rich blubber than to process the meat and bones from a carcase already flensed. It had not proved possible to reach agreement on national quotas which would reduce this wasteful competition within the total catch limit, so the Netherlands and Norway withdrew from the IWC in 1959 in protest. There were no effective catch limits for the next three seasons, although each nation set quotas for their own expeditions.

In response to appeals by the Commission, Norway rejoined the IWC in 1960 and the Netherlands in 1962. Together with Japan, U.S.S.R. and U.K., these five nations still whaling in the Antarctic reached an agreement on national catches within the total quota set by the IWC of 15 000 BWU for the 1962/63 season. The IWC had meanwhile set up the independent Committee of Three scientists to work with the Scientific Committee on assessing the whale stocks and to report on the level of sustainable yield of these stocks and any conservation measures that would increase this sustainable yield. The actions of the IWC on receiving the report of the Committee of Three really marks the beginning of any attempt to manage the whale resources from a background of quantitative scientific knowledge.

The recommendations made by the Committee of Three were for a complete cessation of catching of blue and humpback whales; a reduction of the fin whale catches to 7000 or less; the elimination of the Blue Whale Unit and the establishment of separate catch quotas for each species; and continued population analyses on data provided by all countries engaged in Antarctic whaling (Chapman et al., 1964). The IWC responded by reducing the quota for 1963/64 to 10 000 BWU; by protecting blue whales throughout most of the Antarctic except for the area where the pygmy blue whales were found; and by giving humpback whales complete protection throughout the southern hemisphere. The inadequacy of this half-hearted response was demonstrated by the fulfilment of the prediction by the Committee of Three that the high quota set would not be achieved, when only 8429 BWU were actually taken in the season.

The situation in 1964 was critical. The Scientific Committee proposed a phased reduction in the catches from 4000 BWU in 1964/65 to 3000 and 2000 BWU in the next two seasons. The four remaining nations whaling in the Antarctic, U.K. having dropped out and sold its share of the catch to Japan, found such a low catch unacceptable. No quota was set therefore within the IWC, but a voluntary limit of 8000 BWU was agreed between the whaling countries. Despite a major switch of emphasis to catching sei whales, the catch totalled 6986 BWU.

As a result, a special meeting of the IWC in 1965 recommended that a catch limit of 4500 BWU should be set for 1965/66, with further reductions in the two following seasons to bring the catch below the combined sustainable yields of the fin and sei whales as determined on the basis of continuing scientific assessments. Together with total protection for blue whales, this proposal was formally adopted and implemented, so that for the first time there was a plan for the effective conservation of whales in the Antarctic.

By the 1967/68 season the quota was reduced to 3200 BWU in line with this policy, and only Japan and the U.S.S.R. were left with Antarctic whaling fleets. A new interpretation of age readings in fin whales (p. 297) caused the revision of the stock and yield estimates, and the catch limit was consequently reduced to 2700 BWU for 1969/70. Further revisions of the scientific assessments brought the quota down to 2300 BWU in 1971/72.

The progressive reductions of the quota were not easily achieved. There was not always a unanimous recommendation from the Scientific Committee on the sustainable yields available. This situation sometimes arose from genuine scientific doubts due to inadequate data, or from the presentation of a range of likely values. In these situations the IWC did not act in a thoroughly conservative manner by adopting catch limits based on the lowest estimates, but often used the highest figures because of the pressure applied by the industry. The argument was always advanced that the whaling fleets could not survive without the higher catches. In similar fashion, moves to abolish the Blue Whale Unit system were resisted by the whaling nations because of the operational and economic difficulties this would cause.

Meanwhile, because of the depletion of the stocks in the North Pacific, the four nations whaling there had made agreements outside the IWC on catch limits by species based on scientific advice from 1966. The land stations operated by Canada and the U.S.A. were soon forced to close by the greatly reduced availability of whales, but the pelagic fleets operated by Japan and the U.S.S.R. continued to catch the quota agreed between themselves. The catches from 1969 onwards were designed to be in line with the policy of not exceeding the sustainable yield, and were brought into the formal IWC arrangements for the 1971 season. It was never clear why regulation by species was possible in the North Pacific but not in the Antarctic.

The call from the United Nations Conference on the Human Environment in Stockholm in 1972 for a complete moratorium on whaling for ten years had a considerable impact on the annual meeting of the IWC that year. A total moratorium was not adopted by the IWC, on the grounds that regulation by species and stocks was the only practical method of whale conservation. It was considered that rational quotas, based on the best scientific advice available, would allow the over-exploited stocks to be restored and avoid excessive catches of those whale stocks which were not seriously depleted. The whale species which were totally protected, the right whales, gray, blue and humpbacks, were under a moratorium already. Catch quotas were set for the Antarctic by species for the first time, and at a level below the estimated replacement yield of the fin whales and at that level for the sei whales in both the Antarctic and North Pacific areas. Quotas were also adopted for sperm whales in the southern hemisphere and the North Pacific for the two sexes separately.

The policy of the IWC is now to regulate the catches in such a way that the various stocks will move towards or be held at their MSY levels. For the depleted fin whale populations of the Antarctic and North Pacific, the fastest rate of rebuilding to these levels will be achieved by the complete protection of the whales. There was therefore a commitment to ban fin whaling in the Antarctic from July 1976. Fine control of the distribution of the catches is necessary to manage all the stocks as separate units. The sperm whale quota in the southern hemisphere was subdivided into three regions in 1973, and the quotas for the fin, sei and minke whales similarly partitioned in 1974. The regions were combinations of pairs of the Antarctic statistical Areas, plus their northward extensions to the equator for the sperm whales. Although these are not biological stock units, they were a move towards this degree of control tempered by the reluctance of the whaling industry to lose any more of the flexibility it claims is required to operate economically. For this reason, the sum of the regional catch limits, based on the estimated sustainable yields of each, exceeded the total quota for each species by a factor of 10%; but under no circumstances could the actual catch taken exceed the total quota. Subsequently, in 1976, the southern hemisphere quotas were divided into the six Antarctic Areas extended to the equator for baleen whales and nine divisions (p. 287) for sperm whales, but still with a 10% flexibility allowance. The North Atlantic and North Pacific quotas were also divided between the identifiable stock areas in each.

The enforcement of these regulations was considerably enhanced when in 1972 agreement was finally reached on the implementation of an international observer scheme. Such a scheme had been under consideration for at least fourteen years amongst the Antarctic pelagic whaling nations. The arrangements finally adopted allow for an exchange of observers between nations whaling in the North Atlantic, North Pacific, Antarctic pelagic grounds and from southern hemisphere land stations. They report to the IWC on the catches and national inspection and obviously give added credibility to the catch reports.

Management of the whale resources by the IWC hinges on the sustainable yield model. From 1965 there has been a definite commitment to reduce the catches in the Antarctic and North Pacific to or below the sustainable yields of the various species concerned. In 1974, in response to continuing calls for a moratorium on commercial whaling, a classification of whale stocks was developed to formalize this management policy and to set out criteria by which the various whale stocks will be harvested in the future. The division is into three categories:

Initial management stocks which are unexploited or only lightly exploited and may be reduced in a controlled manner to achieve MSY levels or other optimum levels as these may be defined.

Sustained management stocks which are or should be maintained at or near MSY levels and then at optimum levels as these may be determined.

Protection stocks which are below the level of sustained management stocks and should be fully protected to allow them to rebuild.

The classification of the whale stocks and the level of commercial whaling permitted in the first two categories is to be according to the advice of the Scientific Committee. There is scope for defining MSY in terms other than numbers of whales, perhaps by weight or in combination with economic criteria. But there are very considerable difficulties in carrying out the necessary assessments because of our less than perfect knowledge of the stocks and biology of the whales, even those long studied. It is difficult, in addition, to estimate stock sizes and sustainable yields for a population which has not been previously exploited, as is the case with the minke whales in the Antarctic; or to calculate the MSY of a stock which has remained apparently stable under more-or-less constant exploitation for a long period of years, such as the fin whales off Iceland. The North Atlantic minke whales hunted by the Norwegian small whale fishery also have not been sufficiently studied so far to determine the status of their stocks. However, both the Icelandic and Norwegian governments maintain very strict controls on the catching effort expended in these whale fisheries.

Outside the IWC there have been no attempts at management of any effective kind. Sperm whaling off the west coast of South America expanded considerably in the 1950's. An analysis of the catch and effort data, mainly from Peru but with some Chilean material (Saetersdal *et al.*, 1963), showed that the rate of exploitation had exceeded the level corresponding to the MSY in weight, if not in numbers. The stock was therefore being over-exploited, and a warning was given that further increases in effort might lead to a serious decline in the total catch. Shortly afterwards the fishery collapsed. The catch has increased in size again now, in part through co-operation between Japanese and South American companies.

Ideal management of the whale resources of the world require a unified control of all whaling operations, regulating catches on an individual stock basis. To have some countries operating outside the major governing body is unsatisfactory where the stocks concerned are not completely independent. With so widely-ranging animals as whales, such isolation is hardly likely to occur anywhere in the world. At present the IWC regulations do not distinguish precisely the various stocks within each species. Progress is slowly being made in this direction, but it may not prove possible to identify, separate or manage individual stocks which intermingle at such a fine level. In these cases, extreme caution should always be exercised in setting catch limits so that there is no danger of depleting any stock. The past record of world whaling is poor; the potential value of this resource is such that we can scarcely afford to waste it.

VII. Conclusion

The history of whaling throughout the years is a generally depressing story, with the probable exception of the Southern Whale Fishery for sperm whales in the 18th and 19th centuries. Many stocks have been so reduced by the successive phases of the industry that there is only a small remnant of some of the major species left in the world's oceans. Modern whaling has the power to bring the remaining whale stocks to the point of economic if not biological extinction. It is this repeated sad history and continuing potential for harm which have given rise to the calls for a total cessation of commercial whaling by various conservation groups and governments. Yet this natural renewable resource could make an important contribution amounting to about 10% of the total yield of marine products on a sustainable basis. The problems lie in assessing wild animal populations which inhabit the open oceans and migrate over half the world; and in regulating a multi-national mixed species fishery conducted for the most part in international waters.

Despite the accumulated data on nearly every whale caught this century, the biological knowledge necessary for rational exploitation of the great whales is still far from complete. The problems of stock identification and delineation, and the responses, both physiological and behavioural, of the whales to abundance changes in their own stocks and in other species in the ecosystem, are probably the two most important elements still to be elucidated. In spite of these gaps in our knowledge, our present understanding of the broad outlines of whale biology do provide a basis for management which could restore the depleted stocks to their full productivity, and maintain those stocks which are still at or above their maximum or optimum sustainable yield levels. The problems here are ones of economics and the need for a genuine will to develop the full long-term potential of the resource. A whaling industry which is too large will want to catch more whales now than the populations can withstand. The reproductive capacity of the whales is less than current monetary interest rates, so that it is more profitable to overexploit the stocks, and leave no whales for future generations.

Estimates of the time needed for the southern blue and humpback whale populations to rebuild to MSY levels by numbers under complete protection are of the order of forty years. The southern fin whales will take some twenty-five years to reach this position if no more are caught. The North Pacific populations of blue and fin whales will need ten to fifteen years without any catching. In this situation, the short-term profits of the whaling industry have to be weighed against the long-term benefits to mankind of having large harvestable whale populations providing appreciable amounts of protein, oils and a wide range of other products. This is quite apart from any aesthetic factors surrounding these large mammals and our responsibility not to needlessly or carelessly destroy part of the diversity of the natural world.

Strong, effective and enlightened management based on sound knowledge is needed to achieve the conservation and optimum utilization of the whales. It must encompass all whaling activity throughout the world, and have the support of the best international research. It is particularly important that the expected recoveries of the much depleted and presently protected species are monitored closely, to provide new evidence of the recruitment and mortality mechanisms which operate at low stock levels. The Californian grey whale stock has recovered since the Second World War and apparently stabilized at its current level. The right, blue and humpback stocks should be studied intensively to record their responses for many years to come. This will cost a lot of money, and since these whales are not permitted to be hunted commercially, there will be a strong temptation to miss a unique opportunity of gathering valuable information. The commercial whale fisheries also must be intensively sampled and the data obtained supplemented by research activity directed outside the normal whaling grounds.

On such a basis of knowledge and enlightened intent, the whales can be restored to become abundant and productive components of the marine ecosystem. Otherwise, they may be reduced to the status of further vestigial reminders of man's folly and greed.

References

Aguayo L., A. (1974). Baleen whales off continental Chile. *In* "The Whale Problem: a Status Report" (W. E. Schevill, Ed.), pp. 209–17. Harvard Univ. Press, Cambridge, Mass.

Allen, K. R. (1966). Some methods for estimating exploited populations. *J. Fish. Res. Bd. Canada* **23**(10), 1553–74.

Allen, K. R. (1968). Simplification of a method of computing recruitment rates. *J. Fish. Res. Bd. Canada* **25**(12), 2701–2.

Allen, K. R. (1971). A preliminary assessment of fin whale stocks off the Canadian Atlantic coast. *Rep. int. Commn Whal.* **21**, 64–6.

Allen, K. R. (1973). The computerized sperm whale population model. *Rep. int. Commn Whal.* **23**, 70–4.

Allen, K. R., Gulland, J. A. and Holt, S. J. (1966). Economic assessment. *Rep. int. Commn Whal.* **16**, 62–3.

Ash, C. E. (1956). The fin whales of 1954/55. *Norsk Hvalfangsttid.* **45**(1), 45–7.

Bannister, J. L. (1969). The biology and status of the sperm whale off Western Australia—an extended summary of results of recent work. *Rep. int. Commn Whal.* **19**, 70–6.

Bannister, J. L. and Gambell, R. (1965). The succession and abundance of fin, sei and other whales off Durban. *Norsk Hvalfangsttid.* **54**(3), 45–60.

Bannister, J. L. and Grindley, J. R. (1966). Notes on *Balaenophilus unisetus* P. O. C. Aurivillius, 1879, and its occurrence in the southern hemisphere (Copepoda Harpacticoida). *Crustaceana* **10**(3), 296–302.

Bergersen, B. and Ruud, J. T. (1941). Pelagic whaling in the Antarctic. IX. The season 1938–1939. *Hvalråd. Skr.* **No. 25**, 1–46.

Bergersen, B., Lie, J. and Ruud, J. T. (1939). Pelagic whaling in the Antarctic. VIII. The season 1937–1938. *Hvalråd. Skr.* **No. 20**, 1–42.

Berzin, A. A. (1961). Materialy po razvitiyu zubov i opredeleniyu vozrasta kashalota. *Trudy Soveshch. ikhtiol. Kom.* **12**, 94–103.

Berzin, A. A. (1971). "Kashalot", pp. 1–367. Pishchevaya Promyshlennost, Moskva.

Best, P. B. (1967). The sperm whale (*Physeter catodon*) off the west coast of South Africa. 1. Ovarian changes and their significance. *Investl Rep. Div. Sea Fish. S. Afr.* **No. 61**, 1–27.

Best, P. B. (1968). The sperm whale (*Physeter catodon*) off the west coast of South Africa. 2. Reproduction in the female. *Investl Rep. Div. Sea Fish. S. Afr.* **No. 66**, 1–32.

Best, P. B. (1969a). The sperm whale (*Physeter catodon*) off the west coast of South Africa. 3. Reproduction in the male. *Investl Rep. Div. Sea Fish. S. Afr.* **No. 72**, 1–20.

Best, P. B. (1969b). The sperm whale (*Physeter catodon*) off the west coast of South Africa. 4. Distribution and movements. *Investl Rep. Div. Sea Fish. S. Afr.* **No. 78**, 1–12.

Best, P. B. (1970). The sperm whale (*Physeter catodon*) off the west coast of South Africa. 5. Age, growth and mortality. *Investl Rep. Div. Sea Fish. S. Afr.* **No. 79**, 1–27.

Best, P. B. (1973). Status of whale stocks off South Africa, 1971. *Rep. int. Commn Whal.* **23**, 115–26.

Best, P. B. (1974a). Status of the whale populations off the west coast of South Africa, and current research. *In* "The Whale Problem: A Status Report" (W. E. Schevill, Ed.), pp. 53–81. Harvard Univ. Press, Cambridge, Mass.

Best, P. B. (1974b). The biology of the sperm whale as it relates to stock management. *In* "The Whale Problem: A Status Report" (W. E. Schevill, Ed.), pp. 257–93. Harvard Univ. Press, Cambridge, Mass.

Best, P. B. and Gambell, R. (1968). A comparison of the external characters of sperm whales off South Africa. *Norsk Hvalfangsttid.* **57**(6), 146–64.

Brinkmann, A. (1948). Studies on female fin and blue whales. *Hvalråd Skr.* **No. 31**, 1–38.

Brown, S. G. (1957). Whales observed in the Indian Ocean. Notes on their distribution. *Mar. Obs., London* **27**, 157–65.

Brown, S. G. (1958). Whales observed in the Atlantic Ocean. Notes on their distribution. *Mar. Obs., London* **28**, 142–6, 209–16.

Brown, S. G. (1962a). A note on migration in fin whales. *Norsk Hvalfangsttid.* **51**(1), 13–16.

Brown, S. G. (1962b). The movement of fin and blue whales within the Antarctic zone. *Discovery Rep.* **33**, 1–54.

Brown, S. G. (1962c). Whale marks recovered during Antarctic seasons 1960/61, 1961/62, and in South Africa 1962. *Norsk Hvalfangsttid.* **51**(11), 429–34.

Brown, S. G. (1964). Whale marks recovered in the Antarctic whaling season 1962/63 and in South Africa 1963. *Norsk Hvalfangsttid.* **53**(10), 277–80.

Brown, S. G. (1968a). The results of sei whale marking in the southern ocean to 1967. *Norsk Hvalfangsttid.* **57**(4), 77–83.

Brown, S. G. (1968b). Feeding of sei whales at South Georgia. *Norsk Hvalfangsttid.* **57**(6), 118–25.

Brown, S. G. (1968c). Whale marks recovered in the Antarctic whaling season 1967/68. *Norsk Hvalfangsttid.* **57**(6), 139–40.

Brown, S. G. (1972). Whale marking—progress report, 1971. *Rep. int. Commn Whal.* **22**, 37–40.

Brown, S. G. (1973). Whale marking—progress report 1972. *Rep. int. Commn Whal.* **23**, 49–54.

Caldwell, D. K., Caldwell, M. C. and Rice, D. W. (1966). Behaviour of the sperm whale *Physeter catodon* L. *In* "Whales, Dolphins, and Porpoises" (K. S. Norris, Ed.), pp. 677–717. University of California Press, Berkeley and Los Angeles.

Chapman, D. G. (1970). Re-analysis of Antarctic fin whale population data. *Rep. int. Commn Whal.* **20**, 54–9.

Chapman, D. G. (1974a). Status of Antarctic rorqual stocks. *In* "The Whale Problem: A Status Report" (W. E. Schevill, Ed.), pp. 218–38. Harvard Univ. Press.

Chapman, D. G. (1974b). Estimation of population size and sustainable yield of sei whales in the Antarctic. *Rep. int. Commn Whal.* **24**, 82–90.

[Chapman, D. G., Allen, K. R. and Holt, S. J.] (1964). Reports of the Committee of Three Scientists on the special scientific investigation of the Antarctic whale stocks. *Rep. int. Commn Whal.* **14**, 32–106.

Chittleborough, R. G. (1955). Puberty, physical maturity, and relative growth of the female humpback whale, *Megaptera nodosa* (Bonnaterre), on the Western Australian coast. *Aust. J. mar. Freshwat. Res.* **6**(3), 315–27.

Chittleborough, R. G. (1958). The breeding cycle of the female humpback whale, *Megaptera nodosa* (Bonnaterre). *Aust. J. mar. Feshwat. Res.* **9**(1), 1–18.

Chittleborough, R. G. (1960). Marked humpback of known age. *Nature, Lond.* **187,** 164.

Chittleborough, R. G. (1965). Dynamics of two populations of the humpback whale, *Megaptera novaeangliae* (Borowski). *Aust. J. mar. Freshwat. Res.* **16**(1), 33–128.

Clarke, R. (1956). Sperm whales of the Azores. *Discovery Rep.* **28,** 237–98.

Clarke, R. and Paliza, O. (1972). Sperm whales of the Southeast Pacific. Part III: Morphometry. *Hvalråd. Skr.* **No. 53,** 1–106.

Clarke, R., Aguayo L., A. and Paliza, O. (1968). Sperm whales of the Southeast Pacific. Part I: Introduction. Part II: Size range, external characters and teeth. *Hvalråd. Skr.* **No. 51,** 1–80.

Cushing, J. E., Fujino, K. and Calaprice, N. (1963). The Ju blood typing system of the sperm whales and specific soluble substances. *Scient. Rept. Whales Res. Inst. Tokyo* **17,** 67–77.

Dawbin, W. H. (1959). Evidence on Growth-rates obtained from Two Marked Humpback Whales. *Nature, Lond.* **183,** 1749–50.

Dawbin, W. H. (1966). The seasonal migratory cycle of humpback whales. *In* "Whales, Dolphins, and Porpoises" (K. S. Norris, Ed.), pp. 145–69. University of California Press, Berkeley and Los Angeles.

DeLury, D. B. (1947). On the estimation of biological populations. *Biometrics* **3,** 145–67.

Doi, T. (1974). Further development of whale sighting theory. *In* "The Whale Problem: A Status Report" (W. E. Schevill, Ed.), pp. 359–68. Harvard Univ. Press.

Doi, T. and Ohsumi, S. (1970). On the maximum sustainable yield of sei whales in the Antarctic. *Rep. int. Commn Whal.* **20,** 88–96.

Doi, T., Ohsumi, S. and Nemoto, T. (1967). Population assessment of sei whales in the Antarctic. *Norsk Hvalfangsttid.* **56**(2), 25–41.

Doi, T., Ohsumi, S., Nasu, K. and Shimadzu, Y. (1970). Advanced assessment of the fin whale stock in the Antarctic. *Rep. int. Commn Whal.* **20,** 60–87.

Doi, T., Ohsumi, S. and Shimadzu, Y. (1971). Status of stocks of baleen whales in the Antarctic, 1970/71. *Rep. int. Commn Whal.* **21,** 90–9.

FAO, Fisheries Division (1966). Report on the effects on the whale stocks of pelagic operations in the Antarctic during the 1964/65 season, and on the present status of those stocks. *Rep. int. Commn Whal.* **16,** 25–49.

FAO, Stock Assessment Section (1967). Report on the effects on whale stocks of pelagic operations in the Antarctic during the 1965/66 season and on the present status of those stocks. *Rep. int. Commn Whal.* **17,** 47–69.

Fujino, K. (1960). Immunogenetic and marking approaches to identifying sub-populations of the North Pacific whales. *Scient. Rep. Whales Res. Inst., Tokyo* **No. 15,** 85–142.

Fujino, K. (1963). Identification of breeding subpopulations of the sperm whales in the waters adjacent to Japan and around Aleutian Islands by means of blood typing investigations. *Bull. Jap. Soc. scient. Fish.* **29,** 1057–63.

Fujino, K. (1964). Fin whale sub-populations in the Antarctic whaling Areas II, III and IV. *Sci. Rep. Whales Res. Inst., Tokyo* **No. 18,** 1–27.

Gambell, R. (1964). A pygmy blue whale at Durban. *Norsk Hvalfangsttid.* **53**(3), 66–8.

Gambell, R. (1967). Seasonal movements of sperm whales. *Symp. zool. Soc. Lond.* **19,** 237–54.

Gambell, R. (1968). Seasonal cycles and reproduction in sei whales of the southern hemisphere. *Discovery Rep.* **35,** 31–134.

Gambell, R. (1970). Weight of a sperm whale, whole and in parts. *S. Afr. J. Sci.* **66,** 225–7.

Gambell, R. (1972). Sperm whales off Durban. *Discovery Rep.* **35,** 199–358.

Gambell, R. (1973). Some effects of exploitation on reproduction in whales. *J. Reprod. Fert.* Suppl. **19**, 531–51.

Gambell, R. (1975a). Sperm whale catching effort by shore-based catcher boats at Durban. *Rep. int. Commn Whal.* **25**, 174–81.

Gambell, R. (1975b). Variations in reproduction parameters associated with whale stock sizes. *Rep. int. Commn Whal.* **25**, 182–9.

Gambell, R. (1976). World whale stocks. *Mammal Rev.* **6**(1), 41–53.

Gambell, R. and Grzegorzewska, C. (1967). The rate of lamina formation in sperm whale teeth. *Norsk Hvalfangsttid.* **56**(6), 117–21.

Gaskin, D. E. (1970). Composition of schools of sperm whales *Physeter catodon* Linn. east of New Zealand. *N.Z. Jl. mar. Freshwat. Res.* **4**(4), 456–71.

Gilmore, R. M. (1959). On the mass strandings of sperm whales. *Pacif. Nat.* **1**(10), 9–16.

Gulland, J. A. and Boerema, L. K. (1973). Scientific advice on catch levels. *Rep. int. Commn Whal.* **23**, 200–12.

Gulland, J. A. and Kesteven, G. L. (1964). The effect of weather on catches of whales. *Rep. int. Commn Whal.* **14**, 87–91.

Harmer, S. F. (1931). Southern whaling. *Proc. Linn. Soc. Lond.* Session **142**, 85–163.

Hart, T. J. (1935). On the diatoms of the skin film of whales, and their possible bearing on problems of whale movements. *Discovery Rep.* **10**, 247–82.

Hjort, J., Lie, J. and Ruud, J. T. (1932a). Norwegian pelagic whaling in the Antarctic. I. Whaling grounds in 1929–1930 and 1930–1931. *Hvalråd. Skr.* **No. 3**, 1–37.

Hjort, J., Lie, J. and Ruud, J. T. (1933a). Norwegian pelagic whaling in the Antarctic. II. *Hvalråd. Skr.* **No. 7**, 128–52.

Hjort, J., Lie, J. and Ruud, J. T. (1933b). Norwegian pelagic whaling in the Antarctic. III. The season 1932–1933. *Hvalråd. Skr.* **No. 8**, 1–36.

Hjort, J., Lie, J. and Ruud, J. T. (1934). Pelagic whaling in the Antarctic. IV. The season 1933–1934. *Hvalråd. Skr.* **No. 9**, 1–59.

Hjort, J., Lie, J. and Ruud, J. T. (1935). Pelagic whaling in the Antarctic. V. The season 1934–1935. *Hvalråd. Skr.* **No. 12**, 1–52.

Hjort, J., Lie, J. and Ruud, J. T. (1937). Pelagic whaling in the Antarctic. VI. The season 1935–1936. *Hvalråd. Skr.* **No. 14**, 1–45.

Hjort, J., Lie, J. and Ruud, J. T. (1938). Pelagic whaling in the Antarctic. VII. The season 1936–1937. *Hvalråd. Skr.* **No. 18**, 1–44.

Holt, S. J. and Gulland, J. A. (1964). Measures of abundance of Antarctic whale stocks. *Rapp. P.-v. Réun. Cons. perm. int. Explor. Mer* **155**(27), 147–51.

[Hylen, A.] (1964). Catcher efficiency. *Rep. int. Commn Whal.* **14**, 92.

Ichihara, T. (1957). An application of linear discriminant function to external measurements of fin whale. *Scient. Rep. Whales Res. Inst., Tokyo* **No. 12**, 127–89.

Ichihara, T. (1961). Blue whales in the waters around Kerguelen Island. *Norsk Hvalfangsttid.* **50**(1), 1–20.

Ichihara, T. (1963). Identification of the pygmy blue whale in the Antarctic. *Norsk Hvalfangsttid.* **52**(5), 128–30.

Ichihara, T. (1966a). The pygmy blue whale, *Balaenoptera musculus brevicauda*, a new subspecies from the Antarctic. *In* "Whales, Dolphins and Porpoises" (K. S. Norris, Ed.), pp. 79–111. University of California Press, Berkeley and Los Angeles.

Ichihara, T. (1966b). Criterion for determining age of fin whale with reference to ear plug and baleen plate. *Scient. Rep. Whales Res. Inst., Tokyo* **No. 20**, 17–81.

International Whaling Commission (1967). Report of IWC/FAO joint working party on whale stock assessment held from 26 January to 2 February, 1966 in Seattle. *Rep. int. Commn Whal.* **17**, 27–47.

International Whaling Commission (1969a). Report of the IWC–FAO working group on sperm whale stock assessment. *Rep. int. Commn Whal.* **19**, 39–69.

International Whaling Commission (1969b). Report of the meeting on age determination in whales. *Rep. int. Commn Whal.* **19**, 131–7.

International Whaling Commission (1971a). Report of the special meeting on Antarctic fin whale stock assessment. *Rep. int. Commn Whal.* **21**, 34–9.

International Whaling Commission (1971b). Report of the special meeting on sperm whale biology and stock assessments. *Rep. int. Commn Whal.* **21**, 40–50.

International Whaling Commission (1973). Sperm whale assessment meeting. *Rep. int. Commn Whal.* **23**, 55–88.

International Whaling Commission (1974). International Convention for the Regulation of Whaling, 1946. Schedule amended June 1974. Office of the Commission, London.

International Whaling Commission (1976). Scientific Committee. Report of Special Meeting, La Jolla, 3–13 December 1974. *Rep. int. Commn Whal.* **26**, 60–179.

International Whaling Statistics 1934–1974. Oslo.

Ivashin, M. V. (1969). O lokal'nosti nekotorykh promyslovykh vidov kitov v iuzhnom polusharii. *Rybnoe Khoziaistvo.* **45**(10), 11–13.

Ivashin, M. V. (1973). Marking of whales in the southern hemisphere (Soviet materials). *Rep. int. Commn Whal.* **23**, 174–91.

Ivashin, M. V. and Rovnin, A. A. (1967). Some results of the soviet whale marking in the waters of the North Pacific. *Norsk Hvalfangsttid.* **56**(6), 123–35.

Jones, R. (1973). Population assessments of Antarctic fin and sei whales. *Rep. int. Commn Whal.* **23**, 215–59.

Jonsgård, Å. (1955). The stocks of blue whales (*Balaenoptera musculus*) in the northern Atlantic Ocean and adjacent Arctic waters. *Norsk Hvalfangsttid.* **44**(9), 505–19.

Jonsgård, Å. (1958). Taxation of fin whales (*Balaenoptera physalus* (L)) at land stations on the Norwegian west coast. *Norsk Hvalfangsttid.* **47**(9), 433–9.

Jonsgård, Å. (1966). Biology of the North Atlantic fin whale *Balaenoptera physalus* (L). Taxonomy, distribution, migration and food. *Hvalråd. Skr.* **No. 49**, 1–62.

Jonsgård, Å. (1974). On whale exploitation in the eastern part of the North Atlantic Ocean. *In* "The Whale Problem: A Status Report" (W. E. Schevill, Ed.), pp. 97–107. Harvard Univ. Press, Cambridge, Mass.

Kawamura, A. (1974). Food and feeding ecology in the southern sei whale. *Scient. Rep. Whales Res. Inst., Tokyo* **No. 26**, 25–144.

Kellogg, R. (1929). What is known of the migrations of some of the whalebone whales. *Rep. Smithson. Instn* **1928**, 467–94.

Klevesal, G. A. and Kleinenberg, S. E. (1967). Opredelenie vozrasta mlekopitayushchikh po sloistym strukturam zubov i kosti. *Akad. Nauk SSSR, Moscow* 1–144.

Klevesal, G. A. and Mitchell, E. (1971). O godovykh sloyakh v kosti usatykh kitov. *Zool. Zh.* **50**(7), 1114–16.

Laurie, A. H. (1937). The age of female blue whales and the effect of whaling on the stock. *Discovery Rep.* **15**, 223–84.

Laws, R. M. (1952). A new method of age determination for mammals. *Nature, Lond.* **169**, 972–3.

Laws, R. M. (1959a). The foetal growth rates of whales with special reference to the fin whale, *Balaenoptera physalus* Linn. *Discovery Rep.* **29**, 281–308.

Laws, R. M. (1959b). Accelerated growth in seals, with special reference to the Phocidae. *Norsk Hvalfangsttid.* **48**(9), 425–52.

Laws, R. M. (1960a). Problems of whale conservation. *Trans. N. Amer. Wildl. Conf.* 304–19.

Laws, R. M. (1960b). Laminated structure of bones from some marine mammals. *Nature, Lond.* **187**, 338–9.

Laws, R. M. (1961). Reproduction, growth and age of southern fin whales. *Discovery Rep.* **31**, 327–486.

Laws, R. M. (1962). Some effects of whaling on the southern stocks of baleen whales. *In* "The Exploitation of Natural Animal Populations" (E. D. Le Cren and M. W. Holdgate, Eds), pp. 137–58. Blackwell, Oxford.

Laws, R. M. and Purves, P. E. (1956). The ear plug of the Mysticeti as an indication of age with special reference to the North Atlantic fin whale *Balaenoptera physalus* Linn. *Norsk Hvalfangsttid.* **45**(8), 413–25.

Lillie, D. G. (1915). Cetacea. *Nat. Hist. Rep. Br. antarct. Terra Nova Exped. Zool.* **1**(3), 85–124.

Lockyer, C. (1972a). The age at sexual maturity of the southern fin whale (*Balaenoptera physalus*) using annual layer counts in the ear plug. *J. Cons. int. Explor. Mer.* **34**(2), 276–94.

Lockyer, C. H. (1972b). A review of the weights of cetaceans with estimates of growth and energy budgets of the larger whales. Univ. Lond. M. Phil. thesis 1–196.

Lockyer, C. (1974). Investigation of the ear plug of the southern sei whale, *Balaenoptera borealis*, as a valid means of determining age. *J. Cons. int. Explor. Mer.* **36**(1), 71–81.

Lockyer, C. (1976). Body weights of some species of large whales. *J. Cons. int. Explor. Mer.* **36**(3), 259–73.

Lund, J. (1950a). Charting of whale stocks in the Antarctic on the basis of iodine values. *Norsk Hvalfangsttid.* **39**(2), 53–60.

Lund, J. (1950b). Charting of whale stocks in the Antarctic in the season 1949/50 on the basis of iodine values. *Norsk Hvalfangsttid.* **39**(7), 298–305.

Lund, J. (1951). Charting of whale stocks in the Antarctic 1950/51 on the basis of iodine values. *Norsk Hvalfangsttid.* **40**(8), 384–6.

Machin, D. (1974). A multivariate study of external measurements of the sperm whale (*Physeter catodon*). *J. Zool., Lond.* **172**, 267–88.

Mackintosh, N. A. (1942). The southern stocks of whalebone whales. *Discovery Rep.* **22**, 197–300.

Mackintosh, N. A. (1965). "The Stocks of Whales," pp. 1–232. Fishing News (Books) Ltd., London.

Mackintosh, N. A. and Brown, S. G. (1956). Preliminary estimates of the southern populations of the larger baleen whales. *Norsk Hvalfangsttid.* **45**(9), 469–80.

Mackintosh, N. A. and Wheeler, J. F. G. (1929). Southern blue and fin whales. *Discovery Rep.* **1**, 257–540.

Marr, J. (1962). The natural history and geography of the Antarctic krill (*Euphausia superba* Dana). *Discovery Rep.* **32**, 33–464.

Matsuura, Y. (1940). The constitution of whale populations in the Antarctic. III. Humpback whale. *Bull. Jap. Soc. scient. Fish.* **9**(2), 51–60.

Matthews, L. H. (1937). The humpback whale *Megaptera nodosa*. *Discovery Rep.* **17**, 7–92.

Matthews, L. H. (1938a). The sperm whale, *Physeter catodon*. *Discovery Rep.* **17**, 93–168.

Matthews, L. H. (1938b). The sei whale, *Balaenoptera borealis*. *Discovery Rep.* **17**, 183–290.

Mitchell, E. D. (1973). The status of the world's whales. *Nature Canada* **2**(4), 9–25.

Mitchell, E. D. (1974). Present status of northwest Atlantic fin and other whale stocks. *In* "The Whale Problem: A Status Report" (W. E. Schevill, Ed.), pp. 108–69. Harvard Univ. Press, Cambridge, Mass.

Nasu, K. and Shimadzu, Y. (1970). A method of estimating whale population by sighting observation. *Rep. int. Commn Whal.* **20,** 114–29.

Nemoto, T. (1962). Food of baleen whales collected in recent Japanese Antarctic whaling expeditions. *Scient. Rep. Whales Res. Inst., Tokyo* **No. 16,** 89–103.

Nishiwaki, M. (1966). Distribution and migration of the larger cetaceans in the North Pacific as shown by Japanese whaling results. *In* "Whales, Dolphins, and Porpoises" (K. S. Norris, Ed.), pp. 171–91. University of California Press, Berkeley and Los Angeles.

Nishiwaki, M., Hibiya, T. and Ohsumi (Kimura), S. (1958). Age study of sperm whale based on reading of tooth laminations. *Scient. Rep. Whales Res. Inst., Tokyo* **No. 13,** 135–153.

Nishiwaki, M., Ohsumi, S. and Maeda, Y. (1963). Change of form in the sperm whale accompanied with growth. *Scient. Rep. Whales Res. Inst., Tokyo* **No. 17,** 1–14.

Ohsumi, S. (1964). Examination on age determination of the fin whale. *Scient. Rep. Whales Res. Inst., Tokyo* **No. 18,** 49–88.

Ohsumi, S. (1965). Reproduction of the sperm whale in the North-West Pacific. *Scient. Rep. Whales Res. Inst., Tokyo* **No. 19,** 1–35.

Ohsumi, S. (1966). Sexual segregation of the sperm whale in the North Pacific. *Scient. Rep. Whales Res. Inst., Tokyo* **No. 20,** 1–16.

Ohsumi, S. (1971). Some investigations on the school structure of sperm whale. *Scient. Rep. Whales Res. Inst., Tokyo* **No. 23,** 1–25.

Ohsumi, S. (1972). Examination of the recruitment rate of the Antarctic fin whale stock by use of mathematical models. *Rep. int. Commn Whal.* **22,** 69–90.

Ohsumi, S. (1973). Revised estimates of recruitment rate in the Antarctic fin whales. *Rep. int. Commn Whal.* **23,** 192–9.

Ohsumi, S. and Fukuda, Y. (1972). A population model and its application to the sperm whale in the North Pacific. *Rep. int. Commn Whal.* **22,** 96–110.

Ohsumi (Kimura), S., Nishiwaki, M. and Hibiya, T. (1958). Growth of fin whale in the northern Pacific. *Scient. Rep. Whales Res. Inst., Tokyo* **No. 13,** 97–133.

Ohsumi, S., Kasuya, T. and Nishiwaki, M. (1963). Accumulation rate of dentinal layers in the maxillary tooth of the sperm whale. *Scient. Rep. Whales Res. Inst., Tokyo* **No. 17** 15–35.

Ohsumi, S., Shimadzu, Y. and Doi, T. (1971). The seventh memorandum on the results of Japanese stock assessment of whales in the North Pacific. *Rep. int. Commn Whal.* **21,** 76–89.

Olsen, Ø. (1913). On the external characters and biology of Bryde's Whale (*Balaenoptera brydei*), a new rorqual from the coast of South Africa. *Proc. zool. Soc. Lond.* **1913,** 1073–90.

Omura, H. (1953). Biological study on humpback whales in the Antarctic Whaling Areas IV and V. *Scient. Rep. Whales Res. Inst., Tokyo* **No. 8,** 81–102.

Omura, H. (1959). Bryde's whale from the coast of Japan. *Scient. Rep. Whales Res. Inst., Tokyo* **No. 14,** 1–33.

Omura, H. (1966). Bryde's whale in the Northwest Pacific. *In* "Whales, Dolphins, and Porpoises" (K. S. Norris, Ed.), pp. 70–8. University of California Press, Berkeley and Los Angeles.

Omura, H. and Ohsumi, S. (1974). Research on whale biology of Japan with special reference to the North Pacific stocks. *In* "The Whale Problem: A Status Report" (W. E. Schevill, Ed.), pp. 196–208. Harvard Univ. Press.

Purves, P. E. (1955). The wax plug in the external auditory meatus of the Mysticeti. *Discovery Rep.* **27,** 293–302.

Purves, P. E. and Mountford, M. D. (1959). Ear plug laminations in relation to the age composition of a population of fin whales (*Balaenoptera physalus*). *Bull. Br. Mus. nat. Hist. Zool.* **5**(6), 123–61.

Raynor, G. W. (1940). Whale marking: progress and results to December 1939. *Discovery Rep.* **19**, 245–84.

Rice, D. W. (1974). Whales and whale research in the eastern North Pacific. *In* "The Whale Problem: A Status Report" (W. E. Schevill, Ed.), pp. 170–95. Harvard Univ. Press, Cambridge, Mass.

Risting, S. (1912). Knolhvalen. *Norsk Fisk Tid.* **11**, 437–49.

Roe, H. S. J. (1967). Seasonal formation of laminae in the ear plug of the fin whale. *Discovery Rep.* **35**, 1–30.

Ruud, J. T. (1940). The surface structure of the baleen plates as a possible clue to age in whales. *Hvalråd. Skr.* **No. 23**, 1–24.

Ruud, J. T. (1945). Further studies on the structure of the baleen plates and their application to age determination. *Hvalråd. Skr.* **No. 29**, 1–69.

Saetersdal, G., Mejia, J. and Ramirez, P. (1963). La caza de cachalotes en el Peru. *Boln Inst. Invest. Recurs. mar., Callao* **1**(3), 45–84.

Seber, G. A. F. (1962). The multisample single recapture census. *Biometrika* **49**, 339–50.

Slijper, E. J., van Utrecht, W. L. and Naaktegeboren, C. (1964). Remarks on the distribution and migration of whales based on observations from Netherlands ships. *Bijdr. tot Dierk.* **34**, 3–93.

Townsend, C. H. (1935). The distribution of certain whales as shown by logbook records of American whaleships. *Zoologica, N.Y.* **19**, 1–50.

Vervoort, W. and Tranter, D. (1961). *Balaenophilus unisetus* P.O.C. Aurivillius (Copepoda Harpacticoida) from the southern hemisphere. *Crustaceana* **3**(1), 70–84.

Whales Research Institute, Tokyo (1967). Summarised result of the whale marking in the North Pacific. *Rep. int. Commn Whal.* **17**, 116–19.

Wheeler, J. F. G. (1930). The age of fin whales at physical maturity. *Discovery Rep.* **2**, 403–34.

Wheeler, J. F. G. (1934). On the stock of whales at South Georgia. *Discovery Rep.* **9**, 351–72.

Zemsky, V. A. and Boronin, V. A. (1964). On the question of the pygmy blue whale taxonomic position. *Norsk Hvalfangsttid.* **53**(11), 306–11.

Subject Index

A

Abies alba, 76
Abies concolor, 150
Abies grandis, 68
Acanthis cannabina, 113
Acanthis flammea, 149
Acetylene banger, 99
Acridotheres tristis, 113, 150
Aerial spraying, 120, 121, 131
Age
   distribution, 190–1, 194, 208, 226, 228
   dose response relationship, 193
Agelaius phoeniceus, 127
Agelaius tricolor, 126
Age-lines, 190
Agropyron repens, 34–6, 38, 40, 42
Agrostemma githago, 15, 17
Alauda arvensis, 142
Allium spp, 34
Alopecurus myosuroides, 4, 22
Alpha chloralose, 137, 146
Amaranthus spp, 122
Amazona autumnalis, 130
4-aminopyridine, 124, 127, 131
Ammodytes spp, 152
Anatidae, 93
Anemone nemorosa, 17
Anguilla anguilla, 152
Ankylosis, 309
Anthraquinone, 130, 143
Anti-cholesterol, 105
Anseranas semipalmata, 139
"Anser" geese, 140
Anser anser, 140
Anser brachyrhynchos, 140
Aprosimictus erythropterus, 130
Aquila audax, 145
Aquila chrysaëtos, 144
Arachis hypogaea, 122
Aratinga canicularis, 130
Aratinga pertinax, 130

Arbovirus, 109, 110
Ardeidae, 153
Ardeola ibis, 145
Artificial plantation forestry, 83–4
Artificial population control (birds), 120–1, 134–5, 145, 152, 157–9
Ash (tree), 146
Ashy headed goose, 140
Asio flammeus, 96
Australian X disease, 109
Auxin, 62, 64
Avena fatua, 6, 14, 16 ff, 21, 27
Avertin, 137
Avicides, 121–2
Avitect, 143
Avitrol, 123, 127, 131, 159

B

Bachelor school, 265
Bacterial infections (in birds), 107
Baits, 101, 105, 124, 136–7, 146, 158
Balaena mysticetus, 248
Balaenoptera acuto rostrata, 248
Balaenoptera borealis, 248
Balaenoptera edeni, 248
Balaenoptera musculus, 248
Balaenoptera musculus brevicauda, 268
Balaenoptera physalus, 248
Baleen plate, 247, 269, 277, 282, 295, 303
Baleen whale, 247, 254, 288 ff, 291, 298, 305, 311, 321 ff, 326 ff, 332
   migration, 251, 254–260
   population estimates, 317–19
   stock units, 266 ff, 270
Barnacle goose, 141
Barn owl, 109
Bar-shouldered Dove, 112
Baya weaver, 119
Beech, 54, 61, 70
Belted kingfisher, 153

345

Woodpigeon, 97, 108, 112–14, 131–9, 141–2, 148
Wood science, 83
Wrasse, 154
Wren, 151

X

Xanthocephalus xanthocephalus, 128
Xylem, 62

Y

Yellow-headed blackbird, 128
Yew, 75
Yield,
  in forestry, 53, 69, 78 ff

in Ungulate populations, 184, 220 ff
  maximum sustained, 216–17, 218–20, 225–7, 230–4
  optimum sustained, 221
in Whale populations, 323–7
Yield-parabola method, 231

Z

Zea mays, 111
Zenaida asiatica, 122
Zenaida auriculata, 112, 159
Zenaida doves, 112, 122
Zenaida macruora, 112, 160
Zosterops lateralis, 150